Tantric Traditions in Transmission and Translation

Tantric Traditions in Transmission and Translation

Edited by

DAVID B. GRAY

RYAN RICHARD OVERBEY

OXFORD
UNIVERSITY PRESS

OXFORD
UNIVERSITY PRESS

Oxford University Press is a department of the University of Oxford. It furthers the University's objective of excellence in research, scholarship, and education by publishing worldwide. Oxford is a registered trade mark of Oxford University Press in the UK and certain other countries.

Published in the United States of America by Oxford University Press
198 Madison Avenue, New York, NY 10016, United States of America.

Cataloging-in-Publication data is on file at the Library of Congress
ISBN 978-0-19-976368-9 (hbk.); 978-0-19-976369-6 (pbk.)

3 5 7 9 8 6 4 2
Printed by Webcom, Canada

Contents

Contributors

Naresh Man Bajracharya is the distinguished first Professor of Buddhist Studies at Tribhuvan University, Nepal. He was the founding Chair of the Central Department of Buddhist Studies in the same University. He is also the lineage holder and leading Priest of Newar Buddhism. He was named Fulbright Scholar in Residence (SIR) for 2009–2010. The author of many articles and books on Newar Buddhism, he played a pioneering role in introducing Buddhist Studies in Nepal and in revitalizing Newar Buddhism. Currently he is devoting his life to the construction of a Bajrayana Monastery in the Lumbini Master Plan area, and serving Lumbini Buddhist University in Lumbini, Nepal, as the Vice-Chancellor.

Jacob P. Dalton, PhD (2002) in Buddhist Studies, University of Michigan, is an Associate Professor of Tibetan and Buddhist Studies at the University of California, Berkeley. He works on tantric Buddhism in Tibet, and his publications include *The Taming of the Demons: Violence and Liberation in Tibetan Buddism* (2011).

David B. Gray is an Associate Professor of Religious Studies at Santa Clara University. His research explores the development of tantric Buddhist traditions in South Asia, and their dissemination in Tibet and East Asia, with a focus on the Yoginītantras, a genre of Buddhist tantric literature that focused on female deities and yogic practices involving the subtle body. He is the author of both *The Cakrasamvara Tantra: A Study and Annotated Translation* (2007) and *The Cakrasamvara Tantra: Editions of the Sanskrit and Tibetan Texts* (2012).

Shaman Hatley researches the literature, ritual, and social history of the tantric traditions in medieval India. Now at the University of Massachusetts–Boston, he completed his PhD in 2007 at the University of Pennsylvania under the direction of Harunaga Isaacson, after which he taught at Concordia University, Montréal. His publications concern goddess cults, yoga, tantric ritual, and the technical terminology of the Śaiva *tantras*. Currently, he is preparing a monograph on the Yoginī cults of early medieval India, and a multivolume study and critical edition of the *Brahmayāmalatantra*, one of the earliest surviving works of Śaiva tantric literature focused upon goddesses.

Todd Lewis is the Murray Distinguished Professor of Arts and Humanities in the Religious Studies Department at the College of the Holy Cross. His primary research since 1979 has been on Newar Buddhism in the Kathmandu Valley, Nepal. He is the author of many articles on this tradition, co-author of *World Religions Today* (2014), and editor of the new course book, *Buddhists: Understanding Buddhism Through the Lives of Practitioners* (2014). His most recent translation, *Sugata Saurabha: A Poem on the Life of the Buddha by Chittadhar Hridaya of Nepal*, received awards from the Khyentse Foundation and the Numata Foundation as the best book in Buddhist Studies published in 2011.

Ryan Richard Overbey studies the intellectual and ritual history of Buddhism, with particular emphasis on early medieval Buddhist spells and ritual manuals. He studied at Brown University (AB in Classics & Sanskrit and Religious Studies, 2001) and at Harvard University (PhD in the Study of Religion, 2010). He has worked as an academic researcher for Prof. Dr. Lothar Ledderose's project on Stone Sūtras at the Heidelberger Akademie der Wissenschaften, as a Visiting Assistant Professor of Religious Studies at the College of the Holy Cross, and as the 2013–2015 Shinjō Itō Postdoctoral Fellow in Buddhist Studies at the University of California, Berkeley. He is currently a Visiting Assistant Professor in Religion at Wesleyan University.

Richard K. Payne is the Yehan Numata Professor of Japanese Buddhist Studies, Institute of Buddhist Studies, Berkeley, and a member of the Graduate Theological Union's Core Doctoral Faculty. Recent edited works include *Tantric Buddhism in East Asia* (2005), and the Japan section of *Esoteric Buddhism and the Tantras in East Asia* (2011). He has served as

Editor-in-Chief of Oxford Bibliographies/Buddhism, Co-Editor-in-Chief of Oxford Research Encyclopedia of Religion/Buddhism, Chair of the Editorial Committees of both Pure Land Buddhist Studies series, University of Hawai'i Press, and *Pacific World: Journal of the Institute of Buddhist Studies.* His *homa* research continues, as does a survey of tantric Buddhism.

John Powers is Professor of Asian History in the College of Asia and the Pacific, Australian National University, and a Fellow of the Australian Academy of Humanities. He is the author of fourteen books and more than sixty articles and book chapters. His publications include *A Bull of a Man: Images of Masculinity, Sex, and the Body in Indian Buddhism* (2009) and *Historical Dictionary of Tibet* (with David Templeman, 2012).

Tam Wai Lun is a professor and Chairperson in the Department of Cultural and Religious Studies in the Chinese University of Hong Kong (CUHK). He is a co-investigator of Prof. David Faure's Area of Excellence Project on "Historical Anthropology of Chinese Society" in CUHK. Prof. Tam has been conducting fieldwork researches funded by various competitive funding to study local religion and society in southeast China. He has also collaborated with Dr. Gordon Melton to study the Chinese Tantric "True Buddha School." He has published detailed ethnographic descriptions of local religion in southeast China in Prof. John Lagerwey's Traditional Hakka Society Series.

Abbreviations

D. Situ Chos-kyi 'byung-gnas, ed. sDe-dge par phud Kanjur; facsimile copy of the 1733 blocks; Delhi: Karmapae Chodey Gyalwae Sungrab Partun Khang, 1978. Tibetan Buddhist Resource Centr Volume No. 962.

Q. Suzuki, Daisetz T., ed. *The Tibetan Tripitaka: Peking Edition*. 168 vols. Tokyo-Kyoto: Tibetan Tripitaka Research Institute, 1955–1961.

T. Takakusu Junjirō 高楠順 and Watanabe Kaikyoku 渡邊海旭, eds. 1924–1932. *Taishō shinshū daizōkyō* 大正新修大藏經. 85 vols. Tōkyō 東京: Taishō issaikyō kankōkai 大正一切經刊行會.

To. Ui Hakuju宇井伯壽et al., eds. 1934. *A Complete Catalogue of the Tibetan Buddhist Canons (bkaḥ-ḥgyur and bstan-ḥgyur)*. Sendai仙台: Tōhoku Imperial University.

Tantric Traditions in Transmission and Translation

Introduction

TRACING TANTRIC TRADITIONS THROUGH TIME AND SPACE

David B. Gray and Ryan Richard Overbey

THE PURPOSE OF this volume is to explore the movement of tantric Buddhist traditions through time and space. "Time," of course, indicates a focus on the historical development of tantric traditions, which ranges from the mid-seventh century, when the earliest known tantric work was composed, to the present day. By "space" we refer not only to the obvious focus on movements across cultural boundaries, but also the conceptual "space" of religious traditions. Regarding the former, tantric traditions developed in India but were rapidly disseminated to Southeast, East, and Central Asia, and this dissemination has continued around the globe.

As many of the chapters in this volume discuss, tantric traditions have developed, and are developing, through transmissions across sectarian boundaries as well. Tantric Buddhist traditions in India drew, to varying degrees depending on the tradition, from Hindu textual and ritual sources. But once these traditions were transmitted to other cultural spaces, they continued to develop by exchanges with the native traditions of these spaces, such as the Bön tradition in Tibet, Daoism in China, and the Shintō tradition in Japan.

However, before we move on to explore these topics in more depth, it is important to clearly indicate exactly what we mean by "tantric traditions." The adjective "tantric," an English word derived from the Sanskrit *tāntrika*, means simply that which relates to the *tantras*, the genre of scripture that serves as the canonical source texts for the various traditions of tantric practice. Tantras are works that primarily focus on ritual and meditative practices, so the term "tantric" also envelops the practices associated with these scriptures, and were traditionally disseminated by the *tāntrikas* (the Sanskrit term also designates tantric practitioners), along with the texts (Padoux 2002, 18). So "tantric traditions" are the communities of practitioners who practice, preserve, and transmit, through both time and space, both the texts and the practices that are traditionally associated with them.

It is important to note that we use this term in a plural form. Tantric or esoteric Buddhist traditions are multiple, and also originated as multiple, distinct traditions of both text and practice. Indeed, one of the most important tropes in the history of the dissemination of tantric traditions is that of lineage, the transmission of teachings along an uninterrupted lineage, from master to disciple, the so-called *guruparaṃparā*. Lineages must be distinguished from institutionalized sectarian traditions, as they often are preserved by multiple sects, which typically make claims with respect to lineage to bolster their authority.[1] This focus on lineage is found throughout the tantric Buddhist world; originating in India, this emphasis was transmitted to Tibet and East Asia, and remains an important concern of contemporary tantric communities, as Tam Wai Lun's chapter in this volume clearly indicates.

Eventually, circa the tenth century, advocates of these traditions developed broad rubrics to conceptualize the movement as a whole. These include the well-known South Asian formulation of the Vajrayāna, or "Adamantine Vehicle." The earliest known reference to this term is found in a relatively early esoteric Buddhist work, the *Compendium of the Reality of All Tathāgatas Māhayāna Sūtra*, which interestingly retains an identity as a Māhayāna sūtra while nevertheless advancing the cause of the newly conceived Adamantine Vehicle. The third section of this work contains the following verse: "Well spoken is this sūtra, which is the secret of all Tathāgatas, the unexcelled Adamantine Vehicle, and is the compendium of the Great Vehicle."[2] Another important rubric is the East Asian formulation of "Esoteric Teaching" (密教; Chinese *mijiao*, Japanese *mikkyō*). The labels "Esoteric Teaching" and "Adamantine Vehicle" both appear to have come into common use circa the tenth century, relatively late in the history of these traditions.[3] Broad rubrics, such as "Tantric Buddhism," Vajrayāna, and Esoteric Teaching, are abstractions that have no basis in how actual tantric traditions are organized and practiced. And since there is no term for the tantric traditions as a whole that is universally accepted by all of them, we will use the term "tantric traditions" in this volume, since the terms "tantra" and "tantric" are emic terms that are nonetheless well known in Western academic circles, despite their shortcomings.[4]

The plurality of tantric traditions is reflected by these tradition's own self-understanding. Unlike early Buddhist traditions, which attributed to Śākyamuni Buddha the establishment of their textual and practice traditions, there is no singular point of origin for the tantric traditions, which developed multiple origin myths. These myths typically serve to provide a legendary account of the revelation of key scriptures associated with practice lineages, typically by a divine being such as Vajradhara or Vajrasattva, to a human sage, such as Nāgārjuna, Saraha, Lūipa, and so forth. These myths often invoke the classical Buddhist myth of the decline and eventual disappearance of Buddhadharma.[5] These myths include the myth that key tantric scriptures transmitted to East Asia during the eighth century, namely the *Mahāvairocanābhisaṃbodhi* and *Sarvatathāgatatattvasaṃgraha* tantras, originated in the revelation of these works by Vajradhara Buddha to Nāgārjuna inside an iron stūpa in Central India (Orzech 1995, 314–317), or the claim made by advocates of the Cakrasaṃvara tradition that the key scripture of this tradition, the *Cakrasaṃvara Tantra*, was revealed by Buddhist deities to the great Indian saints Saraha and Lūipa (Gray 2007, 35n107).

While there are many lacunae in our understanding of the early history of tantric Buddhist traditions, available evidence points to the mid-seventh century as the most likely point at which historically datable traditions began to take shape. The earliest known datable tantric text is the *Awakening of Mahāvairocana Tantra* (*Mahāvairocanābhisaṃbodhi-tantra*), which was composed circa the mid-seventh century, and was reportedly one of the texts collected by the Chinese pilgrim Wuxing 無行 circa 680 CE (Hodge 2003, 14–15). Wuxing also commented on the emergence of a new "teaching about mantra" (*zhenyan jiaofa* 真言教法), which was very popular during his time in India (Davidson 2002, 118; Lin 1935), a fact that is confirmed in the account of another Chinese pilgrim who journeyed in India during the late seventh century, Yijing 義淨 (Hodge 2003, 10).

There was rapid growth and dissemination of the newly emerging tantric Buddhist traditions. Within a few decades after their initial composition, early tantric traditions of text and practice were disseminated to East and Southeast Asia. This was facilitated by the active trade and diplomatic exchanges between India and China during the seventh and early eight centuries, via overland trade routes through Central Asia and also maritime trade routes via Southeast Asia (Sen 2003,

203–211). Likewise, there is evidence that the Sarvadurgatipariśodhana and Trailokavijaya maṇḍalas, and, presumably, their associated practice and textual traditions, were introduced to Java circa 700 CE (Nihom 1998, 251). Moreover, the Central Asian monk Amoghavajra, who journeyed from China to India and back via the maritime route during the mid-eighth century, reported that there was a new canon of eighteen tantras, which he attempted to convey back to China, and partially translated into Chinese.[6] This suggests that there was a very rapid production of new tantric texts and practice traditions circa the mid-seventh through mid-eighth centuries.

Tantric traditions were established in China during the Tang dynasty, and thence disseminated to Korea (Sørensen 2011) and Japan.[7] While the institutionalized esoteric Buddhist school did not survive the Wuzong emperor's (武宗, 814–846; r. 840–846) infamous persecution of Buddhism in the mid-ninth century, esoteric Buddhist traditions survived in peripheral areas in China, and many elements of esoteric Buddhist practice were taken up by the "mainstream" non-esoteric traditions, as well as by Daoist traditions.[8]

Tibetan Buddhist traditions view the seventh century as the time when Buddhism first reached Tibet, although there might have been gradual dissemination of Buddhism into the region earlier. Both the development of the Tibetan script and the first Tibetan translations of Buddhist Sanskrit texts are traditionally attributed to Thon-mi Saṃbhoṭa, who was sent to India for these purposes by the great king Srong-btsan-sgam-po (617–649 CE).[9] The translation of Buddhist scriptures began, apparently, during the late seventh century, and continued with imperial support during the eighth and ninth centuries, with most of the "early" translations made between 779–838 CE (Herrmann-Pfandt 2002, 132). As evidenced by imperial catalogues compiled during this period, as well as tantric manuscripts preserved at Dunhuang, all of which predate the second or "latter transmission" of Buddhism to Tibet that commenced in the late tenth century,[10] a significant amount of tantric scriptures and ritual texts were translated into Tibetan during the imperial period.[11] This translation activity slowed with the collapse of the Tibetan empire in 841 CE, but accelerated in the late tenth century, when King Lha-bla-ma Ye-shes-'od is reported to have sent twenty-one novice monks to Kashmir to receive further training. One of them, Rin-chen bZang-po (958–1055 CE), became a renowned translator, thus initiating the second or "latter transmission" (*phyi dar*) of Buddhism to Tibet.[12]

Tibetan Buddhists would later play important roles in the dissemination of Buddhism (and associated tantric traditions) to China and Mongolia, and eventually throughout the world, with the diaspora of Tibetan lamas in the twentieth century following the Chinese invasion and occupation of Tibet in 1950.

The chapters in this volume seek to trace the development of tantric Buddhist traditions both in South Asia and beyond South Asia, as well as their dissemination across both religious and cultural boundaries. In Chapter 1 of this work, "Buddhas, Siddhas, and Indian Masculine Ideals," John Powers explores the history of Buddhism through the lens of masculine studies. In it he traces the changing conceptions of masculinity from early Buddhism through the later tantric traditions. He demonstrates both the continuity and the changes and transformations regarding masculine ideals in Buddhist traditions. His chapter helps ground the volume; tantric Buddhist traditions, after all, developed from earlier Indian Buddhist traditions. It is important to keep this in mind since contemporary tantric Buddhist traditions generally identify with the larger Mahāyāna Buddhist tradition from which the tantric traditions emerged.

In Chapter 2, "Converting the Ḍākinī: Goddess Cults and Tantras of the Yoginīs between Buddhism and Śaivism," Shaman Hatley explores the fascinating but still enigmatic relations between early Śaiva and Buddhist tantric traditions. Over the past two decades Alexis Sanderson, in a series of articles, has argued that Buddhist tantric traditions, particularly those associated with the Yoginītantras, drew from earlier Śaiva textual and practice traditions.[13] Hatley sheds further light on this phenomenon by tracing the development of the worship of goddesses, such as *ḍākinīs* and *yoginīs* in Śaivism circa the fifth century. He then presents evidence for early tantric Buddhist dependence on these traditions, with reference to works such as the *Mahāvairocanābhisaṃbodhi*. He moves on to the issue of the textual dependence of Buddhist Yoginītantras on earlier Śaiva works, deepening our understanding with detailed comparison of the Śaiva *Brahmayāmala* and Buddhist *Laghuśaṃvara Tantra*. Interestingly, he also finds evidence that the *Brahmayāmala*, in turn, drew from an earlier Buddhist source, suggesting that Hindu and Buddhist tantric traditions developed interdependently, each drawing on the other at various points in their histories.

Chapter 3 of this volume features Todd Lewis and Naresh Man Bajracharya's "Vajrayāna Traditions in Nepal." It is the longest chapter in this volume and deservedly so. The Kathmandu Valley, a relatively small region in the foothills of the Himalayas, has played a major role in the preservation and dissemination of tantric Buddhist traditions. It has long been an important center of Buddhist tantric traditions, and it is the only non-ethnic Tibetan region of South Asia in which tantric Buddhist traditions have survived to the present day. The vast majority of surviving Sanskrit Buddhist manuscripts has been preserved there, and most of these works are tantric in nature. The Kathmandu Valley also straddles an important trade route linking India with Tibet. The Newar community there has long played an important role in this trade. As a result, the Kathmandu Valley has also played an important role in the dissemination of Buddhist to Tibet. Moreover, the tantric Buddhist traditions of Nepal have continued to coexist with Hindu traditions, and have thus continued the process of development in dependence upon Hindu traditions that ceased elsewhere when Buddhism disappeared in most of South Asia. Despite the significance of the Kathmandu Valley to the history of Buddhism, the tantric Buddhist traditions preserved there remain among the most poorly studied Buddhist traditions. This chapter seeks to remedy this lacuna by shedding light on the history of these traditions.

In Chapter 4, "How Dhāraṇīs WERE Proto-Tantric: Liturgies, Ritual Manuals, and the Origins of the Tantras," Jacob P. Dalton explores the early development of tantric Buddhist literature. Relying on ritual literature preserved in Chinese translation, as well as early Tibetan ritual literature preserved in Dunhuang, he argues that the rise of the tantric Buddhist traditions was preceded by an important development, namely the rapid development and proliferation of ritual manuals in Indian Buddhist circles during a period ranging from the mid-fifth to mid-seventh centuries. Several of these ritual manuals were retrospectively classified as *kriyātantras* by later Buddhist authors such as Buddhaguhya. Dalton suggests that while the earliest Buddhist tantras did likely appear circa the mid-seventh century, this development in turn is dependent upon two centuries of the development of Buddhist ritual practices and the literature written to inform this practice.

David Gray, in the Chapter 5, "The Purification of Heruka: On the Transmission of a Controversial Buddhist Tradition to Tibet," focuses on a later phase of tantric Buddhist history, the late tenth and early eleventh centuries, at the start of the "later transmission" of Buddhism to Tibet. He focuses on a work attributed to Śraddhākaravarma, a Kashmiri Buddhist scholar with whom Rin-chen bZang-po studied, and translated. This work, entitled "The Purification of Heruka" (*he ru ka'i rnam par dag pa*), is somewhat anomalous. From the title one would expect a meditation manual focus on the purification (*viśuddhi*) process in which one purifies elements of one's psycho-physical continuum, such as one's aggregates and elements, with divinities. Instead, the text focuses on Heruka himself, detailing the symbolism of his iconography. Gray suggests that this text may have been written to alleviate doubts about the authenticity of the Yoginītantras, doubts that were exacerbated by the dependence of these scriptures on "heretical" non-Buddhist works, and the descriptions of rituals in these works, involving violent ritual sacrifice and sex, that challenged the normative limits of Buddhist identity. The chapter thus seeks to shed light on the process by which these challenging texts were successfully defined as Buddhist to effect their transmission to Tibet.

In Chapter 6, "Vicissitudes of Text and Rite in the *Great Peahen Queen of Spells*," Ryan Overbey explores the corpus of Chinese translations of the *Mahāmāyūrīvidyārājñī*, an important early Buddhist apotropaic spell. This spell was translated six times into Chinese from the fifth to eighth centuries CE, and these versions also featured wildly varying ritual manuals. By analyzing Indian materials preserved in the Chinese record, Overbey shows how quickly texts and rituals could change, and reveals how older Buddhist spells and ritual texts were absorbed into the tantric traditions.

Richard Payne, in Chapter 7, "The Homa of the Northern Dipper" explores a fascinating example of multiple layers of borrowing to and from tantric Buddhist traditions. The chapter focuses on the rite of fire sacrifice, *homa*, which was adapted by tantric Buddhists from the ancient Vedic Hindu ritual of the same name, and which was disseminated with tantric Buddhism traditions across Asia. In China, a distinct version of this rite was developed that focused on the Northern Dipper (*beidou* 北斗) constellation, which has long held great significance in Chinese culture, and was the focus of Daoist ritual and contemplative practices. Esoteric Buddhists in China borrowed from Daoists to develop a uniquely Chinese form of the *homa* rite. This was transmitted to Japan by the Shingon tradition, and it was thence appropriated by advocates of the Shintō tradition, who developed their own version of the rite. Payne thus sheds light on the complex manner in which ritual practices were disseminated across both cultural and religious boundaries.

Lastly, in Chapter 8, "The Tantric Teachings and Rituals of the True Buddha School: The Chinese Transformation of the Vajrayāna Buddhism," Tam Wai Lun introduces us to a recently established Chinese tantric Buddhist tradition, the True Buddha School, which was founded in the 1970s by a Taiwanese master named Lu Shengyan (盧勝彥, b. 1945). Raised as a Christian, a spiritual experience in 1969 led him to seek training as a Daoist priest. He founded a religious school in the 1970s that was originally oriented toward Daoist practice, but from 1979 onward he also began receiving transmissions of Tibetan tantric practices from various masters. Over the course of the 1980s he gradually moved toward a greater identification with Vajrayāna Buddhism, changing the name of his school in the process. Currently the True Buddha School is growing into an international movement largely serving the Chinese communities in diaspora. It self-identifies with the larger Vajrayāna tradition, and integrates Daoist, Tibetan Buddhist, and traditional Chinese Buddhist practices. It is a fascinating example of a contemporary tradition that displays the venerable tendency of tantric traditions to cross boundaries.

These chapters as a whole demonstrate the dynamic nature of tantric traditions. From their inception in the mid-first millennium CE to their contemporary manifestations, tantric Buddhist traditions have been in motion, rapidly borrowing and adapting elements from rival religious traditions. And they have quickly crossed cultural boundaries, and have renewed themselves in new milieu by continuing to borrow and adapt elements encountered therein.

Notes

1. Matthew Kapstein provided a very helpful definition of the terms "sect" and "lineage," which are overlapping categories in Tibetan Buddhism and, arguably, other tantric traditions as well: "By *sect,* I mean a religious order that is distinguished from others by virtue of its institutional independence; that is, its unique character is embodied outwardly in the form of an independent hierarchy and administration, independent properties and a recognizable membership of some sort. A *lineage,* on the other hand is a continuous succession of spiritual teachers who have transmitted a given body knowledge over a period of generations but who need not be affiliated with a common sect" (1996, 284n2).
2. My translation of the following Sanskrit text edited in Horiuchi (1974, 490): *subhāṣitam idaṃ sūtraṃ vajrayānam anuttaram/sarvatāthāgataṃ guhyaṃ mahāyānābhisaṃgraham//.* The canonical Tibetan translation reads:*/rdo rje theg pa bla na med//de bzhin gshegs pa kun gyi gsang//theg pa chen po mngon bsdus pa'i// mdo sde 'di ni legs par bshad/*(fol. 48a.2–3). I am indebted to Christian Wedemeyer for bring to my attention this text's use of the term *vajrayāna.*

3. Regarding the development of the "Esoteric Teaching" designation, see Sharf (2002, 269). Regarding "Adamantine Vehicle," the dating of the *Sarvatathāgatattvasaṃgraha-nāma Mahāyāna-sūtra* is a complex problem. While early versions of this or closely related texts such as the *Vajraśekhara Tantra* were disseminated to East Asia during the eighth century, the texts in circulation at this time likely differed substantially from the Sanskrit texts preserved in Nepal centuries later, or the Tibetan translation made in the late tenth century by Rinchen bZang-po and Śraddhākaravarma. The verses of this text containing the term *Vajrayāna* thus cannot be reliably dated earlier than the tenth century.
4. Were this volume to address solely Indian and Tibetan traditions, then the use of the term *Vajrayāna* would be ideal, since this term came into common use on these cultural spheres. However, it did not come into common use in East Asia, where expressions like "Esoteric Teachings" and "Esoteric Buddhism" (*mizong fojiao* 密宗佛教) are more common. These terms, in turn, would be ideal for a volume focusing solely on East Asia (such as Orzech, Sørensen, and Payne 2011), but these expressions are not commonly used in Indian and Tibetan traditions, despite the importance of secrecy in these traditions. While the terms "tantra" and "tantric" derive from Sanskrit terms, it should be noted that they carry negative connotations. As Hugh Urban has shown in his book *Tantra: Sex, Secrecy, Politics, and Power in the Study of Religion* (2003), these terms have negative associations in both India and the West, being particularly associated with black magic in India, and with sex in the West. However, these associations are not entirely unwarranted, as many of the tantras are replete with descriptions of both violent magical rituals as well as sexual practices.
5. Regarding this, see Nattier (1991).
6. Regarding Amoghavajra and his attempt at transmitting this canon of tantric literature see Giebel (1995) and Gray (2009, 12–13).
7. Regarding the establishment of the Shingon school of esoteric Buddhism and the addition of esoteric Buddhist practice to the Tendai school in Japan during the ninth century, see Abé (1999) and Groner (2000).
8. The impact of esoteric Buddhist in China is a major focus of Orzech, Sørensen, and Payne's *Esoteric Buddhism and the Tantras in East Asia* (2011). See especially pp. 421–574.
9. See Skilling (1997, 87–89).
10. Regarding Dunhuang Tibetan tantric manuscripts, see Dalton and van Schaik (2006).
11. According to Tibetan historical sources, three catalogues of translated texts were made during the Tibetan imperial period. These include the *Lhan/lDan kar ma*, which has been dated to 812 CE (Herrmann-Pfandt 2002, 129), and the *'Phang-thang-ma*, which has been dated to 842 CE (Dotson 2007, 4). The third catalogue, the *mchims phu ma*, is apparently lost.
12. See Ronald Davidson's (2005) study of this era of Tibetan religious history.

13. Sanderson recently published a book chapter (2009) that is his most extensive presentation of his argument of the dependence of Buddhist on Śaiva tantric traditions.

References

Abé, Ryūichi. 1999. *The Weaving of Mantra: Kukai and the Construction of Esoteric Buddhist Discourse.* New York: Columbia University Press.

Dalton, Jacob, and Sam van Schaik. 2006. *Tibetan Tantric Manuscripts from Dunhang: A Descriptive Catalogue of the Stein Collection at the British Library.* Leiden and Boston: Brill.

Davidson, Ronald M. 2002. *Indian Esoteric Buddhism: A Social History.* New York: Columbia University Press.

Davidson, Ronald M. 2005. *Tibetan Renaissance: Tantric Buddhism in the Rebirth of Tibetan Culture.* New York: Columbia University Press.

Dotson, Brandon. 2007. "'Emperor' Mu rug btsan and the '*Phang thang ma Catalogue.*" *Journal of the International Association of Tibetan Studies* 3 (December): 1–25. http://www.thlib.org?tid=T3105. Accessed October 22, 2010.

Giebel, Rolf W. 1995. "The Chin-kang-ting ching yü-ch'ieh shih-pa-hui chih-kuei: An Annotated Translation." *Journal of Naritasan Institute for Buddhist Studies* 18: 107–201.

Gray, David. 2007. *The Cakrasamvara Tantra: A Study and Annotated Translation.* New York: AIBS/CBS/THUS [Columbia University Press].

Gray, David. 2009. "On the Very Idea of a Tantric Canon: Myth, Politics, and the Formation of the Bka' 'gyur." *Journal of the International Association of Tibetan Studies* 5: 1–37.

Groner, Paul. 2000. *Saichō: The Establishment of the Japanese Tendai School.* Honolulu: University of Hawai'i Press.

Herrmann-Pfandt, Adelheid. 2002. "The *Lhan Kar Ma* as a Source for the History of Tantric Buddhism." In *The Many Canons of Tibetan Buddhism,* edited by Helmut Eimer and David Germano, 129–149. Leiden: Brill.

Hodge, Stephen. 2003. *The Mahā-vairocana-abhisaṃbodhi Tantra, With Buddhaguhya's Commentary.* London: RoutledgeCurzon.

Horiuchi Kanjin 堀内寛仁. 1974. *Bon-Zō-Kan taishō shoe kongōchōkyō no kenkyū: Bonpon kōtei hen* 梵蔵漢対照初會金剛頂經の研究: 梵本校訂篇. 2 vols. Wakayama-ken Kōya-chō 和歌山県高野町: Mikkyō Bunka Kenkyūjo 密教文化研究所.

Kapstein, Matthew T. 1996. "*gDams ngag*: Tibetan Technologies of the Self." In *Tibetan Literature: Studies in Genre,* edited by José Ignacio Cabezón and Roger R. Jackson, 275–289. Ithaca, NY: Snow Lion.

Lin, Li-Kouang. 1935. "Punyodaya (Na-T'i), un propagateur du tantrisme en Chine et au Cambodge à l'époque de Hiuan-tsang." *Journal Asiatique* 227: 83–100.

Nattier, Jan. 1991. *Once Upon a Future Time: Studies in a Buddhist Prophesy of Decline.* Berkeley, CA: Asian Humanities Press.

Nihom, Max. 1998. "The Maṇḍala of Caṇḍi Gumpung (Sumatra) and the Indo-Tibetan Vajraśekharatantra." *Indo-Iranian Journal* 41 (2): 245–254.

Orzech, Charles D. 1995. "The Legend of the Iron Stūpa." In *Buddhism in Practice,* edited by Donald S. Lopez, 314–317. Princeton, NJ: Princeton University Press.

Orzech, Charles D., Henrik H. Sørensen, and Richard K. Payne, eds. 2011. *Esoteric Buddhism and the Tantras in East Asia.* Leiden: Brill.

Padoux, André. 2002. "What Do We Mean by Tantrism?" In *The Roots of Tantra,* edited by Katherine Anne Harper and Robert L. Brown, 17–24. Albany: State University of New York Press.

Sanderson, Alexis. 2009. "The Śaiva Age: The Rise and Dominance of Śaivism during the Early Medieval Period." In *Genesis and Development of Tantrism,* edited by Shingo Einoo, 41–349. Tokyo: Institute of Oriental Culture, University of Tokyo.

Sarvatathāgatatattvasaṃgraha-nāma-mahāyāna-sūtra. Tōh. 479, sDe-dge rgyud 'bum vol. nya, 1b-142a.

Sen, Tansen. 2003. *Buddhism, Diplomacy, and Trade: The Realignment of Sino-Indian Relations, 600–1400.* Honolulu: University of Hawai'i Press.

Sharf, Robert. 2002. *Coming to Terms with Chinese Buddhism: A Reading of the* Treasure Store Treatise. Honolulu: University of Hawai'i Press.

Skilling, Peter. 1997. "From bKa' bstan bcos to bKa' 'gyur and bsTan 'gyur." In *Transmission of the Tibetan Canon: Papers Presented at a Panel of the 7th Seminar of the International Association for Tibetan Studies,* edited by Helmut Eimer, 87–111. Wien: Österreichische Akademie Der Wissenschaften.

Sørensen, Henrik. 2011. "Early Esoteric Buddhism in Korea: Three Kingdoms and Unified Silla (ca. 600–918)." In *Esoteric Buddhism and the Tantras in East Asia,* edited by Charles D. Orzech, Henrik H. Sørensen and Richard K. Payne, 575–596. Leiden: Brill.

Urban, Hugh B. 2003. *Tantra: Sex, Secrecy, Politics, and Power in the Study of Religion.* Berkeley: University of California Press.

1

Buddhas, Siddhas, *and Indian Masculine Ideals*

John Powers

Masculinities in Conflict

Discursive studies of societies from around the world have shown that notions of gender and bodies vary considerably across cultures and over time. As Judith Butler has noted, sex roles are "performative," not natural (1999, 235). Societies develop and socialize certain traits, attitudes, and behaviors as normative for men or women, and this process is not under the conscious control of people who try to live them. R. W. Connell states that "[m]asculinities come into existence at particular times and places and are always subject to change. Masculinities are, in a word, historical" (2005, 185). For men and women attempting to conform to the sometimes conflicting norms of gender, the contingent nature of these discourses is seldom apparent, and in most cases they are widely hegemonic.

Indic texts that describe the life of the Buddha (ca. fourth to fifth centuries BCE) indicate that there were two primary male ideals during the time when his legend was being constructed: the brahman priest, devoted to religious performance and meditation, and the *kṣatriya* (warrior and ruler), who excels in martial arts, athletics, and warfare. In brahmanical literature, brahmans are portrayed as spiritually inclined and widely respected. Their high social status is a result of their virtuous actions in past lives, but in Buddhist sources there is a recurring counter-discourse in which the Buddha declares that birth alone is not enough: only those who truly act in accordance with religious ideals merit the designation "brahman."[1]

The *kṣatriya* is widely valorized as an ideal type, but brahmanical sources warn of the negative karmic effects of a life devoted to fighting and killing, and they depict brahmans as better suited to the higher goals of religion, particularly liberation (*mokṣa*) from cyclic existence.[2] This tension is never resolved in Indic sources, and though the two groups are presented as essential to the preservation and advancement of society, their contrasting roles and activities are clearly separated. Brahmans should only take up arms in extraordinary circumstances, and the predispositions (*adhikāra*) with which they are born make them uniquely qualified to perform the rituals that preserve social order and maintain the cosmos. *Kṣatriyas* rule states and fight wars, but these activities enmesh them in mundane concerns and actions that lead to negative karma, and thus constitute an impediment to religious pursuits.

This tension also figures in Buddhist texts. Traditional accounts of the Buddha's life report that he was born into a *kṣatriya* family and was named Siddhārtha Gautama. His biographies provide lengthy descriptions of his exploits in athletics and martial arts, in which he easily bests all of his contemporaries. In addition, during his young adulthood he is depicted as a sexual "stallion" who has up to three wives and tens of thousands of courtesans.[3] He sexually satisfies all of them, and each believes that he only spends time with her. In several biographies, his father, King Śuddhodana, tries to keep Siddhārtha involved in worldly affairs and to turn his attention away from the pitfalls of cyclic existence so that he will engage in the activities expected of a *kṣatriya* and not become interested in religious practice. The prince lives in the "women's quarters," where he is surrounded by beautiful females skilled in the erotic arts, whose only task is to keep him entertained.[4] His sexual exploits form a key part of this narrative, and his performance exceeds the wildest dreams of most men. His courtesans all proclaim his erotic proficiency, and his energy never flags. In addition, he outshines all his contemporaries in sports and martial arts.

Masculinity and Sports

An important event in this part of the future Buddha's biography is his marriage to Yaśodharā, the most beautiful princess in the region. Śuddhodana wants his son to wed, produce male heirs, and inherit the kingdom, but

Yaśodharā's father, Daṇḍapāṇi, has doubts regarding the prince's manliness. Because Siddhārtha has grown up in the women's quarters surrounded by courtesans, Daṇḍapāṇi fears that he has become effeminate and has neglected the martial training required of *kṣatriyas*. Warriors are toughened by competition with other warriors and develop masculine traits through rough camaraderie; by spending too much time in sexual dalliances and living among women, Siddhārtha may have become soft and thus unfit to rule and to fight his kingdom's enemies.[5]

When Śuddhodana presents these concerns to his son, Siddhārtha assures him that while he may not have spent much time training or exercising, he can best any rival in sports and martial arts contests. A tournament is arranged and the hand of Yaśodharā is the prize. The strongest, fastest, fittest men compete in "archery, fighting, boxing, cutting, stabbing, speed, and feats of strength, use of elephants, horses, chariots, bows, and spears, and argument."[6] In every event Siddhārtha outshines them all. The *Extensive Sport* summarizes the result: "Then an exhibition was given by prince Siddhārtha in which he displayed his feats in all the [martial] arts. There was no one to equal him in either wrestling or boxing."[7]

None of the accounts that describe the tournament indicates that Siddhārtha trained for this event, nor did he need to lift weights, run sprints, or follow any special diet in preparation for his outstanding manly exploits. He was born with a perfect body, one that was naturally stronger and better coordinated than those of his contemporaries, and no amount of training on their part would have allowed them to match his strength and skill.[8] At the conclusion of the tournament Daṇḍapāṇi is satisfied that Siddhārtha is an outstanding *kṣatriya* and gladly agrees that he should marry Yaśodharā.

The Ultimate Man

Indic sources that describe the Buddha emphasize the idea that he had a perfect male physique, one that completely surpassed the bodies of every man of his time and was testament to his extraordinary spiritual accomplishments in past lives and the vast store of merit he had accumulated through asceticism, generosity, ethics, patience, meditation, and particularly through his willingness to sacrifice his own body for the benefit of others. He is described as "handsome, good looking, graceful, possessing supreme beauty of complexion, with sublime beauty and sublime presence, remarkable to behold."[9] The fruition of his exertions in past lives was a birth with the body of the "ultimate man" (*puruṣottama*), adorned with the physical characteristics of a great man (*mahāpuruṣa-lakṣaṇa*). In the earliest extant descriptions, there are thirty-two major physical characteristics, and later literature adds a further eighty secondary ones.[10]

Indian Buddhist texts devote considerable attention to elaborate descriptions of his unique physiognomy, particularly the details of the physical characteristics of a great man, and also to discussions of the past practices that produced the merit that made their actualization possible. The most extensive description in the Pāli canon is found in the "Discourse on the Physical Characteristics" (*Lakkhaṇa-sutta*).[11] Another detailed account of the Buddha's extraordinary physique is given in the "Brahmāyu Discourse" (*Brahmāyu-sutta*) by a brahman named Uttara, who visits the Buddha intending to ascertain for himself whether or not he really is a "great man" as his followers claim. A great man epitomizes wisdom and has attained the pinnacle of spiritual realization, but his attainments can only be definitively confirmed by his physique. Uttara listens to a sermon by the Buddha but is unconvinced. Fools may parrot words of wisdom, but they cannot fake the body of a great man, and only by verifying the Buddha's possession of the thirty-two physical characteristics can Uttara determine his level of spiritual realization.

Uttara examines the Buddha's body and ascertains that he possesses thirty of the major physical characteristics, which include a fist-sized lump on top of his head (*uṣṇīṣa*); a bright silver tuft of coiled hair between his eyebrows about a meter in length (*ūrṇā*); flat feet with a spoked wheel pattern on the soles; webbed fingers and toes; arms that can reach down to his knees without him bending over; legs like an antelope's; eyelashes like a cow's; and golden colored skin so smooth that no dust or dirt can settle on it. Two crucial features cannot be verified by Uttara's detailed examination: a long, copper-colored tongue and a sheathed penis. Reading his mind, the Buddha allows the audience to view his sheathed penis, and then he extrudes his tongue, touching the tip into each earhole and then covering his forehead with it.[12]

This display—and the Buddha's physique—would probably strike most contemporary readers as freakish, but Uttara is deeply impressed and concludes that there is no doubt that the Buddha is indeed a great man. Brahmāyu, Uttara's teacher, hears his student's description of the Buddha's body and decides to see the ultimate man for himself and also asks to see the master's sheathed penis and tongue, which he links with ideal masculinity: "Upon your body, Gotama, is what is normally concealed by a cloth hidden by a sheath, greatest of men? Though named by a word of the feminine gender, is your tongue really a manly (*narassika*) one?[13] Is your tongue also large? . . . Please stick it out a bit and cure our doubts."[14] The Buddha obliges, and Brahmāyu is also convinced that he is a great man. After a similar display in the "Discourse on the Physical Characteristics," the Buddha informs his audience that he attained this perfect body as a result of "mighty deeds, generosity, discipline, abstinence, honoring parents, ascetics, and brahmans."[15]

The Buddha's sheathed penis figures in a number of accounts. It is associated with stallions, bulls, and elephants, all symbolic of masculinity in Indic sources. In addition to convincing skeptical brahmans of his spiritual attainments, it is used as a basis for religious instruction in some narratives. According to tradition, a "first council" of *arhat*s was convened following the Buddha's death, during which his attendant Ānanda was chastised for lifting up the robes covering the Master's corpse so that a group of female devotees could view his phallus. Ānanda defended his actions on the grounds that upon beholding the Buddha's perfect organ the women would become disgusted with the female form and would set their minds on future male rebirths, which would constitute a significant spiritual advance for them (La Vallée Poussin 1976, 4–7).

In a Mahāyāna text entitled *Discourse on the Ocean-Like Meditation of Buddha Remembrance*, the Buddha uses his penis to convert heretics. He creates a huge mountain and lays on his back, extruding his phallus and wrapping it around the mountain seven times, and then extends it to the heaven of Brahmā. A group of naked Jain ascetics who witness this display are so impressed that they decide to convert.[16]

Interestingly, there is no indication in this or other Indian Buddhist sources that size matters. The Buddha's male organ and tongue may be extended for instructional purposes, but the size of his penis has no bearing on his masculinity, nor is there any indication that it was longer than those of other men in its normal state. Length and diameter are not related to his ability to sexually satisfy his courtesans in his early life. This reflects a general sense in Indic sources that a long penis is not a desirable feature for men. The *Kāma Sūtra*, for example, declares that men with small organs are better lovers and have calm and agreeable personalities, while those with large, bulky bodies and long penises tend to be violent and aggressive.[17] Men fortunate enough to have small phalluses also live longer and enjoy greater happiness.

Female sexual satisfaction is not connected with the size or diameter of the penis in any Indic text I have seen; rather, the key factor is the amount and quality of semen they receive. Women crave semen, and the more a man ejaculates, the greater their sexual pleasure. Caraka indicates that the ideal is ejaculation "like an elephant," in which a copious amount of semen is transferred.[18] Large amounts of semen attest to male virility, and the quantity and quality are directly related to the odds of conceiving a son. Sons are highly valued in India, both in past times and today, and a man who produces large amounts of high-quality semen is more likely to engender a son than others whose output is more meager and of inferior potency. Women desire both semen and sons, so men with copious seminal discharges satisfy their mates and continue their family lines.[19]

An example of the linkage between volume and potency of semen and masculinity is a story from Laos reported by Charles Archaimbault, in which the Buddha overhears some monks gossiping. An evil disciple attempts to besmirch the Master's reputation by stating that the Buddha has no difficulty maintaining celibacy because he is a eunuch, and so lacks the natural desires of other men. Hearing this, some monks become confused and begin to doubt his masculinity. The Buddha asks them, "Do you really question my virility? Do you really think my virtues are a reflection of impotence?" He then walks into a secluded grove and emerges with his cupped hands brimming with semen and declares, "Here is proof of my manhood!" His monastic followers are left with no doubts regarding his manly bona fides, and then he tosses his emission into a nearby river and washes his hands. The seminal discharge is so potent that a female fish that swims through it becomes pregnant, and later gives birth to a human son, who grows up to become the *arhat* Upagupta (Archaimbault 1972, 55).

Similar scenarios recur in a number of accounts of the Buddha's life. He often shrugs off insults that disparage his meditative accomplishments or his claims to have attained awakening, but vigorously defends himself when his consummate masculinity is questioned. An example is a story in the *Monastic Code of the Original Everything Exists School*, in which Siddhārtha is preparing to leave his father's palace and pursue the life of a wandering religious mendicant, but he fears that if he does so before conceiving a son, other *kṣatriyas* might think that he is not a manly man, which would undermine his reputation and that of his monastic order. He then impregnates his wife—after having already resolved to abandon her—in order to forestall this potential problem.[20]

As these stories indicate, Indian Buddhist texts devote considerable attention to the Buddha's body and emphasize his paradigmatic masculinity. His physique elicits admiration from his male compatriots in his early life, and even after he renounces the world and pursues the path of an ascetic seeker of liberation, men, particularly kings, proclaim the perfection of his form and affirm that he has lost none of his strength or athleticism and continues to look the part of a warrior. At the same time, he is described as the ultimate sage who has fully understood the truth (*dharma*) and who possesses perfect eloquence and clarity of insight. He surpasses the religious leaders of his time, and many members of other religious orders who meet him are converted. His body is often the decisive factor. The Buddha's spiritual attainments are also described in detail, and they are linked with the physical attainments of a great man, which proclaim his perfect virtue and wisdom. Buddhaghosa declares that the body of a buddha "impresses worldly people, and because of this he is fit to be relied upon by laypeople."[21]

Because the Buddha is the ultimate man, he must perfectly perform the two apparently contradictory roles of the contemplative, religiously inclined brahman and the vigorous, martial, athletic *kṣatriya*. Indian texts maintain this tension throughout their accounts of the Buddha's life, and neither is downplayed or diminished. Several narratives indicate that even as an old man the Buddha retained exceptional vitality and physical beauty, along with undiminished wisdom and insight.

The physical characteristics of a great man are extolled in Indian Buddhist sources as the perfection of male beauty and are linked with extraordinary acts of virtue in past lives. According to Vasubandhu, each is produced by the cultivation of one hundred merits,[22] and Buddhaghosa states that each "is born from its corresponding action."[23] The *Extensive Sport* indicates that the Buddha's acquisition of a sheathed penis was the consequence of celibacy and generosity in past lives and testifies to his perfection of these qualities.

The Buddha's unusual tongue is also linked with past practice of virtue connected with speech and eating and is a testament to his perfection of truthfulness and eloquence. In one narrative in the *Divine Legends*, the Buddha upbraids a skeptical brahman who doubts his teachings. The Buddha sticks out his tongue and covers his face up to the hairline, and then he asks: "What do you think, brahman, could a man able to extrude his tongue from his mouth and cover the entire surface of his face knowingly lie, even for the sake of hundreds of thousands of kingdoms of universal monarchs?" The chastened brahman agrees that this display proves the Buddha's integrity.[24]

A number of conversion stories begin with an encounter with a doubter who is impressed by the Buddha's physique. Many of these include a head-to-foot description of his body that emphasizes the physical characteristics of a great man and proclaims him to be the epitome of masculine beauty. Several kings who describe the Buddha's body to him lament that such a perfect physical specimen, one clearly suited to ruling a kingdom and subduing enemies, has renounced the life of a *kṣatriya* for religious pursuits. In the *Extensive Sport*, the king of Magadha says to the Buddha, "You are in the flower of your youth! Your complexion is brilliant; you are clearly robust. Accept from me abundant riches and women. Stay here in my kingdom and enjoy yourself!"[25] The Buddha responds that he has overcome any interest in the body and is fully aware of what he has left behind: "I no longer have any impulse of desire. I abandoned everything that is desirable and gave up thousands of beautiful women. I found no happiness in the things of the world and renounced them all in order to gain supreme awakening, the greatest happiness."

The *Acts of the Buddha* dwells on the effect that his body has on women, who are unable to resist staring at him. Even after years of asceticism and living as a wandering mendicant, "his beautiful body was transformed by shaving his head and wearing cast-off garments, but he was still covered in the color of gold [radiating] from his body." A group of women who saw him in a monk's robes opined that he "should be humbling enemy princes" and "be gazed at by hordes of women."[26]

Beauty and Virtue

Indian religious literature assumes a close linkage between physical beauty and virtue. A beautiful body is the result of the successful practice of meritorious actions, while ugliness proclaims moral deficiency. As Daniel Boucher notes, "The classical Indian world . . . formulated an essential connection between bodily and moral attainment. Brahmanical writers . . . regularly saw bodily appearance as an indicator of character and virtue" (2008, 3).

The *Questions of Milinda* posits a direct association between physical endowments and virtue. It states that people who are short-lived, ugly, or sickly display past negative karma on their bodies, while those who suppress evil thoughts and engage in positive actions will be healthy and beautiful.[27] The *arhat* Nāgasena compares acquired merit to a currency that can be used to purchase birth in families of good lineage, a beautiful body, wealth, wisdom, worldly glory, heavenly glory, and even nirvana. He compares the situation of a virtuous person to that of a wealthy man in a bazaar, who can buy whatever he wants, and he adds that the teachings of the Buddha provide people with opportunities to accumulate this currency.[28]

These ideas are linked to notions of karma and rebirth that are commonly accepted by Indian religions, including Buddhism. Practice of virtue results in better rebirths, and this includes enhanced physical endowments, wealth, good fortune, and high social status. Birth as a brahman or *kṣatriya* is due to meritorious deeds in past lives. Several Buddhist sources state that all buddhas are born into either brahman or *kṣatriya* families, depending on which group is most highly regarded at a particular time. In the Buddha's time, *kṣatriya*s had the better reputation, and that is why he chose *kṣatriya* parents.[29]

If we look at the Buddha's life as narrative, other factors are apparent. As the ultimate man, the Buddha must excel in both religious pursuits and in martial arts. Brahmans are forbidden by their social function as priests from engaging in athletic contests and martial pursuits, except in exigent circumstances. Physical contact between a brahman and someone belonging to a lower social group (including *kṣatriya*s) leads to a transfer of ritual pollution from lower to higher, and so if the Buddha were born a brahman, he would not have been able to compete with *kṣatriya*s merely to secure a marriage. *Kṣatriya*s are the group in traditional Indian society that excels in martial arts, and so the Buddha as the ultimate man must be a member of this group in order to prove himself against the best competition. If he were to out-wrestle brahmans and best them in archery, his victory would be a hollow one because brahmans are not warriors or athletes. But *kṣatriya*s are fully capable of entering the religious life and can attain nirvana and other proximate goals, such as supernatural abilities and entry into advanced meditative states. Had the life stories of the Buddha cast him in the role of a brahman, he would have had difficulty proving himself in the martial aspects of the ultimate man's persona, but birth as a *kṣatriya* presents no barrier to his religious pursuits.

In order to perform his role as a buddha, Siddhārtha required a perfect male body that publicly proclaimed his consummate virtue and wisdom. Had he been born with an unattractive physique or in a destitute family, people of the time would have assumed this to be the result of sinful actions in past lives, which would have made it difficult or impossible for him to become established as a religious teacher. As the *Questions of Rāṣṭrapāla Discourse* states, "Fools, due to their arrogance, will be thrown into evil states, destinies among unfortunate rebirths, and rebirths in poor and despised families. They will be blind from birth, ugly, and will have little strength."[30]

Gender is also a factor. A buddha must be male because males are the dominant sex in Indian society. Indian Buddhist sources assume that male bodies are better suited to religious pursuits and are naturally more conducive to cultivation of self-control than those of females. The female body is conceived as oozing fluids and is difficult to control and discipline, and in many sources women are portrayed as slaves to their carnal desires. Men are naturally stronger, hardier, better suited to physical regimens and discipline, and they outperform women in martial pursuits and in withstanding the rigors of religious asceticism.

As noted earlier, one of the physical characteristics of a great man is a sheathed penis, and the eighty secondary physical characteristics include a perfectly formed male organ, and so presumably only men can become buddhas. This reflects the social standing of men in Indian society. A buddha is the most exalted of all beings as a result of past religious practice, and his final life must reflect this status. A buddha cannot be born among the lower classes because the final birth of a bodhisattva (buddha in training) is the culmination of countless lifetimes spent engaging in virtuous deeds and accumulating vast stores of merit. An incipient buddha will have the best of all possible bodies and will be born into a wealthy family at the apex of society. And he must be a man because the social status of males is superior to that of females. The logic is clear, even if the premises are flawed. The creators of the Buddha legend presumed that the main features of their society are reproduced in other worlds and at other times. As we have seen, a number of sources state that buddhas are always born into either brahman or *kṣatriya* families, assuming that Indian social groupings are universal rather than specific to a certain region and time.

Moreover, the gender discourses they assume, while specific to their culture, are deemed to be universal. Descriptions of the Buddha's perfect body differ considerably from current notions of paradigmatic masculinity, but there is no indication that the authors of his legend were aware that there are other possible ideal masculine types.

Performing Masculinity

An emphasis on performance runs through the stories of the Buddha's life. In the *Extensive Sport*, a recurring narrative theme has him reflecting on the standard sequence of events in a buddha's life and considering how best to display the actions expected of him. Gods and sages know this sequence and eagerly anticipate his demonstration of paradigmatic actions. During his mother's pregnancy, gods come to her chamber to watch him enact particular paradigmatic events, and the *Extensive Sport* states that while in her womb he was encased in a transparent crystal casket that allowed others to view him. Throughout this period, gods visit him, and he appears to enjoy the attention.[31] The bodhisattva regularly ponders upcoming events in his progression toward full attainment of buddhahood and considers how his actions will impact on his audiences.

His perfect body is a necessary aspect of this narrative trope because it demonstrates to all that his past practice of virtue resulted in a form that epitomizes the highest development of the human physique, and it is said to surpass even those of the gods in beauty. The physical characteristics of a great man are a crucial distinguishing feature: the bodies of gods may be radiant and powerful, but they lack the major and minor physical characteristics. Their exalted positions are also a result of past practice of virtue, but their lives as deities are merely temporary and will end when their accumulated store of virtue is exhausted. The great man, however, has attained the summit of cyclic existence and is the teacher of gods and humans. His unique physiology is a public statement of his supreme spiritual accomplishments. Despite this emphasis on the spiritual, the fact that stories about his life repeat the themes of his physical beauty, strength, manliness, and athletic prowess, along with descriptions of his supernatural powers and unsurpassed insight, shows that the authors felt a need to maintain both aspects of his ultimate manhood in their development of the literary character of the Buddha.

The Adepts: A New Paradigm

The tropes discussed so far are found throughout Pāli literature and Mahāyāna works. In the tantras, however, some significant conceptual shifts occur, but some earlier discourses are retained. The notion that past practice of virtue is reflected by a person's physique is assumed, but new meditative techniques are presented that allow ill-favored people, members of despised castes, and women to make rapid progress on the path and attain the highest levels of accomplishment. In the *Lives of the Eighty-Four Adepts,* stories of simple, extraordinarily effective, and often personalized instructions enable newly initiated practitioners to reach the supreme attainment after a fortuitous encounter with a yogi who bestows the teachings of the great seal (*mahāmudrā*), followed by a relatively short period of intense practice (commonly twelve years). Many of the adepts have little or no previous familiarity with the dharma, some are brahmans who follow a different path, and some are well advanced in years and in poor health before they receive instructions. The notion that past practice of virtue is proclaimed on a person's physique is articulated in several stories, including that of Anaṅga, who is said to be extremely handsome due to meditating on patience in a past life (Dorje 1979, 2:251). The same is true of Kalapa, who also had a beautiful physique due to past cultivation of patience, but his good looks led to frustration because people constantly stared at him and followed him. To get away from the unwanted attention, he moved to a cemetery (ibid., 2:106–107).

Reflecting assumptions about the linkage between physical attributes and morality in Indian society, negative deeds produce correlative bodily effects. Before encountering the dharma, Thaganapa was a compulsive liar, and he was warned that liars will have bad breath, their tongues will not work properly, and others will not be convinced by their words (ibid., 2:85–87). An underlying message of the stories of the *siddhas* is that for ordinary beings caught up in the karmic whirl, positive and negative actions leave corresponding imprints on both present and future bodies, and these can be read by others as indicators of a person's moral stature.

For those who receive the extraordinary teachings of *mahāmudrā*, however, the situation is different. Catrapa is told, "Your body shows what you have done previously; what happens later depends on the mind" (ibid., 2:97). Adepts who successfully grasp the teachings they receive make rapid progress, and in some cases this is accompanied by physical transformation. Tantipa was an unexceptional person who had reached old age before encountering a teacher. His children banished him to a hut, where he chanced to encounter a yogi who was willing to give him the highest esoteric lore. As a result of his practice, he quickly attained tantric accomplishments (*siddhi*), and one night his family was amazed to see that he was engaged in meditation, surrounded by beautiful celestial maidens. The next day his body was transformed into that of a handsome sixteen-year-old: "From his body immeasurable rays of light arose, and none of the people could bear to look at him. His body was like a clear polished mirror, and everything appeared as light" (ibid., 2:58).

In most of the stories of the adepts, however, their bodies remain unaltered. They may develop greater vigor and their demeanor changes, but there is no indication that any of them acquire the physical characteristics of a great man. At the end of each account, the reader is informed that the *siddha* traveled in that very body to the realm of the *ḍākas*, which is characterized as the ultimate attainment.

Indian tantras often assert that their meditative techniques far surpass those of the common Mahāyāna and enable those fortunate enough to encounter tantric teachings (and practice them effectively) to make rapid progress and greatly shorten the time spent on the path to awakening. They generally assume a linkage between beauty and virtue and the trope of the physical characteristics of the great man as testament to buddhahood, but they also promise that their techniques can result in the highest attainment without the necessity of transformation of one's present body into one resembling that of the Buddha. The Buddha is still depicted in tantric works as having the physical characteristics of a great man, but adepts constitute a new ideal, one that retains some aspects of earlier tropes while downplaying others. The tantras often contain transgressive images and enjoin trainees to engage in actions that were condemned in traditional Indian society, and the lives of the adepts reflect these transgressive tendencies. Several belong to outcaste groups, some like Lūyipa ingest offensive substances (in his case, fish entrails), and they often inhabit liminal places like cemeteries and cremation grounds, which are shunned by ordinary people.

A common narrative element in the tales of the eighty-four *siddhas* depicts a person who is receptive to the dharma encountering an existential crisis. A wandering yogi recognizes this and offers the teachings of the great seal, generally in the form of pithy and personalized verses that provide a template for practice. The focus of this training is the mind, rather than the body, and the resulting transformation is mainly cognitive. Sometimes there are physical benefits, including a return to youth and vitality, but for the most part their exterior appearance remains the same. In the case of Gorakṣa, whose hands and feet had been cut off in punishment for a crime he did not commit, his limbs are restored, and other adepts acquire magical abilities that enable them to alter their physical circumstances and the world around them (ibid., 2:38–43). These powers are testament to their spiritual accomplishments, much as they are in biographies of the Buddha, who assuaged the doubts of skeptics by his performance of magical feats.

Sexual Yogas

Indian tantric texts present a range of practices and paradigms. In the *yoginī* tantras, there is a pervasive emphasis on the extraordinary efficacy of sexual yogas to facilitate spiritual development. This notion is seen in the opening stanzas of several of these works, in which the Buddha appears in sexual embrace with a female consort before a shocked audience. The opening statement of the *Hevajra-tantra* declares that the Buddha was "residing in the vagina (*bhaga*) of the Vajrayoginī who is the essence of the body, speech, and mind of all thus gone ones" (Snellgrove 1959, 2:2). The assembly is scandalized by the sight of the founder of the Buddhist monastic order—who enjoined strict celibacy to his followers as the precondition for effective dharma practice—*in flagrante delicto* and engaged in a public act of coitus. They faint, but are revived by the Buddha's power; he informs them that the earlier discourses of celibacy were merely expedient teachings delivered for practitioners of inferior capacity and that the most advanced trainees have the ability to skillfully use desire as part of the path.

According to tantric medical theory, these sexual yogas make use of a natural phenomenon: at the moment of orgasm, coarser levels of mind fade away and more subtle ones manifest. The subtlest of these is the mind of clear light (*prabhāsvara-citta*), which arises at the time of death and precedes entry into the intermediate state (*antarābhava*). At the moment of orgasm, one also experiences the arising of subtle levels of mind, but most people take no notice of this and may fall asleep or transition back to coarser forms of cognition. Through training, a yogic adept can enhance the manifestation of more profound levels of consciousness and can maintain this state, which creates greater familiarity with the clear light nature of mind and enables one to simulate the world of a buddha.

Buddhas live in the clear light nature of mind, and their actions are spontaneous responses to their environment, informed by the recognition that all appearances are an interplay of luminosity and emptiness (*śūnyatā*). For ordinary beings, sexual activity is born of desire, and engagement in coitus serves to further increase attachment and inauspicious mental states. Adepts, however, learn to channel the energy of desire and incorporate it into the path, and instead of using mental effort to suppress desire, they redirect it in skillful ways. The state of buddhahood is one of bliss; all negative emotions have been eliminated, reality is recognized as empty, and so it no longer has the power to evoke suffering or despair. Actions that lead to craving and pain for ordinary beings become tools of spiritual practice. Thus in the *Great Violent Wrath Tantra* the Buddha advises his disciples:

> In a pleasant place where there are no distractions, in secret, you should take a woman who has desire. . . . You should bring the woman near you and seat her before you. Each should gaze intently on the other, with mutual desire. . . . Then make your throbbing penis (*sphurad-vajra*) enter the opening in the center of the lotus (vagina). Give one thousand thrusts, one hundred thousand, ten million, one hundred million in her three-petalled lotus. . . . Insert your *vajra* and offer your mind with pleasure![32]

The theory behind this practice is that there is nothing inherently wrong with sexual activity. The *yoginī* tantras enjoin practitioners to engage in a plethora of actions that were condemned by brahmanical orthodoxy in ancient India, including eating meat, drinking wine, and even ingesting polluting substances such as urine and feces. From the perspective of the fully awakened, everything is empty, and nothing is either inherently good or bad. The *Great Violent Wrath Tantra* declares, "The mind precedes all things good and bad."[33]

Freedom and Spontaneity

The tantras describe the life of an adept as one that is completely free. Adepts wander from place to place, caring nothing for social conventions, happily exchanging food (and bodily fluids) with anyone from any social situation. Adepts act spontaneously, adapting their actions to the environment, and feel no obligation to live up to the expectations of others. The *Hevajra-tantra* declares, "Free from learning and ceremony and any sense of shame, the yogi wanders wherever he wills, filled with great compassion" (Snellgrove 1959, 20). Nothing has the power to frighten him, and he is secure in the confidence born of supreme power: "Whatever demon should appear before him, even if it is of the rank of Indra, he will have no fear, for he wanders like a lion" (20).

Social norms are ridiculed as the foolish constraints of ordinary beings. Adepts make their own rules and, motivated by pure compassion untainted by ego or the need for approval, work for the benefit of others, but without any expectation of recompense. Even when they demand fees for their services, these only reflect the value of the dharma they maintain and help recipients to recognize this. Their skill in means (*upāya-kauśalya*) allows them to use any aspect of the world for the benefit of themselves and others. In the *Hevajra-tantra*, the Buddha tells Vajragarbha (Snellgrove 1959, 34),

> That by which the world is bound,
> By that very thing it is released from bondage.
> But the world is deluded and does not understand this truth,
> And one who does not grasp this truth cannot attain accomplishments (*siddhi*).

This attitude is contrasted with that of conventional Buddhists, who adhere to lay vows or monastic restrictions. As a result, they are bound by their inferior dharma and fail to grasp the expansive vision of the tantras. They remain ordinary and, while they make plodding progress and develop conventional moral qualities and corresponding improved life situations in future rebirths, their path is a slow and uninspired one. From the standpoint of the *yoginī* tantras, all beings have the potential for buddhahood. The subtlest level of the mind of every sentient being is characterized by pure luminosity, and adventitious defilements are the only thing that prevents the full actualization of this. Thus the *Hevajra-tantra* declares, "beings are buddhas, but this is hidden by adventitious negative factors; when these are removed, beings are then actually buddhas" (Snellgrove 1959, 70).

In addition to quickly attaining the realization of a buddha, adepts acquire mighty magical powers that place them beyond the comprehension even of gods. According to the *Perfect Awakening of Great Radiance Tantra*, adepts are sorcerers (Tib. *rig 'dzin*; Skt. *vidyādhara*) who use their supernatural abilities to benefit others and to convert them through public displays of magical feats:

> When the lord of mantras has eliminated all doubts concerning the nature of the self
> Then he will truly become a benefactor of all beings in the world.
> He will be endowed with various wondrous abilities

And attain the state of a magician (*mig 'phrul can*).[34]
In brief, when action and birth are projected simultaneously
The mantra adept [fulfills] the attainment that arises from mind.
When this is accomplished, he can travel in the sky
Just like one who has no fear of illusions.
He will mystify with a mantra-net
Just like a great sorcerer.[35]

The *Elimination of All Negative Destinies Tantra* proclaims that adepts become the teachers of gods and that deities worship them. At one point during the teaching of this text, the assembled Indic gods proclaim,

> We will attend him like slaves ready to serve and to obey all his commands! We will grant every benefit, happiness, and complete accomplishment. Blessed One, in short, we will wipe the dust of his feet with our heads. Blessed One, we will venerate him. Blessed One, we worship him and follow behind him![36]

In addition, effective tantric practice also produces improved bodies. The *Arising of Supreme Pleasure Tantra* proclaims the maxim that the "first great result" of acquiring good karma is rebirth as a man and adds that those who successfully practice its teachings also develop robust male physiques.[37]

Siddhas' *Bodies*

In other tantric sources, however, there is a significant shift in descriptions of the physical benefits of training. The tales of the eighty-four adepts generally describe physically ordinary men and women. A few are said to be attractive as a result of past practice of virtue, but one important implied message in these stories is that people with little or no previous engagement with the dharma, those born into despised castes as a result of past negative actions, and even women can reach the highest levels of attainment through practice of the meditations of the great seal. Their final apotheosis is a cognitive one, derived from sublimely effective techniques skillfully adapted to their individual proclivities by awakened teachers. They attain the highest realizations and travel to the realm of the *ḍākas* in the bodies in which they were born—many of which are ordinary or even unattractive—although their spiritual transformation enables them to perform extraordinary feats with them.

The notion that the bodies of buddhas are adorned with the physical characteristics of a great man is retained in many tantric texts, but adepts need not acquire them. The *Hevajra-tantra* disparages the notion that a fully awakened being must develop the sort of physique traditionally attributed to buddhas: "great knowledge abides in the body, free from all imaginary constructions, but although it pervades all things and exists in the body, it does not arise in the body" (Snellgrove 1959, 2). The *Secret Assembly Tantra* goes even further, relegating the physical characteristics of buddhas in mainstream Mahāyāna texts to "the stage of the lower accomplishments" (*hīna-siddhi*).[38] It accepts the notion that practitioners who follow the standard path culminating in buddhahood acquire resplendent golden bodies adorned with the characteristics of a great man, but it claims that those who perfect the trainings it describes utterly surpass them. It even avers that the *siddhis* one acquires as a result of its teachings can destroy ordinary buddhas, including Vajradhara, who is associated with yogic power. The *Wheel Binding Tantra* proclaims that adepts acquire the ability to "terrify" ordinary buddhas and can bind them to their will, despite the fact that buddhas are presented in Mahāyāna literature as the most powerful of beings. The tantra describes its path:

> Drinking the water of bliss, the adept makes contact through practice of the nondual yoga of nonduality; through this training all sins are eliminated. Practicing by way of contact and even sexual intercourse, one becomes liberated from all sins and acquires a purified body that is free from illness. Purified of all sins, he attains the level of a thus gone one.[39]

As noted earlier, there is a pervasive concern with bodies in Indian Buddhist literature. The relative level of development of a practitioner is proclaimed by his or her physical attributes. Buddhas have the best possible bodies due to innumerable lifetimes engaged in prodigious acts of virtue, sacrificing their own bodies for the benefit of others, engaging in meditative training, and adhering to the norms of the monastic code. The major and minor marks become sequentially manifest in later lives on their exteriors, following perfection of the corresponding good quality. In their final births they are endowed with perfect male bodies whose beauty demonstrates their spiritual perfection and quells the doubts of skeptics. Stories of the Buddha's life abound with accounts of spontaneous conversions based on merely viewing his perfect body. Similarly, there are numerous stories of his advanced followers converting non-Buddhists who see their beautiful physiques.

The tantras also associate spiritual advancement with increasing physical perfection, but this is mainly internal and is not necessarily reflected in one's outer appearance. Adepts acquire various impressive abilities and may fly through the air, radiate light from their bodies, and transform their shapes, but in most cases their outer forms remain largely unchanged. The real transformation occurs in the "subtle body" (*sūkṣma-deha*), which is contiguous with the physical body and interacts with it.[40] This subtle body has energy channels (*nāḍī*) through which subtle energies called "winds" (*prāṇa*) and "drops" (*bindu*) circulate. With most beings, the movement of these energies operates outside their conscious awareness or control, but tantric adepts develop the ability to control the energies and use powerful meditative techniques to actualize profound states of mind that are conducive to the attainment of *siddhi*s and ultimate awakening.

The *Hevajra-tantra* and other texts describe a mystical physiology of channels and subtle energies that is gradually brought under the conscious control of adepts. There are three main channels: (1) *lalanā*, located on the left side of the spinal column and associated with wisdom; (2) *rasanā*, situated on the right side and associated with method; and (3) *avadhūtī*, which is roughly contiguous with the spine and integrates the two main aspects of practice. A primal energy called *caṇḍālī* normally resides at the base of the central channel, and through visualization one can cause it to rise up through a series of stages (*cakra*) located at the navel, heart, throat, and head, where the left and right channels wrap around the central channel and constrict the flow of energies. This process is accompanied by progressively more sublime experiences of bliss and actualization of subtle minds. According to the *Hevajra-tantra*, as *caṇḍālī*—which is both a subtle energy and a manifestation of a buddha—blazes and rises through the *cakra*s, she burns the buddhas that represent conventional Buddhist teachings and practices, and this enables the adept to transcend them and advance to the vastly more profound techniques of the Hevajra cycle. It denounces Buddhists who cling to conventional teachings and practices and who disparage tantra as misguided. It characterizes those who reject Vajrayāna as heretical as the true heretics, and further claims that only trainees who can leave conventions behind and embrace the radical freedom of the tantric path will be able to attain the ultimate level of awakening.[41]

Some tantric texts make the further claim that in the final analysis *only* their techniques are ultimately effective and that practitioners who remain within the confines of conventional practice will be unable to attain buddhahood. The *Compendium of the Truth of All Buddhas* rewrites the traditional biography of the Buddha and claims that at the penultimate stage of his spiritual trajectory he left his physical body under the Tree of Awakening in Bodhgayā and traveled to a tantric realm in a subtle body after being told by a group of buddhas that his conventional meditations were insufficient to lead him to the final level of buddhahood. Without engaging in sexual yogas, final awakening is impossible; all buddhas of the past performed these practices at this point in their careers. Recognizing the truth of their assertions, Siddhārtha perfected these techniques with a consort named Tilottamā, following which he returned to his physical body.[42]

Concluding Remarks

Indian tantric texts reject the masculine paradigms of brahmans and *kṣatriyas* that are central to discourses relating to the Buddha and buddhahood in the Pāli canon and in Mahāyāna works. Adepts surpass brahmans in their meditative realizations, and because of their magical powers they have no need either for physical strength or mundane *siddhis*. *Siddhas* do as they please and wander at will, and they can attract any women they want with magical spells. Even the gods are no match for them; the *Secret Assembly Tantra* declares,

> In the supreme accomplishment of all sacraments, meditating on the *vajra* body, you will become a sorcerer among the great sacraments. In invisibility and so forth you alone will illumine the thousand worlds, you will steal from all the buddhas and enjoy the women of the gods.[43]

The tantras overturn mainstream assumptions about bodies and virtue. Outward appearance is characterized as false, and the unattractive physiques of adepts often hide their attainments. Ordinary beings commonly fail to recognize their supernatural powers, and adepts who belong to outcaste groups are assumed by the unenlightened masses to be in these positions because of moral failings in past lives. Moreover, the tantras present new images of bodies that are very different from those of mainstream imagination. The Buddha—with his golden skin, perfect male physique, and the major and minor physical characteristics of a great man—appears in this form in tantric texts, but he also introduces new buddhas with strange and sometimes grotesque physiques. The buddha Hevajra is described as having eight faces, four legs, and sixteen arms, and he tramples demons (*māra*) with his feet. He wears a garland of severed human heads around his neck, and his body is smeared with ashes from cremation grounds. His terrifying outer form hides his inner tranquil nature and frightens ordinary beings who are unable to look past appearances.

Śākyamuni's physique publicly proclaims his status as a buddha and his past perfection of virtue and meditative training, but the buddha Vajrabhairava has a body that is replete with things considered terrifying in ancient India: he has fearsome faces on several heads, and his main visage is a ferocious buffalo with sharp fangs that drip blood. His forehead is deeply wrinkled, indicating rage, and his mighty roar causes beings to freeze in terror. He eats human flesh and devours the gods Indra, Brahmā, and Viṣṇu. Like Hevajra, his neck is adorned with a garland of skulls, and he wears a garment of bloody elephant skin. Some of his thirty-four arms hold weapons dripping blood. He is surrounded by fearsome animals and lives in a landscape of barren trees with parts of bodies hanging from their branches.

These images of buddhahood contrast sharply with those of non-tantric Buddhist traditions and reflect the transgressive aspects of tantric literature. Tantric buddhas need not be handsome or physically powerful, and their bodies may repel and terrify ordinary beings. Similarly, tantric adepts make rapid progress toward the highest awakening, and in the process utterly transcend the trainees of mainstream traditions. Even the mainstream buddhas are portrayed as inferior to adepts, who can bind them with their magical spells or terrify them with abilities beyond their imagination, and who are unrestrained by the inferior norms to which others adhere.

As Mary Douglas notes, the body serves as a symbol of society, and it is not surprising that the antinomian and iconoclastic society of the *siddhas* developed alternative images that challenged those of the mainstream (1973, 137–139). The powers and prohibitions of the social structure are reproduced on the bodies of those who adhere to it, while those who reject it often develop alternative discourses of body image as part of their agenda of subversion. As Connell notes, masculinities may shift significantly as a society changes, and gender relations "are inherently historical; and their making and remaking is a political process affecting the balance of interests in society and the direction of social change" (2005, 44). The Indian tantras—particularly the *yoginī* tantras, as well as literature describing the transgressive paradigm of the *siddhas*—overturned core elements of the traditions they viewed as inferior, and in their place created new gender discourses and images of the body as part of their program of subversion.

Notes

1. See, for example, *Udāna*, Steinthal (1948, 5–6).
2. This tension is seen in the *Bhagavad-gītā*, in which the *kṣatriya* Arjuna is faced with the dilemma of fulfilling his dharma and slaying enemies—who include relatives and teachers—and the injunctions of religious codes that warn of negative karmic consequences if one harms relatives, teachers, and others to whom one is closely bound.
3. The Chinese translation of the *Mūlasarvāstivāda-vinaya* (T. 1450, 24:111–112) states that he had three wives and 60,000 courtesans.
4. The *Extensive Sport* (*Lalita-vistara*) and *Deeds of the Buddha* (*Buddha-carita*) both describe Siddhārtha's sexual exploits with his harem. See Vaidya (1958, 84ff). and Johnston (1984, 16ff).
5. *Lalitavistara*, Vaidya (1958, 100).
6. *Mahāvastu*, Senart (1977, 2:73–74).
7. Ibid., 2:75.
8. I discuss this theme at length in Powers (2009b, 67–94). Some of the themes in this chapter are also discussed in my book *A Bull of a Man: Images of Masculinity, Sex, and the Body in Indian Buddhism* (Powers 2009a).
9. *Cankī-sutta, Majjhima-nikāya*, Chalmers (1960, 2:166–167).
10. The eighty secondary physical characteristics are not found in the *Nikāyas* or the *Vinaya*. They first appear in the legends of early Buddhist figures (*Avadāna*). They are also mentioned in the Chinese translation of the *Discourse of the Great Final Release* (*Mahāparinirvāṇa-sūtra*) of the *Dīrghāgama* (T. 1, 1:12b).
11. *Dīgha-nikāya*, Carpenter (1960, 3:144ff).
12. *Brahmāyu-sutta, Majjhima-nikāya*, Chalmers (1960, 2:136–137).
13. *Jivhā*, the Pāli word for tongue, is a feminine noun.
14. *Brahmāyu-sutta, Majjhima-nikāya*, Chalmers (1960, 2:136).
15. *Lakkhaṇa-sutta, Dīgha-nikāya*, Carpenter (1960, 3:145).
16. See Soper (1949, 325). The *Discourse on the Ocean-Like Meditation of Buddha Remembrance* was originally written in Sanskrit but is now only extant in Chinese (*Guānfó sānmèi hǎi jīng* 觀佛三昧海經, T. 643).
17. *Kāmasūtra*, Shastri (1964, 2.1.4–6).

18. *Caraka Saṃhitā*, Sharma and Dash (1999, 3:1364–1369).
19. Ibid., 2:354.
20. *Mūlasarvāstivāda-vinaya* (T. 1450, 24:120).
21. *Visuddhimagga*, Rhys Davids (1975, 211); see also *Samantapāsādikā*, Takakusu and Nagai (1968, 1:124).
22. *Abhidharmakośa-bhāṣya*, Pradhan (1967, 266).
23. *Sumaṅgalavilāsinī*, Rhys Davids, Carpenter, and Stede (1886–1932, 2:448).
24. *Divyāvadāna*, Cowell and Neil (1987, 71).
25. *Lalitavistara*, Vaidya (1958, 177).
26. *Buddhacarita*, Johnston (1984, 47).
27. *Milindapañha*, Trenckner (1986, 1:100).
28. Ibid., 2:341.
29. See *Lalitavistara*, Vaidya (1958, 11–19).
30. *Rāṣṭrapālaparipṛcchā*, Finot (1957, 5:35).
31. See, for example, the *Mahāvastu*, Senart (1977, 1:167–168 and 2:15–17).
32. *Caṇḍamahāroṣaṇa Tantra*, George (1974, 20–28).
33. Ibid., 32.
34. *Mahāvairocana-abhisaṃbodhi-vikurvitādhiṣṭhāna-vaipulya-sūtrendra-rāja-nāma-dharma-paryāya*, 374.6–7.
35. Ibid., 418.3–5.
36. *Sarvadurgatipariśodhana Tantra*, Skorupski (1983, 226–228).
37. *Saṃvarodaya Tantra*, Tsuda (1974, 74).
38. *Guhyasamāja Tantra*, Bagchi (1965, 100).
39. *Tantra-rāja-śrīlaghusamvara-nāma*, 463.7–464.2.
40. This physiology is primarily associated with the *yoginī* tantras, and Tibetan doxographers generally consider it to be exclusive to the highest yoga tantra (*anuttara-yoga-tantra*) class.
41. *Hevajra-tantra*, Snellgrove (1959, 50).
42. *Sarva-tathāgata-tattva-saṃgraha*, Yamada (1981, 531).
43. *Guhyasamāja Tantra*, Bagchi (1965, 45).

References

Archaimbault, Charles. 1972. *La course de pirogues au Laos.* Ascona: Artibus Asiae.

Bagchi, S., ed. 1965. *Guhyasamāja Tantra or Tathāgataguhyaka.* Darbhanga: Mithila Institute.

Boucher, Daniel. 2008. *Bodhisattvas of the Forest and the Formation of the Mahāyāna: A Study and Translation of the Rāṣṭrapālaparipṛcchā-sūtra.* Honolulu: University of Hawai'i Press.

Butler, Judith. 1999. "Bodies That Matter." In *Feminist Theory and the Body: A Reader*, edited by Janet Price and Margrit Shidrick, 235–246. New York: Routledge.

Carpenter, J. Estlin, ed. 1960. *Dīgha-nikāya.* London: Pali Text Society.

Chalmers, Robert, ed. 1960. *Majjhima-nikāya*. London: Pali Text Society.

Connell, R. W. 2005. *Masculinities*. Crows Nest, NSW: Allen & Unwin.

Cowell, Edward B., and Robert Alexander Neil, eds. 1987. *The Divyāvadāna: A Collection of Buddhist Legends*. Delhi: Indological Book House.

Dorje, Acharya Sempa, ed. 1979. *The Biography of Eighty Four Saints by Acharya Abhayadatta Sri*. Varanasi: Central Institute of Higher Tibetan Studies.

Douglas, Mary. 1973. *Natural Symbols: Explorations in Cosmology*. New York: Vintage Books.

Finot, Louis, ed. 1957. *Rāṣṭrapālaparipṛcchā: Sūtra du Mahāyāna*. Gravenhage: Mouton.

George, Christopher S., ed. 1974. *The Caṇḍamahāroṣaṇa Tantra*. New Haven, CT: American Oriental Society.

Johnston, E. H., ed. 1984. *Aśvaghoṣa's Buddhacarita, or Acts of the Buddha*. Delhi: Motilal Banarsidass.

La Vallée Poussin, Louis de. 1976. *The Buddhist Councils*. Calcutta: K. P. Bagchi.

Mahāvairocana-abhisaṃbodhi-vikurvitādhiṣṭhāna-vaipulya-sūtrendra-rāja-nāma-dharma-paryāya (Tib. *rNam par snang mdzad chen po mngon par rdzogs par byang chub pa rnam par sprul pa byin gyis rlab pa shin tu rgyas pa mdo sde'i dbang po'i rgyal po shes bya ba'i chos kyi rnam grangs*). sde dge, vol. *tha*. New York: Tibetan Buddhist Resource Center. W22084-0971.

Powers, John. 2009a. *A Bull of A Man: Images of Masculinity, Sex, and the Body in Indian Buddhism*. Cambridge, MA: Harvard University Press.

Powers, John. 2009b. "You're Only as Good as You Look: Indian Buddhist Associations of Virtue and Physical Appearance." In *Destroying Māra Forever: Buddhist Ethics Essays in Honor of Damien Keown*, edited by John Powers and Charles S. Prebish, 67–94. Ithaca, NY: Snow Lion Publications.

Pradhan, Prahlad, ed. 1967. *Abhidharmakośa-bhāṣya*. Patna: K. P. Jayaswal Research Institute.

Rhys Davids, Caroline, ed. 1975. *Visuddhimagga*. London: Pali Text Society.

Rhys Davids, Thomas William, J. Estlin Carpenter, and William Stede, eds. 1886–1932. *Sumaṅgalavilāsinī of Buddhaghosa*. London: Pāli Text Society.

Senart, Émile, ed. 1977. *Mahāvastu*. Paris: l'Imprimerie Nationale.

Sharma, Ram Karan, and Vaidya Bhagwan Dash, eds. 1999. *Agniveśa's Caraka Saṃhitā*. Varanasi: Chowkhamba Sanskrit Series Office.

Shastri, Devadatta, ed. 1964. *Kāmasūtra of Vātsyāyana*. Varanasi: Caukhamba Sanskrit Sansthan.

Skorupski, Tadeusz, ed. 1983. *The Sarvadurgatipariśodhana Tantra: Elimination of All Evil Destinies*. Delhi: Motilal Banarsidass.

Snellgrove, David, ed. 1959. *The Hevajra Tantra: A Critical Study*. Oxford: Oxford University Press.

Soper, Alexander. 1949. "Aspects of Light Symbolism in Gandhāran Sculpture." *Artibus Asiae* 12 (4): 252–283.

Steinthal, Paul, ed. 1948. *Udāna*. London: Pali Text Society.

Takakusu Junjirō 高楠順次郎 and Nagai Makoto 長井真琴, eds. 1968. *Samantapāsādikā of Buddhaghosa*. London: Pali Text Society.

Tantra-rāja-śrīlaghusamvara-nāma (Tib. *rGyud kyi rgyal po dpal bde mchog nyung ngu*). sde dge rgyud 'bum vol. *ka*. New York: Tibetan Buddhist Resource Center. W22084-0962.

Trenckner, Vilhelm, ed. 1986. *Milindapañha*. London: Pali Text Society.

Tsuda Shin'ichi 津田真一, ed. 1974. *The Saṃvarodaya Tantra: Selected Chapters*. Tokyo: Hokuseido Press.

Vaidya, P. L., ed. 1958. *Lalitavistara*. Darbhanga: Mithila Institute.

Yamada Isshi 山田 一止, ed. 1981. *Sarva-tathāgata-tattva-saṃgraha*. New Delhi: Śata-piṭaka Series.

2

Converting the Ḍākinī

GODDESS CULTS AND TANTRAS OF THE YOGINĪS BETWEEN BUDDHISM AND ŚAIVISM

Shaman Hatley

Introduction

The corpus of Mahāyāna scripture known as *Yoginītantras* ("Tantras of the Yoginīs") or *Yoganiruttaratantras* ("Highest Yoga Tantras"), according to some classification schemas,[1] represents the last major wave of Buddhist literary production in India, along with its exegetical traditions.[2] The pantheons and practices of the *Yoginītantras* assumed considerable prominence in the latter centuries of Indian Buddhism, and characterize the religion as it took root in Tibet. Some texts of this corpus, as Alexis Sanderson has delineated in a pioneering, if somewhat controversial series of articles (1994, 2001, 2009), also have remarkable parallels in another body of tantric literature: scriptures of the *vidyāpīṭha* division of the Śaiva *tantras*. Much as texts of the *vidyāpīṭha* ("Wisdom Mantra Corpus") mark a shift from the pacific deity Sadāśiva to the skull-bearing Bhairava and his wild female companions, maṇḍalas of the Buddhist *Yoginītantras* (and some precursors) center not upon Mahāvairocana, the radiant supreme Buddha of the *Yogatantras*, but upon divinities of the *vajra* clan (*kula*) presided over by the Buddha Akṣobhya. Their iconography is frequently mortuary (*kāpālika*), while their maṇḍalas exhibit increasing emphasis on goddesses, including consorts of the Buddhas. It is within the scriptures and practice systems centered upon divinities of Akṣobhya's clan, especially erotic, *kāpālika* deities such as Cakrasaṃvara and Hevajra, that the goddesses known as *yoginīs* or *ḍākinīs* rise into prominence, parallel to the cult of *yoginīs* evidenced in Śaiva *tantras* of the *vidyāpīṭha*.

Sanderson's contention that the *Yoginītantra* corpus drew heavily upon Śaiva models has generated fresh debate on the nature of Buddhist–Hindu interaction in early medieval India. Undoubtedly some of the most fascinating historiographic issues surrounding Indian tantric traditions lie in the dynamics of this interaction, and the formation of parallel ritual systems across sectarian boundaries focused, to a surprising degree, upon the figure of the *yoginī*. For while there is much that is similar in older forms of Tantric Śaivism and Buddhism, it is with the cult of *yoginīs*, represented by the Śaiva *vidyāpīṭha* and Buddhist *Yoginītantras*, that parallels in ritual, text, and iconography reach their most remarkable levels. Assessment of the enormous body of comparative evidence and its interpretation in light of the social and historical contexts of early medieval India shall require sustained scholarly engagement, admirably begun in the works of Sanderson (1994, 2001, 2009), Davidson (2002), and others (Sferra 2003; Gray 2007, 7–11; Ruegg 2008). Recent scholarship (Davidson 2002; Sanderson 2009) has extended the earlier focus on systemic influences and textual appropriation (cf. Sanderson 1994, 2001) to historical processes and contexts, thereby navigating some of the problems inherent to historiography focused upon origins and influences. For while such analysis seems in some measure integral to historical inquiry, the attendant problems are considerable: excessive focus on the sources and influences involved in complex cultural phenomena risks obscuring both the actual phenomena and the agency of the historical persons involved. Such analysis may also inadvertently depend upon essentialist constructions of religion (e.g., "Original Buddhism" and "syncretism"). Particularly vexing is the problem of implicitly positioning what is under scrutiny in a hierarchy of authenticity. As Carl Ernst (2005, 15) poses the problem, "once influence has been established, it is felt, one has said something of immense significance; the phenomenon has been explained—or rather, explained away. . . . 'Sources' are 'original' while those 'influenced' by them are 'derivative.' " With this predicament in mind, I should like to clarify from the beginning that while this chapter seeks to highlight ways in which certain Vajrayāna Buddhists may have creatively adapted aspects of a competing tradition—one itself having remarkably hybrid roots, including a long history of exchange with Buddhism—I certainly do not intend to contribute to a perception of

Buddhist *Yoginītantra* traditions as "derivative," but rather to explore some of the ways in which they are historically situated.

The present chapter seeks to elaborate on the evolving figure of the *yoginī/ḍākinī* in Indian Tantric Buddhism, tracing its antecedents and shifting representations in relation to non-Buddhist traditions. My aims hence depart from those of Herrmann-Pfandt (2001) and Simmer-Brown (2002), for instance, whose important studies draw predominantly on Tibetan source material and are more synchronic in orientation, advancing interpretations of the cultural, religious, and psychological "meanings" of the Vajrayāna *ḍākinī*. It will be shown that the latter represents a goddess typology shared by contemporaneous Buddhist and Śaiva tantric traditions. The first section of the chapter reviews non-Buddhist conceptions of the *yoginī* and *ḍākinī*, their relationship to deities known as Mother-goddesses (*mātṛ*), and their roles in Tantric Śaivism. Though Buddhist and Śaiva conceptions of *yoginī*s share much in common, there exists a distinction in terminology: while in Śaiva goddess taxonomies (as in earlier Buddhist sources) the term *ḍākinī* frequently connotes a dangerous, often vampiric variety of female being, the Buddhist *Yoginītantra*s by and large treat the word as a synonym of *yoginī*. This terminological choice seems meaningful, reflecting an elevation of the *ḍākinī* consonant with Buddhist precedents for the "conversion" and incorporation of hostile deities, noteworthy examples of which include the early tradition's assimilation of *yakṣa*s and *yakṣī*s, and of the Mother-goddess Hārītī. Within tantric Buddhist literature, transformations in conceptions of *ḍākinī*s and related female deities, especially the Seven Mothers (*sapta mātaraḥ*), appear to provide key indicators for the historical developments culminating in the *Yoginītantra*s. In the second section of this chapter I attempt to map out aspects of this process, limited by reliance upon Sanskrit sources and the scholarship of others on account of my lack of competence in Tibetan and Chinese. The third and final section discusses the relationship between two influential, indeed formative, works of tantric literature focused upon *yoginī*s: the *Brahmayāmala* or *Picumata* of the Śaiva *vidyāpīṭha*, and the *Laghuśaṃvaratantra* or *Herukābhidhāna* of the Buddhist *Yoginītantra*s. I will adduce additional evidence in support of Sanderson's contention that the latter draws upon the former; however, I will also argue that one section of the *Brahmayāmala* shows signs of having been redacted from an unknown Buddhist *Kriyātantra*.

Yoginīs *and* Ḍākinīs *in Non-Buddhist Traditions*

The roots of the figure of the *yoginī* lie above all in ancient Indic goddesses known as *mātṛ*s, "the Mothers" or "Mother-goddesses," as I have attempted to demonstrate elsewhere and summarize in the following text.[3] Much like *yakṣa*s and *yakṣī*s or *yakṣiṇī*s, divinities intimately connected with the natural world, *mātṛ*s were popular deities in ancient India whose identities and worship were not initially circumscribed by a single religious tradition, whether Buddhism or the emergent theistic sects of the early common era. Defined by maternity and a nexus of beliefs concerning nature's feminized powers of sustenance, fecundity, contagion, and mortality, *mātṛ*s figure prominently in Kuṣāṇa-era statuary, early medical literature, and the tale-cycles of Skanda in the *Mahābhārata*. In their early manifestations, especially in the context of the apotropaic cult of Skanda's "seizers" (*skandagrahāḥ*), Mother-goddesses represent potentially dangerous forces who afflict children with disease if not propitiated, hence being intimately associated with not only fertility and life, but also sickness and death. By the fifth century, a particular heptad of Mothers coalesces with identities mirroring those of a series of major Brahmanical gods—Brahmā, Śiva, Skanda, Viṣṇu, Varāha (or Yama), and Indra. In this "Hinduized" form, *mātṛ*s became the focus of a widespread temple cult linked closely to Śiva, which attracted considerable elite patronage in the Gupta era. As do their iconic forms, the names of these Mothers mirror those of their male counterparts: Brāhmī, Māheśvarī, Kaumārī, Vaiṣṇavī, Vārāhī (or Yāmī), and Aindrī, each name having several variants. Exceptional is the seventh goddess, Cāmuṇḍā, the fierce and skeletal hag who is "leader of the Mothers" (*mātṛnāyikā*) and the counterpart of no male deity. Her identity appears closely linked to that of the warrior goddess Caṇḍī or Caṇḍikā,[4] one of the principal ciphers for emergent conceptions of the singular Mahādevī, "the Great Goddess." As a set, they become known as the "Seven Mothers" (*sapta mātaraḥ, saptamātṛkāḥ*), though an eighth member often joins their ranks (e.g., Mahālakṣmī, Yogeśvarī, or Bhairavī).

In addition to the temple cult of the Mothers, *mātṛ*s also emerge among the earliest important tantric goddesses. Their significance extends beyond chronology, for the figure and cult of the *mātṛ* appear to underlie those of *yoginī*s. In the most archaic textual sources of Tantric Śaivism, goddesses have little cultic importance. Such is true of the *Niśvāsatattvasaṃhitā*, one of the earliest surviving Śaiva *tantras*,[5] which refers to the Mother-goddesses not as tantric mantra-deities, but goddesses of public, lay religion (*laukikadharma*) alone.[6] The only evidence for their appropriation as tantric deities occurs in the context of cosmology, rather than ritual. Chapter 5 of its *Guhyasūtra* (5.1–21), a comparatively late stratum of the text, lists several varieties of goddess among the lords of a series of seven netherworlds (*pātāla*). In particular, the *kapālamātṛ*s, "Skull Mothers," who preside over the fourth netherworld, appear to represent a transformation of the Mothers into deities whose *kāpālika* iconography presages that of the *śākta vidyāpīṭha*'s cult goddesses. Positioned higher in the series of netherworlds are the *yogakanyā*s, "yoga maidens" or "daughters of Yoga," of the sixth and seventh *pātāla*s. Powerful, youthful goddesses, they appear to intimate the deities subsequently referred to as *yoginī*s or *yogeśvarī*s. The evidential record is unfortunately fragmentary for Śaiva traditions bridging the gulf between the *Niśvāsatattvasaṃhitā* and Śaiva cult of *yoginī*s, which perhaps first comes into evidence with the cult of the four Sisters of Tumburu (*bhaginī*s), attested as early as the sixth century (Sanderson 2009, 50, 129–130). The (poorly preserved) scriptures of this system were classified as the *vāmasrotas* or "Leftward Stream" of scriptural revelation, spoken by Sadāśiva's northern or leftward face, the feminine Vāmadeva.

Linked by tradition to the Sanskrit verbal root √*ḍī*, "to fly,"[7] *ḍākinī* is the basis for *ḍāin* (Hindi, etc.) and a number of related modern Indo-Aryan terms for "witch" (Turner 1962–1966, 311)—one of the senses it had in the medieval period as well. Like the *yoginī*, the figure of the *ḍākinī* has roots interwoven with Mother-goddesses (*mātṛ*), a connection evident in the early fifth-century inscription of Gaṅgdhār, in western Mālwa district.[8] Dated 423/424 or 424/425 CE, this mentions (v. 23, on lines 35–37) the construction of an "extremely terrible temple of the Mothers" (*mātṝṇāṃ . . . veśmātyugraṃ*) "filled with *ḍākinī*s" (*ḍākinīsaṃprakīrṇṇam*). The inscription speaks of the Mothers as deities "who make the oceans tumultuous through powerful winds arising from tantras" (*tantrodbhūtaprabalapavan odvarttitāmbhonidhīnām*). This description of *mātṛ*s uses imagery suggestive of powerful, "unfettered" tantric goddesses,[9] not at all in the image of the protective World Mothers (*lokamātaraḥ*) mentioned in other Gupta-era inscriptions. Of unspecified number and identity, *mātṛ*s are here associated with *ḍākinī* hordes, a temple cult, and occult spells (*tantra*) and powers,[10] suggesting that some key elements of the subsequent tantric cult of *yoginī*s had come together by the early fifth century. Unfortunately, this inscription is exceptional: we have no other firmly dated evidence for a cult of Mother-goddesses in the company of *ḍākinīs* in the fifth century, which makes the inscription difficult to contextualize.

A tantric tradition foregrounding *ḍākinīs* first comes into evidence in the seventh century, it seems, when the Mādhyamaka philosopher Dharmakīrti makes critical remarks concerning *Ḍākinītantras* and *Bhaginītantras*. The commentary of Karṇakagomin identifies the latter as "Tantras of the Four Sisters" (*caturbhaginītantras*)—in all probability, Sanderson argues (2001, 11–12), scriptures of the Leftward Stream (*vāmasrotas*) of Śaiva revelation. The *Ḍākinītantras* that Dharmakīrti refers to, which appear not to have survived, seem to represent a Śaiva tradition; he implies that these are non-Buddhist, and the existence of Śaiva texts by this designation can be confirmed from other sources.[11] Authors mentioning these texts associate them with parasitic, violent magical practices mirroring activities ascribed to *ḍākinīs*. Descriptions of similar practices do survive in *vidyāpīṭha* sources, and it is possible that the tradition represented by the *Ḍākinītantras* was, at least in part, subsumed within the *yoginī* cult of the *vidyāpīṭha*.[12] While not clearly documented until Dharmakīrti, magical practices centered upon *ḍākinīs* could date to the period of the Gaṅgdhār inscription, and seem to represent an important formative influence in the development of Buddhist and Śaiva *yoginī* cults.

With earlier precedents, Tantric Śaiva goddess cults become prominent in the *Bhairavatantras*, which have two primary divisions: tantras of the *mantrapīṭha* and *vidyāpīṭha*, distinguished by whether their pantheons consist predominantly of mantras (i.e., male mantra-deities) or *vidyās*: the "lores" or "wisdom mantras," which are the female mantra-deities (Sanderson 1988, 668–671; 2009, 19–20, 45–49). Literature of the *vidyāpīṭha* is hence intrinsically concerned with goddesses, and the *vidyāpīṭha/mantrapīṭha* divide appears intended, primarily, for distinguishing *Bhairavatantras* with goddess-dominated pantheons from those centered upon forms of Bhairava (cf. the distinction between Buddhist *Yoganiruttaratantras* and *Mahāyogatantras*). Four major *vidyāpīṭha* works appear to be extant: the *Brahmayāmala*, *Siddhayogeśvarīmata*, *Tantrasadbhāva*, and *Jayadrathayāmala*, none of which has been fully edited.[13] Much as the *vidyāpīṭha* appears to represent a development from the *mantrapīṭha* cult of Bhairava, additional tantric systems referring to themselves as Kaula ("Of the Clans of [Goddesses]") appear to have developed within and have substantial continuity with the *vidyāpīṭha*. Hence, while the earliest attested literature of the Śaiva *yoginī* cult belongs to the *vidyāpīṭha*, a substantial corpus of Śaiva literature concerned with *yoginīs* instead identifies itself with Kaula lineages (*āmnāya*), the lines between the two sometimes being problematic (Sanderson 1988, 679–680; 2009, 45–49).

The close connection between Mother-goddesses and emergent conceptions of *yoginīs* is evident in numerous ways. *Vidyāpīṭha* accounts of "the characteristics of *yoginīs*" (*yoginīlakṣaṇa*)[14] classify these goddesses according to clans (*kula, gotra*) that have the Seven or Eight Mothers as matriarchs, clan mothers in whose natures the *yoginīs* partake as *aṃśas*, "portions," or "partial manifestations." Tantric practitioners too establish kinship with the Mother-goddesses, leaving behind their conventional clan and caste identities and entering into initiatory kinship with the deities, who when propitiated may bestow *siddhi* upon individuals initiated into their own clans.[15] Beyond tantric literature proper, the old *Skandapurāṇa* (circa 6–7th centuries CE) also intimates these connections, linking the temple cult of the Seven Mothers to *yoginīs* and to Śaiva texts it refers to as Tantras of the Mother-goddesses (*mātṛtantra*) or Union Tantras (*yāmala*). These include the *Brahmayāmala*, an extant scripture of the *vidyāpīṭha* with extensive parallel passages in the Buddhist *Laghuśaṃvaratantra*. While the *Brahmayāmala* may have been reworked in the interval between the copying of its earliest extant manuscript (mid eleventh-century) and its mention in the *Skandapurāṇa*, its attestation in the latter is an important pieces of evidence pointing toward the development of a Śaiva cult of *yoginīs* by, at the latest, the early eighth century (Hatley 2007).

Representations of *yoginīs* in tantric Śaiva literature are extremely diverse, but some of the most common characteristics of this deity typology include occurrence in groups (e.g., sextets, with configurations of sixty-four becoming common by the tenth century), organization into "clans" of the Mother-goddesses, theriomorphism and shapeshifting, the ability to fly, association with guarding and/or transmitting tantric teachings, and potency as sources of both grave danger and immense power. In addition, *yoginīs* often blur the boundaries between human and divine, for through perfection in tantric ritual, it was held that female practitioners could join the ranks of these sky-traveling (*khecarī*) goddesses (Hatley 2007, 11–17; cf. White 2003, 27). In tantras of the *vidyāpīṭha*, the entire edifice of tantric ritual appears oriented toward the aim of power-bestowing "union" or encounter (*melaka, melāpa*) with *yoginīs*, a communion through which the *sādhaka* assumes the powers of Bhairava himself. Originally esoteric deities, from the tenth century *yoginīs* became prominent in the wider Indic religious landscape, as attested by their entry into purāṇic literature and the unique circular, open-air temples enshrining them across the subcontinent (Dehejia 1986; Hatley 2014).

Though connected intimately with the Seven Mothers, *yoginīs* demonstrate remarkable continuity with more ancient Mother-goddess conceptions. Their theriomorphism, shapeshifting, multiplicity, extraordinarily variegated appearances, bellicosity, independence, and simultaneous beauty and danger all find precedent in the *Mahābhārata*'s representation of the Mother-goddesses, as does, suggests White (2003, 39, 205), their connection with flight. While taking on the powerful iconography of tantric deities, *yoginīs* also maintain clear visual continuity with the Kuṣāṇa-era Mother-goddess, as reflected in statuary. Other ancient feminine deities figure in their formation as well: White (2003, 27–66) highlights notable continuities with the *apsaras* ("celestial maiden") and the *yakṣī* or *yakṣiṇī* ("dryad"), in addition to early *mātṛs* and other *grahas* ("seizers"). Other significant sources for conceptions of *yoginīs* include *vidyādharīs* (flying, semi-divine sorceresses), and in particular, Śiva's *gaṇas*: male deities whose theriomorphic or otherwise bizarre forms, multiplicity, variety, and engagement in activities such as warfare are highly suggestive of *yoginīs*. Serbaeva (2006, 71) also points out that *gaṇas* and *yoginīs* share an important similarity in representing states of being that Śaiva practitioners sought to attain.

Beyond *yoginī* taxonomies based on clans of the Mother-goddesses, *vidyāpīṭha* and Kaula sources develop additional classificatory schemata that order a much more diverse cast of divine and semi-divine female beings, based, for instance, upon notions of "habitat" (e.g., *yoginīs* who are aerial, terrestrial, aquatic, of the netherworlds, or who inhabit sacred places), degrees of divinity, or disposition.[16] Prominent in such taxonomies is the figure of the *ḍākinī*, which the *Brahmayāmala*, among other sources, associates with cruelty and ritual violence. Attainment of their state of being transpires though "perverse" (*viloma*) methods.[17] The Śaiva *ḍākinī* appears closely linked to, and sometimes is synonymous with, the decidedly non-vegetarian *śākinī*, of which Kṣemarāja quotes the following definition from the *Tantrasadbhāva*:

> A female who, for the purpose of shapeshifting, ever drinks the fluids of living beings after drawing them close by artifice, and who after obtaining [that fluid] slays the creatures—she should be known as a *śākinī*, ever delighting in dreadful places.[18]

The conflation of the *ḍākinī* and *śākinī* is evident in a verse occurring in multiple *vidyāpīṭha* sources, with minor variations, which in some cases defines the *rudraḍākinī* but elsewhere the *rudraśākinī*.[19] Note also, for instance, that a taboo on uttering the word "*ḍākinī*" (*Siddhayogeśvarīmata* 6.51) is applied by other sources to the word "*śākinī*."[20]

Representations of the *ḍākinī* as a vampiric, *śākinī*-like being also find expression in period non-tantric literature, especially the *Kathāsaritsāgara* of eleventh-century Kashmir. The colorful *yoginī*s of its tales range from powerful goddesses to impetuous, even vile, "witches" as well as virtuous and accomplished female tantric adepts.[21] Reflecting *yoginī* taxonomies from tantric Śaiva literature, those referred to with the epithets *ḍākinī* or *śākinī* are invariably malevolent, while *yoginī*s not given such qualifiers are benevolent, or at least ambivalent. The *yoginī* Citralekhā, for instance, utilizes her prowess in flight to facilitate the union of the princess Uṣā with Aniruddha of Dvāravatī.[22] Another well-meaning *yoginī* instructs her friend in mantras for turning her illicit lover into a monkey, and for restoring her pet to human form on demand.[23] In contrast, the *ḍākinī* Kālarātri, the grotesque and lusty wife of an orthodox brahman teacher (*upādhyāya*), possesses the power of flight through mantra-practice and consumption of human flesh, and acts secretly as guru to a coven of *ḍākinī*s.[24] Another story tells of a weary traveler who unknowingly accepts the hospitality of a *śākinī*. He thwarts her attempt to use enchanted barley to turn him into a goat, but ends up being turned into a peacock by the butcher's wife, a "wicked" (*duṣṭa*) *yoginī*.[25] Elsewhere, a jealous queen, a greedy female renunciant, and clever barber conspire to make the king think his newest bride is secretly a *ḍākinī*, who sucks out his vitals while he sleeps.[26] Book seven tells of Bhavaśarman of Vārāṇasī, who had an affair with a fickle brahman woman, Somadā, a "secret *yoginī*" (*guptayoginī*, 150d) of the worst sort—a "petty *śākinī*" (*kṣudraśākinī*, 168b) who eventually turns him into an ox. After his sale as a beast of burden, the *yoginī* Bandhamocinī spots him and restores him to human form.[27] In another, parallel episode, a certain Vāmadatta discovers that his wife, Śaśiprabhā, is secretly both an adultress and a *śākinī*. Caught in the act with a herdsman, she turns her enraged husband into a buffalo, beats him, and sells him off. A "perfected" (*siddhā*) *yoginī*, however, recognizes him in animal form and restores his humanness, eventually imparting to him the *vidyā*-mantra of goddess Kālasaṃkarṣaṇī, the supreme deity of Krama Śaivism.[28] In these tales, the *yoginī*/*ḍākinī* dichotomy functions virtually to demarcate the "good witch" from the "bad," echoing *yoginī* taxonomies of Tantric Śaivism. In light of this, it is remarkable that the categories came to be largely interchangeable in the Vajrayāna *Yoginītantras*.

Mother-Goddesses and Ḍākinīs *in Early Buddhist Tantric Literature*

Significant uncertainties surround the chronology of Buddhist tantric literature, though attenuated by the assistance that Chinese and Tibetan sources offer in dating specific works. Of particular value, we know the periods of early learned authors such as Buddhaguhya and Vilāsavajra, active in the mid- and late eighth century, respectively, who quote or comment upon tantric scriptural sources; for extant, reliably pre-tenth century commentary on Tantric Śaiva scripture, we have only Sadyojyotis, who may have been active in the period circa 675–725 (Sanderson 2006a).[29] As is well known, "proto-tantric" Buddhist literature of the variety later classified as *Kriyātantras* survives from the early centuries of the common era, often only in Chinese translation. Concerned largely with accomplishing worldly aims, this literature contains much that is characteristic of later tantric ritual, yet without articulating mantra-practice within a Mahāyāna soteriological framework.[30] Evidence for a developed tantric literature and eyewitness reports concerning the prevalence of tantric Buddhist traditions in India emerge only in the middle or latter half of the seventh century.[31]

Cultic emphasis upon the figure of the *yoginī* is not yet evident in the *Mahāvairocanābhisaṃbodhi(-tantra/sūtra)*—hereafter *Vairocanābhisaṃbodhi*—though closely related goddesses register a presence. This is one of the few extant Buddhist texts of the transitional variety sometimes classified as *Caryātantras*, similar in many respects to the subsequent *Yogatantras* but appearing to lack a developed soteriological vision of tantric ritual.[32] Composed, according to Stephen Hodge, around 640 CE or somewhat earlier, this survives primarily in Chinese and Tibetan translations.[33] Prominent in the maṇḍala of the supreme Buddha Mahāvairocana, as delineated in the second chapter, are goddesses such as Tārā. In the same maṇḍala appear "wrathful Mother-goddesses" headed by the goddess Kālarātri, who form the retinue of Yama, lord of Death and guardian of the southern direction (II.50). Kālarātri is accompanied by Raudrī, Brahmī, Kaumārī, Vaiṣṇavī, Cāmuṇḍā, and Kauberī (XIII.89)—an unusual heptad, being a variant upon the Seven Mothers: Brāhmī, Raudrī/Māheśvarī, Kaumarī, Vaiṣṇavī, Vārāhī, Indrāṇī, and Cāmuṇḍā. In this case, Kauberī replaces Indrāṇī/Aindrī, while Cāmuṇḍā's preeminent position is usurped by Kālarātri, who appears to be identified with Yāmī, the female counterpart of Yama.[34] That they are tantric divinities, however minor, is evidenced by occurrence within the maṇḍala and their invocation by mantra.[35] Kālarātri and seven unspecified Mother-goddesses also figure in the entourage of Śākyamuni,[36] while elsewhere Mothers are included in an enumeration of potentially dangerous spirits.[37] Chapter 6 links them to mantras for causing illness, bridging the goddesses' roots as *grahas* ("Seizers") in the entourage of Skanda, as described in the *Mahābhārata* and early medical literature, with tantric "magical" practices.[38] Furthermore, as do the Śaiva *Niśvāsatattvasaṃhitā* and a variety of other tantric sources, the *Vairocanābhisaṃbodhi* lists Mother shrines—as well as temples of Śiva—among the places appropriate for performing solitary *sādhana*, though without cultic emphasis on these deities.[39]

In addition to Mother-goddesses, the *Vairocanābhisaṃbodhi* contains several references to *ḍākinīs* and female divinities such as the *yakṣiṇī* ("dryad"), while the text's "appendix *tantra*" (*Uttaratantra*) describes rites for bringing the latter and female denizens of the netherworlds under one's power.[40] While in *Yoginītantras* of the subsequent period *ḍākinīs* would become prominent deities, the *Vairocanābhisaṃbodhi* groups them with minor, potentially pernicious beings such as the *rākṣasa*, *yakṣa*, and *piśāca*, consistent with early non-Buddhist conceptions of the *ḍākinī*. Early Buddhist works also emphasize the malevolence and predatory violence of the *ḍākinī*, with the *Laṅkāvatārasūtra* linking them to the nocturnal, flesh-eating *rākṣasī* of Indic folklore.[41] No evidence for the figure of the *yoginī* is present in the *Vairocanābhisaṃbodhi*, although the vocative-case epithets *yogini* and *yogeśvari* appear in a mantra; the deity is not named.[42] In this text we hence find evidence for interest in some of the divinities prominent in the later *Yoginītantras*, in particular a limited appropriation of the Mothers as tantric deities. This accords with roughly contemporaneous sculptural evidence for Buddhist interest in these goddesses, for a shrine of the Mothers is present in the Buddhist cave temple complex at Aurangabad (Hatley 2007, 68–69).

The *Mañjuśriyamūlakalpa*[43] attests a similar, yet broader range of female deities and spirits. Classified within the tradition as a *Kriyātantra*, a portion of this heterogeneous text has been shown to date to the middle of the eighth century, the period in which some sections appear in Chinese translation (Matsunaga 1985). In its opening chapter, the *Mañjuśriyamūlakalpa* enumerates a vast pantheon of divine, semi-divine, and human beings who assemble to hear the Dharma, among whom are an array of female divinities that include *pūtanās* ("Stinkers"), *bhaginīs* ("Sisters"), *ḍākinīs*, *rūpiṇīs* ("Beauties"), *yakṣiṇīs* ("Dryads"), and *ākāśamātṛs* ("Sky Mothers"). Each of these beings is said to have ordinary and "greater" (*mahā-*) varieties; the "Great [Sky] Mothers" include the standard Seven, augmented by Yāmyā, Vāruṇī, Pūtanā, and others, with retinues of innumerable nameless Mothers.[44] This is highly suggestive of the range of female divinities described in literature of the Śaiva and Buddhist *yoginī* cults.

Although they are not prominent in the ritual of this text, the *Mañjuśriyamūlakalpa*, like the *Vairocanābhisaṃbodhi*, positions the Seven Mothers in the retinue of Yama among the non-Buddhist deities in the outer layers of the maṇḍala.[45] The effort to give them a Buddhist identity is suggested by the addition of "Vajracāmuṇḍi" to their ranks.[46] In general, the depiction of the Mothers is consonant with the ancient cult of Skanda's countless *grahas*, with whom their connection is made explicit: most of the *Mañjuśriyamūlakalpa*'s copious references to the Mothers point toward their identity as dangerous female spirits, and only rarely as the seven Brahmanical goddesses. Mother-goddesses are mentioned among the spirits by whom one may become possessed, alongside beings such as the *piśāca* and *ḍākinī*,[47] while the "Mothers of Skanda" (*skandamātaraḥ*) are mentioned in 22.24b (TSS edition vol. 1, p. 233)—a chapter rich in its accounts of beings fabulous and dangerous. As for *ḍākinīs*, their characterization is entirely that of pernicious, possessing female spirits, against whom one requires mantras for protection; no indications are present of the positive associations and prominence assigned to them in *Yoginītantras*. One *vidyā*-mantra, for instance, is said to have the power to conjure a *yakṣiṇī*, or else to destroy *ḍākinīs*.[48] Among a number of other references is described a curious rite for removing the breasts and genitalia of proud, wicked *ḍākinīs* and women. Used on a man, it changes his gender.[49] Of additional interest in this *tantra* is its incorporation, as tantric deities, of Tumburu and the Four Sisters—Jayā, Vijayā, Ajitā, Aparājitā—the core pantheon of Śaiva *tantras* of the Leftward Stream (*vāmasrotas*). Chapters 47–49 are devoted to practices connected with these deities, and include the tale of their conversion to Buddhism.[50]

Further developments toward a cult of *yoginīs* are evident in the *Sarvatathāgatatattvasaṃgraha* (hereafter *Tattvasaṃgraha*), among the earliest extant scriptures classified as *Yogatantras* and representative of a developed Buddhist soteriological vision of tantric ritual. Its composition had apparently commenced by the last quarter of the seventh century, and the text was partially translated into Chinese in 753.[51] Although the *Tattvasaṃgraha* thus does not necessarily postdate the *Mañjuśriyamūlakalpa*, it takes the "conversion" of goddesses considerably further, and its range of female deities even more clearly intimates that of the *Yoginītantras*. Here, for instance, we find reference to Mother-goddesses classified under the categories *antarīkṣacāri* ("aethereal"), *khecarī* ("aerial"), *bhūcarī* ("terrestrial"), and *pātālavāsinī* ("denizens of the netherworlds")—closely related to categories applied in later classifications of *yoginīs*.[52] Along with a host of other erstwhile hostile deities, headed by Śiva, Vajrapāṇi confers upon them tantric initiation and initiatory names; thus Jātahāriṇī becomes Vajramekhalā, Māraṇī becomes Vajravilayā, Kauberī becomes Vajravikaṭā, and Cāmuṇḍā becomes Vajrakālī, to name one from each respective class.[53] The latter goddess, adorned with a garland of skulls and bearing a skull-staff, is once addressed as Vajraḍākinī.[54] Leaving behind their identities as *grahas* of Skanda or as maternal, Brahmanical goddesses, the Mothers here explicitly take on identities as goddesses of the "Adamantine Vehicle," the Vajrayāna.

In the *Tattvasaṃgraha*, we are presented with perhaps the earliest narrative of the conversion and accommodation of *ḍākinīs*. Charged with quelling wicked beings, Vajrapāṇi utters the "Heart Mantra for Drawing Down All Ḍākinīs and other Wicked Possessing Spirits," upon which the *ḍākinīs* and other *grahas* assemble in a circle, supplicate, and express concern about the dietary restrictions their new allegiance will entail:

> Then Vajrapāṇi, the great Bodhisattva, again spoke the Heart Mantra for Drawing Down All Ḍākinīs and other Wicked Possessing Spirits: 'OṂ VAJRA quickly draw down all wicked possessing spirits by the word of Vajradhara HUṂ JAḤ'! Then, as soon as this had been uttered, all the *ḍākinīs* and other wicked possessing spirits formed a ring around the summit of Mt. Meru and remained there. Then Vajrapāṇi, the great Bodhisattva, summoned the *ḍākinīs* and other wicked possessing spirits, and said, 'Resort, O friends, to the assembly of the pledge of teaching abstention from slaughter, lest I should incinerate your clans with my burning *vajra*, [when it has] become a single, blazing flame.' Then the *ḍākinīs* and other wicked possessing spirits, folding their hands to where the Lord was, entreated the Lord: 'O lord, we eat meat; hence direct [us] how [this] should be obtained.'[55]

Advised by Vajrasattva, the supreme Buddha, the compassionate Vajrapāṇi does indeed provide appropriate means:

> Next, the Lord spoke to Vajrapāṇi thus: 'O Vajrapāṇi, after generating great compassion for these beings, assent to give them a means.' Then Vajrapāṇi, possessing great compassion, spoke this, the Heart Mantra of the Mudrā for Knowing the Deaths of All Living Beings: 'OṂ VAJRA seize extract the heart if this being dies within a fortnight then let its heart emerge SAMAYA HŪṂ JJAḤ.' Now this is the binding of the *mudrā*: . . . Through this *mudrā*, you may extract hearts from all living beings and eat them.' Then the *ḍākinī*s and other wicked possessing spirits made clamorous *hulu hulu* sounds and returned home.[56]

The episode, a conversion story of sorts, suggests growing concern with the figure of the *ḍākinī*, and perhaps also the entry of mantra techniques associated with them into the battery of those available to practitioners. An early eighth-century Chinese commentary on the *Vairocanābhisaṃbodhi* provides a closely related narrative, wherein the association of *ḍākinī*s and their practices with Śiva and Śaivism is made explicit.[57] While this signals a process of providing Buddhist identities to *ḍākinī*s and connected practices—techniques presumably similar to those described in the lost (presumably Śaiva) *Ḍākinītantra*s referred to by Dharmakīrti—there is as yet little indication in the *Tattvasaṃgraha* of their transformation into the wild and ambivalent, yet supremely powerful and potentially beneficent, sky-wanderers of the *Yoginītantra*s.

A scripture completed perhaps in the latter half of the eighth century, the *Guhyasamājatantra* evidences a marked increase in engagement with the erotic and the impure, intimating developments carried even further in the *Yoginītantra*s. Its ritual has a significant *kāpālika* dimension and incorporates both coitus and the ingestion of impure substances, while erotic imagery distinguishes the iconography of its deities.[58] Focused upon the Buddha Akṣobhya, patriarch of the *vajra*-clan deities, the transitional status of this and closely related literature is reflected in its classification, frequently, as neither *Yoga-* nor *Yoginī-*, but *Mahāyogatantra*s (Tribe 2000, 210–213). In chapter 17 of the *Guhyasamāja* occurs an important early reference to *vajraḍākinī*s—transformations of these hostile beings into wielders of the *vajra* scepter, marking their entry into the Vajrayāna pantheon. Vajrapāṇi discloses a series of initiatory pledges (*samaya*) connected with specific deities, among whom are female beings: *yakṣiṇīs*, *nāga* queens (*bhujagendrarājñī*), *asura* maidens, *rākṣasīs*, and *vajraḍākinīs*. The pledge connected with the latter is as follows:

> Next, Vajrapāṇi, lord of all Buddhas, sent forth from the *vajras* of his body, speech, and mind the Pledge of All *Vajraḍākinīs*:
>
> > 'One should always eat urine, feces, and blood, and drink wine and so forth. One should slay through the *vajraḍākinī* yoga, through *padalakṣaṇas* (?). Arisen by their very nature, they [*ḍākinīs*] roam the triple universe. One should observe this pledge wholly, desiring the good of all beings'.
>
> [Then Vajrapāṇi entered?] the meditative trance called 'The Assembly of the Entire Triple Universe.'"[59]

That the "Pledge of All Adamantine Ḍākinīs" binds one to the consumption of urine, feces, blood, and alcohol, and to magical slaying suggests as yet little fundamental transformation in conceptions of *ḍākinīs*, despite their conversion. Some evidence points toward the emergence of material with close affinity to the *Yoginītantras* in the eighth century, separated little in time from the *Yogatantras*. Amoghavajra wrote a description of the *Sarvabuddhasamāyogaḍākinījālasaṃvara*, a text referred to in some scholarship as a "proto-*Yoginītantra*" (English 2002, 5), after his return to China in 746 CE (Giebel 1995, 179–182); it seems likely that, with possible exceptions, most other *Yoginītantras* date to the ninth century and beyond. The *Yoginītantras* and their exegetical literature constitute a vast corpus, much of which survives only in Tibetan translation and relatively little of which has been published, in cases where the Sanskrit original is preserved. Among the most important *Yoginītantras* are the *Laghuśaṃvaratantra* or *Herukābhidhāna*, and the *Śrīhevajraḍākinījālasaṃvara* (i.e., the *Hevajratantra*), texts considered foundational to the systems of practice and cycles of scripture focused upon Cakrasaṃvara and Hevajra, respectively. Other important texts of this genre include, for instance, the *Caṇḍamahāroṣaṇatantra* and *Kṛṣṇayamāritantra*—although the latter is perhaps more commonly considered a *Mahāyogatantra*[60]—texts teaching the cults of their namesake deities.

While the dating of the major *Yoginītantras* is problematic, most undoubtedly belong to the period prior to the *Laghukālacakratantra* and its important commentary, the *Vimalaprabhā*, which date between 1025 and circa 1040 CE, as Newman (1998, 319–349) shows convincingly. It has been observed that the late eighth-century commentator Vilāsavajra may quote from the *Laghuśaṃvara* (Davidson 1981, 6–7), probably the earliest and most authorative scripture in the cycle of *Yoginītantras* focused upon Cakrasaṃvara. Gray (2007, 12–14), however, demonstrates that most of the citations at issue are shared with and could instead derive from the *Sarvabuddhasamāyoga*; evidently only two cases cannot be accounted for in this manner, with Sanderson (2009, 161–163) suggesting that these offer "no more than a possibility that Vilāsavajra knew the *Laghuśaṃvara*"—though this possibility still seems significant. In addition, Sanderson (2009, 158–161) argues that Jayabhadra, an abbot of Vikramaśīla and probably the text's earliest commentator, was active in the tenth century, rather than the ninth, as had previously been supposed (Gray 2005, 62). While these considerations are inconclusive, they raise questions concerning the extent of Buddhist incorporation of the figure of the *yoginī* prior to the ninth century.

The cult of *yoginīs* thoroughly permeates the literature and ritual of the Cakrasaṃvara tradition. I shall focus on the *Laghuśaṃvaratantra,*[61] one of the foundational scriptures of the *Yoginītantra* corpus, to illustrate representations of goddesses in the *Yoginītantras*, for this text's parallels and relationship with the *Brahmayāmala* of the Śaiva *vidyāpīṭha* form the focus of the subsequent section. In the *Laghuśaṃvara*, the cult deities comprise a *kāpālika* male divinity, Cakrasaṃvara or Heruka, and his consort, Vajravārāhī or Vajrayoginī, who preside over a maṇḍala primarily of goddesses referred to as *ḍākinīs*, *vajraḍākinīs*, or *dūtīs* ("consorts").[62] While the maṇḍala *ḍākinīs* have male counterparts in the twenty-four "heroes" (*vīra*), the latter have only secondary significance.[63] The *Laghuśaṃvara*'s *ḍākinīs* are fully representative of the *yoginī* typology evident in the Śaiva *vidyāpīṭha*, combining in their *kāpālika*, theriomorphic iconography images of power and eroticism. They "pervade the universe,"[64] a wild horde with names such as Khagānanā ("Bird-face"), Surābhakṣī ("Drunkard"), Cakravegā ("Wheel-speed"), Vāyuvegā ("Wind-speed"), Mahābalā ("Mighty"), Mahānāsā ("Big-nose"), and Caṇḍākṣī ("Grim-eyes"). All but the first two of these names are held in common with goddesses mentioned in the *Brahmayāmala*, while the remaining names reflect general typological congruence,[65] illustrating the shared Śaiva-Buddhist image of the *yoginī* or *ḍākinī*.

As goddesses of the clan of Vajrayoginī/Vajravārāhī, the *Laghuśaṃvara*'s maṇḍala *ḍākinīs* represent a single class among the spectrum of female beings with which the text is concerned—deities whose principal varieties are the *yoginī, ḍākinī, rūpiṇī, lāmā,* and *khaṇḍarohā*.[66] Collectively, they comprise the "web" or "matrix" (*jāla*) of *ḍākinī*s that pervades the universe. They take cultic form in the "great maṇḍala" of deities (*mahācakra*) described in chapter 48, the abode of all *ḍākinī*s (*sarvaḍākinyālaya*);[67] based upon the "heart mantra of all *yoginī*s," this incorporates goddesses of the five classes together with the twenty-four male heroes. "Consisting of all *ḍākinī*s," the whole constitutes the supreme Buddha himself, Vajrasattva, the highest Bliss.[68] The nature of the goddesses' manifestation and movement (*sañcāra*) on the earth forms a central focus, reflected in the several chapters of the *Laghuśaṃvara* delineating typologies of the clans of goddesses. The text devotes several chapters to the subject of *chommā* as well, the secret verbal and nonverbal codes for communication between practitioners and the deities, or between initiates mutually.[69] Sacred geography forms a concern as well, a mapping of the powerful places where the goddesses are said to manifest.[70] As with the Śaiva *vidyāpīṭha*, the *yoginī* cult of the *Laghuśaṃvara* is thoroughly *kāpālika* in character,[71] and this text's rites of fire sacrifice utilize a battery of meats and other things impure, largely with aggressive magical aims.[72] Prominent among the goals of ritual is the attainment of encounters with *ḍākinī*s; to the heroic *sādhaka*, they may bestow the power of flight and freedom from old age and death.[73] Enabled by the *ḍākinī*s, the *sādhaka* comes to traverse the entire world as their master.[74] Significant attention is devoted, furthermore, to rites of bodily transformation, a domain of magic characteristic of the shapeshifting, theriomorphic *yoginī*.[75]

While in the *Yogatantra*s deities were organized according to clans (*kula*) of the five Buddhas of the Vajradhātu maṇḍala, *Yoginītantra*s sometimes introduce new, in some cases matriarchal, deity clans for the classification of *yoginī*s. In the case of the *Laghuśaṃvara*, the chapters concerned with *yoginī* classification are among those which Sanderson claims drew most heavily from Śaiva exemplars (2001, 42–43): chapters 16–19, and 23. It would appear that chapters 16, 18, and 19 reduce a taxonomy of seven or eight deity clans—in all likelihood, those of the Seven Mothers—to a smaller set of clans with distinctively Buddhist names, including clans of Śrīheruka, Vajravārāhī, and the Tathāgatas. The resultant overlap and lack of coherent systematization seem consonant with a non-Buddhist pedigree. *Laghuśaṃvara* chapter 17, in contrast, parallel to and possibly based on *Jayadrathayāmala* III, 32.137ff, provides an unusual taxonomy of deity clans neither based upon the Mothers nor obviously "Śaiva" or "Buddhist" in sectarian identity. In the cases of *Laghuśaṃvara* chapters 16 and 19, the apparent *vidyāpīṭha* exemplars are the extant *Jayadrathayāmala* (III, 32.119cd–127ab) and *Siddhayogeśvarīmata* (ch. 29), respectively, which delineate *yoginī* taxonomies based upon the Seven Mothers. Törzsök's (1999, 192–196) careful comparison of the latter and *Laghuśaṃvara* chapter 19 (identical to *Abhidhānottaratantra* ch. 38) finds multiple indications that the direction of redaction was from the Śaiva source to the Buddhist, her observations including "changes of non-Buddhist references to Buddhist ones" (cf. Gray 2007, 9–10), alterations that render a metrical verse in the Śaiva text unmetrical in the Buddhist, and "Śaiva iconographic features left unchanged in the Buddhist version."[76] Such intertextuality, irrespective of the direction of influence, highlights common patterns of representing *yoginīs*, and illustrates the degree to which their cult and figure come to stand at the intersection of Buddhism and Śaivism in early medieval India.

Buddhist and Śaiva Yoginītantras*: The Case of the* Laghuśaṃvaratantra *and the* Brahmayāmala

In a pioneering article of 2001, Sanderson identified extensive parallel passages in tantric literature within and across sectarian boundaries, and argued that substantial portions of important Buddhist *Yoginītantras* were redacted from Śaiva sources, largely unpublished (Sanderson 2001, especially 41–47). This constitutes some of the most important evidence marshaled in support of his thesis concerning the historical relationship between Śaivism and the esoteric Buddhism of the *Yoginītantras*, first argued in an article of 1994, where he asserts, "almost everything concrete in the system is non-Buddhist in origin even though the whole is entirely Buddhist in its function" (92). More recently (2009), he has added substantially to the text-critical evidence, and framed his findings within a broader hypothesis on the reasons for Śaivism's efflorescence in the early medieval period. While Sanderson's examples concern several Buddhist texts, the most remarkable case is that of the *Laghuśaṃvaratantra*, nearly half the contents of which he holds "can be seen to have been redacted from Śaiva originals found in texts of the Vidyāpīṭha division" of the *Bhairavatantras*—namely, the *Brahmayāmala*, *Siddhayogeśvarīmata*, *Tantrasadbhāva*, *Niśisañcāra*, and the *Yoginīsañcāraprakaraṇa* of the

Jayadrathayāmala (Sanderson 2001, 41–47 [quotation on p. 42]; 2009, 187–220).

In the present discussion I shall confine myself to a specific case of textual history, rather than attempt to address the larger picture of Śaiva–Buddhist interactions. The longest of the passages that Sanderson identifies as shared by the *Brahmayāmala* (/*Picumata*) and *Laghuśaṃvara* belongs to the first portion of chapter 88 of the *Brahmayāmala*, entitled "The Section on the Pledges" (*samayādhikārapaṭala*),[77] and to the greater part of chapters 26–29 of the *Laghuśaṃvara*. He notes that this intertextuality extends to the *Abhidhānottara* as well, a text of the Cakrasaṃvara cycle, in which the *Laghuśaṃvara* is fundamental: chapter 43 begins with text corresponding to *Laghuśaṃvara* 26.6 and *Brahmayāmala* 88.9. Though the text of *Abhidhānottara* chapter 43 closely parallels *Laghuśaṃvara* chapters 26–29—fortuitously so, given that this section of the *Laghuśaṃvara* does not survive in Sanskrit—the former contains none of the latter's divisions into chapters.[78] In addition to shared passages, the *Brahmayāmala* and *Laghuśaṃvara* share a number of idiomatic expressions, to a degree unlikely to be coincidental.[79]

To the passages identified by Sanderson I can add the final five verses of *Brahmayāmala* chapter 87, which correspond to the opening verses of *Laghuśaṃvara* chapter 26 (Table 2.1). Hence, *Laghuśaṃvara* chapters 26–29 roughly correspond, more or less in sequence, to the last several verses of *Brahmayāmala* chapter 87 and the first fifty-odd verses of 88, although individual verses and several short sections in both have no parallels in the other. The crucial Baroda codex of the *Laghuśaṃvara* is unfortunately lacunose from the third verse of chapter 22 up to the colophon of 29.[80] Pandey (2002) has attempted a reconstruction of the Sanskrit, utilizing the Tibetan translation, the commentary of Bhavabhaṭṭa, and parallels in the *Saṃpuṭatantra* and *Abhidhānottara*. This has been improved upon considerably in the new edition of Gray (2013), who utilizes testimonia from additional Sanskrit commentaries and *vyākhyātantras*. Interestingly, though Gray does not utilize Śaiva testimonia in constituting the text (cf. Sugiki 2008), his well-considered reconstruction of the opening passage of chapter 26 brings it much closer to the parallel passage of the *Brahmayāmala* than Pandey's does, particularly where he follows the oldest commentary: Jayabhadra's *Cakrasaṃvarapañjikā*. Jayabhadra appears to have commented on an early version of the *Laghuśaṃvara* lacking chapter divisions—much like the parallel text of *Abhidhānottara* chapter 43—as well as the concluding section of the received text. The latter includes some of the passages most recognizably "Buddhist" in content (Sanderson 2009, 158–159).

Table 2.1 places the passage from *Brahmayāmala* chapter 87 alongside the corresponding verses of *Laghuśaṃvara* chapter 26, as given in Gray's edition. The passage in question is also shared by the *Brahmayāmalasāra*, a short recension of the *Brahmayāmala* preserved in two Nepalese codices.[81]

Table 2.1 A Parallel Passage in *Brahmayāmala*, ch. 87, and *Laghuśaṃvara*, ch. 26

Brahmayāmala 87.222–28	*Laghuśaṃvaratantra* 26.1–5
nātaḥ parataraṃ kiñcit	ataḥ paraṃ mantrapadaṃ
triṣu[123] lokeṣu vidyate |	triṣu lokeṣu na vidyate |
jñātvā picumataṃ tantraṃ	śrīherukamantraṃ jñātvā
sarvatantrān[124] parityajet ||222||	sarvān mantrān parityajet ||1||
carvāhāravibhāge[125] 'pi	
tālakārādhake[126] tathā |	
sarvātmake ca yogo 'yaṃ	
sarvataḥ svānurūpataḥ ||223||	
dūtīyogātmayogāc ca	
prakriyāyogayojanāt |	
sarvatra ca caturṇāṃ tu	
yogo 'yam parikīrtitaḥ ||224||	
anulomavilomena	anulomavilomena
dūtayaḥ saṃvyavasthitāḥ |	dūtayaḥ saṃvyavasthitāḥ |
adhordhvasiddhidā devi	adhordhvasiddhidā nityam
ātmadūtī[127] tu sarvadā ||225||	ātmadūtīṃ tu sarvagām ||2||
taddravyaṃ sarvadā siddhaṃ[128]	taṃ dūtīṃ sarvasiddhidāṃ
darśanāt[129] sparśabhakṣaṇāt |	darśanaṃ sparśanaṃ tathā |
cumbanā gūhanāc caiva[130]	cumbanāvagūhanā nityaṃ
śivapīṭhe[131] viśeṣataḥ ||226||	yogapīṭhe viśeṣataḥ ||3||
yāvato dravyasaṃghātaḥ[132]	yāvanto yogasaṅghātāḥ
sarvasiddhikaraḥ param[133] |	sarvasiddhikarāḥ smṛtāḥ[134] |
dātavyaṃ mantrasadbhāvaṃ	dātavyaṃ sarvasadbhāvaṃ
nānyathā tu kadā cana[135] ||227||	nānyathā tu kadā cana ||4||
mātā ca bhaginī putrī	mātā bhaginī putrī vā
bhāryā vai[136] dūtayaḥ smṛtāḥ[137] |	bhāryā vai dūtayaḥ sthitāḥ[138] |
yasyā mantraṃ daden nityaṃ	yasya[139] mantraṃ daden nityaṃ
tasyaiṣo hi vidhiḥ smṛtaḥ ||228||	tasya so hi vidhiḥ smṛtaḥ ||5||

This short recension presupposes the existence of the twelve-thousand verse recension—although not precisely as transmitted in its oldest extant manuscript, for several readings of the *Brahmayāmalasāra*, as reported in the annotation in Table 2.1, are closer to those of the *Laghuśaṃvara*, and may derive from an earlier stage in the *Brahmayāmala*'s transmission.

In the *Brahmayāmala*, this passage concludes the first chapter of the *Uttaratantra*, an "addendum *tantra*" to the *Brahmayāmala* probably belonging to a comparatively late stratum of the text. Parallels for the some of the passage's obscure terminology occur earlier in the chapter and elsewhere in the *Brahmayāmala*.[82] In the *Laghuśaṃvara*, this passage instead opens chapter 26. With the negative particle *na* not in the initial position, as in the *Brahmayāmala*, but in the hypermetrical second verse-quarter, the opening gives the appearance of having been awkwardly rewritten to introduce a new topic. That the verse is unclear semantically is suggested by its divergent interpretations.[83] The *Laghuśaṃvara* passage as a whole, or so it seems to me, reads as a tract of decontextualized text, assembled with scant regard for meter and still less for grammar, the interpretation of which challenges the imagination. In verse six, the subject shifts to the Eight Pledges, with a passage parallel to *Brahmayāmala* 88.1–42.[84]

There are multiple and clear indications of the dependence of *Laghuśaṃvara* chapters 26–29 upon *Brahmayāmala* chapters 87–88, for the redactors appear to have been less than successful in removing traces of technical terminology distinctive to their source text. One case that Sanderson (2001, 44–47) has discussed in detail is a reference to the *smaraṇa*, a word in ordinary parlance meaning "recollection," but in the *Brahmayāmala*, a technical term for the seed-mantra of Kapālīśabhairava (HŪṂ). An ostensibly neutral word, the Buddhist redactors allowed this to remain, unconcerned with or perhaps unaware of its significance in the source text.[85] In addition to the *smaraṇa*, I would single out another case in which characteristic jargon from the *Brahmayāmala* has not been redacted out of the *Laghuśaṃvara*: 26.15, which corresponds to *Brahmayāmala* 88.9. This verse concerns a typology of the practitioner (*sādhaka*) that is, as far as I can determine, distinctive to the *Brahmayāmala*—and certainly alien to the *Laghuśaṃvara*. The text of the *Laghuśaṃvara* version of the verse is as follows, in Gray's reconstruction:

> *śuddho 'śuddho 'tha miśraś ca sādhakāś ca trividhā sthitāḥ |*
> *ārādhako viśuddhaś ca dīpako guṇavān naraḥ ||*

Jayabhadra, the earliest commentator on the *Laghuśaṃvara*, recognized that this verse should concern a classification of practitioners, and offers the following interpretation:

> The "man of virtue" (*guṇavān naraḥ*)—the yogin—has a threefold division. *Ārādhaka* means "one in whom understanding has not arisen"; *viśuddha* means "one in whom capacity has arisen"; *dīpaka* ("lamplight") means the *madhyadīpaka* ("average luminary"): one in whom some understanding has arisen, and who enlightens himself and others. Or else, *ārādhaka* means "worshipper of the deity through practice of mantra and yoga," *guṇavān* means "one who understands the meaning of scripture," [while] *dīpaka* means "capable of fulfilling the goals of all living beings," like a lamp (*pradīpa*).[86]

Jayabhadra's creative yet incongruent attempts to find three *sādhaka*s in the second line testify to the fact that this verse lacks context; a threefold classification of this nature is otherwise absent from the *Laghuśaṃvara* and related literature.

In contrast, the triad of "pure," "impure," and "mixed" comprises a key conceptual framework in the *Brahmayāmala*: practitioners, ritual, scripture, and the Three Śaktis are patterned accordingly.[87] *Ārādhaka*, too, has a specific, contextually germane meaning. In the *Brahmayāmala*, the verse in question occurs in a passage that follows the enumeration of initiatory Pledges (*samaya*):

. . . ity aṣṭau samayāḥ[88] *parāḥ* || 7 ||
jñātavyāḥ[89] *sādhakair nityaṃ*[90] *sādhanārādhanasthitaiḥ*[91] |
sāmānyāḥ sarvatantrāṇāṃ na hantavyās tu hetubhiḥ || 8 ||
śuddhāśuddhavimiśras[92] *tu sādhakas trividhaḥ*[93] *smṛtaḥ* |
ārādhako viśuddhas tu dīpakādiguṇair vinā || 9 ||
grāme grāme vrataṃ tasya devatārūpalakṣaṇam |
unmattam asidhārañ ca pavitrakṣetravarjitaḥ || 10 ||
sādhakas tu dvidhā proktaś carumārgo 'tha tālakaḥ |
tālamārgaratānāṃ tu na carur naiva saṃyamaḥ || 11 ||
vidyāvrataviśuddhis tu triṣaṣṭivratam[94] *eva ca* |
abhedyatvaṃ tatas tasya tālādau sādhane vidhau || 12 ||
carumārgaikadeśo hi tālaḥ sarvātmako bhavet |
kṣetrasthānāni siddhāni yoginyo yatra saṃgatāḥ || 13 ||
teṣu sthitvā japaṃ kuryāc carum ālabhate dvijaḥ |

> . . . these are the supreme eight Pledges. [7d] They should always be known by *sādhakas* [whether] engaged in [mantra-]*sādhana* or [deity] worship (*ārādhana*). They are common to all the *tantras*, and should not be assailed with reasoned arguments. [8] The *sādhaka* is threefold—pure, impure, and mixed[95]—while the *ārādhaka* is very pure, free from the qualities of 'lamplight' and so forth (?).[96] [9] From village to village, his observance (*vrata*) is [that of taking on] the form and characteristics of the deities, and the 'madman' and 'razor's edge' [observances],[97] avoiding the sacred fields. [10] But the *sādhaka* is [actually] twofold: the one following the path of *caru* ('oblation gruel'), and the *tālaka*. For those on the *tālaka* path, there is neither *caru* nor self-restraint. [11] [After engaging in] purification by the *vidyā*-mantra observance and the 'sixty-three observance',[98] he then [reaches] the state of [making] no distinction between the ritual procedures of the *tālaka*, etc. [12] Following the way of the *caru*, having a single location, the *tālaka* would become a *sarvātman* ("universal") [*sādhaka*].[99] Remaining in the sacred, empowered places where the *yoginīs* assemble, he should perform his mantra recitation in those; the twice-born one obtains an oblation (*caru*) [from the *yoginīs*].[100] [13–14ab]

Here *ārādhaka*, "worshipper," refers to a specific category of practitioner. In its core chapters, the *Brahmayāmala* describes a threefold typology of the *sādhaka*: pure, impure, and impure-*cum*-pure, for which the primary designations are *tālaka*, *carubhojin* ("eater of the oblation gruel"), and *miśra* ("mixed"), respectively.[101] This classification receives detailed elaboration in the text's massive forty-fourth chapter, "the section on the *sādhaka*" (*sādhakādhikāra*). However, the latter chapters of the *Brahmayāmala*—chapters 87–104, comprising the *Uttara*- and *Uttarottaratantras*—introduce a new fourfold taxonomy of initiates: the *ārādhaka*, *carubhojin*, *tālaka*, and *sarvātman* ("universal"), whose activities and subdivisions comprise the respective subjects of *Brahmayāmala* chapters 94–97. This typology differs from the threefold insofar as the category of *miśraka*, the practitioner of "mixed" purity, appears to be reconfigured as the highest grade, the *sarvātman*—above the *tālaka*.[102] On the other hand, the *ārādhaka* represents a variety of householder practitioner.[103]

That the redactors of the *Laghuśaṃvara* had intended to remove references to a Śaiva typology of practitioners is suggested by comparison; in Table 2.1, note that *Brahmayāmala* 87.223–224, which makes specific reference to the classification of *sādhakas* in question, has no parallel in the *Laghuśaṃvara* (nor in the *Brahmayāmalasāra*, which also omits this passage). Yet *Laghuśaṃvara* 26.15 nonetheless contains a reference to what is, in the *Brahmayāmala*, the same typology expressed with different terminology: the designations pure, impure, mixed, and "worshipper" (*ārādhaka*), as opposed to the more distinctive "oblation eater" (*carubhojin*), *tālaka*, "worshipper" (*ārādhaka*), and "universal" (*sarvātman*).[104] Verse 26.15 was perhaps retained by the Buddhist redactor either under the assumption that the more neutral terminology would not appear alien, or on account of ignorance of the jargon.

Considered alongside the already strong evidence adduced by Sanderson, the presence of a typology of practitioners distinctive to the *Brahmayāmala* in the *Laghuśaṃvara*, where it lacks not only context but also a plausible interpretation, provides strong indication of the direction of redaction in the passages shared by these texts. That the *Laghuśaṃvara* has drawn from the *Brahmayāmala*, whether directly or through another derivative source, seems the most plausible explanation for the relationship between the material in question. Derivation from an unknown common source is not impossible, but this would in all likelihood have been a Śaiva text intimately related to the *Brahmayāmala*, to the extent of sharing unusual terminological similarities.

Although the case for the *Laghuśaṃvara* drawing on Śaiva source material seems compelling, this proposal and especially Sanderson's broader claims have elicited controversy. Davidson (2002), in particular, has questioned the plausibility of extant *tantric* Śaiva texts being significant sources of material found in the Buddhist *Yoginītantras*, though he highlights the influence of the (non-tantric) Kāpālika and Pāśupata Śaiva ascetic orders on the Vajrayāna. One of his principal objections is chronological: he considers problematic the evidence attesting specific, extant works of tantric Śaiva literature prior to the ninth and tenth centuries.[105] He questions, for instance, whether the mid-eleventh-century Cambodian Sdok Kak Thoṃ inscription should be taken as an accurate record for the existence in the ninth century of the Śaiva texts it mentions—several texts of the Leftward Stream (*vāmasrotas*) of the cult of Tumburu and the Four Sisters (*bhaginī*)—which the inscription associates with a brahman in the court of that period. While such caution may be laudable in principle, here it is perhaps excessive: the existence of Śaiva *tantras* of the *vāmasrotas* prior to the ninth century may be inferred in multiple manners, including Dharmakīrti's reference to the genre and the presence of two loose folios of an exegetical work of this tradition among the Gilgit manuscripts (perhaps mid-sixth century). The texts mentioned in the inscription, including the extant *Vīṇāśikhātantra*, are known to have been fundamental scriptures of this genre.[106] In fact, Davidson's objection appears inconsistent considering that he himself draws upon a single reference in the *Kālikāpurāṇa* for reconstructing the allegedly pre-Buddhist origins of the deity Heruka, relying heavily on a mythological text for reconstructing history, perhaps at a remove of well more than half a millennium. His speculations concerning the origins of Bhairava raise similar problems.[107]

Critiquing Sanderson's thesis of the Buddhist *Yoginītantras*' indebtedness to Śaivism, Davidson (2002, 217) counters that "a more fruitful model would appear to be that both heavily influenced the final formations of the agonistic other and that each had alternative sources as well." A model of mutual influence certainly has appeal when considering Buddhist-Śaiva interactions broadly over the course of the first millennium,[108] yet such cannot be assumed a priori in any particular case; indeed, most of what Davidson cites as examples of Tantric Śaiva texts having syncretic sources appear to be post twelfth-century works, and accordingly have little bearing on the relation between the Śaiva *vidyāpīṭha* and Buddhist *Yoginītantras*. A potential exception is the *Jayadrathayāmala*, a *vidyāpīṭha* scripture which, as Davidson points out, shows awareness of the Vajrayāna in its account of the scriptural canon.[109] The *Jayadrathayāmala*, Sanderson argues, is a historically layered composition that, though assimilating early material, took its final form in Kashmir at some point prior to the period of Jayaratha (thirteenth century).[110] That sections of the text reveal awareness of Tantric Buddhism is neither surprising nor unusual, and Davidson's assertion (2002, 217) that this suggests "dependence on Buddhist tantras" should require demonstration of the nature of such dependence. Among the other Śaiva texts Davidson singles out is "the *Brahmayāmala*"; but what he refers to is in fact a late medieval east Indian composition by this title, rather than the early *vidyāpīṭha* scripture.[111] It would indeed appear that the late medieval *śākta* tradition of Śaivism, particularly in east India, appropriated much from Tantric Buddhism during the centuries of the latter's decline. This is dramatized, for instance, in tales of the brahmanical sage Vaśiṣṭha's sojourn to Mahācīna ("Greater China") in order to learn worship of Tārā from the inebriated Buddha, and evidenced by the emergence of syncretic pantheons such as the "Ten Great Wisdom-mantra Goddesses" (*daśa mahāvidyāḥ*), who include Tārā (Bühnemann 1996; Sanderson 2009, 240–243).

Regrettably, Davidson goes so far as to suggest that Sanderson's model of the *vidyāpīṭha* is informed by a "curious theology of scripture," contending that "while it is seldom that a received body of texts reflects no influence at all, this seems to be Sanderson's ultimate position on the *vidyāpīṭha* Śaiva scriptures" (2002, 386n105). This assertion appears entirely unsustainable in light of Sanderson's research into the complex genealogies of Śaiva scriptures, including those of the *vidyāpīṭha*. Concerning the *Tantrasadbhāva*, a Trika text of the *vidyāpīṭha*, he demonstrates that it has incorporated and expanded upon cosmological material from the *Svacchandatantra*—an extensive tract of text which the latter, in turn, drew in part from the *Guhyasūtra* of the *Niśvāsatattvasaṃhitā*, transforming this in the process within its own cultic system (Sanderson 2001, 23–32). He argues, moreover, that the *Niśvāsatattvasaṃhitā* itself—perhaps the earliest extant tantric Śaiva scripture—is heavily indebted to pre- and proto-tantric Śaiva sects of the Atimārga.[112] Particularly noteworthy is Sanderson's more recent investigation (2005) into the formation of the *Netratantra*, a Śaiva text that he argues was produced in the milieu of an eighth- or early ninth-century Kashmiri court. Note also his demonstration that the *Bṛhatkālottara*, a Kashmiri-provenance *tantra* of the Śaivasiddhānta, has incorporated material from a Vaiṣṇava scripture of the Pāñcarātra (Sanderson 2001, 38–41). In light of this obvious commitment to identifying agents, circumstances, and sources involved in the formation of Śaiva scriptural literature, it hardly seems defensible to attribute bias to Sanderson for failing to unearth examples of the indebtedness of early texts of the *vidyāpīṭha* to Buddhist *Yoginītantras*.

Nonetheless, the picture may well be more complex, for it is possible that the *Brahmayāmala* has itself drawn upon material redacted from an unknown Buddhist source—most probably not a *Yoginītantra*, but a more archaic text of the *Kriyātantra* variety. The principal chapter (*paṭala*) in question is *Brahmayāmala* chapter 65,[113] the "chapter on the practices for mastering dryads" (*yakṣiṇīsādhanapaṭalaḥ*). This delineates a fourfold classification of *yakṣiṇīs* (*yakṣiṇīkulacatuṣṭaya*): those belonging to the clans (*kula*) of *yakṣas*, Brahmā (*brahmakula*), the lotus (*padma*), and *vajra*. The designations arouse immediate suspicion, for clans of the *padma* and *vajra* feature prominently in deity taxonomies of the *Kriyātantras*, and have no evident precedent or obvious rationale in Śaivism. While the Buddhist *Mañjuśriyamūlakalpa*, for instance, attests a variety of mantra-deity taxonomies, constant are the clans of the Buddhas/Tathāgatas, *padma* (associated with Avalokiteśvara), and *vajra* (associated with Vajrapāṇi);

a *yakṣa* or *guhyaka* clan is attested as well.[114] Another *Kriyātantra*, the *Amoghapāśakalparāja*, provides a fourfold clan system with deity clans of the *vajra, tathāgata*, gem (*maṇi*), and lotus (*padma*).[115] It is possible that the *Brahmayāmala* draws upon a similar fourfold system, its Brahmā-clan *yakṣiṇī* perhaps supplanting what was, in the hypothetical Buddhist exemplar, a dryad of the clan of the Buddhas (*tathāgatakula*).

I am presently unaware of a classification of dryads comparable to the *Brahmayāmala*'s in a Buddhist source, though one does find the expressions *padmayakṣiṇī* and *vajrayakṣiṇī*.[116] The closest parallel for the *Brahmayāmala*'s fourfold classification is found instead in another Śaiva, *vidyāpīṭha* source: the *Jayadrathayāmala*.[117] Here the *yakṣiṇī* clans are designated lotus (*padma*), red (*rakta*), white (*śveta*), and *vajra*. Though this, too, lacks precise Buddhist parallels, the occurrence of clans of the *padma* and *vajra* arouses similar suspicion. That such suspicion may indeed have strong grounds finds support in another Śaiva text—the *Uḍḍāmareśvaratantra*—in the case of its instructions for conjuring a divine maiden (*surasundarī*). Here the Buddhist pedigree of the passage in question is suggested by the fact that the practitioner is instructed to perform the rite in a temple of [the *bodhisattva*] Vajrapāṇi.[118]

The *Brahmayāmala* shows signs of being a composite document, and chapter 65 belongs to a textual stratum that I have argued (Hatley 2007, 200–211) has incorporated materials from disparate sources. Chapters 51–104 have in some respects a miscellaneous character, containing a large number of short, often untitled chapters, many of which are devoted to deities marginal to the text's primary mantra-deity systems. These include chapters that might originally have circulated as independent works: the *Tilakatantra* (ch. 62) and *Utphullakamata*/tantra (ch. 83), titles matching those of texts quoted by Abhinavagupta. Chapter 62, for its part, has incorporated material apparently from the *Uttarasūtra* of the *Niśvāsatattvasaṃhitā* (Hatley 2007, 219–220). In most cases, the passages redacted into the *Brahmayāmala* appear to have undergone substantial modification, being reasonably well integrated in terms of both content and style of expression (the latter being a rather dubious distinction). This is evident in the treatment of *yakṣiṇīs*, too, where one encounters the idea that one purpose of attracting a *yakṣiṇī* is for generating the sexual fluids required as offerings for the deities—a distinctive dimension of the ritual system of the *Brahmayāmala*. By and large, however, the *Brahmayāmala*'s treatment of rites for controlling dryads is remarkably free of identifiably Śaiva content.

Chapters 63–66 of the *Brahmayāmala* appear closely related, forming a distinctive unit: the end of chapter 64 (vv. 162–164) intimates the subject of chapter 65, while the corpse ritual (*kaṅkālavratasādhana*) of chapter 63 appears, inexplicably, to find closure in the final verses of chapter 66, tacked on at the end of a discussion of recipes for magical pills (*guḍikā*). The mantras delineated in chapters 64–65 also share a common structure, one not elsewhere attested in the *Brahmayāmala*.[119] If chapter 65's rites for subjugating *yakṣiṇīs* draw on a Buddhist *Kriyātantra*, one might hence expect this to be true of material in the adjacent chapters as well. Chapter 66 may in fact suggest this possibility in its description of procedures for preparing magical pills. After readying the substances and wrapping them with pipal (*aśvattha*) leaves, one engages in mantra recitation until success (*siddhi*) is signaled by one of three "signs" (*cihna*): heat, smoke, or fire (*uṣman, dhūma, jvalana*), which betoken increasingly greater degrees of magical attainment. Isaacson (2007) has drawn attention to this passage, pointing out that its threefold typology of signs and levels of *siddhi* finds attestation in the *Niśvāsatattvasaṃhitā*, perhaps the earliest extant Śaiva *tantra*, but is otherwise rare in Śaiva sources; on the other hand, it pervades the Buddhist *Mañjuśriyamūlakalpa*.[120] While the mere presence of the tripartite typology in the *Brahmayāmala* might not intimate a Buddhist source, the presence of similarly suspicious material in the adjacent chapter lends greater weight to the possibility. In addition, the passage referring to the threefold *siddhi* contains another potential link to the *Kriyātantras*: the use of seven pipal leaves to wrap or cover the empowered substances has close and extensive parallels in the *Mañjuśriyamūlakalpa*, where the procedure is remarkably similar to that outlined in the *Brahmayāmala*.[121] In this case, too, a similar practice is outlined in the *Niśvāsatattvasaṃhitā* (*Guhyasūtra*, especially 10.30), leaving open multiple historical scenarios.

Identifying the possible origins of the *Brahmayāmala*'s *yakṣiṇī* rites in an unknown Buddhist source complexifies the issue of Śaiva *vidyāpīṭha* influence upon the *Yoginītantras*. While Sanderson's thesis remains compelling, the case of the *Brahmayāmala* highlights the complex redactional histories of *vidyāpīṭha* literature, and suggests that the textual "flow" may have been multidirectional in some cases. Finding potential intertextuality at the level of Buddhist *Kriyātantra* and early *vidyāpīṭha* points toward what is likely to be a history of interaction, shared ritual paradigms, and textual appropriation extending back to early strata of Śaiva and Buddhist tantric literatures. Indeed, the extant *Kriyātantra* offering the most useful parallels to *Brahmayāmala*, chapters 63–66—the *Mañjuśriyamūlakalpa*—itself appears to have drawn extensively from Tantric Śaivism, as is especially evident in its wholesale incorporation of the cult of Tumburu and his Four Sisters (*caturbhaginī*), principal deities of the archaic Leftward Stream (*vāmasrotas*) of Śaiva scriptural revelation.[122] Severe losses of early Śaiva scripture—especially those of the *vāmasrotas*, as well as *Bhūta-* and *Gāruḍatantras*, which among Śaiva sources perhaps exhibit the closest affinity to the Buddhist *Kriyātantras*—suggest that much of this history is likely to remain opaque.

Notes

1. For an insightful study of classifications of the Buddhist tantric canon in India and Tibet, see Dalton (2005).
2. I would like to thank Jacob Dalton, David Gray, Harunaga Isaacson, and Iain Sinclair for their comments on this chapter, the shortcomings of which are my responsibility alone.
3. Hatley (2012); see also White (2003, 27–66).
4. Note, for instance, that the *Brahmayāmala* uses the names Caṇḍikā, Carcikā (or Carcā), and Cāmuṇḍā interchangeably (Hatley 2007, 376).
5. Goodall and Isaacson's preliminary assessment would place "the earlier parts of the text between 450–550 AD" (2007, 6).
6. *Niśvāsatattvasaṃhitā, Mukhāgama* 2.28, 3.33–34ab.
7. The derivation of "*ḍākinī*" is discussed by Herrmann-Pfandt (1992, 115–116). The etymological link to the root √*ḍī* or √*ḍai* is traditional; H. Isaacson (personal communication) points out that the connection is drawn in chapter 1 of the *Sarvabuddhasamāyoga*, in a verse quoted widely (e.g., p. 3 in Ratnākaraśānti's *Guṇavatī* commentary on the *Mahāmāyātantra*). Bhavabhaṭṭa and Jayabhadra, commentators on the *Laghuśaṃvaratantra*, also both connect the word *ḍākinī* to √*ḍai*; see Bhavabhaṭṭa ad *Laghuśaṃvara* 1.2, Sarnath edition, p. 6; and Jayabhadra commenting on the same verse, p. 107 in Sugiki's edition of the *Cakrasaṃvarapañjikā*.
8. This inscription was first published by John F. Fleet in Corpus Inscriptionum Indicarum, vol. III (1888, 72–78), and subsequently by Sircar 1965, 1:399–405.
9. Borrowing an expression from the title of an article of Chitgopekar (2002).
10. The inscription's use of the word *tantra* is probably, as D. C. Sircar recognized (1965, 1:405), in the well-attested sense of "spell," such as in the expression *tantramantra* (cf., e.g., *Mālatīmādhava* IX.52). It seems improbable that the word could refer here to tantric scripture, as "powerful winds" (*prabalapavana*) would not be described as having arisen (*udbhūta*) from

texts. My interpretation of this passage undoubtedly has been influenced by H. Isaacson's remarks on the subject, in a lecture given at the University of Pennsylvania in January 2003.

11. See Sanderson (2001, 12n10), who identifies several other references to *Ḍākinītantras*, including Kṣemarāja's *Netroddyota*, ad *Netratantra* 20.39.
12. It seems likely that *Ḍākinītantras* taught practices such as *pañcāmṛtākarṣaṇa*, "extraction of the five [bodily] nectars," said in the *Mālatīmādhava* to be the source of the wicked *yoginī* Kapālakuṇḍalā's flight. On the bodily nectars (blood, semen, etc.) and the methods of their extraction, yogic and otherwise, see *Tantrikābhidhānakośa*, vol. 3 (Rastelli and Goodall 2013), s.vv. "*dikcarī*," "*nāḍyudaya*," "*pañcāmṛta* (3)," and "*pañcāmṛtākarṣaṇa*."
13. Among these, most of the *Siddhayogeśvarīmata* has been edited by Törzsök (1999), while the present author has edited several chapters of the *Brahmayāmala* (Hatley 2007)—both in doctoral theses yet unpublished.
14. *Siddhayogeśvarīmata*, ch. 29; *Brahmayāmala*, ch. 74; and *Tantrasadbhāva*, ch. 16.
15. A *yoginī* of the clan of Brāhmī/Brahmāṇī is said to be *brahmāṇyaṃśā*, "possessing a portion of Brahmāṇī." See, e.g., *Tantrasadbhāva* 16.253cd. An initiate too is said to be "connected to" or "possess" (*yukta*) an *aṃśa* of a Mother-goddess. Note, e.g., *Brahmayāmala* 74.47cd: *brahmāṇīkulajā devi svāṃśasiddhipradāyikā* ("[She is] a yoginī of the clan of Brahmāṇī, O Goddess, who bestows *siddhi* upon those [*sādhakas*] of her own [Mother-goddess] *aṃśa*").
16. Note, for instance, chapters 56 and 101 of the *Brahmayāmala*, both of which concern the classification of goddess clans.
17. For descriptions of the *ḍākinī* as a dangerous variety of female spirit, see, e.g., *Brahmayāmala* 56.12, 56.43–44, and 101.38–39. Cf. Sanderson 2001, 12n10.
18. *Netroddyota*, quoted in the commentary on *Netratantra* 2.71:

    chalenākṛṣya pibati kṣudrā prāṇipayaḥ sadā |
    rūpaparivartanārthaṃ labdhvā pātayati paśūn |
    śākinī sā tu vijñeyā raudrasthānaratā sadā |

    With minor variants and corruptions, this corresponds to 16.163cd–64 in Dyczkowski's draft edition of the *Tantrasadbhāva*. Cf. *Tantrasadbhāva* 16.181–218, which describes the pernicious activities of several varieties of *yoginī*, such as the *adhoniśvāsikā* and its subtypes; several verses from this passage are quoted by Kṣemarāja ad *Netratantra* 19.55.
19. The verse defines the *rudraḍākinī* in *Siddhayogeśvarīmata* 26.14 and the *Sarvavīratantra* (as quoted by Kṣemarāja in *Netratantroddyota*, ad *Netratantra* 2.16); it defines the *rudraśākinī* in *Tantrasadbhāva* 16.165, also quoted by Kṣemarāja ad *Netratantra* 19.71.
20. *Tantrāloka* 15.552ab and *Tantrasadbhāva* 9.544ab; see Törzsök 1999, 18.
21. For more detailed discussions, see Herrmann-Pfandt (1996) and Hatley (2007, 101–106).

22. *Kathāsaritsāgara* VI, 5.1–36. Cf. *Bhāgavatapurāṇa* X, 62.
23. *Kathāsaritsāgara*, VII.107–118.
24. Ibid., III, 6.102–218.
25. Ibid., XII, 4.263–277.
26. Ibid., VI, 6, especially vv. 153–80.
27. This episode occurs as *Kathāsaritsāgara* VII, 3.147–169.
28. Ibid., XII, 1.31–72.
29. On the dating of Buddhaguhya, see Hodge (2003, 22–23); see also Sanderson (2009, 128–132). Concerning Vilāsavajra, I follow Davidson (1981, 6–7). Evidence Sanderson (2006a) cites for dating Sadyojyotis includes the fact that he was known to Somānanda (early tenth century), appears to have been familiar with Kumārila (but not Dharmakīrti), that his commentary on the *Svāyambhuvasūtrasaṃgraha* is paraphrased in the *Haravijaya* (circa 830 CE), and that in his critique of the Vedāntins, he displays no awareness of the *vivartavāda* or "illusionism" associated with Śaṅkara (fl. c. 800 CE?) and Maṇḍanamiśra. See also Watson (2006, 111–114).
30. Hodge (2003, 5–8) provides a valuable account of the chronology of the Chinese translations of early tantric literature. Buddhist *Kriyātantras* in all likelihood drew upon ancient and perhaps nonsectarian magical traditions, such as the *vidyā* practices attested in an early Jaina narrative, the *Vasudevahiṇḍī* (on which see Hatley [2007, 95–101]).
31. Hodge (2003, 9–11) points out that a Chinese traveler, Xuanzang, gives no indication that Buddhist tantric traditions were prevalent in India in the period up to 645 CE. On the other hand, there are firsthand reports concerning tantric practices and scripture from the latter half of the century.
32. See Tribe (2007, 207–210). Hodge, offering a different assessment of the soteriological dimension of the *Vairocanābhisaṃbodhi*, considers this text "likely to have been one of the first, if not actually the first *fully* developed tantra to be compiled, that has survived in some form to the present day" (2003, 29 [quotation], 33–39). In my discussion of this text, I rely entirely upon Hodge's English translation from the Chinese and Tibetan.
33. Concerning the dating, see Hodge (2003, 14–17). Translated into Chinese in 724 CE, the *Vairocanābhisaṃbodhi* appears to have been among the manuscripts collected by Wuxing in India at some point during the eight years prior to his death in 674.
34. "Wrathful Mothers" perhaps translates the Sanskrit *rudramātaraḥ* ("Rudra/Śaiva's Mother-goddesses"). That this could refer specifically to the Seven Mothers is suggested by Kṣemarāja's explanation of the term as it occurs in *Netratantra* 2.13c (he glosses *rudramātaraḥ* with *brahmyādyās*—"Brahmī, etc."). The identification of Yāmī with Kālarātri is suggested in the Chinese translation of I.19; see Hodge's note thereon (2003, 63). Yāmī and the sow-faced Vārāhī alternate in textual accounts of the Seven Mothers, while sculpted sets appear as a rule to depict Vārāhī.

35. Note also their association with a series of drawn insignia (*mudrā*), as with the other maṇḍala deities (XIII.89). While Kālarātri is invoked with her own mantra, the others are paid reverence with the generic NAMAḤ SAMANTABUDDHĀNĀṂ MĀTṚBHYAḤ SVĀHĀ (IV.11).
36. See *Vairocanābhisaṃbodhi* IV.11.
37. *Vairocanābhisaṃbodhi* XVII.13; also mentioned are, e.g., *piśācas* and *rākṣasas*.
38. VI.15: "Then, for example, the Asuras manifest illusions with mantras. Or, for example, there are [mundane] mantras which counteract poison and fevers. Or else there are the mantras with which the Mothers send sickness upon people . . ." (Hodge 2003, 170–171).
39. Lists of suitable locations are present in V.9 and VI.30. In *Vairocanābhisaṃbodhi, Uttaratantra* III.2, Mother shrines are listed among the places appropriate for fire sacrifice having as its goal "subduing" (Sanskrit *vaśīkaraṇa*, presumably).
40. A short series of mantras for minor divinities and spirits such as *rākṣasas*, *ḍākinīs*, and *asuras* is provided in IV.16, while *mudrās* and mantras for a larger series, including *ḍākinīs*, are listed in XI.98–99. A list of dangerous beings in the *Uttaratantra* includes both *ḍākinīs* and what Hodge translates as "witches" (IV.1). As described in III.9 of the *Uttaratantra*, through fire sacrifice one may "draw to himself *yakṣiṇīs* and likewise girls of the subterranean realm with the male and female assistants."
41. *Laṅkāvatārasūtra* 8.10–16 (verse version) speaks of birth from the womb of a *ḍākinī* or *rākṣasī* as a potential fate for the carnivore. See the discussion of Gray (2005, 50–51).
42. XV.10; the mantra for the "Mudrā of Upholding the Bhagavat's Yoga" is given as NAMAḤ SAMANTABUDDHĀNĀṂ MAHĀYOGAYOGINI YOGEŚVARI KHĀÑJALIKA SVĀHĀ.
43. The text is better known as the *Mañjuśrīmūlakalpa*. While both titles occur in manuscript colophons, I follow the convention preferred by Martin Delhey, who is currently preparing a critical edition of sections of the text.
44. *Mañjuśriyamūlakalpa* 1, vol. 1, pp. 20–21 (Trivandrum Sanskrit Series edition).
45. The Seven Mothers (precise identities unspecified) occupy a position in the southeastern direction, adjacent to Yama in the south, and are also among the deities around the perimeter of that layer of the maṇḍala; their company includes major brahmanical gods, *gaṇa*-lords such as Mahākāla, sages, Tumburu and the Four Sisters, the Planets, and so forth. *Mañjuśriyamūlakalpa* 2, vol. 1, pp. 44–45.
46. *Mañjuśriyamūlakalpa* 45 provides *mudrās* connected to and named after the Mothers, and includes both Cāmuṇḍi (45.229cd–30ab) and Vajracāmuṇḍi (45.228cd–229ab). Vol. 2, p. 510. Verse numbers here and elsewhere are given as per the reprint edited by P. L. Vaidya, while volume and page numbers are those of the Trivandrum Sanskrit Series edition.
47. See, for example, *Mañjuśriyamūlakalpa* 3, vol. 1, p. 53, and chapter 9, vol. 1, p. 82. Cf., e.g., 22.229 (vol. 1, p. 249), in a vivid description of the activities of Mother-goddesses.

48. *Mañjuśriyamūlakalpa* 2.4–5, vol. 1, p. 30.
49. Chapter 52, vol. 3, p. 563–564.
50. The *vidyā*-mantras of these deities are first given in 2.15–17, where they are said to be "attendants of the Bodhisattva" (*bodhisattvānucārikā[ḥ]*, 2.16b). Vol. 1, p. 32. *Mañjuśriyamūlakalpa* ch. 47 presents a brief narrative of their taking refuge in the Dharma, after which begin instructions on their worship. See also the discussion of Sanderson (2009, 129–130).
51. Elements of this text were introduced in China by an Indian, Vajrabodhi, who would have learned the teachings around 700 CE; Amoghavajra partially translated the text in 753. See the discussion of Hodge (2003, 11–12).
52. Among Buddhist sources, note, for instance, *Laghuśaṃvaratantra* 2.26–27, referring to *ḍākinīs* of the skies, earth, and netherworlds, as well as Mother-goddesses of the eight directions. (*Laghuśaṃvara* verse numbers are given as per the 2013 edition of David Gray.) On the Śaiva classification of *yoginīs* as aerial, terrestrial, and so forth, cf., e.g., the Śaiva *Kulasāra*, discussed by Törzsök (Rastelli and Goodall 2013, s.v. "*dikcarī*").
53. *Tattvasaṃgraha* 6, p. 173 (lines 3–21). I cite the text from the edition of Yamada (1981).
54. *Tattvasaṃgraha* 14, pp. 306–307 (lines 10–14, 1–4); Cāmuṇḍā/Vajrakālī is addressed as, e.g., *kapālamālālaṅkṛtā* ("adorned with a garland of skulls") and *vajrakhaṭvāṅgadhāriṇī* ("bearer of a *vajra* and skull-staff").
55. *Tattvasaṃhgraha* 6, p. 180–181 (lines 8–17, 1–3):

> *atha vajrapāṇir mahābodhisattvaḥ punar api sarvaḍākinyādiduṣṭagrahāk arṣaṇahṛdayam abhāṣat* / OṂ VAJRĀKARṢAYA ŚĪGHRAṂ SARVADUṢṬAGRAHĀN VAJRADHARASATYENA HUṂ JAḤ // *athāsmin bhāṣitamātre ḍākinyādayaḥ sarvaduṣṭagrahāḥ sumerugirimūrdhni bāhyato maṇḍalībhūtvāvasthitā iti // atha vajrapāṇir mahābodhisattvaḥ tāṃ ḍākinyādīn sarvaduṣṭagrahān āhūyaivam āha / pratipadyata mārṣāḥ prāṇātipātavairamaṇyaśikṣāsa mayasaṃvare mā vo vajreṇādīptena pradīptenaikajvālībhūtena kulāni nirdaheyam / atha te ḍākinyādayaḥ sarvaduṣṭagrahā yena bhagavān tenāñjaliṃ baddhvā bhagavantaṃ vijñāpayām āsuḥ / vayaṃ bhagavan māṃsāśinas tad ājñāpayasva kathaṃ pratipattavyam iti*

Concerning *vairamaṇya*, see its lexical entry in Edgerton (1953, vol. 2).

56. *Tattvasaṃgraha* 6, p. 181 (lines 4–12, 15–18):

> *atha bhagavān vajrapāṇim evam āha / pratipadyasva vajrapāṇe eṣāṃ sattvānāṃ mahākaruṇām utpādyopāyaṃ dātum iti / atha vajrapāṇir mahākāruṇika idaṃ sarvasattvamaraṇanimittajñānamudrāhṛda yam abhāṣat* / OṂ VAJRA PRATIGṚHṆA HṚDAYAM ĀKARṢAYA YADY AYAṂ SATTVO MĀSĀD ARDHENA MRIYATE TAD ASYA HṚDAYAN NIṢKRAMATU SAMAYA HŪṂ JJAḤ // *athāsya mudrābandho bhavati / . . . anayā*

mudrayā bhavadbhiḥ sarvasattvahṛdayāny apakṛṣya bhoktavyānīti |
atha te ḍākinyādayaḥ sarvaduṣṭagrahā hulu hulu prakṣveḍitāni kṛtvā svabhavanam gatā iti ||

57. This passage from the commentary of Śubhakarasiṃha and his disciple Yixing is translated and discussed by Gray (2005, 47–49). The commentators' remarks concern *Vairocanābhisaṃbodhi* IV.16, mentioned earlier (n. 40).
58. On the dating of the *Guhyasamāja*, I follow Matsunaga (1978, xxiii–xxvi). On eroticism in the iconography and ritual of the *Guhyasamāja*, see Sanderson (2009, 141–142).
59. *Guhyasamāja* XVII, p. 99:

atha vajrapāṇiḥ sarvatathāgatādhipatiḥ sarvavajraḍākinīsamayaṃ svakāyavākcittavajrebhyo niścārayām āsa |
viṇmūtrarudhiraṃ bhakṣed madyādīṃś ca pibet sadā |
vajraḍākinīyogena mārayet padalakṣaṇaiḥ ||24||
svabhāvenaiva sambhūtā vicaranti tridhātuke |
ācaret samayaṃ kṛtsnaṃ sarvasattvahitaiṣiṇā ||25||
sarvatraidhātukasamayasamavasaraṇo nāma samādhiḥ |

Aspects of this seem puzzling; *vajraḍākinīyoga* might refer to the invasive yogic processes by which *ḍākinīs* prey upon victims (cf., e.g., Rastelli and Goodall 2013, s.v. "*pañcāmṛtākarṣaṇa*"); *padalakṣaṇaiḥ* suggests no plausible interpretation to me, while the interpretation of the next verse-quarter is unclear as well. Candrakīrti, commenting on this verse, glosses *vajraḍākinīyogena* with "the yoga of Gaurī, etc." (*gauryādiyogena*). His remarks on *padalakṣaṇaiḥ* are unfortunately corrupt, but contain clear reference to the parasitic practices of *ḍākinīs* (***padalakṣaṇaiḥ*** *duṣṭānām †uḍya†raktāk[r]ṣṭyādiprayogaiḥ* ***mārayet***, "One should slay with *padalakṣaṇas*, i.e. the application of ... extraction of blood from the wicked"). *Pradīpoddyotana*, p. 206.
60. H. Isaacson, personal communication (May 2007).
61. The orthographies *-saṃvara* and *-śaṃvara* sometimes alternate in the names of the text and its deity. I have adopted the convention Sanderson argues for (2009, 166–168) in referring to the deity as Cakrasaṃvara but the text as the *Laghuśaṃvara(-tantra)*.
62. The primary maṇḍala is described in chapter 2 of the *Laghuśaṃvara*, while the twenty-four *ḍākinīs* are listed in chapter 4. For a discussion of the maṇḍala, see Gray (2007, 54–76); see also Sanderson (2009, 170).
63. Mentioned first in 2.19cd, the *vīras* are not named until chapter 48.
64. *Laghuśaṃvara* 4.1ab, ... *ḍākinyo bhuvanāni vijṛmbhayanti*. Cf. 41.16ab, *caturviṃśatir ḍākinya etābhiḥ sarvavyāptaṃ sacarācaram*.
65. The names of the twenty-four are given in *Laghuśaṃvara* 4.1–4. While Khagānanā has no precise counterpart in the *Brahmayāmala*, for avian imagery, note Lohatuṇḍī, "Iron-beak." Surābhakṣī, too, does not figure in the *Brahmayāmala*;

however, the principal Six Yoginīs are said to be fond of alcohol (*madirāsavapriyā nityaṃ yoginyaḥ ṣaṭ prakīrtitāḥ*, 54.15ab).

66. Lists of the five goddess classes occur in, e.g., 13.3 and 14.2. Additional subcategories of *ḍākinī* are described in chapters 16–19 and 23. The twenty-four maṇḍala *ḍākinīs* are said to belong to the *vārāhīkula* in 2.18cd (*ḍākinyas tu caturviṃśā vārāhyā[ḥ] kulasambhavāḥ*).

67. The description of the *sarvaḍākinyālaya* ("abode of all *ḍākinīs*") begins in 48.8, and is based upon the pantheon of the *hṛdaya* mantra stated in 48.3. The "great cakra" is also described as *ḍākinījālasaṃvara* ("the assembly [?] of the matrix of *ḍākinīs*") in 48.16 (*pūrvoktena vidhānena yajeḍ ḍākinījālasaṃvaram | mahācakraṃ sarvasiddhyālayaṃ tathā*).

68. *Laghuśaṃvara* 1.3ab: *sarvaḍākinīmayaḥ sattvo vajrasattvaḥ paraṃ sukham.*

69. Chapters on *chommā* include *Laghuśaṃvara* 15 (single-syllable *chommās*), 20 (communication through pointing at parts of the body), 21 (similar gestures plus their correct responses), 22 (gestures made only with the fingers), and 24 (single-syllable and other verbal codes).

70. Lists of *pīṭhas* occur in *Laghuśaṃvara* 41, which associates specific sets of goddesses with these; and *Laghuśaṃvara* 50.19ff.

71. Note, for instance, that the initiatory maṇḍala described in chapter 2 is constructed with mortuary materials such as cremation ashes.

72. Particularly noteworthy are the *homa* rites described in *Laghuśaṃvara* 50.

73. See, for instance, the brief chapter 39; the heroic *sādhaka* is promised attainment of the state of a Sky-wanderer (*nīyate khecarīpadam*, 4b [Pandey edition]), and freedom from old age and death (*na jarāmṛtyuḥ sarvatra sādhako mantravigrahaḥ*, 5ab).

74. *Laghuśaṃvara* 3.16:

   ḍākinyo lāmayaś caiva khaṇḍarohā tu rūpiṇī |
   etair vicarej jagat sarvaṃ ḍākinyaiḥ saha sādhakaḥ ||16 ||
   sarvā kiṅkarī tasya sādhakasya na saṃśayaḥ |

   Highly irregular grammatical forms such as *etaiḥ* (masculine, for the feminine *etābhiḥ*) and *ḍākinyaiḥ* (for *ḍākinībhiḥ*) are none too rare in this text, while the metrical irregularities of 16c and 17a are even more typical.

75. Note in particular the rituals of *Laghuśaṃvara* 49, which promise the yogin the power to transform himself at will (*kāmarūpo mahāvīrya yogī syān nātra saṃśayaḥ*, 49.15cd, Pandey edition).

76. Regarding *Laghuśaṃvara* ch. 16, Sanderson claims that this is based upon a passage from the *Yoginīsañcāraprakaraṇa* of the *Jayadrathayāmala*. The parallel text comprises *Jayadrathayāmala* III, 32.119cd–127ab (= *Yoginīsañcāraprakaraṇa* 9.119cd–127ab). The texts differ substantively primarily in the verse-quarters providing clan-names; the actual descriptions of the *yoginīs* differ relatively little. The Buddhist version is sometimes unmetrical or nonsensical

precisely where the texts differ: compare especially *Jayadrathayāmala* III, 32.120cd (*śivagoṣṭhīratā caiva sā jñeyā śivagotrajā*) with *Laghuśaṃvara* 16.3cd: *saugatagoṣṭhīratā caiva sā jñeyā kulagotrajā*; 3c has metrical faults (short syllables in both positions 2 and 3, as well as hypermetricism), while 3d challenges interpretation ("born in the clan of the clan"?). I am grateful to Alexis Sanderson for sharing his draft edition of the *Yoginīsañcāraprakaraṇa* with me, and to Olga Serbaeva for sharing her transcription of other portions of the vast *Jayadrathayāmala*.

77. The colophon reads, in the oldest manuscript (NAK 3-370), *samayādhikāro nāmañcāśītimaḥ paṭalaḥ*—with *nāmañcāśītimaḥ* no doubt corrupt for *nāma pañcāśītimaḥ*. Sanderson evidently follows the emended colophon in numbering this chapter 85 rather than 88, the latter being its number in order of occurrence (an estimate, given that several folia are missing).

78. I have consulted two manuscripts of the *Abhidhānottara*, as detailed in the list of references.

79. For instance, *Laghuśaṃvara* 26.13cd (*aprakāśyam idaṃ guhyaṃ gopanīyaṃ prayatnataḥ*), which occurs again as 31.14ab, is parallel to *Brahmayāmala* 90.2cd (*aprakāśyam idaṃ devi gopanīyaṃ prayatnataḥ*); variants of this phrase appear in chapters 21, 22, 45, and 46 of the *Brahmayāmala* as well. Note the absence of the (contextually inappropriate) vocative *devi* in the *Laghuśaṃvara* version. There are other similarities of idiom: another phrase shared by the *Brahmayāmala* and *Laghuśaṃvara*, and not with other Buddhist sources I am aware of, is *nātaḥ parataraṃ kiñcit triṣu lokeṣu vidyate*. This occurs as *Laghuśaṃvara* 5.25cd and 50.14ab (cf. 26.1ab and 48.7ab), and *Brahmayāmala* 14.262ab and 87.222ab (cf., e.g., the *Revākhaṇḍa* attributed to the *Skandapurāṇa*, 71.1cd: *nātaḥ parataraṃ kiṃcit triṣu lokeṣu viśrutam*). Other idiomatic expressions shared by the *Brahmayāmala* and the *Laghuśaṃvara* include variations upon the following (*Laghuśaṃvara* 3.20cd–21ab):

adṛṣṭamaṇḍalo yogī yogitvaṃ yaḥ samīhate ||
hanyate muṣṭinākāśaṃ pibate mṛgatṛṣṇikām |

Striking the sky and drinking from a mirage are proverbial expressions for futile endeavor. My attention was first drawn to this verse by Harunaga Isaacson in the autumn of 2003. Compare, e.g., *Brahmayāmala* 91.44:

aviditvā -d- imaṃ sarvaṃ yaḥ pūjāṃ kartum arhati |
hanate muṣṭinākāśam īhate mṛgatṛṣṇikām ||

Verses with remarkable similarities occur as *Brahmayāmala* 3.5, 11.44cd–45ab, 22.106, 75.212, 85.50, and 90.56. These parallels are not, however, unique to the *Brahmayāmala*; note also *Tantrasadbhāva* 28.88ab and *Niśvāsakārikā* (T.17) 44.241cd (*hanate muṣṭinākāśaṃ pibate mṛgatṛṣṇikām*).

80. Oriental Institute of Baroda manuscript no. 13290.

81. The short recension is transmitted in two manuscripts, as detailed in the list of references, one of which is incomplete. In its final chapter (81), the text refers to itself as the *sāra* ("essence") of the twelve-thousand verse *Brahmayāmala*, just as the latter was drawn from the (putative) recension of 125,000 verses. I hence refer to the shorter recension as the *Brahmayāmalasāra*.

82. Note, for instance, that the reference to consorts (*dūtī*) being "with the grain" or "against the grain" (225ab) is apparently explained in 87.14cd: *ṛtuyogaviyogena anulomavilomajā[ḥ]*, which seems to mean, "[consorts either] go with or against the grain, according to whether or not they are in their menstrual period (*ṛtu*)."

83. Gray (2007, 265) translates, "Furthermore, having known Śrī Heruka's mantra, which does not exist in the triple world, all [other] mantras should be disregarded." Cf. Bhavabhaṭṭa's gloss: ***ato** mūlamantrāt śreṣṭha**mantrapadam*** | *vidyatā vajravārāhī tasyāḥ sambodhanaṃ **vidyate*** | ***nāstī**tyasya nirdeśo vā* | ***mantraṃ** mūlamantrādikam* | ***jñātvā sarvān mantrān parityajet*** | ("'From/ than this' [*ataḥ*] refers to the root mantra; [*paraṃ mantrapadaṃ*] means 'most excellent mantra word'. *vidyate* is the vocative of *vidyatā*, which refers to Vajravārāhī. Or else, [*na vidyate*] specifies, 'does not exist' (*nāsti*). *mantra* refers to the root mantra and so forth. Having learnt [it], one should abandon all [other] mantras"). It is striking that Bhavabhaṭṭa would go so far as to seek a vocative epithet of Vajravārāhī in the commonplace verb *vidyate* ("exists"), illustrating his predicament in making sense of some of the *Laghuśaṃvara*'s more obscure passages.

84. Preceding *Brahmayāmala* 88.1 is a short series of mantras in prose, the text of which is badly damaged. These have no precise counterpart in the *Laghuśaṃvara*. There may, however, be a structural parallel, for the short chapter preceding *Laghuśaṃvara* ch. 26 consists of a single long mantra.

85. The term *smaraṇa* occurs in *Laghuśaṃvara* 29.3c. Concerning the *smaraṇa* and mantra-deities of the *Brahmayāmala*, see also Hatley (2007, 251–258).

86. Jayabhadra, *Cakraśaṃvarapañjikā*: ***ārādhako viśuddhaś ca dīpako guṇavān nara** iti **guṇavān naro** yogī **tridhā** bhidyate* [em. H. Isaacson; *vidyate* Ed.] ***ārādhaka** ity anutpannapratibhaḥ **viśuddha** ity utpannasāmarthyaḥ **dīpaka** iti madhyadīpakaḥ kiṃcidutpannapratibhaḥ svaparārthabodhakaś ca* || *athav**ārādhako** mantrayogābhyāsena devātāradhakaḥ **guṇavān** śāstrārthavettā **dīpakaḥ** pradīpavat sarvasattvārthakriyāsamarthaḥ* ||

87. On the classification of scripture in relation to the *śaktis*, see Hatley (2007, 264–268); see discussion later in this chapter concerning the threefold classification of *sādhakas*.

88. samayāḥ] *corr.;* samayā MS.

89. jñātavyāḥ] *corr.;* jñātavyā MS.

90. sādhakair nityaṃ] *em.*; sādhakai nnityaṃ MS (*tops damaged*).

91. °sthitaiḥ] *conj.* (Cs. Kiss); °sthitau MS.

92. °vimiśras tu] *em.*; °vimuktas tu MS.
93. trividhaḥ] *corr.;* tṛvidhaḥ MS.
94. triṣaṣṭi°] *em.*; ttriṣaṣṭhi° MS.
95. There are strong grounds for emending *śuddhāśuddhavimuktas* to *°vimiśras*, as I have done, for this threefold classification of *sādhaka*s based upon degrees of "purity" pervades the *Brahmayāmala* and fits the present context. Cf., e.g., *Brahmayāmala* 33.331c, *śuddhāśuddhavimiśreṣu*. Furthermore, several Buddhist sources support the emendation: Gray (2013) reads *śuddho 'śuddho 'tha miśraś ca* in *Laghuśaṃvara* 26.15a, reporting as testimonia, for the last three syllables, *misras ca, miśra vaiḥ*, and *mimra vai* (apparatus ad 26.15a). In 9b, one could consider emending to *sādhakaḥ trividhā smṛtaḥ*, or to *sādhakās trividhā sthitāḥ*; a range of variants are attested in the Buddhist parallels (see Gray 2013, apparatus at 26.15b).
96. I am unable to determine the probable intended sense of 9d, *dīpakādiguṇair vinā*, as transmitted in the codex. The parallel text in *Laghuśaṃvara* 26.15d provides no assistance obvious to me.
97. The *unmattakavrata* is fourth of the Nine Observances described in *Brahmayāmala* ch. 21, involving feigned insanity, as the name implies. The *asidhāravrata* ("observance of the sword's edge") for its part comprises the subject of *Brahmayāmala* ch. 40 (edited by Hatley, forthcoming).
98. While the various observances taught in *Brahmayāmala* ch. 21 are referred to collectively as *vidyāvratas*, "observances of the [nine-syllable] *vidyā*," this term is primarily used for the final and most important of these, a *kāpālika* observance also called the *mahāvrata* (108a) or *bhairavavrata* (109ab). As for the *triṣaṣṭivrata*, this appears to be connected with a mantra-deity pantheon (*yāga*) of the same name; yet while the "*yāga* of the sixty-three" and its *vrata* are mentioned in several chapters, I have not identified a detailed description.
99. The implication is that the *sarvātman sādhaka* is bound by no single discipline and may engage at will in practices associated with the lower grades of initiate. This is consistent with the description of the *sarvātman* found in *Brahmayāmala* ch. 97.
100. The notion that one may attain *siddhi* through consuming oblation gruel (*caru*) offered directly by the *yoginīs* is mentioned in, e.g., *Brahmayāmala* 104.29, and is in all likelihood alluded to here in 14b. For a detailed description, see *Kaulajñānanirṇaya* 11.7cd–10.
101. The terms for the threefold *sādhaka* are provided in *Brahmayāmala* 45.10cd–11ab:

    śuddhas tu tālakaḥ proktaś [corr.; proktaṃś MS*] carubhojī tv aśuddhakaḥ || 10 ||*
    śuddhāśuddho bhaven miśraḥ [em.; misraṃ MS*] sādhakas tu na saṃśayaḥ |*

    On the term *tālaka*, see the entry in Rastelli and Goodall (2013). A detailed study of the *Brahmayāmala*'s threefold typology of *sādhaka*s has been published by Csaba Kiss (2015).

102. It is evident from the descriptions in *Brahmayāmala* 45 that the *miśraka*, as one might expect, constitutes the middle grade of *sādhaka*. Hence in 45.472, it is said that a *miśraka* purified through constant practice may become a *tālaka* (*kadācin miśrako devi karmayogena nityaśaḥ | tālamārga[ṃ] samāpnoti yadā śuddhaḥ prajāyate*). However, the *sarvātman sādhaka* is "mixed" in an entirely different sense: he is free from all regulations, engaging at will in the disciplines associated with lower practitioners.

103. It appears that the *ārādhaka* might not be considered a *sādhaka*, per se; their characteristic modes of ritual, *ārādhana* ("worship") and *sādhana*, are placed in contrast. See, e.g., 88.8b above. Nonetheless, the term *ārādhaka* figures in later Śaiva typologies of the *sādhaka*. In the *Kulasāra*, the *ārādhaka* features as fourth of the five grades of *sādhaka*, above the *tālaka*, *cumbaka*, and *cārvāka* (= *carubhojin*, presumably); transcending the *ārādhaka* is the *śivodbhūta*:

tālako cuṃbakaś caiva cārvākārādhakas [em.; °*korādhakas* MS] *tathā* |

śivodbhūta -m- [em. (Vasudeva); *śivobhūtam* MS] *ataḥ proktaḥ pāṃcabhedo 'pi sādhakaḥ* |

I am grateful to Somadeva Vasudeva for providing me his draft edition of this passage. Given the terminological continuities, it seems possible that this fivefold typology develops out of the threefold classification present in the *Brahmayāmala*, the addition of the *ārādhaka* reflecting an intermediate stage.

104. Reference to the fourfold typology of practitioners is clearly present in *Brahmayāmala* 87.223, although out of sequence: *carvāhāra* (= *aśuddha* or *carubhojin*), *tālaka* (= *śuddha*), *ārādhaka* (by emendation of °*ārādhane*; = *viśuddha*), and *sarvātmaka* (= *miśra*). The point of 224cd is that the yoga expounded in this chapter is applicable to all four (*caturṇām*) types of practitioner.

105. On the evidence for pre-eleventh-century works of Śaiva literature, see Sanderson (2001, 2–19; 2009, 45–53). Davidson's cautious views on the chronology of Śaiva literature occasionally veer to the extreme, as when he refers to "the fact that most Kaula works appear composed after the sites [of the *circa* 9th–13th century *yoginī* temples] were constructed" (2002, 180).

106. Davidson addresses Sanderson's remarks on this inscription as they were presented in Sanderson (2001, 7–8). Sanderson has subsequently discussed this material in greater detail (2003–2004, 355–357). On the Gilgit fragment of an exegetical work of the *vāmasrotas*, see Sanderson (2009, 50–51). On early evidence for the *vāmasrotas*, see all of the preceding. Recently, Tomabechi (2007) has identified a passage in the *Sarvabuddhasamāyoga*—sometimes spoken of as a proto-*Yoginītantra*—as being shared with the *Vīṇāśikhatantra*, apparently the only extant *tantra* of the *vāmasrotas*. He does not venture an opinion concerning the direction of redaction, but notes also that the text's mantra code results in the supreme buddha, Vajrasattva, being given the mantra HAṂSA,

"... the famous mantra representing the Śaiva Tantras' supreme being, which is often identified with the movement of vital energy (*prāṇa*) within the human body" (918).

107. Davidson's attempts to show that Bhairava and "his Buddhist counterpart, Heruka" have (independent) roots in tribal or local divinities seem unconvincing. The *Kālikāpurāṇa*, which may contain old material but which in its current form is unlikely to predate the sixteenth century (Stapelfeldt 2001, 35–40), associates a cremation ground called Heruka with Kāmākhyā; Davidson identifies this (plausibly) as the modern site called Masānbhairo (*śmaśānabhairava*). He further postulates that "Buddhists apparently appropriated a local term [Heruka] for a specific Assamese ghost or cemetery divinity and reconfigured it into the mythic enemy of evil beings in general" (Davidson 2002, 211–216 [quotations on 211, 214]). Even if it could be demonstrated that the reference to Heruka comes from a comparatively early stratum of the *Kālikāpurāṇa*, to argue that he was originally an Assamese cremation-spirit deity on this basis calls to mind what Davidson (2002, 206) elsewhere describes as "sustained special pleading about single reference citations, a questionable method of arguing history." For another view on the origin of the name Heruka, see Sanderson (2009, 148n340).

As for Bhairava, Davidson (2002, 211) asserts that he "seems to have been little more than a local ferocious divinity at one time ... eventually appropriated by Śaivas, much as they aggressively appropriated so much other tribal and outcaste lore for their own ends." He cites little evidence for this, beyond origin myths found in the *Kālikāpurāṇa* for a *liṅga* called "Bhairava" near Guwahati. While the roots of Bhairava remain unclear, the evidence extends back well before the *Kālikāpurāṇa*. Mahābhairava ("The Great Terrifier") is named as a Śaiva place of pilgrimage in the *Niśvāsatattvasaṃhitā* (*Mukhāgama* 3.21d and *Guhyasūtra* 7.115d) as well as the old *Skandapurāṇa* (chapter 167); the latter source makes clear that the site is named after the form of Śaiva enshrined there (cf. Mahākāla of Ujjayinī). A fourth-century Vākāṭaka king is described as a devotee of Mahābhairava in an inscription of the fifth century, on which see Sanderson (2003–2004, 443–444) and Bisschop (2006, 192–193). The emergence of Bhairava in the tantric Śaiva pantheon, whatever his roots may be, appears to have involved some degree of identification with Aghora, the southern, fierce face of Sadāśiva who is said to reveal the *Bhairavatantras*.

108. Note, for instance, Davidson's (2002, 183–186) plausible suggestion that Pāśupata monasticism is a response to the *śramaṇa* ascetic orders. One should also mention the influence of Mahāyāna Buddhist thought upon the nondualist Śaiva exegetical tradition. For a recent and insightful study, see Ratié (2010); see also Torella (1992).

109. Davidson (2002, 217), citing Dyczkowski (1987, 102), also claims that the *Jayadrathayāmala* names the Buddhist *Guhyasamājatantra*. This is Dyczkowski's

interpretation of the compound *Guhyādi* ("those [scriptures] beginning with the *Guhya*"). The verse Dyczkowski might have had in mind reads differently in the version quoted and discussed by Sanderson (2007, 233): *bhairavaṃ vajrayānaṃ ca guhyātantraṃ sagāruḍaṃ || bhūtatantrāditantraṃ ca viśeṣataram ucyate* |. Here *vajrayāna* is mentioned as a class of scripture in the *viśeṣatara* ("more esoteric/ restricted") category, but the compound following it, *guhyātantra*, appears not to be its adjective but to represent another, distinct class of scripture—*tantras* of the Leftward Stream (*vāmasrotas*) of Śaiva relevation, according to Sanderson (2007, 233).

110. Sanderson sees within the *Jayadrathayāmala* multiple texts that might originally have been independent: the *Śiraścheda*, an early *Vāmatantra* (2001, 31–32n33; 2002, 1–2); the *Mādhavakula*, a text cited by Abhinavagupta and incorporated into the fourth book (*ṣaṭka*) of the *Jayadrathayāmala* (2002, 1–2); and the *Yoginīsañcāra* of *Jayadrathayāmala*, book three (2009, 187). See also Sanderson (1990, 32n6; 2002, 2). He has recently argued (2009, 203–212) in detail that a passage from the eighth chapter of the latter is "an expanded variant" of the Śaiva source for *Laghuśaṃvara* 8.3–28. Cf. Sanderson (2001, 41–43).
111. Davidson refers to the *Rudrayāmala*, *Tārātantra*, and *Brahmayāmala* as texts transmitting the legend of Vaśiṣṭha learning "*cīnācāra*" ("the Chinese method") from the Buddha (2002, 216, citing Bhattacharya 1925–1928, 2:cxi–ii [in fact cxli–ii]; 1930). In this matter Bhattacharya drew upon Sanskrit textual materials edited from Bengali manuscripts by Vedāntatīrtha (1913). This publication includes excerpts from the first two chapters of a certain "*Brahmayāmala*" preserved in a manuscript of the Varendra Research Society. I find no indication that the text is related to the *vidyāpīṭha* scripture of the same name.
112. The windows afforded by the *Niśvāsatattvasaṃhitā* into early Śaiva systems and its own dependence upon these comprise the subject of Sanderson (2006b). See also Sanderson (2001, 29).
113. While the chapter is the 65th in sequence, it is numbered 60 in its colophon (*iti mahābhairave yakṣiṇīsādhanapaṭala ṣaṣṭhimaḥ*); chapter 63 in sequence is likewise numbered 60 (*iti kaṅkālabhairavādhikāro nāma ṣaṣṭhimaḥ paṭalaḥ*). A critical edition of chapter 65 is currently under preparation.
114. A *yakṣakula* is mentioned in 30.31ab, 38.22cd, and throughout chapter 37.
115. *Amoghapāśakalparāja*, p. 114 (folio 25a, line 7): *taṃ gṛhya ākāśenotpatati | ye ca vajrakulā tathāgatakulā maṇikulā padmakulā sarvve te mukhāgre 'vatiṣṭhanti* | ("After taking hold of that [empowered noose], he flies into the air; and all [deities] of the Vajra clan, the clan of the Buddhas, the Gem clan, and the Lotus clan stand before him").
116. Padmayakṣiṇī is the name of a *mudrā* in *Sarvatathāgatatattvasaṃgraha* 1605 (edition Horiuchi, 2:37); in 1638 (2:49), it occurs as an epithet of Padmanarteśvarī. Padmoccā (Sanskrit Padmotsā, "lotus-born") occurs as the

name of a *yakṣiṇī* in *Mañjuśriyamūlakalpa* ch. 52. The expression *vajrayakṣiṇī* occurs in *Sarvatathāgatatattvasaṃgraha* 1137 (edition Horiuchi, 1:465).

117. The material on *yakṣiṇīs* occurs in *ṣaṭka* II, chapters 25 (vv. 457ff) and 26. I am grateful to Olga Serbaeva for allowing me to consult her electronic transcription.

118. *Uḍḍāmareśvaratantra* 9, p. 34:

> *atha surasundarīsādhanam—oṃ hrīṃ āgaccha āgaccha surasundari svāhā / vajrapāṇigṛhaṃ gatvā gugguladhūpaṃ dattvā trisaṃdhyaṃ pūjayet sahasraṃ trisaṃdhyaṃ māsaparyantaṃ japet tato māsābhyantare pratyakṣā bhavati antimadine raktacandanenārghyaṃ dadyāt / tata āgatya mātā bhaginī bhāryā vā bhavati tāsāṃ yāni karmāṇi tāny eva karoti / yadi mātā bhavati tadā siddhadravyāṇi rasāyanāni dadāti / yadi bhaginī bhavati tadā pūrvavad amūlyaṃ vastraṃ dadāti / yadi bhāryā bhavati tadā sarvam aiśvaryaṃ paripūrayati /*

119. Note, for instance, the mantra of the *yakṣa*-clan dryad given in *Brahmayāmala* 65.6cd–8ab: OṂ YAKṢAKUMĀRIKE YAKṢAMUKHI EHY EHI RUDRO JÑĀPAYATE NIṂ SVĀHĀ. (Cf. the much simpler YAKṢAKUMĀRIKE SVĀHĀ of *Mañjuśriyamūlakalpa* ch. 52, *saptayakṣiṇyaḥ* section.) Compare this with the mantra for enslavement (*kiṅkarasādhana*) in *Brahmayāmala* ch. 64, which I reconstruct as follows: OṂ NAMO MAHĀKIṄKARĀYA KIRI KIRI KHAḌGAHASTĀYA VIḌĀLAVAKTRĀYA BHUJAṄGAHASTARAUDRĀYA [] EHY EHI RE RE RE RE RUDRO JÑĀPAYATE ṬAK[A?] SVĀHĀ. The formula RUDRO JÑĀPAYATI SVĀHĀ occurs with great frequency in the *Kriyākālaguṇottara*, one of the few surviving works of *Gāruḍatantra* variety. A similar expression occurs several times in the *Mañjuśriyamūlakalpa*, e.g., after 2.29: OṂ GARUḌAVĀHANA CAKRAPĀṆI CATURBHUJA HUṂ HUṂ SAMAYAM ANUSMARA BODHISATTVO JÑĀPAYATI SVĀHĀ.

120. Note, for instance, the following passage from *Mañjuśriyamūlakalpa* ch. 55:

> *tāṃ gṛhyātmano mukhe prakṣipya sarvabhūtikabalim upāhṛtya dakṣiṇamūrtau sthitaḥ haritālamanaḥśilāñjanamañjiṣṭhārocanām ekatrayaṃ gṛhya aśvatthapatrāntaritāṃ kṛtvā tāvaj japed yāvat trividhā siddhir iti ūṣmāyati dhūmāyati jvalati / ūṣmāyamāne pādapracārikāṃ pañcavarṣasahasrāyur bhavati / sarvasattvavaśīkaraṇam / dhūmāyamāne 'ntardhānaṃ daśavarṣasahasrāyur bhavati / jvalitena sarvavidyādharo bhavati /*

121. Note, for instance, the following passage from *Mañjuśriyamūlakalpa* ch. 29:

> *kapilāyāḥ samānavatsāyāḥ ghṛtaṃ gṛhya tāmrabhājanaṃ saptabhir aśvatthapatraiḥ sthāpya tāvaj japed yāvat trividhā siddhir iti / taṃ pītvā śrutidharam antardhānākāśagamanam iti //*

My attention was drawn to this use of *aśvattha* leaves by Harunaga Isaacson at the Third International Workshop on Early Tantra in Hamburg, July 2010. Compare with a procedure for preparing magical pills (*guḍikā*) in *Brahmayāmala* 66.4–5:

kṛtayatnaḥ sudhīrātmā patrair aśvatthasaṃbhavaiḥ |
tribhis tu rocanāliptair vistṛtai rugvivar[j]itaiḥ ||
saṃsthāpya guḍikāṃ tatra cchādaye[t] tu tataḥ punaḥ |
caturbhir upariṣṭā[t] tu rocanāmbuyutais tathā ||

122. As mentioned previously, this comes into evidence as early as the sixth century (Sanderson 2009, 50, 129–130).
123. triṣu] *corr.*; tṛṣu MS (= National Archives of Kathmandu ms. no. 3-370).
124. Here the *Brahmayāmalasāra* (NGMPP reel no. E1527/6) reads *mantrāṃ sarvvāṃ*, rather closer to the *Laghuśaṃvara*'s *sarvān mantrān.*
125. carvāhāravibhāge] *em.*; °vibhāgo MS.
126. °ārādhake] *em.*; °ārādhane MS.
127. The *Brahmayāmalasāra* reads *ātmadūtin.*
128. siddhaṃ] *em.*; siddha MS.
129. The *Brahmayāmalasāra* reads *darśanā.*
130. cumbanā gūhanāc caiva] *em.*; cumbanā gūhanañ caiva MS. Understand *cumbanā* as ablative, with elision of the final *-d* (cf. Edgerton 1953, 1:§8.46–48). The *Brahmayāmalasāra* agrees in reading *cumbanā gūhanañ* (the latter probably corrupt for the ablative), but, like the *Laghuśaṃvara*, reads *nityaṃ* rather than *caiva.*
131. The *Brahmayāmalasāra* reads *tatpīṭhañ*, which is hypometrical and presumably secondary.
132. *yāvato dravyasaṅghātaḥ* is supported by the *Brahmayāmalasāra*; understand *yāvato* as singular (cf. Edgerton 1953, 1:§18.33).
133. °siddhikaraḥ param] *conj.*; siddhikaraḥ paraḥ MS. The *Brahmayāmalasāra* reads *°siddhikara smṛtaḥ*; the latter lexeme is shared with the *Laghuśaṃvara*, and might represent the older reading.
134. In 4ab, there is evidence that some versions of the *Laghuśaṃvara* read the singular, as the *Brahmayāmala* appears to; see Gray (2013, apparatus ad 26.4ab).
135. kadā cana] *em.*; kadā canaḥ MS. The *Brahmayāmalasāra* reads *kathañ canaḥ.*
136. The *Brahmayāmalasāra* reads *vā.*
137. For *smṛtāḥ*, the *Brahmayāmalasāra* reads *sthitāḥ*, which is shared by the *Laghuśaṃvara* and possibly original.
138. See the previous note.
139. Jayabhadra reads *yasyā*, as does the *Brahmayāmala*, while the *Brahmayāmalasāra* reads *tasya.*

References

PRIMARY SOURCES

Abhidhānottara. Institute for Advanced Studies of World Religions, Buddhist Sanskrit Manuscripts film-strip no. MBB-1971-100.

Abhidhānottara. Lokesh Chandra, ed. 1981. *Abhidhānottara-tantra: A Sanskrit Manuscript from Nepal.* Śata-piṭaka series 263. New Delhi.

Amoghapāśakalparāja. Mikkyō seiten kenkyūkai, eds. 1999. "Transcribed Sanskrit Text of the Amoghapāśakalparāja. Part II," *Annual of the Institute for Comprehensive Study of Buddhism, Taishō University* 21: 81–128.

Uḍḍāmareśvaratantra. Pandit Jagad Dhar Zadoo, ed. 1947. *The Uddamareshvara Tantram (A Book on Magical Rites)*. Kashmir Series of Texts and Studies 70. Srinagar: Research Department of Jammu and Kashmir State.

Kulasāra. National Archives of Kathmandu ms. no. 4-137; Nepal-German Manuscript Preservation Project reel no. A40/11. Electronic transcription of Somadeva Vasudeva.

Kaulajñānanirṇaya. Prabodh Candra Bagchi, ed. 1934. *Kaulajñānanirṇaya and Some Minor Texts of the School of Matsyendranātha*. Calcutta Sanskrit Series 3. Kolkata: Metropolitan Printing and Publishing House.

Kṛṣṇayamāritantra. Samdhong Rinpoche and Vrajvallabh Dwivedi, eds. 1992. *Kṛṣṇayamāritantram, with Ratnāvalīpañjikā of Kumāracandra*. Rare Buddhist Texts Series 9. Sarnath, Varanasi: Central Institute of Higher Tibetan Studies.

Kriyākālaguṇottara. Draft edition of Michael Slober.

Guhyasamājatantra. Benoytosh Bhattacharya, ed. 1967. *Guhyasamāja Tantra or Tathāgataguhyaka*. Gaekwad Oriental Series 53. Baroda: Oriental Institute.

Guhyasamājatantra. Matsunaga Yūkei, ed. 1978. *The Guhyasamāja Tantra: A New Critical Edition*. Osaka: Tōhō Shuppan.

Guhyasamājatantrapradīpoddyotanaṭīkāṣaṭkoṭīvyākhyā of Candrakīrti. Chintaharan Chakravarti, ed. 1984. Bhoṭadeśīyasaṃkṛtagranthamālā 25. Patna: Kashi Prasad Jayaswal Research Institute.

Cakrasaṃvarapañjikā of Jayabhadra. Sugiki Tsunehiko, ed. 2001. "On the Making of *Śrīcakrasaṃvaratantra*—with a critical Sanskrit text of Jayabhadra's *Śrīcakrasaṃvarapañjikā*." *Journal of Chisan Studies* 50 (3): 91–141.

Caṇḍamahāroṣaṇatantra. Christopher S. George, ed. 1974. *The Caṇḍamahāroṣaṇa Tantra, Chapters I–VIII: A Critical Edition and English Translation*. American Oriental Series 56. New Haven, CT: American Oriental Society.

Jayadrathayāmala. Electronic transcription prepared by Olga Serbaeva.

Jayadrathayāmala, Yoginīsañcāraprakaraṇa. Draft edition of Alexis Sanderson.

Tantrasadbhāvatantra. Marc Dyczkowski, ed. 2006. "Partially and provisionally edited" e-text available from the Digital Library of the Muktabodha Indological Research Institute. http://www.muktabodhalib.org/digital_library.htm.

Tārātantram. Girīśacandra Vedāntatīrtha, ed. 1983 [1913]. *Tārātantram. Śrīgirīścandravedāntatīrthasaṅkalitam*. With an Introduction by A. K. Maitra. Reprint, Delhi: Bani Prakashan.

Niśvāsakārikā. Institut Français de Pondichéry Transcript nos. 17, 127, and 150. Electronic transcriptions 2006 by S. A. S. Sarma, Nibedita Rao, and R. Sathyanarayanan.

Niśvāsatattvasaṃhitā. Electronic transcription and draft edition 2006 by Dominic Goodall, Peter Bisschop, Diwakar Acharya, and Nirajan Kafle, based on National

Archives of Kathmandu ms. no. 1–227 (Nepal-German Manuscript Preservation Project reel A41/14), and two apographs: NAK 5-2406 (NGMPP reel A159/18), and Wellcome Institute Sanskrit ms. I.33.

Niśvāsatattvasaṃhitā. Dominic Goodall, Alexis Sanderson, Harunaga Isaacson, et al., eds. 2015. *The Niśvāsatattvasaṃhitā. The Earliest Surviving Śaiva Tantra. Volume 1. A Critical Edition and Annotated Translation of the Mūlasūtra, Uttarāsūtra, & Nayasūtra*. Collection Indologie 128. Early Tantra Series 1. Pondichéry: Institut Français de Pondichéry / École française d'Extrême-Orient / Asien-Afrika-Institut, Universität Hamburg.

Netratantra. Madhusūdan Kaul Shāstrī, ed. 1926, 1939. *The Netra Tantram, with Commentary by Kshemarāja*. 2 vols. Kashmir Series of Texts and Studies 46, 61. Bombay: The Research Department of Jammu and Kashmir State.

Pradīpoddyotana. See *Guhyasamājatantrapradīpoddyotanaṭīkāṣaṭkoṭīvyākhyā*.

Brahmayāmala/Picumata. National Archives of Kathmandu ms. no. 3-370; Nepal-German Manuscript Preservation Project reel no. A42/6.

Brahmayāmala/Picumata. See Hatley (2007).

*Brahmayāmalasāra**. Nepal-German Manuscript Preservation Project reel no. E1527/6 (private collection).

Brahmayāmalasāra. National Archives of Kathmandu ms. no. 1-1557; Nepal-German Manuscript Preservation Project reel no. A165/16. Incomplete manuscript.

Bhāgavatapurāṇa. Electronic text input by Ulrich Stiehl, 2001 (edition unknown).

Mañjuśriyamūlakalpa. T. Gaṇapati Śāstrī, ed. 1920–1925. *The Âryamanjusrîmûlakalpa*. Trivandrum Sanskrit Series 70, 76, 84. Trivandrum: Government Press.

Mahāmāyātantra. Janardan Pandey, et al., eds. 1992. *Mahāmāyātantram Guṇavatī-ṭīkāsahitam*. Rare Buddhist Texts Series 10. Sarnath: Central Institute of Higher Tibetan Studies.

Mahāvairocanābhisaṃbodhisūtra. See Hodge (2003).

Revākhaṇḍa (attributed to the *Skandapurāṇa*). Oṅkārānanda Giri, ed. 1994. *Bṛhat Śrīnarmadāpurāṇam Revākhaṇḍam*. 3rd edition. Hoshangabad: Jñānasatra Prakāśana Nyāsa.

Laghuśaṃvaratantra. Janardan Shastri Pandey, ed. 2002. *Śrīherukābhidhānam Cakrasaṃvaratantram, with the Commentary of Bhavabhaṭṭa*. 2 vols. Rare Buddhist Texts Series 26. Sarnath, Varanasi: Central Institute of Higher Tibetan Studies.

Laghuśaṃvaratantra. Oriental Institute of Baroda, ms. 13290.

Laghuśaṃvaratantra. David Gray, ed. 2013. *The Cakrasamvara Tantra (The Discourse of Śrī Heruka): Editions of the Sanskrit and Tibetan Texts*. New York: American Institute of Buddhist Studies/Columbia University Press.

Laṅkāvatārasūtra. Nanjio Bunyiu, ed. 1923. Bibliotheca Otaniensis 1. Kyoto: Otani University Press.

Saṃvarodaya. Tsuda Shin'ichi, ed. 1974. *The Saṃvarodaya-Tantra. Selected Chapters*. Tokyo: The Hokuseido Press.

Saṃvarodaya. Tokyo University Library ms. no. 404.

Sarvatathāgatatattvasaṃgraha. Isshi Yamada, ed. 1981. *Sarva-tathāgata-tattva-saṅgraha Nāma Mahāyāna-sūtra: A Critical Edition Based on a Sanskrit Manuscript and Chinese and Tibetan Translations*. Śatapiṭakam: Indo-Asian Literature 262. New Delhi: International Academy of Indian Culture.

Sarvatathāgatatattvasaṃgraha. Horiuchi Kanjin, ed. 1983. 2 vols. *Sarva-tathāgata-tattvasaṃgrahaṃ nāma Mahā-yāna-sūtram*. Kōyasan University: Mikkyō Bunka Kenkyūjo.

Siddhayogeśvarīmata. See Törzsök (1999).

Hevajratantra. D. L. Snellgrove, ed. 1959. *The Hevajra Tantra: A Critical Study*. 2 vols. London Oriental Series, vol. 6. London: Oxford University Press.

SECONDARY LITERATURE

Bhattacharya, Benoytosh, ed. 1925–1928. *Sādhanamālā*. 2 vols. Gaekwad Oriental Series 26, 41. Baroda: Oriental Institute.

Bhattacharya, Benoytosh. 1930. "Buddhist Deities in Hindu Garb." In *Proceedings and Transactions of the Fifth Indian Oriental Conference*, 2:1277–1298. Lahore: University of the Punjab.

Bisschop, Peter. 2006. *Early Śaivism and the Skandapurāṇa: Sects and Centers*. Groningen Oriental Studies 21. Groningen: Egbert Forsten Publishing.

Bühnemann, Gudrun. 1996. "The Goddess Mahācīnakrama-Tārā (Ugra-Tārā) in Buddhist and Hindu Tantrism." *Bulletin of the School of Oriental and African Studies* 59 (3): 472–493.

Dalton, Jacob. 2005. "A Crisis of Doxography: How Tibetans Organized Tantra during the 8th–12th Centuries." *Journal of the International Association of Buddhist Studies* 28 (1): 115–181.

Davidson, Ronald. 1981. "The Litany of Names of Mañjuśrī: Text and Translation of the *Mañjuśrīnāmasaṃgīti*." In *Tantric and Taoist Studies in Honour of R. A. Stein*, edited by Michel Strickmann, 1–69. Bruxelles: Institut belge des hautes études chinoises.

Davidson, Ronald. 2002. *Indian Esoteric Buddhism: A Social History of the Tantric Movement*. New York: Columbia University Press.

Dyczkowski, Mark S. G. 1987. *The Canon of the Śaivāgama and the Kubjikā Tantras of the Western Kaula Tradition*. Albany: State University of New York.

Edgerton, Franklin. 1953. *Buddhist Hybrid Sanskrit Grammar and Dictionary*. 2 vols. Reprint, Delhi: Motilal Banarsidass, 1998.

English, Elizabeth. 2002. *Vajrayoginī: Her Visualizations, Rituals and Forms. A Study of the Cult of Vajrayoginī in India*. Studies in Indian and Tibetan Buddhism. Boston: Wisdom Publications.

Ernst, Carl. 2005. "Situating Sufism and Yoga." *Journal of the Royal Asiatic Society* 15 (1): 15–43.

Fleet, John Faithful, ed. 1888. *Inscriptions of the Early Gupta Kings and Their Successors*. Corpus Inscriptionum Indicarum 3. Calcutta: Office of the Superintendent of Government Printing.

Giebel, Rolf. 1995. "The Chin-kang-ting ching yü-ch'ieh shih-pa-hui chih-kuei: An Annotated Translation." *Journal of the Naritasan Institute for Buddhist Studies* 18: 179–182.

Gray, David. 2005. "Eating the Heart of the Brahmin: Representations of Alterity and the Formation of Identity in Tantric Buddhist Discourse." *History of Religions* 45: 45–69.

Gray, David. 2007. *The Cakrasamvara Tantra (The Discourse of Śrī Heruka): A Study and Annotated Translation*. New York: American Institute of Buddhist Studies/ Columbia University Press.

Gray, David. 2013. See *Laghuśaṃvaratantra*.

Hatley, Shaman. 2007. "The *Brahmayāmalatantra* and Early Śaiva Cult of Yoginīs." PhD thesis, The University of Pennsylvania.

Hatley, Shaman. 2012. "From *Mātṛ* to *Yoginī*: Continuity and Transformation in the South Asian Cults of the Mother Goddesses." In *Transformations and Transfer of Tantra in Asia and Beyond*, edited by István Keul, 99–129. Berlin: Walter de Gruyter.

Hatley, Shaman. 2014. "Goddesses in Text and Stone: Temples of the Yoginīs in Light of Tantric and Purāṇic Literature." In *History and Material Culture in Asian Religions*, edited by Benjamin Fleming and Richard Mann, 195–225. London: Routledge.

Hatley, Shaman. Forthcoming. "Erotic Asceticism: the Knife's Edge Observance (*asidhārāvrata*) and the Early History of Tantric Coital Ritual." *Bulletin of the School of Oriental and African Studies*.

Herrmann-Pfandt, Adelheid. 1996. "The Good Woman's Shadow: Some Aspects of the Dark Nature of Ḍākinīs and Śākinīs in Hinduism." In *Wild Goddess in India and Nepal*, edited by Cornelia Vogelsanger and Anette Wilke, 39–70. Bern: Peter Lang.

Herrmann-Pfandt, Adelheid. 2001. *Ḍākinīs: zur Stellung und Symbolik des Weiblichen im tantrischen Buddhismus*. Indica et Tibetica, band 20. Marburg: Indica et Tibetica-Verlag.

Hodge, Stephen, trans. 2003. *The Mahā-Vairocana-Abhisambodhi Tantra: With Buddhaguhya's Commentary*. New York; London: Routledge Curzon.

Isaacson, Harunaga. 2007. "Language and Formulae in the Niśvāsa-corpus." Presentation made at the Early Śaivism Workshop, Pondicherry Centre of the École française d'Extrême-Orient, January 2007.

Kiss, Csaba. 2015. *The Brahmayāmalatantra or Picumata. Volume II. The Religious Observances and Sexual Rituals of the Tantric Practitioner: Chapters 3, 21, and 45. A Critical Edition and Annotated Translation*. Collection Indologie 130. Early Tantric Series 3. Pondichéry: Institut Français de Pondichéry / École française d'Extrême-Orient / Asien-Afrika-Institut, Universität Hamburg.

Matsunaga Yūkei. 1978. See *Guhyasamājatantra.*

Matsunaga Yūkei. 1985. "On the Date of the Mañjuśrīmūlakalpa." In *Tantric and Taoist Studies in Honour of R. A. Stein*, edited by Michel Strickmann, 3:882–894. Bruxelles: Institut belge des hautes études chinoises.

Newman, John. 1987. "The Outer Wheel of Time: Vajrayāna Buddhist Cosmology in the Kālacakra Tantra." PhD dissertation, University of Wisconsin-Madison.

Pandey, Janardan Shastri. 2002. See *Laghuśaṃvaratantra.*

Rastelli, Marion, and Dominic Goodall, eds. 2013. *Tāntrikābhidhānakośa. Dictionnaire des terms techniques de la littérature hindoue tantrique*, vol. 3. Sitzungsberichte der philosophisch-historischen Klasse, Band 839. Beiträge zur Kultur- und Geistesgeschichte Asiens 76. Vienna: Verlag der Österreichischen Akademie der Wissenschaften.

Ratié, Isabelle. 2010. "The Dreamer and the Yogin: On the Relationship Between Buddhist and Śaiva Idealisms." *Bulletin of the School of Oriental and African Studies* 73 (3): 437–478.

Ruegg, David Seyfort. 2008. *The Symbiosis of Buddhism with Brahmanism/Hinduism in South Asia and of Buddhism with 'Local Cults' in Tibet and the Himalayan Region.* Vienna: Verlag der Österreichischen Akademie der Wissenschaften.

Sanderson, Alexis. 1985. "Purity and Power among the Brahmans of Kashmir." In *The Category of the Person: Anthropology, Philosophy and History*, edited by Steven Collins, Michael Carrithers, and Steven Lukes, 190–216. Cambridge: Cambridge University Press.

Sanderson, Alexis. 1990. "The Visualization of the Deities of the Trika." In *L'Image Divine: Culte et Meditation dans l'Hinduisme*, edited by Andre Padoux, 31–88. Paris: Editions du CNRS.

Sanderson, Alexis. 1994. "Vajrayāna: Origin and Function." In *Buddhism into the Year 2000. International Conference Proceedings*, 87–102. Bangkok: Dhammakaya Foundation.

Sanderson, Alexis. 2001. "History Through Textual Criticism in the Study of Śaivism, the Pañcarātra and the Buddhist Yoginītantras." In *Les Sources et le Temps. Sources and Time. A Colloquium. Pondicherry 11–13 January 1997*, edited by François Grimal, 1–47. Pondicherry: Institut Français de Pondicherry/École française d'Extrême-Orient.

Sanderson, Alexis. 2002. "Remarks on the Text of the Kubjikāmatatantra." *Indo-Iranian Journal* 45: 1–24.

Sanderson, Alexis. 2003–2004. "The Śaiva Religion among the Khmers, Part I." *Bulletin de l'Ecole française d'Extrême-Orient* 90–91: 349–463.

Sanderson, Alexis. 2005. "Religion and the State: Śaiva Officiants in the Territory of the King's Brahmanical Chaplain (with an appendix on the provenance and date of the *Netratantra*)." *Indo-Iranian Journal* 47: 229–300.

Sanderson, Alexis. 2006a. "The Date of Sadyojyotis and Bṛhaspati." *Cracow Indological Studies* 8: 39–91.

Sanderson, Alexis. 2006b. "The Lākulas: New Evidence of a System Intermediate Between Pāñcārthika Pāśupatism and Āgamic Śaivism." Ramalinga Reddy Memorial Lectures, 1997. *The Indian Philosophical Annual* 24: 143–217.

Sanderson, Alexis. 2007. "The Śaiva Exegesis of Kashmir." In *Mélanges tantriques à la mémoire d'Hélène Brunner/Tantric Studies in Memory of Hélène Brunner*, edited by Dominic Goodall and André Padoux, 231–442. Collection Indologie 106. Pondicherry: Institut Français de Pondichéry/École française d'Extrême-Orient.

Sanderson, Alexis. 2009. "The Śaiva Age." In *Genesis and Development of Tantrism*, edited by Shingo Einoo, 41–350. Institute of Oriental Culture Special Series 23. Tokyo: Institute of Oriental Culture, University of Tokyo.

Serbaeva, Olga. 2006. "*Yoginīs* in *Śaiva Purāṇas* and *Tantras*: Their Role in Transformative Experiences in a Historical and Comparative Perspective." PhD dissertation, Université de Lausanne.

Sferra, Francesco. 2003. "Some Considerations on the Relationship Between Hindu and Buddhist Tantras." In *Buddhist Asia 1. Papers from the First Conference of Buddhist Studies Held in Naples in May 2001*, edited by Giovanni Verardi and Silvio Vita, 57–84. Kyoto: Italian School of East Asian Studies.

Sircar, D. C., ed. 1965. *Select Inscriptions Bearing on Indian History and Civilization*, vol. 1. 2nd edition. Kolkata: University of Calcutta.

Simmer-Brown, Judith. 2002. *Dakini's Warm Breath: The Feminine Principle in Tibetan Buddhism*. Boston: Shambhala Publications.

Stapelfeldt, Sylvia. 2001. *Kāmākhyā–Satī–Mahāmāyā: Konzeptionen der Groß en Göttin im Kālikāpurāṇa*. Reihe/Series XXVII, Asiatische und Africanische Studien. Frankfurt am Main: Peter Lang.

Sugiki, Tsunehiko. 2008. Review of: David B. Gray, *The Cakrasamvara Tantra (The Discourses of Śrī Heruka): A Study and Annotated Translation* (New York: The American Institute of Buddhist Studies/Center for Buddhist Studies and Tibet House, 2007). *Journal of the International Association of Buddhist Studies* 31 (1–2): 505–541.

Tomabechi, Toru. 2007. "The Extraction of Mantra (*mantroddhāra*) in the *Sarvabud dhasamāyogatantra*." In *Pramāṇakīrtiḥ. Papers dedicated to Ernst Steinkellner on the Occasion of his 70th Birthday*, edited by B. Kellner et al., 2:903–923. Wiener Studien zur Tibetologie und Buddhismuskunde 70.1–2. Vienna: Arbeitskreis für tibetische und buddhistische Studien, Universität Wien.

Torella, Raffaele. 1992. "The Pratyabhijñā and the Logical-Epistemological School of Buddhism." In *Ritual and Speculation in Early Tantrism: Studies in Honor of André Padoux*, edited by Teun Goudriaan, 327–346. Albany: State University of New York Press.

Törzsök, Judit. 1999. "'The Doctrine of Magic Female Spirits': A Critical Edition of Selected Chapters of the *Siddhayogeśvarīmata(tantra)* with Annotated Translation and Analysis." PhD dissertation, University of Oxford.

Tribe, Anthony. 2000. "Mantranaya/Vajrayāna: Tantric Buddhism in India." In *Buddhist Thought: A Complete Introduction to the Indian Tradition*, by Paul Williams and Anthony Tribe. London; New York: Routledge.

Turner, Sir R. L. 1962–1966. *A Comparative Dictionary of the Indo-Aryan Languages*. London: Oxford University Press.

Vedāntatīrtha, Girīśacandra, ed. 1913. See *Tārātantram*.

Watson, Alex. 2006. *The Self's Awareness of Itself: Bhaṭṭa Rāmakaṇṭha's Arguments Against the Buddhist Doctrine of No-self.* Vienna: Sammlung de Nobili Institut für Südasien-, Tibet- und Buddhismuskunde der Universität Wien.

3

Vajrayāna Traditions in Nepal

Todd Lewis and Naresh Man Bajracharya

Introduction

The existence of tantric traditions in the Kathmandu Valley dates back at least a thousand years and has been integral to the Hindu–Buddhist civilization of the Newars, its indigenous people, until the present day. This chapter introduces what is known about the history of the tantric Buddhist tradition there, then presents an analysis of its development in the premodern era during the Malla period (1200–1768 CE), and then charts changes under Shah rule (1769–2007). We then sketch Newar Vajrayāna Buddhism's current characteristics, its leading tantric masters,[1] and efforts in recent decades to revitalize it among Newar practitioners. This portrait,[2] especially its history of Newar Buddhism, cannot yet be more than tentative in many places, since scholarship has not even adequately documented the textual and epigraphic sources, much less analyzed them systematically.[3] The epigraphic record includes over a thousand inscriptions, the earliest dating back to 464 CE, tens of thousands of manuscripts, the earliest dating back to 998 CE, as well as the myriad cultural traditions related to them, from art and architecture, to music and ritual.

The religious traditions still practiced by the Newars of the Kathmandu Valley represent a unique, continuing survival of Indic religions, including Mahāyāna-Vajrayāna forms of Buddhism (Lienhard 1984; Gellner 1992). Rivaling in historical importance the Sanskrit texts in Nepal's libraries that informed the Western "discovery" of Buddhism in the nineteenth century (Hodgson 1868; Levi 1905–1908; Locke 1980, 1985), Newar Vajrayāna tradition in the Kathmandu Valley preserves a rich legacy of vernacular texts, rituals, and institutions.

Historical Background: Licchavi (459–780 CE) and Post-Licchavi Eras (900–1200 CE)

Beginning with Sanskrit inscriptions dating from the fifth century CE, the large mid-montane Himalayan Valley called "Nepal" has been a vibrant cultural center where both Hindu and Buddhist traditions have flourished. What is called "Nepal" today is the modern nation-state that was formed after 1769, when the Shah dynasty of Gorkha district expanded across the region, conquering the Valley city-states and making Kathmandu its capital.

The earliest cities and religious monuments of this Valley were built by people who were ruled by those calling themselves *Licchavis*. They were progenitors of the Newars, the earliest attested ethnic group of the Valley, whose name derives simply from the early place name of the Valley. Newars speak a non-tonal Tibeto-Burman language called "Newari" in the Euro-American world, but referred to by Newars as *Nepāl Bhāsā*, using Sanskrit terminology, or *Newā: Bhay* in the spoken vernacular, or *Newā* in the latest fashion. This language has been thoroughly influenced by Sanskrit vocabulary, especially in the technical terms imported from the Indic traditions.

This Valley from its first historical records was a Himalayan trade and pilgrimage center, and later a refuge for Buddhist monks (and others) migrating north, especially in the wake of the rapid decline and fall of the great monasteries in the Gangetic Plain following the Muslim conquest of North India. By this time, monasteries in Kathmandu, Bhaktapur, and Patan became centers of Mahāyāna-Vajrayāna culture. Even before this time, and increasingly afterward, Tibetan monk-scholars visited Nepal[4] to obtain initiations, Sanskrit manuscripts and, in some cases, to confer with Nepalese *paṇḍitas*. There have been many Newar Buddhist scholars from then until the present day who read and utilize Sanskrit, making it an important literary and religious language for the indigenous elite. Some notable *paṇḍitas* and poets up through the modern era also composed works in Sanskrit. Manuscript veneration, archiving, and copying grew in importance. Tibetan historical and hagiographic sources provide additional information about this outpost of Indic Buddhism, its history over the last millennium, and the diffusion of traditions in both directions, that is, between the Kathmandu Valley and centers of Tibetan civilization.

The Newar saṅgha elite's familiarity with Sanskrit, and especially the use of Sanskrit mantras and religious terminology, explains the existence of the many hundreds of Buddhist manuscripts rendered in a Sanskrit–Newari format.[5] While the virtuoso ritualists, adepts, and scholars used Sanskrit texts to guide their ritual practices, tantric meditations, musical compositions, or philosophical studies, they also redacted relevant Indic works into their own language and composed treatises in it as well.

The earliest attested historical records[6] for the Nepal Valley begin in mid-fifth century CE in the Sanskrit inscriptions by kings who titled themselves Licchavi. These indicate that Nepal was part of the northeast Gangetic Plain cultural region. Rendered in high Sanskrit and Brahmi script, they record the existence of a hundred settlements (mostly villages [*grāma*]), a caste-ordered society, and twenty named *goṣṭhī*, which are social institutions dedicated to specific, often religious, purposes.[7] Licchavi society was ruled by Hindu kings who are recorded as supporting brahmans and temple institutions, as well as Buddhist *vihāras*. There is only one inscription[8] that may contradict the terse report by the Chinese pilgrim Xuanzang, around 640 CE, that these traditions coexisted harmoniously, with sanctuaries located side by side.

The Licchavi inscriptions also reveal continuity and connections between the Nepal Valley and the traditions of monasticism and patronage that originated across the Gangetic Plain going back to the time of the Buddha. Among over two hundred recorded inscriptions, there are references to monks and nuns enjoying support by prominent local merchants and caravan traders.[9] The only saṅgha specifically mentioned is that of the Mahāsamghikas.

These inscriptions also indicate an early formation of Mahāyāna culture. Monastic precincts reveal verses of praise addressed to Śākyamuni and other Buddhas, as well as shrines to the celestial bodhisattvas Mañjuśrī, Vajrapāṇi, Samantabhadra, and—most frequently—Avalokiteśvara. The names of thirteen *vihāras* are cited. The Buddhist donative formulae found in the Valley are similar to those at sites across South Asia, including the practice of monks making offerings for the welfare of their parents.[10] Also cited are donations of stūpas, images, and lands to *vihāras*, in several instances by nuns, as in the name of one text, the *Kinnari Jātaka*.

Unusual for ancient Indic Buddhist monasticism, however, was the custom of monks in Nepal's Licchavi monasteries being assigned responsibility from the maintenance of law and civic order in settlements built around the monasteries and on lands donated to them.[11] If a criminal (thief, adulterer, murderer, etc.) under monastic jurisdiction is apprehended, one inscription allows "the noble community of monks" residing in the prominent Śivadeva Vihāra to take possession of the miscreant's "house, fields, his wives, and all his wealth. . . ."[12]

The presence of the term *śākya-bhikṣu* likely indicates that there was a Mahāyāna presence in the early saṅgha.[13] The term *vajrayāna* is found only once and in fragmentary form in the known corpus of inscriptions during the reign of the powerful Amshuvarman (ruled 605–631), but it is on a shard that allows no scope for serious speculation. The term *Vajradhara* is found in a long hymn praising Śākyamuni and a group of Mahāyāna bodhisattvas.[14] A recent study of the Licchavi inscriptions has suggested the presence of a "Sukhāvatī cult" in ancient Nepal. However, the evidence is merely a hymn praising Śākyamuni with a group of bodhisattvas; but this may be read just as a term of praise, not as the name of the cosmic Buddha of the later Vajrayāna cosmology.[15]

The conclusion about this period for this study is that Buddhism in the Kathmandu Valley seems to have been typical of the culture area of northeast Indian Buddhism of the late Gupta period. It was a location where Mahāyāna Buddhism was established, and where the development of a widespread Vajrayāna tradition, by 700 CE, was not yet evident.

After the Licchavi era, there are no epigraphic records for another four hundred years, a curious lacuna. Historical data so far discovered[16] comes exclusively from art objects and the colophons of texts that have survived and that modern textual scholars have culled for basic information (Petech 1958; Petech 1984). With this record still being assembled, to date there has been no comprehensive effort to analyze in a systematic manner the vast archival holdings of texts extant in the various libraries, much of which has been microfilmed or, more recently, digitally scanned; nor have art historians, much less scholars of Buddhism, assembled or comprehensively analyzed the cumulative set of material objects that can illuminate the Buddhist culture that produced these expressions.

Tibetan Sources on Newar Vajrayāna Buddhism

The Tibetan sources contain accounts of eminent monks and *siddhas* from the lowlands (e.g., Atiśa in 1041; Jñānakāra in 1054; Vanaratna c. 1425) who transited Nepal to reach points in Tibet, as well as a series of Tibetans who traversed Nepal to reach the great centers of Buddhism in the Gangetic region (e.g., Marpa in 1065; Rwa Lotsava in 1076; Khyrin po in 1090; Dharmasvāmin in 1226–1234 and 1241–1242). While the number of Tibetans traveling south declined greatly after 1200, Tibetan monks and *siddhas* continued to visit Nepal from this time onward into the Malla era, and then right up to the present.[17]

What is clear from the existing accounts is that tantric teachers in the Kathmandu Valley were sought out as charismatic and authoritative masters of major Vajrayāna traditions, and that they gave tantric initiation to whomever they felt worthy. Ron Davidson has concluded that the *mahāsiddha* Marpa received his major teachings in Nāropa's lineage from Newar and Indian masters resident in the town of Pharping, located in the southwest of the Kathmandu Valley, in the eleventh century (2005, 146); he also highlights other credible Tibetan sources that have Sanskrit texts being translated into Tibetan in the Kathmandu Valley with Newar Sanskrit Buddhist pandits involved (126). In exposing the history of the career of the southern Tibetan Ralo Dorje drak (1016–1072), Davidson also provides a wealth of new information on Newar Buddhism then, as found in Patan: a depiction of this city as a Buddhist paradise, "a residence of scholars and *siddhas*" (130); the spiritual guidance granted to Ralo from a Newar householder named Kunda Bhāro, who was both a *Bajrācārya* and "a titled aristocrat with landed estates . . ." (141). The Newar master[18] bestowed on him tantric teachings centered on Vajravārāhī and Vajrabhairava; he also gave him the initiation of the *vajra* and *vajra*-bell. Empowered to perform rituals, Ralo became the family ritualist of a prominent Newar merchant named Chandra Bhadra.

This account's image of Kunda Bhāro's monastery is clearly "a lay-based institution," with the presence of wives and family figuring in the account. Indeed, this type of institution has also been shown in a palm leaf manuscript translated by K. P. Malla for Ukū Bāhā in Patan that describes how monastery funds must be allotted "for the children and wives of the monks . . ." (1990, 18).[19]

The Ralo biography also states that a Newar named Mandzu-lingpa was the abbot at Nālandā in this era, for Ralo studied extensively with him when he ventured to the famous Indian monastery and took ordination (Davidson, 138). Once additional Tibetan sources are brought into this arena, the medieval history of Newar Buddhism will be clearer still. [20]

What is certain is that the Kathmandu Valley had become a major regional center of the late Indian Buddhist world, and Vajrayāna traditions—texts, art objects, and ritual practices such as initiation rites—crossed through the ethnic lines of Newars and Tibetans. There were Tibetan monasteries at Svayambhū and Bauddha where the celibate monastic traditions continued, institutions where Newars interested in this spiritual path could be ordained. Thus, after the Indian Buddhist holy land was lost for teachers and pilgrimage, Himalayan Buddhists now had to organize their own Buddhist societies based upon their inheritance of the Indic cultural resources.

Evidence from the Textual Archives

The genres the extant texts can shed light on the history of post-Licchavi Buddhism. Over the last 150 years, these collections were spread across the world, from Kathmandu to Japan, from India to Europe; to date, there has never been a systematic examination of the totality of attested texts. For its heuristic value, we offer here (and document in Appendix 1) an analysis of the colophons surveyed by Petech (1958). The number of early, extant Sanskrit texts copied by Newars found in Sakya, Tibet, is noteworthy, a confirmation of active religious exchange that also included art and artisans (e.g., Lo Bue 1985, 1988; Petech 1958, 99). A thoroughgoing aggregate accounting of the Buddhist texts copied in the Valley would provide one means to assess the popularity of "working texts" over the time span from 998 until 1479 CE (See Figure 3.1).

What do these works provide as evidence for surmising the nature of the formative era of Newar Mahāyāna–Vajrayāna culture? There are the expected narratives concerning the life of the Buddha, the *Lalitavistara* (extant 1036 CE), as well as collections of rebirth stories such as *Avadānakalpalatā* (1302 CE), and the *Mahākarmavibhaṅga* (1410 CE). Some of the great works explicating the nature of cosmic Buddhahood that are attested include the *Saddharmapuṇḍarīka* (1039 CE, 1065, 1066, 1082, 1093), *Gaṇḍavyūha* (1166 CE), *Kāraṇḍavyūha* (1196 CE) and the *Ārya-Amoghapāśa-Sūtra* (1360 CE). Another major text emphasizing the bodhisattva life was the *Bodhicaryāvatāra* (1078 CE].

What were the works of which the most copies were made? These would be the great, earliest works of Mahāyāna philosophy, *Prajñāpāramitā* (998 CE, 1008, 1015, 1069, 1071, 1093, 1120, 1148, 1164, 1165–2, 1166, 1200, 1246, 1253, 1284, 1395), and then the important

FIGURE 3.1 Buddhist text from the library of a Newar householder. All images in this chapter have been photographed by Todd Lewis.

pan-Asian work of ritual protections, the *Pañcarakṣā* (1063 CE, 1138, 1140, 1155, 1192, 1247, 1282, 1374, 1384, 1386, 1389, 1470, 1476, 1479). Both of these works have been the object of a recent study by Jinah Kim (2013) on the illustrated Buddhist manuscripts of Pāla-era India and Nepal. Kim shows that the Vajrayāna tradition was being grafted into the local textual scribal traditions with tantric images inserted into these venerable, and central, philosophical and apotropaic texts of Mahāyāna Buddhism. Other texts focusing on mantra recitation were the *Ārya-Uṣṇīṣavijāya Nāma-Dhāraṇī* (1099 CE), the *Vasundhārā Dhāraṇī* (1123 CE, 1429), and the *Nāmasaṅgīti*. The *Kriyāsaṃgraha*'s presence was found after 1216 CE (then, 1217, 1252).

The extant Buddhist tantras were, in order of the dates in their colophons: the *Mahāmanthāna Bhairava Tantra* (1180 CE, 1084), a *Sādhanasamuccaya* (1216 CE), the *Vajrāvalī* (1220 CE, 1429), and the *Caṇḍamahāroṣaṇa Tantra-pañjikā* (1297 CE). There are also many Hindu tantras in this collection,[21] giving a clear indication of the pluralistic context in which Buddhism developed. However many problems there are in interpreting this record of extant texts,[22] they do help to establish what constituted the general shape of the textual corpus that the Malla-era Buddhists had in circulation among their scribes and archives.

Historical Narrative: Early Malla Nepal to 1495

The Kathmandu Valley has always been shaped by its regional and geographical contexts, as well as its connections to centers of civilization in regions in every direction. What is certain is that the regional formation of Buddhism was undergoing significant innovations amidst profound political changes. The great centers of Indic Buddhism to the south were fallen or in steep decline, as travel to remaining outlying Buddhist sites across North India was risky. Only with the triumph of the Mughals (1526–1857) would stability and prosperity in the subcontinent leave the Himalayan region in peace. To the north, the polities of central Tibet were also changing, sometimes violently, under Mongol interventions; highland Buddhist institutions accrued growing secular power, organized by monastic networks loyal to lineages begun by great scholars. The Gelugpa school eventually consolidated central power by the seventeenth century.

In Nepal, the long silence of inscriptions ends with all the markers of major political formation and cultural activity. A group with the surname Malla consolidates power in the foremost city Bhaktapur; the rise of other major unified settlements, notably Patan and Kathmandu, is also clearly attested. Ancient sanctuaries from the Licchavi period endured: the Svayambhū stūpa on its western hill, the Paśupati temple to Śiva, and the Chāngu Nārāyan temple on its eastern hill. These small city-states possessed Buddhist *vihāras*; their urban spaces were built around monastic courtyards, with palace precincts ornamented with temples to the great gods of the Indic pantheon and brahman officials, their boundaries walled and pierced by gateways.

The rule of Bhaktapur king Sthiti Malla (1367–1395) consolidated power, especially in the aftermath of invasions and natural disasters, and is reputed in later histories to have done so, in part, by enhancing the Hindu factions in Newar society. His grandson, Yaksha Malla (1408–1482), decided to divide his realm among three sons, and henceforth determined that his descendants would be Malla kings ruling from the three small city-states: Bhaktapur, the most Hindu city; Patan, the most Buddhist city; and Kathmandu, mixed but more Buddhist than Hindu, and with a profusion of Buddhist merchants.

A major trauma to Newar civilization occurred in 1349 CE, when the Kathmandu Valley suffered a destructive raid by the Bengali Sultan, Shams ud-Dīn. After looting the precious metals and temple-monastic treasures, the invaders committed atrocities and set the cities ablaze; the great Buddhist center, the Svayambhū stūpa, and the great Paśupati Śiva temple were also plundered and desecrated. Thus, in the next centuries, Newar civilization had to be materially restored, and at just the same time, its Buddhist cultural foundations—with Buddhism to the south fallen—needed to be redefined.[23] Three texts reflect just this new development, and remain central to the formation of the Mahāyāna–Vajrayāna Newar Buddhist culture that endures until today.

Gopālarājavaṃśāvalī

Centered on the history of kings, this text was compiled during the reign of Jayasthiti Malla (1382–1395), probably by his court astrologer in Bhaktapur (Vajracarya and Malla 1985). It covers events that occurred from 1057 to 1389 CE. This text, written in an unpolished Sanskrit, records significant events, such as the invasions of the country, intrigues by local petty-rulers, and major buildings constructed under royal patronage. It is also interspersed with reports about down-to-earth happenings in the realm, from famines to epidemics, earthquakes to unusual weather, weddings to staging of court dramas.

While it is at times difficult to recognize names of places and people based on modern usage, the *Gopālarājavaṃśāvalī* is a key source of Kathmandu Valley history. The author's individual voice sometimes breaks through, but the content seems to have been subjects that were of interest to the royal palace of Bhaktapur: mainly concerned with the kings, their courtiers, and their sponsorship of building projects and religious donations.

One of the *Gopālarājavaṃśāvalī*'s main interests is the donations to the Paśupati temple of Śiva, a protector of their realm, and its mention is recurrent. Also indicative of the nature of Jayasthiti Malla's religious identity are entries noting his donations to and his wife's going in a great procession to worship Viṣṇu at the Chāngu Nārāyana temple (Vajracarya and Malla 1985, 162), and together performing a *Lakṣmī vrata* and taking tantric initiation from a brahman in 1379. There are also records of ritual offerings made to Svayambhū and at the Bungamati Lokeśvara festival. The text notes in one place that the king "is like an incarnation of the virtuous Rāma" (133); in another his scribe pronounces that "He was an incarnation of Buddha, blessed with the grace of Svayambhū in the Kali Yuga, as well as an incarnation of the eight *Lokapālas* . . . of all sentient beings"

(131). Such was the reality of Malla royalty situating themselves amidst the two Indic religions in their realm. Another text composed in the Valley at about this time (Uebach 1970, 13–15), the Śaivite *Nepālamāhātmya*, contains a section about pilgrimage to Svayambhū, and makes the following observation, "Monks live there who have left their descendents and relatives and enjoy the bliss of knowledge [*jñānānanda*], and who are dedicated [only] to beholding the Buddha" (Brinkhaus 1980, 281).

Guṇakāraṇḍavyūha

A text in verse that was created in Nepal by a Newar pandit in the Malla era, the *Guṇakāraṇḍavyūha* is based on the *Kāraṇḍavyūha*, a Sanskrit Mahāyāna text written almost a thousand years earlier. With Newar traditional opening and concluding chapters (I and XIX), the unknown author reframes the text and introduces themes such as the Ādi Buddha that resonate with those in the *Svayambhū Purāṇa*. As noted in Tuladhar-Douglas's treatment of this Newar text,[24] the *Guṇakāraṇḍavyūha* features seventeen central tales[25] recounting a series of compassionate exploits of the bodhisattva Avalokiteśvara, with other nested tales inserted; it is a "retelling" of the earlier work, "adapted for a different historical context, using the skillful means best suited to its own time and place" (2006, 116). Large portions of the *Bodhicaryāvatāra* are also inserted in two chapters; the salvific work of Avalokiteśvara in the hells and among non-humans is the focus of separate chapters, covering all domains in the Buddhist wheel of life: hells, hungry ghosts, asuras, yakṣas, animals (including worms in sewage), heavens, and the human domain, including students! The narrative arrangement as stories inserted that suddenly switch into frames to hear from previous Buddhas and visit pure lands is a feature that makes it consistent with the Buddhist cosmology in the *Svayambhū Purāṇa* (see later discussion in this chapter).

Mahāyāna doctrines highlighted include the *pāramitā*s, the supreme rewards of donations to the saṅgha, and the possibility of rebirth in Sukhāvatī. A recurring theme is the practice of the six-syllable mantra, the *ṣaḍakṣarī vidyā*, as "the essence of Avalokiteśvara,"[26] as is the practice of other "methods and *samādhi*s, . . . *dhārāṇī*s, *vidyā*s. . . ." There is also the recurring promotion of one particular ritual, the *uposatha vrata*. This is a distinctively Newar ritual and ritual genre, unknown elsewhere in the Buddhist world in its form, designed to be performed by householders on the Buddhist holy days. It is still the most common householder ritual in the Newar Buddhist tradition.[27]

Devotion to Mahāyāna sūtras, especially the *Kāraṇḍavyūha*, is especially lauded, as is the meritorious act of building stūpas and organizing chariot festivals. The text ends with verses exhorting the power of *Guṇakāraṇḍavyūha* recitation to help in securing worldly prosperity, including its ability to bring good luck, protect children, safeguard ocean voyagers, promote political stability, and ensure rainfall. This text[28] has doubtless been the basis of local Buddhist masters composing many local adaptations of Avalokiteśvara narratives, and these characteristically laud and promote the performance of this aforementioned *uposatha vrata*. The most important of these drawn from this text is the *Simhalasārthabāhu Avadāna*.

Of special note for reckoning the inter-religious history of the later Malla and succeeding eras are chapters introducing, and subjugating, the Hindu gods. In the third chapter, the *Guṇakāraṇḍavyūha* conveys a cosmology that identify all reality as, in fact, the body of Avalokiteśvara, with all the gods emanating from it: Maheśvara from the eyes, Viṣṇu from the heart, and so on.[29] It later has Śiva ask the bodhisattva just how they should act given this reality, and he assigns them and all the Indic divinities realms and tasks. They also are told that in the Kali Yuga, Avalokiteśvara will reside in the Formless Realm, Brahmā will rule the Realm of Form, and Viṣṇu will rule the Realm of Desire, whereas Śiva will be worshiped only by "deluded people." The celestial bodhisattva then exhorts all the deities to help the unhappy and confused people, and to inspire them by taking up the path to realization.

Another chapter has Avalokiteśvara provide spiritual guidance to Bali, the demon who was trampled by the dwarf *avatāra* of Viṣṇu. Engagement with the major Hindu gods includes having Śiva and Pārvatī ask for religious instruction, an encounter that ends with Avalokiteśvara predicting their future attainment of Buddhahood. This subordination of Hindu deities and traditions is especially significant in understanding the text's context, and its role as a resource for Newar Buddhists in framing their relationships with Hindu kings over ensuing centuries, a topic we will revisit.

Svayambhū Purāṇa

Another strand in the development of post-Licchavi Buddhism was a tradition that made the strong claim that the Kathmandu Valley itself is a sacred

Mahāyāna land made habitable by tantric *siddhas*. The formative text for subsequent Newar Buddhism is one that is usually titled *Svayambhū Purāṇa*.[30] It is a fully Newar text that has over one hundred attested copies extant today, the earliest dated back to 1558.[31]

The content of this text is central to defining the Newar Buddhist tradition for at least the past five centuries. Asserting its origins as the discourse of Śākyamuni during a visit to Nepal while sitting near the great stūpa, this text recounts the Buddhist origins of the Valley as a hierophany of the ultimate reality or Ādi Buddha, whose presence is indicated by a flaming, jeweled lotus in what was then a lake. The text asserts that this site was subsequently visited by a series of Buddhas of former ages of the world. What is the most significant in the Newar reading of this account is that this lake was finally drained by the bodhisattva Mañjuśrī[32] who arrives "from Mahācīna"[33] to manifest the Kathmandu Valley by cutting open the southern enclosing mountains with a cut of his sword. Having opened this newly fertile, divine land to settlement by his disciples, he instructs them in modes of living and religious practice. Later in the text, after other interventions in Nepal and India, he is said to leave his mortal remains in the Valley, while his divine form returns to Wutai Shan, in China.

Several of the final chapters recount the visits of various Indic *siddhas* to the Valley.[34] The text relates the narrative of Dharmaśrīmitra, a scholar-professor at the great monastery Vikramaśīla, who was famous for his lecture on the central mantra in the *Mañjuśrī Nāmasaṅgīti* (Figure 3.2). But one day when advanced seekers asked him about the text's "inner meaning," he could not answer and set off to seek the assistance of Mañjuśrī at Wutai Shan in China. When he broke his journey early on to rest in Nepal, Mañjuśrī (also called Mañjudeva) discerned his quest and appeared to him as a farmer who had yoked a lion and tiger to plow his fields. When Dharmaśrīmitra asked him for directions, Mañjudeva told him he would give them to him in the morning and offered him shelter.

While lodged in the house of the plowman, who is also referred to in this text as "Bajrācārya Mañjudeva," Dharmaśrīmitra overhears the master explain the inner meaning of the *Mañjuśrī Nāmasaṅgīti* to his two wives. When he begs Bajrācārya Mañjudeva for an initiation into the practices associated with the text's mantra, his wish is granted. He is initiated into the *dharmadhātu* maṇḍala, is taught the bodhisattva vows, and has the *Mañjuśrī Nāmasaṅgīti*'s mantra explained to him in full.

Mañjudeva then commands that Dharmaśrīmitra return to Vikramaśīla and promises to visit him one day to ascertain the nature of his spiritual

FIGURE 3.2 Malla-era stone sculpture of Nāmasaṅgīti, Jana Bāhā.

understanding. When Mañjudeva comes there disguised as a beggar, Dharmaśrīmitra first ignores him, and later claims that he had not noticed him. As a result, he goes blind; even after repenting, he remains blinded as the fruit of his bad karma, but is told that his "eye of *prajñā*" can reveal all things. From this time, presumably due to subsequent attainment, his name is changed to Jñānaśrīmitra.

A second key figure in the later *Svayambhū Purāṇa* is Śāntaśrī. He at first is described as a monk who later took initiation as a *Bajrācārya*, then concealed the flame of Svayambhū and erected a stūpa over it. Afterward, he erected a stūpa on a nearby hill to enshrine the remains of Mañjuśrī. As a result, the land was blessed and was very auspicious for the observance of dharma and tantric practice. When an evil king arose and sought his guidance, Śāntaśrī taught him to honor the local holy sites, especially the two great stūpas, and to perform the *uposatha vrata*. When a famine arose, Śāntaśrī performed a *nāga* ritual using *sādhana* and maṇḍala to cause rainfall, ending the Valley's suffering. After this, he was also known as Shantikar Ācārya. Later, he renounced entering final nirvāṇa, and sat

FIGURE 3.3 *Bajrācārya* and patron.

suspended in the state of *vajrayoga samādhi*, residing in a cave near the Svayambhū stūpa, where he still stays hidden in a refuge from which he will re-emerge to aid humanity when the Dharma declines in the world.[35] (See Figure 3.3.)

The *Svayambhū Purāṇa*,[36] thus, is a work simultaneously of Mahāyāna–Vajrayāna Buddhology, Newar ethnic origins, and a narrative of Newar Vajrayāna legitimacy. Like many *Purāṇa*s devoted to the Hindu gods, the text contains long sections denoting how a series of local sites became sacred Buddhist places, at river *tīrtha*s, mountains, caves, and other notable places.

The details of precisely when and why the Mañjuśrī legend was first localized in the Kathmandu Valley are unclear, although further study of the cross-named figures in the text might provide a basis for a more precise reckoning of its composition. A refocusing of Buddhist identity on the Valley is likely related to the closing down of the once-thriving silk routes that linked Buddhist traders and pilgrims, as Islamic states spread and Muslim diaspora merchants came to dominate these lucrative mercantile networks linking India to central Asia, and points beyond. Nepalese Buddhist monks, merchants, and monasteries, once connected to this international world of Indic Buddhism, were cut off from it.

The old centers of authority, both the institutions and the charismatic teachers, were in disarray. Facing this, the *Svayambhū Purāṇa* invokes a Mahāyāna pattern of revelation centered on Mañjuśrī to identify Newar home territory as a sacred zone that dates back in time, even before Śākyamuni. No need to travel a whole year to reach and return from China's Wutai Shan—the Kathmandu Valley now offered a similar realm of revelation, sanctity, and access to the great bodhisattva's grace.

These texts as a whole present the emergence of Newar Mahāyāna–Vajrayāna tradition in the context of later Indic Buddhist history, spanning the Indus-Gangetic region. Just as Nepal is a direct descendent of the artistic traditions that were found to its immediate south in the later Pāla-Sena regions, so do its texts reflect this former connection: the mass appeal of Mahāyāna Buddhism in the form of popular devotion to celestial bodhisattvas Avalokiteśvara and Tārā (S. Dutt 1962, 389), and the virtuosi in a small minority concerned with a great variety of Vajrayāna texts, doctrines, and meditation practices. Yet this tantric elite exerted a formative influence in the new Buddhist culture, designing the rituals that were performed in the Buddhist monasteries, their temples, and the homes of their devotees. These Indic *Bajrācāryas*—some monks, others free agents—served as gurus, healers, and artists.[37] Their presence is evident in the literal handiwork of the many extraordinary illustrated manuscripts created in Nepal in this period (Kim 2013).

Texts highlighting Mahāyāna *bhakti* teachings are among the earliest attested in the Valley, such as the *Saddharmapuṇḍarīka* and the *Bodhicaryāvatāra*; significantly, each contains chapters concerned with Buddhist *pūjā* and its rewards. Their concern with ritual signifies their applicability to Buddhist communities, and it is clear that the saṅghas in early Malla Nepal had adopted this inheritance. They focused on celestial bodhisattvas and the bodhisattva ethos, while its elite absorbed tantric *sādhana* traditions, its saṅgha serving the householder community with rituals built on tantric theory as the medium.[38] Collections of *jātaka* and *avadāna* were made that redacted the heroes to be bodhisattvas, not Śākyamuni, in line with the local domestication of the Mahāyāna tradition.[39]

The establishment of Buddhist temples to these bodhisattvas in the new Newar cities created the need for an attending priesthood and the development of proper ritual procedures to order the community's connections to them. The welter of ritual guidebooks that were copied and composed in subsequent centuries and survived in the Kathmandu Valley collections bears witness to this extensive development of rituals in the Newar tradition.

By the time that the Valley's polity had developed into three city-states, a common central Buddhist tradition had developed around each city's localizations of the celestial bodhisattva Avalokiteśvara (Figure 3.4). Begun first in the earliest center for "Red Avalokiteśvara" in the small town of Bungamati, the kings in Patan wrested this tradition into their domain; decades later, the kings of Kathmandu found that its Buddhist pandits had located another native Avalokiteśvara image, this one white, outside its own town walls. Based on the Indic texts containing narrative traditions about this bodhisattva, such as the *Kāraṇḍavyūha* and *Guṇakāraṇḍavyūha*

FIGURE 3.4 Stone sculpture of Avalokiteśvara, late Licchavi era.

discussed earlier, Newar scholars melded the textual precedents with site-specific legends. What probably began as a cult to a local rain god in the Licchavi era developed as the localization of the most popular universal Buddhist divinity (Locke 1979; Owens 1989). While the exact historical unfolding of this remains unclear, what is clear is that in the towns of Patan, Bungamati, and Kathmandu, and then in other leading Newar towns, temples, priesthoods, land endowments, and festivals became focused on this divinity.

The early Malla kings in each polity made religious connections and participated in these Buddhist traditions, despite the fact that they and their Brahmanical courts came to control the political life of the Valley and established temples to the major Hindu gods. They saw the wisdom in joining in the devotions with their Buddhist majority populations, and the Buddhist leaders seem to have accorded them legitimating gestures in return. The saṅgha leaders of the Mahāyāna-Vajrayāna Buddhist tradition also developed original ritual practices that they invented to manage the temple-centered festivals, and applied them to other areas of life as well, especially individual Buddhist life cycle rites, a topic to which we will return.

Historical Narrative: The Era of the Malla Three Kingdoms (1482–1768)

As the Valley fissured politically after 1495, the three petty kingdoms/city-states were ruled by Malla who, though related, went into battle with each other periodically, and competed jealously among themselves for prestige. This often was contested in acts of conspicuous religious piety, especially at the major temples and stūpas that remained common focal points of devotion.

With its wealth growing from profitable trade with the Mughal Empire to south, and central Tibet to the north, Newar civilization underwent a cultural efflorescence. The abundance of wealth garnered in this era underwrote the cultural vitality evident in the later Malla era (1495–1768). Newar artisans and builders created magnificent art and architecture across the Kathmandu Valley (Pal 1974; Slusser 1982); local writers composed treatises, poems, and dramas, while manuscript copyists were so employed as the establish one of the greatest archives of literature in Asia, especially in libraries of Sanskrit manuscripts (Burnouf 1844; Hodgson 1874).[40] Hindu and Buddhist elites contended to express the nature of local religious identity; constructions and restorations soon became abundant in the now extensive historical record. The Newar religious revitalization that followed was certainly rooted, in part, in the Newar elite's wish to install religious sanctuaries for deities—Hindu and Buddhist—whose roles would be to protect the Kathmandu Valley's sacred territory and its citizens, and to show its leaders as pious devotees.

The same vitality and prosperity were applied to other cultural domains as well. Hindu and Buddhist Newars—kings, priests, merchants, and commoners—maintained an almost continuous yearly round of festival observances for their society. Likewise, their priests arranged complex rites to mark all significant events in an individual's lifetime: from conception to long after death, in celebration and in mourning, rituals have long been integral to the Newar lifestyle.

The context of the formation of Newar Mahāyāna–Vajrayāna tradition up to the present day occurred in petty kingdoms that were evolving to be more inclined toward the various forms of "Hindu" culture, as brahman officials, new Hindu temples, Rāmāyana theatrical performances,[41] tantric ascetics, and Indic law were in the ascendancy and foremost in royal patronage (Slusser 1982; Bledsoe 2004).[42] This development was certainly related to the migration of brahmans, pandits, and other virtuosi from the Hindu kingdom of Mithilā located to the south, in what are today the northern portions of Bihar and Bengal. This region had influenced the Nepal Valley, both for good and for ill, since 900 CE (Slusser 1982, 45–56), but as it came under the sovereignty of Muslim states, refugees moved north into Nepal, where independent Hindu states remained. Cultural forms and practices found in Malla Nepal show this unmistakable effect, most clearly in the use of Mithilā language at court, as well as in the import of theater traditions and poetry that have been preserved in the Valley archives.[43] Just as the political landscape changed and the new independent Malla rulers needed legitimation, these migrants provided the cultural expertise to shift the religious character of the Kathmandu Valley more toward Hindu rule and brahmanical traditions.

There is a wealth of materials that suggest how brahmanical orthopraxy, caste norms, and new assertions of Hindu identity were being articulated in the newly independent Malla royal courts of Bhaktapur, Patan, and Kathmandu. At the palace centers of these city-states, each Malla king proclaimed his allegiance to Śiva-Paśupati in the ancient temple located on the upper Bāgmati River, and to Viṣṇu at the ancient center in Chāngu

FIGURE 3.5 Statue of Bhupatindra Malla.

(Figure 3.5). The various rulers made repeated donations, as recorded in the *Gopālarājavaṃśāvalī*.

Another Malla innovation was to adopt Talegu, a form of the goddess Durgā favored in the Mithilā culture area, as their own family protector deity. In each capital one can still see their large, ornate palace temples that towered over the old city landscapes; each had active, well-supported Hindu priests who performed a regular cycle of rituals, most extensively during the fall festival of Dashara/Dassain. Spatially as well as figuratively, all citizens in the city were placed under her protection, and this, in the Indic ritual imagination, entails obligations. Prominent groups seem to have been obliged to take part in this new devotional enterprise, including two Buddhist merchant castes, the Tulādhars and Kansakārs. Each community was required to supply ritual dancers and horn players (respectively) when the annual rituals for Talegu were being performed in the palace, a relationship that informants thought went back to the Malla courts. While it is uncertain when Buddhist householders in Kathmandu were first required to take part in this worship of the Mallas' protectoress, the practice continued into the twenty-first century.[44]

The second case study is Newar *Bare* caste and its relationship to the Malla royal courts through the cult of the royal *kumārī* (Allen 1975). It was only from these communities that prepubescent girls could be recruited to serve as living embodiments of the goddess for a host of palace rituals.[45] Whether these tasks of serving the palace were taken as a burden or an honor, the attempts to integrate the Buddhist community into a Hindu cult and court were inevitably dissonant to the Buddhist community at large.

In addition to expressing their identity as a Hindu state protected by Śiva and Taleju, the Malla-era redacted *purāṇas* reflect the sectarian direction of this era. As the Vaiṣṇava tradition grew in significance through the Malla period, influenced by movements in Bihar and Bengal (Brinkhaus 1987, 78–79), these provided a counter myth to the *Svayambhū Purāṇa* about the Vajrayāna-infused Buddhist religious identity of the Kathmandu Valley itself. Attested to have been extant in 1504 CE, but with its first articulation thought to be centuries earlier, are stories about Kṛṣṇa and his son, Pradyumnā, in the Kathmandu Valley. Accounts extol the sanctity of the Bāgmati River, and relate that demons dammed up the river, forming a lake; after his son slew a demon guarding the dam, Kṛṣṇa then released the river, breaking open the demon dam with his discus.[46] When the demon Virāda tries to resist, several accounts have Kṛṣṇa pinning him down by placing Śiva-liṅgas on his body. Additional episodes relate, in standard *purāṇa* form, how holy places in the region's established religious geography came to be (Brinkhaus 1987, 10).

The other Hindu texts composed in Nepal in the Malla period that recount this story—*Nepālamāhātmya, Himavatkhaṇḍa*—are strong evidence of Malla royalty attempting to consolidate a more orthodox Hindu identity.[47] The former text contains three passages that express the classical mode of religious contestation in South Asia: the ontological acceptance of other divinities, but under the higher, totalizing reality of one's own ultimate reality.[48] The *Nepālamāhātmya*'s mention of Valley pilgrimages[49] directs Śaiva devotees to visit Buddhist shrines, particularly Vajrayoginī in Sankhu, a "Kāruṇikeśvara" temple in Patan, and then Svayambhū. Yet these places are overlain with a superior, preexisting, presence of Śiva, a sage in this text states to the Buddha, "This country was created by Śiva ... in this the best of lands, at the confluence of the Vāgmatī and the Maṇimatī, honor Śiva's dharma and erect a liṅga ... and he did set up the *liṅga Kāruṇikeśvara* [there] ..."(Brinkhaus 1970, 277).[50] As Horst Brinkhaus pointed out, this text belies the cliché popular in earlier scholarship, and omnipresent in popular literature about it, that religious harmony and syncretism is the timeless record of inter-religious relations in the Kathmandu Valley.

The Malla palace and court dramas give strong testimony of the primary religious focus there being Hindu, in a formulation that is largely Vaiṣṇava in content, but with Kṛṣṇa and Viṣṇu always, in the end, being subordinated by Śiva and Devī. Not only were court-affiliated playwrights active in writing and staging over forty known dramas, records indicate that several Malla kings penned their own dance dramas (Malla 1982). A few attested plays that enact the very narratives of Hindu gods making the Kathmandu Valley from the new texts just discussed.

While the religious figures who offered theological innovations are as yet unknown, their effects are clear in these dramas as well as in new texts, such as the *Nepālamāhātmya*, which declares in one place, "with a positively martial spirit" (Malla 1982, 7) that Viṣṇu and Śiva are identical, and also introduces a story of Viṣṇu declaring that a brahman sage (*muni*) named Nemi should now be the protector (*pāla*) of this sacred Valley, explaining the origin of its name place: Ne[mi]-pāla —> Nepāl. Paintings illustrating aspects of this story were made in Hindu *mathas* in Bhaktapur, and were on display in rest houses and other movable media.

This attempt to insert another foundation into Newar civilization, as we will see, was not an anomaly; but it indicates how brahman *paṇḍitas*, patronized by the royal courts, challenged the Buddhist cultural world and the Buddhist community, subtly contradicting their definition of the Newar homeland. Other paintings dating to this time also suggest the subordination of Buddhist reality to Hindu theology, which found expression in the paintings of the incarnations of Viṣṇu, with the Buddha shown among the group of ten.

Another action that can be read in terms of contestation with local Buddhism was the Malla rulers' continuing support for Śaivite Hindu ascetics, the Nāthas. A group that may have its roots in the ancient Pāśupata and medieval tantric Kāpālika orders (the latter are attested in late Licchavi Nepal), they mark their distinct identity by their practice of slitting their earlobes to accommodate the large earrings that are worn after initiation, and hence the Nāthas are also known as Kānphaṭas ("split ear"). The Nātha texts recount that the yogin Gorakhnātha, a pupil of the tenth-century sage Matsyendranath, and identified as an incarnation of the god Śiva, wandered across regions of India, gathering converts and granting initiations.

The popularity of Gorakhnātha and his order in Nepal reached a pinnacle at the time of Yakṣa Malla (1428–1482), when images of his foot imprints were placed at sites across the Valley, and his yogis were recipients of prominent royal donations, such as ownership of the great rest house in the central city called Kāṣṭamaṇḍapa, the building from which Kathmandu gets its name. This Nātha presence was at the center of a tradition of overlaying a tantric Śaivite identity over every Buddhist sacred center in the Kathmandu Valley. Exponents proposed a new history of the Buddhist bodhisattva of Bungamati-Patan and identified the deity previously known as the Red Bunga-dyaḥ-Avalokiteśvara with the Nātha yogin Matsyendranāth (Locke 1973), backing this claim with a new backstory of his local settlement.[51] This relabeling and assertion of subordination were extended by Yaksha Malla to the Kathmandu realm, as the Jana-Baha Avalokiteśvara became "White Matsyendranātha." This Śaivite challenge was extended to many sacred sites that had the name "*-nātha*" appended to them: "Paśupati-nātha," "Svayambhū-nātha." This suffix and the name Matsyendranātha are usages that Newar Buddhists resisted, and most still do not use them to this day.

Finally comes the issue of Hindu law and ritual orthopraxy. In the *Gopālarājavaṃśāvalī,* there is a recurring expression, noted from the Bhaktapur court, that the Mallas were "adherents of the *Dharmaśāstra*" and were inspired by the norms of Rāma. Just as the new Taleju temples provided a new superior vertical place for Durgā in the Newar city, the Mallas enhanced the horizontal order of their society with gradations in their expectations of proper caste observances, and brahmanical purity orthopraxy, moving from the center outward. In the Newar walled towns, the ceremonial area of the palace and brahman-dominated court became the purest sector of the domain, just as, moving outward, the town walls constituted a pollution boundary, beyond which the very lowest castes, rendered "unclean," had to dwell.

The Emergence of a Malla Vajrayāna Buddhist Counterculture

Malla cities in the Kathmandu Valley expanded their boundaries and were enriched by new constructions in architectural monuments, and in expressions of religious art in every medium. The record suggests that Newar Buddhists were confronted by lavish new Hindu temple constructions and partisan cultural innovations, and so undertook their own revitalizations to counter expressions of Hindu superiority, while conforming to their new cultural expectations in their caste norms.

It was primarily Buddhist merchants and artisans who through their patronage took actions to defend their Buddhist identity and tradition. They built dozens of new Buddhist monasteries that came to define the expanding city spaces, employed Buddhist *Bajrācāryas* to adapt rituals to mirror those favored by the local Malla court, and celebrated with new vigor the festivals—long established and newly created—to express their Buddhist identity. Exactly who the Newar Buddhist leaders were in the early Malla era who composed and "trans-created" new texts and traditions remains largely unknown, but we can attempt a rough sketch of their innovations in literature and material culture. This dialectical opposition pattern may not yet completely explain why the two new Newar Buddhist texts were composed, but it makes understandable why they were accepted, read, and copied, and why they formed the basis of a new localized vital Buddhist identity. The major counter-Hindu/pro-Buddhist elements in these two texts bear summarizing in Table 3.1.

Thus, with these texts Newar Buddhist masters and leaders pushed back in their own ways to assert what to them was the natural order of the religious field, placing the Buddha and the Buddhist cosmos in the superior position, admitting the great gods of Hindu theism as part of the world of beings in *saṃsāra*, but in a clearly subordinate position. Images that have never been attested to elsewhere in the Buddhist world drew on, or were inspired by, both of these texts. The following four icons—cast in metal, sculpted in stone, and painted in hanging scrolls—depict the major

Table 3.1 Buddhist Elements in the *Svayambhū Purāṇa* and *Guṇakāraṇḍavyūha*

Svayambhū Purāṇa	*Guṇakāraṇḍavyūha*
Kathmandu Valley and pre-Valley lake, the site of cosmic Buddha hierophany of Ādi Buddha	Avalokiteśvara cosmology, in which all Hindu gods are merely emanations
Relics and grace of imminent celestial bodhisattva Mañjuśrī	Submission of Śiva and Pārvatī to take refuge in Buddhist refuges
Gaṇeśa and the *nāgas* assist Mañjuśrī in draining the lake	Defines Kali Yuga as one in which Śiva will be worshipped by deluded people
Founding *siddha* still in existence, providing means to control *nāgas*, rain, and life in Valley	
Newar homeland blessed, very auspicious for the observance of dharma and tantric practice	Lauds *uposatha vrata* as central Buddhist rite, a local tradition
Newars are descended from Mañjuśrī's disciples, hence innately, primordially Buddhist	

landmarks in the Newar Buddhist landscape and express a clear vision of Buddhism's religious preeminence:

1. *Śākyamuni's return to Lumbini* (Figure 3.6): As the sage travels by road to reach his home territory and the place of his birth, the entourage forms that includes the usual monks, but also has the Hindu gods Śiva, Viṣṇu, Gaṇeśa, and others attending to him as protectors and acolytes.
2. *Śṛīstīkantha Lokeśvara* (Figure 3.7): A depiction of the revelation found early in the *Guṇakāraṇḍavyūha* that portrays Avalokiteśvara as the ultimate reality, denoting Śiva, Viṣṇu, and the entire pantheon as emanations.
3. *Mañjuśrī drains the Lake* (Figure 3.8), creating the Kathmandu Valley; as in the *Svayambhū Purāṇa*, this moment depicts Gaṇeśa and the *nāgas* cooperating in the enterprise.
4. *Harihariharivāhana Lokeśvara* (Figure 3.9):[52] An Avalokiteśvara superiority myth based on the story of a battle between Garuḍa and a *nāga* leads to the former calling upon his lord Viṣṇu to save him; hearing

FIGURE 3.6 Buddha Returns to Lumbini.

> this, the *nāga* calls upon his lord, Avalokiteśvara, to whom Viṣṇu submits. An icon shows this resolution, with the bodhisattva atop Viṣṇu, who rides Garuḍa, above the *nāga*. The vertical placement, with feet each lower bring, makes a clear statement about Buddhist superiority.

This array of imagery, combined with the new texts, provides the dialectical reply of Buddhists to the Malla Hindu depiction of the Buddha as an incarnation of Viṣṇu, Śiva as supreme reality, of Kṛṣṇa as the real actor who drained the lake that opened the Valley, and of Matsyendranāth as the real identity of Avalokiteśvara. Each has remained popular in the Kathmandu Valley until the present day.

There were two Malla-era vortexes of interaction wherein the Vajrayāna Buddhists expressed their relationship with the theistic Malla kings. Both caused the palace officials and kings to make major commitments to attend and be patrons of their major Buddhist constructions, rituals of renewal, and festivals. Given that the majority of the population then was almost certainly strongly supportive of Buddhism, and that their own wealth was drawn in a major way from the taxes on Tibetan traders, who

FIGURE 3.7 Śṛīstīkantha Lokeśvara.

were almost all prominent Buddhists in their city-states, the Malla kings had every reason, religiously and materially, to show inter-religious support. This pattern is evident in two major events that recur periodically in Kathmandu, where wealthy merchants, Vajrayāna rituals and Buddhist *paṇḍitas* staged dramatic public interactions.

FIGURE 3.8 *Mañjuśrī Drains the Lake.*

Samyak

One major festival that links the Newar saṅgha to Malla royalty is *Samyak*, likely a survival of an ancient Indic tradition called *pañcavārṣika*. Noted by Chinese pilgrims across the central Asian and Indic world, this special event entailed kings joining with merchants to make extraordinary offerings to the monks and their monasteries every five years (*pañca-varṣa*). In Kathmandu, the entire Buddhist community organizes by caste and neighborhood to perform the myriad tasks involving the procession of large, human-occupied Buddha images, the feeding of the saṅgha members from the entire Kathmandu Valley, and, in Kathmandu, the personal appearance of the king (Figure 3.10). Here, then, was a classical scenario that played out across the Buddhist world: a king was given special recognition and legitimation by the Newar Buddhist saṅgha leaders, in return for his patronage and recognition. In Kathmandu, the festival is now celebrated every twelfth year, as well as whenever individual families step up to sponsor their own *Samyak*, at substantial cost. These individual Samyak festivals could be done at any time. While one text suggests that this tradition goes back to 1312,[53] what is clear is that wealthy individual sponsors were numerous in the late Malla era and onward. In effect, then, Buddhist merchants and their *Bajrācārya* priests of Kathmandu regularly compelled

FIGURE 3.9 *Hariharihariv̄āhana Lokeśvara.*

the kings to witness and contribute to their Samyak events, over forty times since 1500 (Shakya 1979, 67–69). This festival of display and donation still exists as a major celebration in Kathmandu[54] and Patan.

Patronage and Restoration at Svayambhū

The record of patronage and restorations at Svayambhū provide a focal point for considering the nature of Newar Buddhism under Malla rule and in its pan-Buddhist context in this era. Just as the analysis of the Malla-era monastery (*bāhā*) will show it as a total architectural creation mirroring the historical Mahāyāna to Vajrayāna development of

FIGURE 3.10 Samyak images of Dīpankara Buddha.

the tradition, so can the cumulative expression of the later renovations and adaptations to this great stūpa do so as well, leaving it today, as it has been for the past 500 years, a statement of tantric Buddhism. The Mahācaitya also has been a site where the Tibetan and Newar traditions have intersected, most notably whenever the monument has been damaged by invaders or lightning, or when the central pillar inevitably rots and needs replacement. With the studies by F. K. Ehrhard (1989, 1991) on the Tibetan sources, and Alexander von Rospatt (2009) on the Newar records, the intricate and ad hoc negotiations for each intervention to this stūpa, averaging once every fifty years, offer insight on the state of local and regional Vajrayāna traditions, as well as the communities that step up to engage in the costly, but prestigious, enterprise. During the period of the Three City-States after 1595, up until 1758, the Malla kings granted permission only to Newars from Kathmandu to renovate the stūpa. The inscription recording the staging of the 1605 restoration authorized by Śivasiṃha Malla of Kathmandu (ruled 1583–1620) expresses the manner in which Newar Buddhists cooperated with the king, who is made to officiate at the rituals of reinvigoration and dedication. When the work was initially completed, the king celebrated by making offerings to brahmans and sponsoring *homa* sacrifices, but lightning struck the stūpa and destroyed the upper portions, an event interpreted as an act of jealous wrath on the part of the Vedic god Indra. Praising the king's repetition of the necessary work up to the completion of the rites, as directed by the leading *Bajrācārya*s, the dedicatory inscription states: "Then, though kings think themselves capable of many works, even acting together they are not able to build a stūpa, which is the auspicious Embodiment of the Method [*vidhitānum*]. This one, which is four-faced and supremely auspicious, with its parts all bejeweled, was suddenly Self-Born all at once, because of Śivasiṃha."[55] The Newar Buddhists' relentlessness brought the ruler along the path of Dharma in their greatest festival, and in renewing their greatest monument from this time, until the end of the Shah dynasty.

Buddhist Building Initiatives

Newar Buddhists welcomed the independence of their city-state and the success of their own kings. They built up the areas between the two former towns, uniting them into one through the construction of new monastery courtyards linked by new lanes that met in neighborhood open centers, each equipped with temples dedicated to Gaṇeśa, rest houses, performance stages, and stūpas paid for by their own family or caste contributions. The Newar saṅgha's population by this era established a central organization of major and branch monasteries living within the city walls.

The later Malla era is marked by the building of many new *vihāras*, as the wealth coming into Nepal from regional trade, especially trade with Tibet, underwrote both royal and Buddhist merchant patronage. While again the records for this remain largely unanalyzed *in toto* since John Locke's landmark documentary study (1985), the number of branch *vihāras* built since 1500 far outnumber those built before; there was, in fact, a surge in the construction of small branch monasteries, and expansions of existing *bāhās*, both upward and with fine arts embellishments, all under the patronage of the Newar upper class. Several examples[56] in Table 3.2 suffice to show the pattern.

The question that follows from these records is, inevitably, why the expansion? Now from the very beginning of Buddhism, the making of

Table 3.2 Main and Branch Monasteries

Main Monastery	Branch Monasteries	Date founded
Kwā Bāhā		1206
	Chusyā Bāhā	1648
	Hāku Bāhā	1650
	Jyoti Bāhā	
Takse Bāhā		1490
	Dagu Bāhā	1683
	Tekan Bāhā	1650
Lagan Bāhā		1380
	Wanta Bāhā	1486
	Ta Bāhā	1486
	Khālā Chen Bāhā	1676
	Kacā Bāhā	1678
	Na Bāhā	1690?
Tadhan Bāhā		1044
	Cidhan Bāhā	1539
	Pinche Bāhā	1590
	Pyukhā Bāhā	1546

FIGURE 3.11 Wooden gong being struck in Itum Bāhā.

monasteries (such as Itum Bāhā, Figure 3.11) as refuges for monks and nuns, supporting their spiritual practice, is praised by the Buddha as the "best of gifts." This factor was doubtless well known in medieval Newar Buddhist culture. But a sudden increase in building branch monasteries could also have been related to an expansion in the saṅgha, such as to accommodate a rising monastic population in the form of wives, children, and patrilineage expansion.

It is clear that the final, and literal, "domestication of the saṅgha" occurred by the end of the Malla period, as the saṅgha by this time consisted almost entirely of married householders.[57] Being a Newar "monk" was no longer a voluntary association, but came to be defined—for all—by birth into endogamous castes that were known collectively as *Bare*[58] in Newari, but that were divided into groups with the Sanskrit surnames *Śākyabhikṣu* and *Bajrācārya*.[59] By 1850, this left only into the local Tibetan saṅghas as communities into which Newars could seek ordination into celibate monastic life; in the twentieth century, modern Theravāda monastic traditions added to this diversity.

The legal and cultural press of Malla rulers and their brahmanical courts led both the saṅgha and the entire Buddhist population to conform to brahmanically normative caste laws. Acting in unison as a group was ideal for impression management outwardly, and to promote conformity within the caste. Their elders and leaders transformed their traditions of monastic life and householder ritual activity, including extensive monastic landholdings.

The Development of "Buddhist–Brahman" Ritualism[60]

Just as Newar Buddhists built new stūpas, monasteries, and images adorned in astonishing detail in wood, precious metals, and stone, so too did they skillfully craft new cultural performances, drawing on Vajrayāna doctrines, techniques, and practices. They inherited an immense wealth of later Indic Buddhist texts, rituals, and spiritual practices, and they applied them to the new sociopolitical circumstances.[61]

It is, in our view, essential to return to the sociocultural context of the later Malla cities to understand the distinctive pattern of evolution that determined the characteristics of Newar Vajrayāna Buddhism. In the city-states ruled by the Malla kings, to have access to the palace had great importance for nearly everyone: for merchants wishing to sell to the royal stores, supply building materials to palace builders, armaments to the army, or metal to the mint; for talented individuals hoping to offer their services (as scribe, advisor, ritualist, artist) in the palace; for access to officials in charge of land registry, for dispute resolution; and to promote one's networking for influential friends—all this entailed relationships with high caste officials, and especially court brahmans. Thus, to succeed as this perennial arrangement swerved toward greater observance of the norms, axioms, and expectations found in the ancient *dharmaśāstra* represented a challenge to Newar Buddhists.

Once they began appointing a *Bajrācārya* as "palace *rājguru*," a person who guided the court in dealing with its Buddhist citizens, as well as in its involvement with prominent Buddhist rituals and restorations, the Malla rulers may have also, intentionally or not, gained an avenue of effecting their cultural goals among their entire polity, working through the *Bajrācārya* community networks that formed across their Kathmandu saṅghas. The promulgation of new rituals and practices to ensure good standing for the Buddhist priests at court could well have exerted a strong influence on how the Buddhists would react to conform with, and subtly resist, the Malla's theistic activities.

This was best done by those known to be "from good families," groups that made it plain that they adhered to acceptable standards of food choices (with whom they ate, with whom they didn't); it required publicly recognized standards of symbolic cleanliness, and expressions of ritual refinement in the brahman-defined Indic mode.

While the exact historical factors that led Newar Buddhists to develop a set of *saṃskāras* in concordance with those in the brahmanical *dharmaśāstras* remain obscure, the fact is that only in Nepal did this development occur, as there is no textual or traditional Buddhist "press" elsewhere for Buddhists to organize their lives on these terms. Thus, the cause for these *dharmaśāstra* innovations must be of local origin and part of the Malla polity's matrix of new cultural ideals and social expectations. A large succession of rites created by *Bajrācārya* masters came to be universally performed for Newar Buddhist householders, with a clear and dual social function: to define their having high caste status while also sustaining strong Buddhist identity. Malla-era ritual *Bajrācārya* masters masterfully created standard brahmanical rites, such as the *homa* fire sacrifice (Figure 3.12), but in a Vajrayāna Buddhist modality. This means that householders sit for life cycle and worship rituals that use Buddhist ritual objects and call on the powers of the Buddhist cosmos, performed by members of the Buddhist saṅgha. Aligning their community in outward conformity with the ideal brahmanical life marked by *saṃskāras*, these virtuosos skillfully created an alternative identity using ritual, one that did not confirm its core theistic beliefs and yet did follow Buddhist tradition in generating worldly benefits and good karma.

A prominent example of this process is evident in the Ihi ritual of "Symbolic Marriage" for young girls, an Indic rite of passage. In the brahmanical performance, girls long before menarche are "married" to Viṣṇu, using the *byāh* fruit as symbolic of the deity. In the Buddhist reworking of this ritual, the girls are infused with *bodhicitta* ("the thought of

FIGURE 3.12 Painting with a *Bajrācārya* performing a *homa* ritual for patrons.

enlightenment") symbolized with the same *byāh* fruit. They are now on the path to human marriage, while also affirming their Buddhist identity.[62]

While the Newar saṅgha continued to have specialists whose focus was manuscript copying, it is evident that the performance of Vajrayāna rituals were also of special interest to some who called themselves *Bajrācāryas*. Ritual priests in early Malla Nepal had the texts needed to devote themselves to adapting Mahāyāna–Vajrayāna religious understandings and ritual technology to every human context: to build temples, hold festivals, and serve the needs of Buddhist families (Figure 3.13). This pattern of development may explain why Newar tradition seems to lack a strong philosophical/scholastic dimension.

What *is* carefully elaborated is the ritualism that expresses and interjects the Mahāyāna–Vajrayāna worldview into every conceivable juncture: for relating to deities, celebrating festivals, moving an individual through his lifetime, seeking the best afterlife destiny, and reaching nirvāṇa. Lacking in philosophical inquiry, the "genius" of Newar Buddhism lies in its pervasive orchestration of Vajrayāna rituals and teachings, which channel blessings, well-being, and—for those householders willing to practice—movement toward enlightenment.

For Newar *upāsakas* (devout laymen), their expression of distinct Buddhist identity was primarily effected via adherence to this ritually

FIGURE 3.13 *Bajrācārya* performing a house foundation stone ritual, dedicated to local *nāgas*.

centered lifestyle, support for their saṅgha, showing devotion to Mahāyāna saviors, and having faith in the *siddhas* who discovered the highest path. Ritual linked Newar householders to the saṅgha, and Newar Buddhism successfully adapted to the cultural milieu of small states ruled by Hindu kings. The maximum development of such Buddhist rituals for non-Bare Newars was accomplished for the Urāy,[63] a grouping of upper castes in Kathmandu. Since their mercantile activities brought them in regular contact with the royal courts, their moral and ritual lives had to conform to orthoprax brahmanical practices. To sustain their social connections with these rulers, protect their wealth, and express their high social status, the wealthy Urāy subjects depended, in part, on their demonstrations of ritual purity in an Indic framework, even if in a Buddhist modality. Among other Buddhists, they were generous, if at times ostentatious, patrons, sometimes competing with kings and Tibetan nobility to build or renovate major monuments.

Shah Era (1769–2006) to the Present: Vajrayāna and the Newar Saṅgha

Newar Buddhism suffered a serious decline with the conquest of the Valley in 1769 by a royal lineage of *parbatiya kṣatriyas* from the neighboring region of Gorkha. This led to further massive transformations in Kathmandu Valley society, as the divided polity of medieval city-states became the single capital region of the new nation. The modern Nepalese nation stretches across 500 miles of mountainous terrain, and the new rulers began far-reaching changes in many spheres.

The Shah royal court was established in the palace of the former Malla kings of Kathmandu. They wanted to secure the loyalty of Newar Buddhist merchants by supporting their trans-Himalayan trade. But they also sought to legitimate their rule based primarily upon their adherence to Hindu law shaped by the *dharmaśāstras*; their patronage favored brahmans, Hindu temples, and related traditions; and their court propounded the doctrines that the Shah king was an incarnation of Viṣṇu who ruled a country protected by Śiva in the royally patronized temple of Śiva-Paśupati.

Shah policy took specific measures to undermine Newar Buddhist institutions, sanctuaries, and landholdings. It became increasingly difficult for the cultural life fashioned under the Newar Malla in the medieval era to still be celebrated, and it was Buddhist religious traditions that suffered the most precipitous decline. Today there is no widespread doctrinal understanding of the most common rituals still performed. Few *Bajrācāryas* grasp even the most basic underlying philosophic assumptions or relate to the rituals beyond the procedural level of proper order and mantra recitations. Nonetheless, many of these traditions are so deeply embedded in Newar life that they continue to survive. Even though many observances have been lost in the last century, the vast cumulative tradition of Mahāyāna–Vajrayāna ritual remains one of the most distinctive characteristics of Newar culture.

Buddhism in modern Nepal was affected by the conquest of the Kathmandu Valley by the Shah dynasty, hill *chettris* (Skt. *kṣatriyas*) who had unified the petty kingdoms across the middle hills, whose own state was found in the town of Gorkha. The Shah's partisan support of Hindu traditions, and their disestablishment of land tenure and other Malla laws that supported Buddhist monasticism and culture, undermined the material culture of Newar Buddhism on every level. By the end of the Rāṇā period (1846–1951), a century when a *kṣatriya* (Nep. *Chetri*) caste family seized control of the state, reducing the Shah kings to mere figureheads, discrimination against Newar language and rituals reached its peak.[64]

The anti-Rāṇā movement for democracy in Nepal and anti-colonialist struggles in India throughout the first half of twentieth century brought new ideas into the Kathmandu Valley, and these affected the religious awareness of the Newar public. Newars, disenchanted with their older Mahāyāna-Vajrayāna traditions, helped bring a few leading Tibetan teachers to teach; they also underwrote the establishment of reformist Theravāda Buddhism in modern Nepal. Influenced by "Protestant Buddhist" groups such as the Mahābodhi Society in Calcutta, the newly imported Theravāda movement commented strongly against the older traditions of Vajrayāna ritual practice. Its exponents also offered clear philosophical expositions and accessible meditation practices (*vipassanā*) that appealed to many in the Newar middle class. Thus, just as a century of harsh rule favoring Hindu traditions had weakened the economic and educational foundations of traditional Newar tradition, the Theravādin reformists entered the marketplace of religious traditions in the Kathmandu Valley to draw away followers and patrons from the older Mahāyāna–Vajrayāna Buddhism maintained by the Newar saṅgha.[65] We will return to discuss the current state of the Newar Buddhist religious field in the final section of the chapter.

Newar Tantric Buddhism since 1950

Our portrait of Newar Vajrayāna tradition in the modern era uses the emic, or indigenous, categories that are used to define the tradition across the Buddhist world: the *triratna*, or "Three Jewels." As prelude to this exposition of the Newar Mahāyāna–Vajrayāna understanding of the Buddha, Dharma, and saṅgha, we introduce the context, the contemporary Newar Buddhist community.

Organized in castes, the contemporary Newar Buddhist community combines a householder saṅgha and laity. Masters in the former serve the majority in several areas: as spiritual master teaching meditation; as priests performing rituals; as doctors using herbs and mantras to promote community health; as astrologers conjuring the best time for marriages and other events. The saṅgha of the Śākya caste do not serve as priests for other groups, only for their own monasteries; only *Bajrācārya*s do rituals for patrons. In the past thirty years, very few Śākyas or Bajrācāryas engage solely in ritual service, having other sources of livelihood.[66]

The Newar laity community is ordered by caste communities, and is divided by religious loyalty, as indicated by choice of family priest. This social ordering is indicated in Table 3.3. The last name of each is titled after their traditional professions. Today, these names are rarely indicative of occupation, as there have been many new possibilities opened by modern education, especially in government service, development work, or the tourism industry.

The Three Refuges in Contemporary Newar Tradition

At the start of every ritual performed by a *Bajrācārya*, he performs a preliminary ritual called the *Guru Maṇḍala Pūjā* that has the patron take refuge in the Buddha, Dharma, and saṅgha. Characteristically, the meaning of these refuges can be understood in both the mundane and supramundane senses.

Buddha

The dominant conception of the Buddha is that of later Indic tradition: cosmic Buddhahood ordered by the three bodies of the Buddha schema; this conception finds universal expression in the Vajradhātu stūpas that possess

Table 3.3 Newar Social Ordering

Buddhist Castes	DUAL	Hindu Castes
Bajrācārya Śākya Urāy (9 sub-groups: Tuladhar, Tamrakar, Kansakar, etc.)	Jośī (astrologers)	Brahman Karmācārya Śreṣṭha (sub-groups: Pradhan, Maskey, etc.)
Citrakār (painters)	Jyāpu (farmers)	
Manandhar (oil pressers)		
	Nau (barbers), Kasai (butchers), Dhobya (washermen), Damai (tailors)	Jogi (householders and former ascetics)
	Chamkala (sweepers)	

the *pañca buddhas*, with four iconographically distinct forms placed in a regular directional, with the fifth (Vairocana) understood as dwelling within.

The Newar understanding about the nature of ultimate Buddhahood, as codified in the *Svayambhū Purāṇa*, can be summarized under a variety of themes expressed in this text. The manifestation of Buddha reality is conveyed in the concept of the Ādi Buddha, or *dharmakāya* Buddha. This reality explains the life of Śākyamuni as an incarnation of the Dharmakāya; the tradition understands Buddhahood as the self-realization ("*svayambhū*") of Śākyamuni, who attained enlightenment through his own efforts. As with the image of the text's teaching of a lotus manifested on the great lake, so, too, is Buddhahood present in the soiled waters of *saṃsāra*, an abode of *nāgas*. Just as this Valley was created by the bodhisattva Mañjuśrī, it naturally became a realm where bodhisattva practices were cultivated. This identity, with its shrines encoding this understanding, was established and shaped in the religious landscape by a tantric master, an *ācārya* named Śāntikāra, as recounted in the *Svayambhū Purāṇa* discussed earlier.

Other texts call this exceptional realm "*Nepāla maṇḍala*"; Newar tradition, thus, is rooted in the view that primal Buddhism existed in this Valley long before Śākyamuni.

Dharma

As is normative for traditional Buddhists across Asia, the understanding of Dharma is founded in moral practices and making merit through ritual offerings and pious donations. What subtle teachings the great philosophers taught in the monasteries or whatever theory of reality gifted Newar ritualists based their practices on, for most Newars "doing Dharma" has meant completing the ritual acts that tradition prescribed. This is seen in the legacy of popular stories in Newar culture that teach the law of karma and its effects.

A central view of Dharma is a conception of the universe that recognizes and reveres the living presence of buddhas, bodhisattvas, and other enlightened beings (*siddhas*, *yoginīs*) and invokes their blessings. Newar Buddhists chant mantras and sing hymns of praise dedicated to them, as handed down from their tradition. For those who are most devout, including the *Bajrācārya* ritualists and those possessing initiations, following the "dharma" also implies access to a series of potent cosmic powers gifted to humans by these Buddhist saints in the form of *dhāraṇīs* and mantras.

The primary focal points of dharma practice in Newar tradition are *caityas* representing the cosmic Buddha, and images of bodhisattvas, with Avalokiteśvara by far the most important (Figure 3.14). These beings are present in this world, so immanent that they answer petitions from devotees with compassion in this world.

The typical Newar Buddhist also views these great beings not as abstract realities, but as having been established in the Kathmandu Valley landscape, with temples serving as their homes. Sacred landscape surrounds them, as mentioned already regarding the *Svayambhū Purāṇa*; the entire landscape of the Kathmandu Valley was made sacred as a manifestation of the ultimate reality, the *dharmakāya* of the cosmic Buddha. Most family stūpas found in monastic and family courtyards are in their form symbolic of this, with the greatest center of Newar Buddhism the stūpa on Svayambhū hill.[67]

The bodhisattva Avalokiteśvara has also become a locally established divinity at two great centers where temples have been built in Patan and Kathmandu. In the latter case, an image signifying the bodhisattva's local manifestation was found just outside the old town walls to northeast;

FIGURE 3.14 Modern stūpa based on the directional Buddhas in the Vajradhātu Maṇḍala.

and this revelation led to a temple being built in Jana Bāhā, and an elaborate annual ritual cycle and chariot festival. Another instantiation of this bodhisattva's wish to be present in Nepal is associated with the towns of Bungamati and Patan; in the legends associated with the two temples in these towns, the bodhisattva is brought to the Valley from Kāmarupa (Assam), by emissaries skilled in tantric ritual. Here, too, there is an even more elaborate annual ritual cycle and a chariot festival that is held to honor this bodhisattva. It is significant that Newar Buddhists commonly use place names to refer to these celestial bodhisattvas: Bunga Dyaḥ ("the deity of Bungamati") for the latter, Jana Bāhā Dyaḥ ("the deity [*dyaḥ*] of Jana Bāhā") for the former.

This sense of localized divinity applies even to the previous incarnations of the future Buddha, whose exemplary lives were lived out locally. There was Maṇicūḍa, a king who gave his life to assist those suffering from an epidemic in a distant land, whose kingdom existed in the vicinity of the old town, Sankhu. Then there was Prince Mahāsattva, among the most famous incarnations of the future Buddha, who sacrificed his life to save a litter of tiger cubs on a hillside outside the town of Dhulikhel, done to perfect his commitment to giving and bodily renunciation.

Newar Buddhists also admit the presence of other divinities that exist that are not strictly Buddhist; while the Buddhist pantheon is supreme, these other beings are powerful and deserve respect, and so they, too, are worshipped. As we have seen, the fact that bodhisattvas are called *dyaḥ*, just as the gods Gaṇeśa and Śiva are, is an important marker of religious perception. The Newar Buddhist understanding of "living according to the Dharma" entails the obligation to respect all divinities in their Valley through ritual service.

Saṅgha: The Logic of Ritual, the Arc of Valley Vajrayāna History

Unlike the monastic institutions of Tibet that fostered in-depth philosophical inquiry and vast commentarial writings, Newar monks produced few original contributions to Buddhist scholarship.[68] The Newar saṅgha's special focus was the performance of rituals drawing upon the deities and powers of the Mahāyāna–Vajrayāna Buddhist tradition. Like married Tibetan monks of the Nyingmapa order, the Newar *Bajrācāryas* came to serve the community's ritual needs, with some specializing in textual study, medicine, astrology, and meditation.

Lifelong ritual relations link householders to a family *Bajrācārya* priest, colloquially called *guru-ju* in colloquial usage. The ritual services provided are vast in scope, and the variations include Buddhist life-cycle rites (*saṃskāras*),[69] fire rites (*homa*), daily temple rituals (*nitya pūjās*), mantra-chanting protection rites, merit-producing donation rites, chariot festivals (*ratha jātras*), and tantric initiations (*abhiṣekas*). Some of these cultural practices were noted 1,500 years ago in India. For example, the ways Newars worship at stūpas today—with offerings and accompanied by drums and musical instruments—are similar to devotional scenes depicted at Sanchi. Another example is visible daily in Kathmandu's Itum Bāhā, where one can still see the ritual of marking time by a Śākya ritualist rapping on a wooden gong, a monastic custom noted in pre-Gupta India. In addition, during the Buddhist holy month of Gunlā, householders make offerings to a large, hand-copied *Prajñāpāramitā* text that is placed in a monastery, continuing "the cult of the Mahāyāna book."[70] In these and many other traditions, Newars continue the cultural practices of later Indic Buddhism.[71]

Newar Monasteries: An Architecture of Vajrayāna Monasticism

More than three hundred *vihāras* (Buddhist monasteries) are in existence today in the Kathmandu Valley, the architectural form reflecting the evolution of Newar Buddhism as a Mahāyāna–Vajrayāna tradition. Each has two names; one is in Sanskrit, the other in the Newar language.[72] The *vihāras* are categorized as the *mu-bāhā* ("main monastery"), each with satellite *kacha-bāhās* ("branch monasteries"). The large cities also have a much smaller but similar set of monasteries called *bāhi* and these, too, have *kacha-bāhi*.[73] But all Newar *vihāras* have a title that includes "*Mahā Vihāra*."[74]

In some *mu bāhās*, the saṅgha is made up only of Bajrācaryas; in others, there is a joint saṅgha of Bajrācāryas and Śākyas. In still other *bāhās*, there are only Śākyas in the saṅgha, who are independent from the Śākyas of the *bāhis*. In *bāhis*, the saṅgha is composed only of Śākyas.

Across the Newar settlements in the Kathmandu Valley and in some cities across Nepal,[75] the *vihāra* is a four-sided monastic building, built around an open courtyard. It is a brick and wooden structure, usually of two stories. Their foundation, walls, and pillars are brick; doors and windows are made of wood, many with intricate carving. Wooden struts support clay-tile roofs. Defined by a ground floor plinth that is a foot or more above it, the courtyard is laid out with oiled bricks. Most have shrines known as *vajradhātu caityas*[76] installed at the center of the courtyard. Many *vihāras* have other caityas located there, the donations of local families.

The typical Newar *bāhā* has a main entrance that is ornamented by a tympanum; there are niche shrines immediately inside, containing images of the monastery guardians Gaṇeśa and Mahākāla. Opposite the entrance, and across the courtyard, is the main shrine building, which has two or more stories (Figure 3.15). On its ground floor is the *kwāpa dyaḥ*, usually an image of Akṣobhya or Śākyamuni Buddha, which is flanked by images of his two great human disciples, Maudgalāyana and Śāriputra. The tantric shrine above can only be reached by indoor stairs. This is the *āgama*, a ritual room open only for adults who have received the appropriate Vajrayāna initiation. There are usually elaborate woodcarvings adorning its outside windows, including another tympanum.

Only members of the saṅgha of each *vihāra* are allowed to enter into the ground-story shrine to perform rituals, but all individuals can view the *kwāpa dyaḥ* from outside when the doors are open. All *vihāras* in the Valley have been renovated periodically, but due to the decline of monastic landholdings and the prevalence of theft of the artistic masterpieces

FIGURE 3.15 Lagan Bāhā, with Avalokiteśvara temple and votive caityas in courtyard.

from them, few monasteries in the Valley still possess well-maintained and intact architecture.

Newar monastic architecture reflects the cumulative history of Indic Buddhism: a foundational, ground-level center to revere Śākyamuni and his disciples, in the *kwāpa-dyaḥ* icon and *caityas*; the presence of Mahāyāna-style *caityas* and maṇḍalas in the courtyard; and the final level, in the upper-story secret chamber, a Vajrayāna image and space for initiation-based *sādhana* practices open to initiates.

The Social Organization of the Newar Saṅgha

It has already been mentioned that *vihāras* are categorized according to the type of saṅgha that has its lineage located in the *vihāra*. Architectural differences are matched by differences in the saṅgha membership of those inhabiting them. The Newar saṅgha is divided into two parts, Śākya and Bajrācārya. Males born into these families become Śākya and members of Śākya saṅgha by obtaining the Buddhist ordination called *pravajya*; those born into Bajrācārya families become members of the Bajrācārya Saṅgha by obtaining the Vajrayāna initiation called the *ācārya abhiṣeka* after the *pravajya*.

The saṅgha of that *mu-bāhā* is also popularly known as a *bajrācārya saṅgha*. A few *mu-bāhās* are mixed, consisting of male Bajrācāryas and Śākya-bhikṣus as their members. All monasteries referred to as *bāhi* have saṅghas that consist of Śākya-bhikṣu caste members only. The Bajrācāryas are colloquially called "Gubhāju"; Śākyabhikṣus affiliated with of *mu-bāhās* and *bāhās* are known as "Bare"; and the Śākya-bhikṣus connected with the *bāhi* are known as "Bikṣu Bare." "Guruju" is the generic term used for all men in the Newar saṅgha.

Each saṅgha is organized according to age seniority and possession of tantric initiation. In some *vihāras* the first five, in some the first ten, in some the first twenty, and in some the first thirty saṅgha members are referred to as *sthāvira* ("elders"). Any male wishing to be promoted to the *sthāvira* rank must take the Cakrasaṃvara initiation. The use of this term thus shows the centrality of tantric tradition in the Newar. After a *sthāvira* dies, the eldest qualified junior member of that saṅgha is promoted into this rank. In the case of the Bajrācārya saṅgha, the seniormost *sthāvira* in each monastery is called *cakreśvara*. The senior-most *cakeśvara* in a city is regarded as *mūla-cakreśvara*. The committee of *sthāviras* in each *vihāra* is authorized to make decisions for its own saṅgha.

For the past two centuries, and likely for some back to early Malla times, some saṅgha members of each *vihāra* married and had children. In the twentieth century, wives of Śākyas and Bajrācāryas are also regarded as Śākya-bhikṣuṇīs and Bajrācāryas, respectively. In practice up to the present, Śākya-bhikṣus of one monastery prefer to arrange marriages with Śākya-bhikṣuṇīs of other monasteries. Similarly, male Bajrācāryas of a monastery prefer to arrange marriages with female Bajrācāryas of other monasteries.[77]

It is mandatory for the male children of Śākyabhikṣus to take Buddhist ordination in their respective *vihāra*; otherwise they forfeit their right and ability to worship in the monastery shrine.[78]

Tantric Buddhist Ordination and Ācārya Initiation

Ordination is one of the main monastic activities in Newar Buddhist communities. It takes place as needed, that is, when there are enough young men who want to complete this passage of life ritual. In some *vihāras*, the saṅgha elders organize the ordination program; in others, an individual family will organize it when its sons come of age. A team of the *sthāviras* gives the ordination and then, typically, an *ācārya-abhiṣeka* initiation follows. Male children in both Śākya and Bajrācārya families become the members of their saṅghas by obtaining the *pravajya* Buddhist ordination (Figure 3.16). It has been well documented by scholars, entailing first (in local parlance) a *śrāvaka*-styled celibate ordination (usually taking four days), then Mahāyāna-styled initiation into what is referred to as the "bodhisattva saṅgha" in which they obtain release from Vinaya rules of celibacy.

Male children of Bajrācārya families obtain this same first ordination, but then do the second, the *ācārya-abhiṣeka*, in their father's home monastery. After obtaining the *ācārya-abhiṣeka*, the new Bajrācāryas are trained in performing the most common ritual, the Buddhist *homa*, and from that time afterward they are empowered to perform it for patrons.[79] From this point onward, Bajrācāryas can follow their own inclination to pursue knowledge of other forms of ritual practice, including competency to do life-cycle rituals, make *maṇḍalas* of colored powder by hand with molds (Figures 3.17 and 3.18), or pursue tantric initiations.

Family Ritualist and Clients System

Each Bajrācārya family, until recently, had a circle of followers for whom its adult, initiated men performed rituals. The Buddhist family priest

FIGURE 3.16 *Bajrācārya* boy holding monastic staff and bowl, during *pravajya* ordination.

FIGURE 3.17 *Bajrācārya* makes maṇḍala with colored powders.

FIGURE 3.18 Making a Basundhara maṇḍala with a mold.

would come to homes at both happy (birth, marriage, etc.) and sorrowful events (sickness and death). Most of the major Buddhist practices are observed in the presence and under the guidance of the family Bajrācārya priest. At present, this Buddhist priest's work cannot suffice with a head of household's need to meet his family's material needs and the costs of education. Most Bajrācāryas have given up their priestly profession, as have their followers. Today, Newar householders depend on a small number of individuals who still know and understand the old traditions. The former *jajman* system now is largely defunct.[80]

Regular and Tantric Rituals in Newar Monasteries

A daily ritual takes place in every Newar Buddhist monastery.[81] Each member of the saṅgha performs the particular monastery's routine by rotation. The full traditional daily ritual takes place thrice in a day, at morning, at afternoon, and at evening, for the main shrine (*kvāpa-dyaḥ*). But today, only a few monasteries observe the thrice-daily ritual strictly. Saṅgha members used to recite several Mahāyāna sūtras and praising verses (*stotras*) jointly in all monasteries daily, and only a few still do so today. Most do this twice in a month; one on every eighth day of the bright half of a month (*śuklapakṣa aṣṭami*), and the other on every full moon day. Further, an esoteric ritual, the *ca:re pūjā* or *auṃśi pūjā*, is conducted on the fourteenth or fifteenth day of the dark half of a month (*ca:re/auṃśi tithi*) for the secret shrine (*āgam dyaḥ*) in every monastery.

The yearly monastic observance is called *Saṃvarodaya Parva*, an esoteric ritual, observed on the waning tenth day of Paush month (*Paush Kṛṣṇa Dashami*). This ritual commemorates the accomplishment (*sādhana*) of Hevajra-Nairātmyā by the legendary *ācārya* Mañjudeva, who protected the Nepal kingdom in the past, as recounted in the *Svayambhū Purāṇa*.

Each active Newar monastery holds a collective member assembly once in a year. At these gatherings, the *sthāvira* membership is updated and a feast is held.[82] In Kathmandu, there are eighteen *mu-bāhā*s (main monasteries), and these are grouped into three divisions according to their location in the city: uptown (northern), midtown, and downtown (southern). Each group conducts its regional assembly, known as *Puiṃ Ācārya Guthi*, once a year. During the *Puiṃ Ācārya* gathering, the newly ordained saṅgha members of each monastery will gain formal entry into the regional assembly. Similarly, they will be registered into the *De Ācārya Guthi* ("Country Ācārya Assembly").[83]

Finally, all saṅgha members unite to conduct a city assembly once a year, known as the aforementioned *De Ācārya Guthi*. The yearly assembly is conducted for two days. The first day is observed at the Shantipur tantric temple atop the Svayambhū stūpa hill; the next day it takes place in the home monastery of the eldest *thayepas* in the city. In an assembly closed to all outsiders, the senior-most *Bajrācārya*s perform a series of rituals, especially the *caryāgīti* (Figure 3.19). It is followed by *dāna* given by the householders living proximate to the *bāhā*. Finally, the chairmanship of the local saṅgha is passed over to the next *Bajrācārya* according to a system of rotation through member families. On the final day, it is noteworthy that the entire assembly is served buttered-salt tea in the Tibetan style. Usually, it is a small group of Bajrācāryas and Urāy who undertake the responsibility for preparing and serving this tea.[84]

Newar Vajrayāna in Modern Practice

Buddhist Castes and Tantric Understanding

Particularly striking in the Newar tantric tradition is the acceptance of caste categories in ritual reckoning. The ritual texts avow that birth into a Śākya caste family is a necessary prerequisite for entry into the Newar

FIGURE 3.19 Senior *Bajrācārya* perform caryāgīti dance.

saṅgha and that rebirth into a particular human group reflects karmic retribution.

When the courts of the later Malla rulers shifted toward the cultural tide supported in the royal courts, which seem to have come under greater Hindu influence, administered by brahmans at court and the rule by Hindu law (*dharmaśāstra*), this affected the Buddhist community. To get along in business, foster political ties, and sustain "respectful" social status, the Newar Buddhist were pressed to observe pollution and purity norms to a degree found nowhere else in Asia. The Newar ritual masters seem to have made the best of this situation, adapting Mahāyāna principles and Vajrayāna practices to create new rituals that conformed to brahmanical temple practices and their long-established high caste *saṃskāras*, rites of passage.[85] Some, if not all, of the monasteries had their monks marry and reckon their sons to be in a monastic patrilineage, thereby closing off ordination as "monks" only to their male descendants, a pattern that continues to the present day. It is easy to imagine how changing the details of practice to ensure the survival of the Dharma, what the Mahāyāna tradition would celebrate as *upāya-kauśalya*, would have been a conscious ideal in the minds of ancient Buddhist monastic leaders.

Vajrayāna Life-Cycle Rituals

There are a host of ritual texts dating back over a century that outline to a great extent Buddhist life-passage rituals. These were composed to utilize the powers of Vajrayāna practice by its *Bajrācāryas* for the benefit of the Newar people. In this pre-modern context, what the Newar masters were doing was a form of medieval "engaged Buddhism," skillfully adapting the faith to new times, using ritual practices in ways that applied the *triratna* to meet the daily life needs of a pre-modern community. In short, these *Bajrācārya* masters harnessed the powers of tantra to better the lives of practitioners, both in terms of curing diseases and maximizing worldly protections, and the new rituals provided Newar Buddhists with expressions of "cultural capital" that allowed them to flourish in the Hindu kingdoms of Malla and then Shah rulers.

The elaboration of Buddhist ceremonies in this community is truly immense: one widely used procedural handbook (Vajracarya 1980) on rituals lists over 120 "major" *pūjās*. The vast orchestration of such performances apparently goes far beyond the repertoire of Buddhist monks in the last phases of Buddhism in the Gangetic Plains. Whenever this began, and given the paucity of understanding of the last phase of Mahāyāna Buddhism in the Pāla-Sena Kingdoms, it is difficult to know as yet just how many of the later Newar practices (purity practices, caste norms, ritual procedures, etc.) were adopted from points south, and which were of purely local origination.

Another twentieth-century ritual guidebook, the *Nepāl Jana Jīvan Kriya Paddhati*, comments on the background of the life-cycle rites that Newar *Bajrācāryas* still practice (Lewis 1994). In them, there are patterns of regularity: most life cycle and other rituals can be broken into core "units" that tend to be assembled in consistent structural patterns. This cumulative ritual tradition is so vast that even the best of priests must refer to ritual texts to do all but the most common *pūjās*. From the first passages of this text, the application of core Vajrayāna concepts is apparent. Conception is described in terms of tantric physiology, and the priest's *sādhana* is often cited as the basis for the rituals performed. Generation of *amṛta prasād* ("ambrosia") through the *sādhanas* that are part of the *Bajrācārya pūjās* became integral to a "medical-religious system" (Stablein 1978) that linked priests to laymen.

In the context of the brahmanically maintained Hindu traditions that gained increasing support in both the Malla palaces and among certain influential groups, Buddhist Newars have also combined many non-Buddhist strands of Indian culture with their own, fashioning both continuities and divergences from the classic Mahāyāna–Vajrayāna ideals.

The Newar Buddhist *saṃskāras* outlined in the *Jana Jīvan* manual closely follow the classical paradigms of Indian brahmanical tradition (Pandey 1969), marking the key points in a person's life with Vajrayāna rituals that both empower and remove forces that threaten an individual's transition, while eliminating any incurred pollution. These Buddhist *pūjās* follow many ancient brahmanical ritual procedures, but have been transformed with alternative Buddhist gestures (*mūdras*), incantations (mantras, *dhāraṇīs*), and meanings. We mention only several central traditions of ritual practice, like the narrative texts discussed earlier, that reflect the main outlines of Newar Vajrayāna Buddhism.

The *Guru Maṇḍala Arcana* Ritual

The *Guru-Maṇḍala-Arcana* (Figure 3.20) is a very common and popular ritual procedure, practiced early in the morning each day by Bajrācāryas

FIGURE 3.20 *Bajrācārya* Chini Kaji performing the *Guru-Maṇḍala-Arcana* ritual.

and Śākyas in their monasteries. *Bajrācārya* priests also perform the *Guru-Maṇḍala-Arcana* for their followers at the start of all rituals: in happy and as well as sorrowful occasions, from birth to death, as part of most rites and life-cycle rituals. It is performed at home, in the cremation grounds, and at all places. Every Newar Buddhist ritual commences with the *guru-maṇḍala-arcana.*[86] To follow its content is to grasp the fundamental terms of understanding the Newar Vajrayāna tradition.

The ritual begins with a salutation to one's gurus and ends with *lokapāla-bali* ("offering oblations to guardian deities"). It consists of a series of the ritual steps like taking a holy bath, purifying the body, overcoming all obstacles, discarding all non-virtuous deeds, protecting oneself, and reminding the disciple of cultivating the six perfections (*pāramitās*) along with their fruits, and the attainment of *samyaksaṃbodhi,* complete enlightenment. To this end, the ritual falls into four modes, sacrificing one's own body, speech, and mind, as summarized here in four stages.

Pūjā Saṃkalpa: (Pūjā Materials on an Offering Plate)

Assemble a *pūjā* plate that contains water, flowers, incense, lamp, *tika* (red and yellow powder), food (rice, sweet, fruits), drinks (like cow's milk, spirits), and a thread-garland. All *pūjā* materials represent the five essential elements: earth, water, light, air, and space, and all of these denote the five sensual objects: sight, sound, smell, taste, and touch. The *pūjā* material denotes not only the totality of sensual objects but also all that the five sense organs can perceive, that is, through the eyes, ears, nose, tongue, and body, respectively.[87] Essential equipment by the ritualist include the set—bell, *vajra,* and rosary—that is utilized in relation to the *pūjā* plate and follower(s).[88] The *pūjā saṃkalpa* means to take a vow to sacrifice sensual objects; it is done to show the individual's strong determination to sacrifice all sensual objects for spiritual blessings.

Ratnamaṇḍala Niryātana: *Offering the* Ratnamaṇḍala *to the Gurus*

The *Ratnamaṇḍala* refers to the totality of creation, following an early Buddhist assumption about the world's cosmology.[89] The *Ratnamaṇḍala* is considered very holy and precious, like a jewel. The offering of it to the Gurus is regarded as the highest honor and sacrifice. A Buddhist disciple who has been initiated in the Vajrayāna esoteric practices devotedly offers the *Ratnamaṇḍala* to the Gurus daily in gratitude for what he or she has learned from all the Gurus. It is also offered to the Gurus when seeking higher levels of tantric Buddhist practices. Offering the *Ratnamaṇḍala* shows great faith in one's Gurus. Similarly, the offering indicates dedication to lifelong Buddhist learning and practice.

Saptavidhānuttara Pūjā: *Sevenfold supreme offering*[90]

There are seven steps in this supreme offering. This is not an ordinary but supreme offering because it is performed only by those beings who wish to become a Buddha in the future. The seven steps of the offering are as follows:

1. *Vandana*: reverent salutation to the Three Jewels—all Buddhas, Dharma, and saṅgha—by body, speech, mind;
2. *Pujāna*: offerings for all the senses;
3. *Pāpadeśanā*: confession of demeritorious actions in body, speech, and mind and vowing not to repeat them;[91]
4. *Anumodana*: expression of appreciation for all virtues possessed by the *śrāvakas*, *pratyekabuddhas*, bodhisattvas, and the buddhas;
5. *Adhyeṣaṇa*: requesting all bodhisattvas to turn the wheel of law in the future, taking future rebirth;
6. *Bodhicitta-utpāda*: causing the altruistic mind to arise, cultivating the *pāramitās*, seeking an enlightened mind;
7. *Puṇya-Pariṇamana*: dedicating the merits, accumulated by doing the above six steps of supreme offering, to become a Buddha in the future and for the welfare of all sentient beings. Thus, the goal of this rite is to make people strongly seek the ultimate goal in life: to become a Buddha for the welfare of all sentient beings.

Lokapāla Bali-Arcana: *Offering oblations to Protective Deities*

In Tantric Buddhism, *Bali-arcana* means sacrificing one's own sensual organs and offering objects related to each sense, an act that has the spiritual benefit of dispersing attachments in the individual's mind.[92] The second meaning is to sacrifice/dedicate oneself and one's worldly objects for the welfare of other living beings. Offering oblations to guardian deities means offering worldly objects to all the sentient beings who are around him- or herself, putting into action the vow earlier to become a Buddha for the welfare of all the sentient beings.[93]

Rituals for Elders

Newar Buddhists do large-scale rituals to strengthen the life force and make massive quantities of merit for their elders when they reach certain ages. At the age of 77 years, 7 months, and 7 days, the family will do the *bhīma ratha jaṁko*, which includes a small chariot procession for the elder, and for which a *Bajrācārya* will chant from the *graha mātṛkā* section of the *Graha Sādhana* text. He will then perform an elaborate pūjā on a graha *maṇḍala*. At 80 (or 88) years, 8 months, and 8 days, there is the *devaratha jaṁko*, for which the *Bajrācārya* does a special ritual dedicated to the Buddhist earth goddess Basundhārā. Finally, when an elder reaches 90 years, 9 months, and 9 days, families do the *Mahāratha Jaṁko*, which features the *Bajrācārya* priest doing a ritual on the maṇḍala of Uṣṇiṣavijāya, the goddess who resides within the stūpa (Figure 3.21). As it is typical to have a painting or repoussé metal image made for use in these special life-cycle occasions, many are found in the museum collections of Newar art.

Death Rituals

As is true elsewhere in Asia, the Newar Buddhist tradition provides strong responses to the dead. The actions taken for the dead by the Newar *Bajrācāryas*, including a host of mantras and *dhāraṇīs* chanted immediately afterward, and during the Newar Buddhist *śrāddha* rituals, are also based on the *Durgatipariśodhana Tantra*. There are some rites done immediately after death, including the drawing of a maṇḍala on the floor near the place of death, which directly steady the mind of the dead person to go on to a next life in good realm (*sadgati*) as soon as possible. There are other rituals that make merit (*puṇya*) and cause it to be dedicated (*puṇyapariṇāmanā*) to the name of the dead. The family *Bajrācārya* acts and utters the common sentiment that this merit be accumulated so that the dead individual "may get eternal happiness in the realm of Sukhāvatī." Later the family offers items owned by the dead to the *Bajrācārya*, in part to lessen the attachment of the deceased individual's consciousness to its former residence, and also to make another meritorious donation to a saṅgha member. Both help the dead one (sometimes referred to as a *preta*) to pass out from the intermediate state, and go on to its next life.

In the aforementioned ritual guidebook for modern *Bajrācāryas*, the *Nepāl Janajīvan Kriya Paddhati*, there appears an explanation and outline

FIGURE 3.21 Metal sculpture of a stūpa, with the goddess Uṣṇiṣavijāya.

of the Newar Buddhist life cycle rituals. It details the extensive agenda for Newar *Bajrācārya* ritualists who perform Buddhist *śrāddha* rituals for their *jajmans* before cremation, to end the initial mourning period, every month on the lunar death anniversary date during the first year of mourning, then yearly on the death anniversary date. During this ritual, male heads of households don Buddhist sacred threads for the only time in their lives, make *piṇḍa* (rice ball) offerings, and, at the conclusion of the rite, deposit all offerings either at a riverside *tīrtha* or in a monastic depository.

What is striking, and apparently not dissonant to Newar Buddhist minds over many generations, was the fact that this ritual—even in modern ritual guidebooks—adopts Vedic terms and assumes a Vedic afterlife metaphysic. What is remarkable, and evidence of Nepal's creative ritual tradition, is how the modern Newar Buddhist *śrāddha tradition* has been meshed clearly with the tantric text that otherwise guides Newar Buddhist death rites, the *Durgatipariśodhana*, and the worship of a form of Avalokiteśvara also unique to Nepal, Sukhāvatī Lokeśvara.

Yet it is difficult to ignore the congruence with the brahmanical construction of the *śrāddha*'s instrumental purpose of the "Ten *Piṇḍa* Rite." As presented in the *Nepāl Janajīvan* text:

> Why do the *dasa piṇḍa?* On the 1st day, *piṇḍa* is for the head; the second day for the eye; the 3rd day for the nose; 4th for the ears. On the 5th day, for the heart; 6th for hand; 7th for stomach; 8th for sense faculties/ organs. On the 9th day for the leg; 10th day for hair, nails. If the ten are completely done, [the dead one] will be complete in manifesting [new] body parts. (Bajracharya 1973, 28)

What is abundantly clear, despite this formulation, is that this Newar Buddhist *śrāddha* is not a classical brahmanical rite in any significant sense (Figure 3.22). This Newars' ritual assimilation uses the doctrines and vocabulary of Vajrayāna Buddhist mantras, utensils, and framing rites (such as the *gurumaṇḍala pūjā*). It makes merit by building *caitya*s and has the family dedicate it to the dead. It draws upon the ideal of Buddhist universalism by offering nourishment and merit to any other hungry ghosts. The Kathmandu rite documented in this study emphasizes the role of one of the 108/360 manifestations of Lokeśvara, Sukhāvatī Lokeśvara, which is prominent in Newar tradition. This celestial bodhisattva is asked to sit on *kuśa* grass and is placed directly in front of the *Bajrācārya* priest; he

FIGURE 3.22 *Bajrācārya* performing a Buddhist Shraddha ritual. The householder wears a Buddhist "sacred thread."

witnesses the *guru maṇḍala pūjā*, receives offerings, and remains for the various and long *Durgatipariśodhana dhāraṇī* recitations on behalf of the deceased. For the "Sixteen *Piṇḍa* Rite," performed at riverside sacred sites, Sukhāvatī Lokeśvara is similarly honored. The *śrāddha* rite's instrumental orchestration is quite explicit: it seeks this bodhisattva's compassionate, salvific actions on behalf of the deceased.

Here again, evidence regarding the singular Newar Buddhist practice suggests that strong cultural and political forces were at work in Malla Nepal that led to *śrāddha* practice being adopted by most Newar Buddhist castes.[94] In pursuit of this originally brahmanical desideratum, Newars spend vast time and resources on their *śrāddha* rituals. Thus, this Buddhist tradition plays to both sides of the Indian question of whether one's destiny is based strictly upon the individual's own karma from past and present lifetimes, or whether rituals can overrule this and manipulate rebirth destiny. Like most Indic religious systems founded on the doctrine that the cosmos is governed by karmic law, Newar tradition naturally looks to death as the critical time when causal mechanisms operate. It is not surprising that the very highly ritualized Buddhism of the Newars has applied Vajrayāna ritual expertise to this time as well.[95] So proficient were their after-death tantric rituals in the popular imagination that until recent times most otherwise high-caste Hindu Newar families regularly called *Bajrācāryas* to perform their death rites.

Vratas

The *vrata* is a package of practices devoted to a particular deity focused on a maṇḍala, a ritual form common to the Indic traditions. The main Buddhist *vratas*[96] are focused on Mañjuśrī, Avalokiteśvara, Tārā, Vasudharā, Dharmadhātu, Lakṣacaitya (100,000 clay caityas), Mahākāla, and so on; the main contents of Buddhist *vrata* entail following the eight moral precepts (*aṣṭaśīla*), a discourse on ten misdeeds, a recitation of narratives from the *vrata-kathā* (from sūtra, *jātaka, avadāna*), and making meritorious *dāna* (offerings). Followers observe a day-long *vrata* on a particular date, according to the deity, under the guidance of priest. It is observed either once a year or once a month for a year or two years (or more). *Vratas* are observed in residence courtyards, residences, monasteries, *tīrthas*, and other pilgrimage sites.

Buddhist Temple Visits and Pilgrimage

Visiting *vihāras* and temples is a frequent and central practice. Many people visit temples and monasteries near their residence daily. Every eighth day of waxing half of each month and full moon day are considered the most auspicious days for these visits. People visit stūpas/*caityas* and monasteries systematically for the holy month of Gumlā.

There is also a tradition of devotees visiting all the Valley's main bodhisattva temples for a month of Kārttika. Occasionally people plan a pilgrimage program of visiting all the monasteries in a city on a single day, singing devotional songs while accompanied by musical instruments and makings offerings. There are also pilgrimage practices directed to the conjunction of rivers (*tīrtha*), natural wells/ponds, hills, mountains, and so on. Taking a meritorious bath in the conjunction of sacred rivers, or in the waters of natural wells or ponds, is the one of the ritual objectives of Newar Buddhist pilgrimages. A *Bajrācārya* priest leads the group, narrating the history and legends, including those in the *Svayambhū Pūraṇa*. Pilgrims receive moral precepts in the holy places and may observe *vrata* rituals while at the sites, too.

Saptavidhānuttara Pūjā

This "Seven Element Ritual" is a very popular Newar householder practice, one that conjoins meditation and ritual offerings. It is performed for any

Buddhist deity, but is most popularly directed to *caityas*, and bodhisattva images such as Avalokiteśvara or Tārā. Performed in monasteries, temples, or private residences, the ritual involves setting up either 108, 360, or 1,000 of the following:

1. begging bowls filled with rice (*gulupa, piṇḍapātra*);
2. ghee lamps (*deva:*) with wicks;
3. water bowls with water colored by saffron (*tiṃca*); and
4. simple wheat-powder sculptures (*torma*).

The central ritual focuses on a water jar (*kalaśa*) surrounded by the eight auspicious symbols (*aṣṭamaṅgala*) that symbolize the eight bodhisattvas.[97]

The purpose of this *pujā* is to take refuge in Triple gems, offer sensory objects, confess misdeeds with vows not to commit them again, rejoicing in the good deeds of *śrāvakas*, bodhisattvas, and Buddhas, and finally, requesting that the latter not enter nirvāṇa, but remain in *saṃsāra* for the welfare of living beings. Those doing the ritual then take a bodhisattva vow to seek Buddhahood in the future; the *Saptavidhanuttara pūjā* reaches completion after all are given the bodhisattva initiation (*abhiṣeka*).

Homa Pūjā

Newar Buddhist fire sacrifice, or *homa*, is a type of *pūjā* that has many varieties (see Figure 3.23). It is an adaptation of the Vedic ritual practice that has been thoroughly reshaped and redefined to express Buddhist metaphysical concepts and religious goals.[98] Newar rituals are sometimes performed along with *homa pūjā*, and it is considered the most prestigious form of offering by Newar Buddhists. In some cases *homa pūjā* is compulsory, at other times optional.

Sūtra Patha, or the "Cult of the Book"

Chanting and listening to sūtras like the *Prajñāpāramitā Sūtra* or the *Pañcarākṣa Sūtra*, a meritorious deed mentioned in many Mahāyāna sūtras, is a traditional Newar Buddhist practice. On full moon or *aṣṭamī* days, many *Bajrācārya* priests sit at major monastic shrines to read these sūtras and allow householders to hear them chanted. Many give small

FIGURE 3.23 Modern *homa.*

offerings to have the text itself touched to their heads. Sūtras are also read on special occasions, such as at different phases in the dedication of a *caitya*/stūpa, the construction of monastery, or for birthday celebrations by honoring family members.

These Newar texts have been written using North Indian–derived scripts, the earliest on palm leaves (*tāra patra*), and then from the seventeenth century onward on layers of paper made from the *daphne* plant. In the latter form, the texts were written on stacked rectangular pages, some with gold letters on dark blue pages; others are in the format of a folded book (*thyā sāphu*). Many texts are interspersed with finely rendered miniature paintings (Kim 2013).

Hārītī Pūjā

A ritual widely done by *Bajrācāryas* and householders today, this reflects how Newar Buddhist tradition has long incorporated the goddess Hārītī into the local pantheon, with temples housing her icon found adjacent to major stūpas and monasteries such as Tha Bāhi. As recounted in the *Mūlasarvāstivāda Vinaya*, Śākyamuni Buddha transformed the *yakṣī* Hārītī from being a killer of children to being their protector. In the Newar tradition, Hārītī's identity overlaps with that of the smallpox goddess Ajimā. The *Bajrācāryas'* priestly veneration of Hārītī takes the form of, and draws upon, their *sādhana* with this reformed *yakṣī*. Drawing on Vajrayāna techniques, the *Bajrācāryas* cultivate power and seek prosperity for living beings, an example of Newar ritual as a working of *upāya*.

Virtuosi Traditions in Newar Vajrayāna

Hnikam: Daily Newar Buddhist Practice

As the name implies,[99] this is a daily practice limited only to Bajrācārya, Śākya, Urāy, and some in the Citrakār artist community. It is the first formal entry point into Vajrayāna spiritual practice. It is also a marker of Buddhist adulthood, as well as a mark of social status. The timing of young people receiving this varies by group.

In the case of the householders in the Urāy and Citrakār castes, the family elders usually organize *hnikam biyegu* ("*hnikam* giving [program]," or initiation) for a group of male and female children. Usually *hnikam* is given immediate after the boys complete their *kayeta-pūjā* rite and girls complete their *ihi* and *bahra-pikāyegu*. If it is not done then, it is usually taken before marriage. But more recently, a growing number wait to take it until after marriage.

The ritual entails the family's *Bajrācārya* priest and his wife (*gurumā-ju*) coming to their home. First, the priest couple performs a long ritual in the secret room (*abhyantar*) where the people who have not received *hnikam* cannot enter. With the recipients fasting, the eldest woman of the house welcomes the couple there with a special ceremonial welcome called *lasa kus*.[100] After the usual *gurumaṇḍala* ritual is done, the family priest instructs the initiates to draw a *ratnamaṇḍala* on a bronze plate[101] and continues with the *pañcābhiṣeka*, which is initiation into worship practice of the five Buddhas, each conveying one of the five *jñānas*.

Following this is the *mantra abhiṣeka*, when the *guru-ju* whispers the mantra softly into their ear of the young men, *gurumā-ju* (his wife) doing so for the young women. Before this, however, an assistant priest collects each person's new 108-bead rosary so that the main *Bajrācārya* can purify them with a mantra. Only then does he whisper the *hnikam* mantra to each initiate, handing back each rosary to the recipient (Figure 3.24). After receiving the mantra and rosary, the initiates show their respect by touching the *guru-ju*'s and *gurumā-ju*'s feet with their forehead (*bhāgi-yāyegu*)

FIGURE 3.24 *Bajrācārya* reveals the mantra to a disciple.

and giving a donation that consists of clothes (*lam-pa*), pots (*thalabala*), and money. This particular payment to the *Bajrācārya* priest and his wife is called *mantra dakṣiṇa*.

Hnikam initiation ends with the group receiving and consuming the *vajrayāna prasād* called *gokudahana*.[102] The next two days, the new *hnikam* practitioners must go the home of the *guru-ju* and *guru-mā* to have *hnikam* practice and mantra enunciation checked. The expectation is that this *hnikam* practice will be done every morning throughout life.

The time at which the eligible Buddhist caste groups take this step into daily practice varies by the group's own traditions. In the case of the Bajrācārya community, the male children get their *hnikam* initiation after the end of their *pravajya* four-day ordination, and they abandon their monastic robes for the householder's life and then receive their *Bajrācārya abhiṣeka*. The members of this group receive their *hnikam* in the course of this initiation. Their home monastery's *cakreśvara* and his wife, the senior-most *Bajrācārya* couple of the monastery, grant them *hnikam* within the precincts. From the next day onward, the new *Bajrācāryas* practice it and have their method checked. As for the female *Bajrācāryas*—who are not given *pravajya*—they do get a separate *hnikam* initiation. Families organize *hnikam biyegu* ceremonies for them, either in the home monastery complex or in their home, where the family priest conducts the ritual.

In the case of Śākya boys, since they take only the *pravajya,* their family's Buddhist priest can organize the *hnikam biyegu* for their male and female children a few days or a few years after their caste-specific initiation. The family priest and his wife grant the *hnikam* to them in the home monastery complex or in their home.

One noteworthy practice associated with the Newar *hnikam* tradition unfolds at the death of an individual. At the end of the *Gha:su* rite—on seventh day after death in Bajrācārya and Śākya communities, and on the twelfth day after the death in Urāy and Citrakār communities—the *hnikam mantra* is "returned" to the family priest from the dead who had *hnikam,* in a short ritual called *hnikam litatayegu* ("returning the *hnikam*").[103]

In recent years, some individual *Bajrācārya* priests and new Newar Buddhist organizations have been organizing *hnikam* initiations outside the normal family priest relationship.

Dekka: Tantric Initiation

Śākyas and Bajrācārya used to undertake several initiations and train in several Vajrayāna practices. At present, some members of the Newar saṅgha take the initiations associated with—in order of modern frequency—Avalokiteśvara, Cakrasaṃvara (Śrī-Heruka; see Figure 3.25), Vajravārāhī, and Caṇḍamahāroṣaṇa (Acala), and Mahākāla.[104] *Cakrasaṃvara trisamādhi, caṇḍalī-yoga,* Candamahāroṣaṇa *trisamādhi, balyarcanā* yoga, *śmāśāna* yoga, and *utkranti* yogas are all still practiced under strict rules of secrecy. All these initiations are now still taken by a very few Śākyas and Bajrācāryas, as well as by individuals in the Urāy community of Kathmandu, who have long been admitted into these initiations and practice the meditations in their own family shrine rooms, their household *āgamas*.

A summary of recent initiations bestowed by a leading *Bajrācārya* master of Kathmandu is given in Table 3.4.

Despite the impracticality of surveying for this information, the number of living Newar Buddhists who possess Vajrayāna tantric initiation today by active *Bajrācārya* masters can be estimated to around 1,500 in Kathmandu, 1,000 in Patan, 500 in Bhaktapur, and 100 in Kirtipur. This would represent less than one percent of high-caste Newar Buddhists.

FIGURE 3.25 Print from large glass negative for initiates of Cakrasaṃvara.

Table 3.4 Recent Initiations Conducted in Kathmandu

Restricted Empowerments/Initiation	Public Visualization Meditation of Training
2011	**2011**
Pañca abhiṣeka in Kathmandu	Ṣaḍakṣarī Lokeśvara, Svayambhū- Kathmandu
2008	Saptavidhānuttara Dhyāna, Patan
Ṣaḍakṣarī Lokeśvara in Bhaktapur, Patan, and Kathmandu	**2010**
Cakrasaṃvara in Bhaktapur	Ṣaḍakṣarī Lokeśvara, MD, USA
Vajravārāhi in Bhaktapur	**2008**
Candamahāroṣaṇa, Patan, Bhaktapur	Ṣaḍakṣarī Lokeśvara, Bhaktapur, Kirtipur
2007	**2007**
Ṣaḍakṣarī Lokeśvara, Kathmandu, Patan	Ṣaḍakṣarī Lokeśvara, Kathmandu
Cakrasaṃvara, Kathmandu, Patan	Saptavidhānuttara Dhyāna, Kirtipur, Bhaktapur
Vajravārāhi, Kathmandu and Patan	**2006**
Caṇḍamahāroṣaṇa, Kathmandu	Ṣaḍakṣarī Lokeśvara, Patan
	Saptavidhānuttara Dhyāna, Kirtipur

Puruścaraṇa Cvanegu

"*Puraścaraṇa*" (New. *puruśan*) is a Vajrayāna practice that enhances an individual's spiritual power and understanding, usually in a retreat site (Figure 3.26). It was a central practice in medieval Indic Vajrayāna tradition.[105] Passed down from teacher to disciple as an advanced and secret practice, men[106] undertake it for three different reasons.

First, it is a compulsory practice for the renovation of Buddhist figures such as the *kvāpa dyaḥ* (the main shrine in a monastery), the *vajrayāna āgam dyaḥ* (secret shrine in a monastery), and *yoginīs* like Vajrayoginī and others. In this case, this entails very secret rituals and *jāpa yoga* practice.[107] The time duration or the number of days for *puruśan* depends on sacrality of the objects to be renovated and the preference of the *upādhyāya guru-ju*, the director for the renovation ritual. The people who undergo the practice of *puruśan* are not allowed to see or talk to others outside the circle of initiation until the end of the retreat. After the completion of the *puruśan*, those completing it go to a *tīrtha* at midnight without letting others know; afterward, they bathe and make offerings

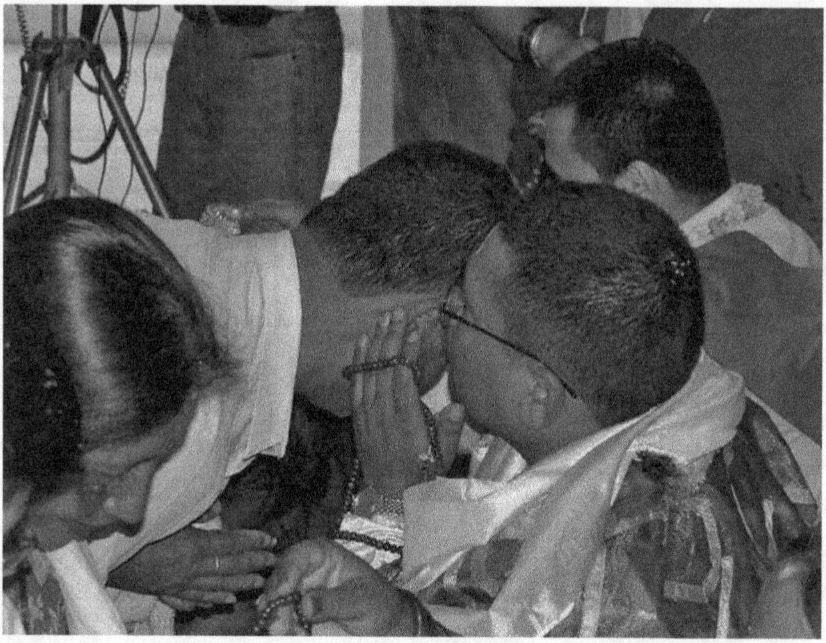

FIGURE 3.26 *Bajrācārya* practice of doing a *Puraścaraṇa* (New. *puruśan*) retreat, Naresh.

to *caityas* made of sand (*baluka-caitya*) and the local *nāgas*, who are represented by sand icons. After completing other necessary rituals, they finally fill special jars with river water and bring them into the venue where the *nyāsa pūjā* for the renovated image will take place. The water jar will be brought at the same night. This is the sacralized water jar in which the *nyāsa* will be inserted.[108]

The second occasion for going on *puruśan* is when a leading *Bajrācārya* teacher needs to prepare for the extraordinary empowerment rituals that he must do to initiate new *Bajrācāryas* into positions of spiritual authority, such as their becoming *mulācārya, upādhyāya, karmācārya,* or *dighācārya gurujus*, as well as for the main sponsor (*mu-jajman*) in an upcoming tantric initiation.

Third, *puraścaraṇa* can be a private, personal practice. It is done in an isolated place like a home or monastery *āgama* shrine, or in a mountain cave. This practice includes both ritual and yoga. The duration depends on the person and the master who is guiding the practitioner. When done, this individual *puraścaraṇa* practice is ended with a *homa* ritual.[109]

Legendary and Modern Nepalese Bajrācāryas

Śāśvat Vajra

There once dwelled in Mantrasiddhi Mahāvihāra a *Bajrācārya* named Śāśvat Vajra.[110] One winter day he was sitting in the sun on his rooftop after getting an oil massage. Just then, a large cloud mass came floating by up in the sky, cutting off his sunlight. When Śāśvat Vajra looked up, he saw that the clouds had remained stationary. He then left the *vihāra* and went to the open field in the Tundikhel, to try to bring the cloud down. By means of a secret ritual utilizing his *mantrasiddhi,* he succeeded in bringing the cloud to earth and then saw Mahākāla inside it. Śāśvat Vajra then worshipped Mahākala with a hymn of his own composition. Once he discerned that this deity always moved between Tibet and Kāśi, he made Mahākāla a promise to stop in this very place during his travels in the future. Once the *pūjā* was complete, Mahākāla blessed Śāśvat Vajra, ascended skyward, then disappeared. The temple to Mahākāla still standing today was built on this location.[111]

Surat Vajra

Surat Vajra was a Buddhist priest. He went, one time, to Lhasa in Tibet, and one day when he was having tea with a great lama of that city, he silently emptied his cup on the floor. He filled the cup and again threw away the tea. Surprised, the lama asked the reason for his strange behavior. Stranger still was the explanation of Surat Vajra. He told the lama that his house in Nepal had caught fire and was burning at that moment, so he was extinguishing the flames.

Lest it should offend his guest's feelings, the lama said nothing just then, but he had misgivings and made a note of the day and time. As soon as his guest was gone, the lama dispatched a messenger to Nepal to verify the truth of Surat Vajra's statement. Months later, the messenger returned to Lhasa and reported to the lama that Surat Vajra's house had actually caught fire at the time noted by him, but thanks to a timely rain, it was saved. The lama could hardly believe the report, but now he was filled with jealousy over the power and knowledge that the Nepalese priest possessed.

When the lama heard that Surat Vajra was preparing to return to his own country, he thought of harming him in some way. He sent word privately to

Nepal, saying that Surat Vajra had died on his way home from Lhasa. The lama then ordered that no boatmen should give passage to the Nepalese priest across the Brahmaputra River. Meanwhile, Surat Vajra took leave of his friends in Lhasa and departed. When he arrived at the river and found that no one would take him across it, he threw a sheet of cloth on the water. Then, to the amazement of the boatmen, he stood on it and crossed the Brahmaputra.

Frustrated to find Surat Vajra equal to this situation, the lama become even angrier; overtaking the homeward-bound priest, he challenged him to a contest of knowledge. Faced with the determined lama, Surat Vajra asked him what sort of contest he proposed. The lama replied that both of them should change themselves into sparrows and perch upon stalks of wheat growing near the roadside. The heavier would be declared the loser. Surat Vajra agreed. At once, both men became sparrows and alighted in a nearby wheat field. To his chagrin, the stalk upon which the lama-sparrow perched was weighed down heavily, while the other, upon which perched the Nepalese priest, was not even slightly bent. Then to show that his burden of bad karma was far less than that of the lama, Surat Vajra changed himself in the next moment into a pigeon. And yet the stalk of wheat still did not bend under him.

Seeing this, the lama becoming enraged, changed himself the next moment into a hawk, the enemy of all pigeons, and then swooped down murderously toward Surat Vajra. But seeing this attack, the pigeon flew into a cave and regained his human shape. Meanwhile, the lama changed himself into a snake and slithered inside. Cornered, Surat Vajra invoked the goddess Guhyeśvarī and she gave him a sword with which he cut the snake to pieces.[112]

After this, the priest resumed his journey without further trouble. But on his arrival in Kathmandu, Surat Vajra learned that he had been reported as dead; since his family had completed all the last rites for him, he could not go home. So to let his family know that he had not really died, he removed his shoes and sent them to his former house. Then he went to the Guhyeśvarī temple and was never seen again.[113]

Śrī Siddhiharṣa Bajrācārya

Śrī Siddhiharṣa Bajrācārya (New. Babukaji Guruju; Figure 3.27) (1879–1951), of Surata Śrī Mahāvihāra (New. Takshe Bāhā) in northeast Kathmandu, was an expert in Sanskrit, Buddhist philosophy, and tantric ritual, especially *caryāgīti*. He was a lineage holder in the Cakrasaṃvara Yoga, and one of the first to publish the important Newar Buddhist ritual text, the *Gurumaṇḍalārcana*. Like many Buddhist masters, Babukaji studied Sanskrit

FIGURE 3.27 Siddhiharṣa Bajrācārya.

with a brahman pandit, Gangadatta Sharma of Kathmandu, and took Buddhist teachings from the Patan master Kula Man Bajrācārya. Making his career as resident expert in the Vir Library Archive in Kathmandu, this scholar worked with a long list of visiting scholars, beginning with Sylvain Lévi of France, and including such noted scholars as Guiseppe Tucci of Italy, professors Rosambi Sokaki and Kawaguchi of Japan, and scholars Hariprasad Shastri, Benatosa Bhattacharya, Rahul Sankrtyayana, and P. C. Bagchi of India.

Pandit Ratna Bahadur Bajrācārya

Ratna Bahadur Bajrācārya (New. Ratna Bahadur Pandit; Figure 3.28) (1892–1956) was a member of the saṅgha of Yaśodhāra Mahāvihāra (New. Bu Bāhā)

FIGURE 3.28 Ratna Bahadur Bajrācārya.

in Patan. He was noted for his work in Sanskrit and local epigraphy, and in Buddhism from Pandit Kulaman Shimha Bajrācārya of Patan, who was his maternal grandfather. At the age of fourteen, Ratna Bahadur visited Tibet in association with his father's business; during his ten years there, he studied the Tibetan language and then sūtras and tantras with Tibetan lamas. After the great earthquake of 1934, he performed the rituals for the extensive renovations of Patan's Avalokiteśvara-Karunamāya and Kumbheśvara temples. Ratna Bahadur Guruju went on tantric retreat (New. *puraśan*) in Rishisvar (New. *Tamana*)[114] and practiced *utkranti yoga* there. This death practice he later taught to thirty-four Bajrācārya and Śākya disciples for a month[115] in this same place; every evening he taught about the *Sukhāvatīvyūha Sūtra*.

Throughout his life he preached to audiences in various places across Nepal, most often during the summer Buddhist holy month, Gumlā,[116] and at the Dharmodaya Pathashala, an institution he founded where Buddhism could be taught. Ratna Bahadur Guruju gave public lectures on Buddhism regularly throughout his life. These included programs based on the *Guṇakāraṇḍavyūuha* in Kuti, a town on a major trade route to Lhasa, just over the border in Tibet; on the *Navakhanda sūtras* ("Nine Texts")[117] in a private residence in Patan; on the *Prajñāpāramitā* for another group in Patan; on the subject of tantra ("*tantrātmaka rahasya*") in Ikha Chen, Patan; on the *Svayambhū Purāṇa*, in Tanga Bāhā, Lalitpur, a series that lasted three years; on the *Aśokāvadāna*, held in Nah tva neighborhood, Patan; on the *Lalitavistara* in Bu Bāhā, Patan; on the *Nāmasaṃgīti* in his own monastic residence (*bāhā*). He performed initiations for individuals in the *Cakrasaṃvara Tantra* in his residence. His most famous foreign scholar was Rahul Sanskrityayan, who studied with him for three months. This extraordinary scholar is reputed to have said, "Pandit Ratna Bahadur Bajrācārya is a true Gem (*ratna*) of Nepal."[118]

In addition to his work in the Department of Nepal Bhasa and Tibetan in the Vir Library, Ratna Bahadur Guruju was a long-serving president of the scholarly institution the Sanskrit Maṇḍala. He compiled a trilingual dictionary of Newari-Sanskrit-Tibetan. His main scholarly work was in doing translations from Sanskrit into Newari and writing treatises in the local vernacular. These modern publications included the *Bodhicaryāvatāra* (published 1958), the *Mahāyāni Nityācara vidhi* (1962 [NS 1083]), the *Ye dharma Gatha* (1972 NS 1093), a *Nityācāravidhi* (NS1102), the *Āryanāmasaṅgīti* (NS1113), and he worked on the *Aṣṭasāhasrikā Prajñāpāramitā*, the *Bodhisattvāvadānakalpalatā*, and the *Śatasāhasrikā Prajñāpāramitā* (all unpublished). According to local tradition, he is said to have also completed partial translations into Newari of the *Daśabhūmīśvara Sūtra*, the *Samādhirāja Sūtra*, the *Guṇakāraṇḍavyūha*, the *Vrihat Svayambhū Purāṇa*, the *Aśokāvadāna*, and the *Jātakamālā*.

His unpublished ritual manuals include the *Sahasrāhuti vidhi, Daśakarma Vidhi, Dikṣā vidhi, Āryabhadracārigāthā*, a *Cakrasaṃvara Samādhi, Triskandha Papadeśana, Pañcarakṣa, Saṃvarodaya Tantra, Karavīra Tantra, Tārā Pūjā Vidhi*, the *Kriyāsaṃgraha* (partial edition), and the *Mañjuśrīpārājikā*. Those published include the *Guru Maṇḍala Arcana Vidhi* (NS 1069), an *Āryagrahamātṛkānāma Dhāraṇī* (NS 1080), and the combined *Yogāmbara Samādhi and Kalaśapūjā* (NS 1099). Additional books on Buddhist thought were the *Puṇyagraduta* (NS 1068) and the

Bauddha Prathama Sikṣā (NS 1092); unpublished manuscripts bear the titles *Śrīstikrama, Bodhicaryā,* and the *Śrāvakācārya Nirdeśa.* Later Newar scholars based many of their writings on those of Ratna Bahadur Guruju.

Amogha Bajra Bajrācārya

Popularly known as Amogha Guruju (Figure 3.29), he was born in 1910, and was a member of the saṅgha in Hemavarṇa Mahāvihāra (New. Gam Bāhā) in Kathmandu. His training in Buddhism began when he was five years old when he completed his initiation into the saṅgha; it continued when he received the Cakrasaṃvara initiation from his father at the age of fourteen, just after his marriage. His training also included Sanskrit study, the *Kriyāsaṃgraha, vajragīti,* and *vajranṛtya.* Around the age of twenty, he studied the *jātakas* and other Buddhist texts with the Kathmandu pandit Siddhiharsha Bajrācārya (Bābukaji Guruju). Studies with Pandit Dambarudeva focused on astronomy and Āyurveda. At age twenty-seven, he learned Vāyu Yoga from a reincarnate Tibetan teacher

FIGURE 3.29 Amogha Bajra Bajrācārya.

(*tulku*). At age twenty-nine, he learned and participated in Gaṇacakrapūjā under the Guhyaharṣa Bajrācārya, the Guruju of Takṣa Bāhā. At age thirty-nine, after completing the tantric pilgrimage called *purva-sevā* at Cakrasaṃvara-maṇḍala sites across Nepal, Amogha Guruju initiated seventy-five disciples in the *Cakrasaṃvara Tantra* and from this time he continued to teach Vajrayāna rituals and Yoga practices to many disciples and performed *utkranti yoga* to benefit the dead. At the age of forty-five, he became the Sthāvira (Cakreśvara), the most senior in his monastery, Hemavarna Mahāvihāra. At the age of fifty-nine, Amogha Guruju renovated the main shrine room of his monastery, performing the major rituals as the *Mūlācārya*. At the age of sixty-one, he participated as the *karmācārya* ritualist in the *ahoratra homa pūjā* that occurred in course of the renovation of the Vajrayoginī temple in Pharping. Amogha Guruju also performed the main rituals for the renovation of many temples in the Kathmandu Valley. Among these were the tantric rituals for both the ground floor and tantric shrine rooms at Ca Bāhā, Kathmandu; for the Carumati Vihāra's main shrine in Chabil; for the temple for Phulabari Guhyeśvari in Deopatan; and for the roof of the Hārītī temple at Svayambhū. At sixty-six, he was the *mulācārya* who performed an *ayuta ahuti homa* ritual for the royal initiation of King Birendra. Takawaka, a Japanese Buddhist priest, studied extensively with Amogha Guruju; he sponsored and accompanied Amogha Guruju on pilgrimages to sacred Buddhist sites in India and Japan. He passed away in 1979.

Amogha Guruju's publications on Newar Buddhist ritual practices established standards in terms of language, methodology, and procedure that unified practices in Kathmandu. His main publications include *Māragharṣaṇa* (a chapter from *Lalitvistara*) NS1074; *Catrisamvaradi Catu sasthi samvara stotram* NS1076; and in *Nepal Bhasa Sahit Dānagatha* NS1086; *Āryatārā stotra Arthasahit*, 1095; *Durgatipariśodhana kalpoddesa*, 1095; *Saptavarapustakam*, 1096; the *Guru maṇḍala arcana pustakam*, NS1101, second edition; the *Piṇḍavidhāna*, NS1094; the *Kalaśārcana vidhi yajnā vidhana*; and a Newari introduction to the *Aṣṭottaraśata Lokeśvara Paricaya* (1979). Amogha Guruju's transmission of the *Cakrasaṃvara Tantra* established this lineage as the major tantric lineage in twentieth-century Kathmandu.

Pandit Divyabajra Bajrācārya

Pandit Divyabajra Bajrācārya (Figure 3.30; 1920–2000) of Kanakacaitya Mahāvihāra (Jana Bāhā), Kathmandu, was a master of Sanskrit, Pali, and

FIGURE 3.30 Pandit Divyabajra Bajrācārya (in white) and senior-most city Bajrācārya Anandamuni at a ceremony organized at the school for Buddhist priests founded by Pandit Badri Ratna Bajrācārya (at far left) in 1980.

Āyurveda who taught many students, including Pali to Theravāda monks and nuns, as well as Sanskrit to Newar saṅgha members. Divya Guruju's scholarly specialization was Buddhist philosophy, and he gave many lecture series on various Mahāyāna and Vajrayāna schools of thought. Noted programs were on the *Bodhicaryāvatāra* at Pyangatham in Patan; on the *Prajñāpāramitā* in Hiraṇyavarṇa Mahāvihāra, Patan; and on the *Abhidharmakośa, Vicitrakarṇikāvadāna*, and *Aṣṭasāhasrikā Prajñāpāramitā* in his home monastery. Divya Bajra received a Cakrasaṃvara initiation at Mulaśrī Mahāvihāra (Mu Bāhā) in Kantipur from Guhyaharṣa Bajrācārya of Takshe Bāhā, one of the renowned *ācārya*s popularly known as Sanukaji

Guruju. It is said that the initiation was conducted with a special focus on him and thus was more advanced than the ritual usually conducted. He was noted for his articulation of the key contrast between the Theravāda and Vajrayāna traditions—"The Theravādins see *duḥkha* (suffering) everywhere; Vajrayānists see *sukha* (happiness) everywhere . . ."—and seeing his own Vajrayāna tradition as having arisen to give householders the chance to fully practice Buddhism.[119]

Divya Guruju's articles and books have been well received by Newar readers, especially Mahāyāna works that he translated from Sanskrit into vernacular Newari. His major published works were editions of the *Bodhicaryāvatāra Catustava, Prajñāpāramitā Piṇḍārtha, Sukhāvatīvyūha Sūtra, Nirvedhābhāgīya, Laṅkāvatāra Sūtra, Gaṇḍavyūha Sūtra, Guhyasamājatantra, Daśabhūmika Sūtra*, and *Ācaryācandrakīrtikṛta Guh yasamājatantrapradīpoddyotanaṭīkā Ṣaṭkoti- vyākhyā-sahita*. His own treatises included the *Nava Sūtra Saṃgraha, Dharmasaṃgrahakośa, Prathama Dhyāna*, and the *Pañcarakṣā Kathāsara*.

Pandit Badri Ratna Bajrācārya

Pandit Badri Ratna Bajrācārya (Figure 3.31; 1946–) is one of the renowned living masters of contemporary Newar Buddhism in Kathmandu. A saṅgha member of Mantrasiddhi Mahāvihāra in Kathmandu, Badri Guruju from a young age began his training in ritual performances from Paramasiddhi Bajrācārya and Motiratna Bajrācārya, and began serving patrons from the age of eleven. He also learned Sanskrit from Buddhist and brahman pandits. In course of learning Sanskrit, he was given the name Bajri Ratna by his brahman teacher. He also studied rhetoric with a brahman teacher, Muralidhara Bhattarai, and astrology with another brahman pandit from Janakpur. He also studied Āyurvedic medicine.

Badri Ratna's expertise as a ritual master continued with training in sand-maṇḍala construction from his maternal uncle Macapaju Bajrācārya. He learned the *vajragīti* (Vajrayāna Buddhist song) from Guru Paramānanda Bajrācārya. He learned the *vajranṛtya* (Vajrayāna Buddhist dance) and *pañcatala* (playing Vajrayāna musical instruments) from Guru Siddhi Ratna Bajrācārya.

Badri Guruju was a lineage disciple of the afore-mentioned Amogha Bajra Bajrācārya. He was greatly inspired by Pandit Amogha Bajra due to his expertise in Buddhist philosophy and yoga, and his mastery of ritual. This teacher kindly accepted and trained him for an extended period in the

FIGURE 3.31 Pandit Badri Ratna Bajrācārya.

master-disciple lineage of Cakrasamvara Yoga, and then later in the fields of Kriyā-tantra, Caryā-tantra, and Yoga-tantra.

After his marriage, Badri Guruju and his wife Asamaya Bajrācārya obtained the Consecration of Ārya Avalokiteśvara, Cakrasaṃvara, Vajradevī, and Acala from Guru Anandamuni Bajrācārya of Kathmandu. After Asamaya's death, he married Tirthakumāri Bajrācārya of Patan.

Badri Guruju continued his spiritual development by going on a series of pilgrimages (called *pīṭha-sevā* or *pūrva-sevā*) to various Vajrayāna Buddhist sites in Nepal under the training of the Kathmandu Buddhist guru Bhajuratna Bajrācārya. He was given many special mantras and learned the *tri-samādhi* (yoga) of Acala from this same teacher. He later took initiation in the *tri-samādhi* practice of Cakrasaṃvara from Amoghabajra Bajrācārya. He also was initiated in the *dharmadhātu* mantra practices by Sakalananda Bajrācārya.

Over the past three decades, Badri Guruju has transmitted the consecrations he received—to Avalokitesvara, Cakrasaṃvara, Vajradevī, Acala, Dharmadhātu, and Vajradhātu—to hundreds of his Newar disciples belonging to Bajrācārya, Śākya, and Urāy castes. He has also transmitted the traditions of Cakrasaṃvara-samādhi, Acala-samādhiyoga, Dharmadhātu-samādhi, Vajradhātu-samādhi, Caṇḍālī-yoga, Balyārcana-yoga, Śmāśāna-yoga, and Utkranti-yoga to a select few disciples.

Badri Ratna has for decades been a prominent ritualist in major public rituals dedicated to the renovation of images and temples. These included the renovation of Khadga Yoginī in Sankhu, and the restorations at the great stūpa, Svayambhū. He also performed as well the essential secret rites at these sites as well. He is the recognized master of the secret *gaṇacakra-pūjā* in the traditions of the *Cakrasaṃvara, Hevajra, Mahāsaṃvarodaya*, and *Kālacakra Tantras*, and has performed these rites across the Kathmandu Valley.

Dedicated to the preservation and revitalization of his own tradition, Badri Guruju has edited more than fifty Buddhist ritual instruction manuals; the publication of these works brought uniformity in ritual performance among Kathmandu *Bajrācāryas*. He has also translated into Newari from Sanskrit many Buddhist narratives from the *avadānas*, *jātakas*, and *vrata* texts. This focus on popular literature has been lifelong, since from the age of fifteen he walked across the region's villages and cities to recount the tales of the future Buddha's previous lives. Large crowds will assemble to listen to his riveting, theatrical, renditions of these tales. Badri Guruju also worked to establish images of the Buddha, Bodhisattvas, *Prajñāpāramitā*, and stūpas to help people to develop their faith and moral practices.

To address the decline in the doctrinal understanding and ritual competence evident among the *Bajrācārya* ritualists in late twentieth century Nepal, in 1980 Badri Guruju established a Nepalese Buddhist ritual training center named the Bajrācārya Adhyana Maṇḍala. He trained young Bajrācāryas and a few of Śākyas in the performance of rituals, making sand maṇḍalas, astrology, preaching, and so on, according to his own vision of the future. Hundreds attended, and he enlisted other *Bajrācārya* pandits such as Divya Guruju (see earlier discussion) to teach them Sanskrit. This work continued more in a more organized and formal manner in 1990, when Badri Guruju introduced the same training at the Mahendra Sanskrit University in Kathmandu, which later added a Department of Buddhist Philosophy through his leadership.

Badri Guruju also established nearly half a dozen other Buddhist organizations to continue and preserve Newar Buddhist traditions of Nepal. He was honored for this work by His Majesty's Government of Nepal with the *Dhanavajra Rastriya Pratibha Puraskar* and *Gorakha Daksinabahu* awards. He has visited India, Bhutan, South Korea, and the United States. At the behest of the king of Bhutan, he performed funeral rites after the death of the late royal priest of Bhutan, Lama Dilgo Khyentse Rinpoche. In order to participate in the Buddha's birthday celebrations, he visited South Korea; he also visited the United States in 2003 as the main Newar master to perform rituals and bestow the first Newar Buddhist Vajradhātu initiations in America, as part of the "Circle of Bliss" Exhibition at the Los Angeles County Museum.

Conclusion: Nepalese Vajrayāna Buddhism in Contemporary Nepal

The Mahāyāna–Vajrayāna Buddhist tradition in South Asia crossed or blurred the lines of Hindu, Jain, and Buddhist traditions, probably as early as 500 CE in South Asia, affecting in subsequent centuries traditions across the region in many dimensions of belief and practice. Whether it really had its origins, as some of its texts suggest, on the peripheries of society and settlement, or among ascetics and others who ignored the caste system and Dharmaśāstra norms of gender, or was formatively influenced by Chinese alchemy traditions (White 1998), what is clear is that a new Buddhist lineage of discourse, yoga practices, and textual writing formed within its Mahāyāna monastic communities (Wedemeyer 2012).[120] It was the tantric Buddhist traditions that, by 1000 CE, when Buddhism was in decline in many regions, dominated in a new reformation of the tradition in the Pāla-Sena region of North India, as well as in Orissa and Nepal, where it then was adopted and underwent further development in Tibet (Davidson 2003, 2005).

By 1100, it seems clear that Buddhism in Nepal was in the midst of a process of reformation and domestication centered on Mahāyāna–Vajrayāna traditions that were being imported by Indic masters, and adopted by circles of both local and Tibetan practitioners.[121] As Jinah Kim has shown for the history of manuscript illumination found in North India and Nepal (2013), tantric paintings were inserted into *Prajñāparamitā* texts, and their placement reflects the conceptualization of the text as maṇḍala: Is this material cultural pattern a simulacrum for how the Pala–Sena–Nepal Vajrayāna tradition was grafted into Mahāyāna monasticism?

The records of Buddhism in the Kathmandu Valley after 1000 show that tantric initiation had become, as it is today, the carefully guarded possession of the elite groups in society: kings, priests (brahman and Bajrācārya), merchants, and virtuoso artists. It is certain that tantric traditions captured the imagination and shaped the elite's belief systems among Buddhists in Nepal. The thousands of ritual texts in the Kathmandu Valley archives far outnumber works devoted to philosophy, signifying the comparative scale of its popularity. Newar Buddhists for centuries have regarded mantras and *dhāraṇīs* as capable of giving extraordinary abilities to individuals by giving them access to great cosmic powers. The stories of the *siddhas* and *yoginīs* in the tantras recount how individuals seeking the experience of enlightenment also gain a host of supernormal powers (*siddhis*), from telekinesis to clairvoyance, from healing to harming enemies at a distance. It is natural that those with political power sought to use this exceptionally potent "classified" knowledge. Initiation into Newar Vajrayāna practices in later centuries, and certainly by the later Malla era, excluded members of the lower castes, since the saṅgha had, as we have seen, hardened into membership by birth only. So while there is a rhetoric of anomic philosophical belief in Vajrayāna Buddhism, directed to nirvāṇa-seeking individuals, the tantric Buddhist traditions in Newar society seemed to have been, since the Malla era, the cultural possession of the Kathmandu Valley's elite, both Hindu and Buddhist.

By 2015 in Nepal, the monarchy is finished, new avenues to wealth are being found, Kathmandu is staggering under an urban population growth rate that is the highest in Asia, and global media are affecting the knowledge horizons of Newar Buddhists. With hill in-migration, the Newars are now a minority in the Valley once dominated by their civilization. It is not surprising that different norms regarding hierarchy and status have been introduced, and that the singularity of traditional Newar Buddhism faces a host of challenges. Simply stated, the world that sustained the Vajrayāna tradition in the urban centers of the Kathmandu Valley since the Malla "Three Kingdoms" is no more.

Amidst contending Buddhist traditions in 2015 and the breakdowns of urban life in the Kathmandu Valley, the future of Newar Mahāyāna–Vajrayāna Buddhism is difficult to anticipate with any precision. Some challenges come from other Buddhist traditions. Present since the early twentieth century, Theravāda reformers introduced celibate monastic traditions in the Valley. At first their Newar exponents directly attacked the

Newar Mahāyāna–Vajrayāna traditions, winning many prominent householders, but alienating others. As one tract by an early Newar who took ordination fulminated:

> The Five Buddhas, Apāramitā, Karuṇāmaya, Tārā, Heruka, Cakrasaṃvara, Vajrasattva, etc. . . . these are all personified representations of metaphysical knowledge and ideas. The so-called teachers who made such representations on canvas or stones, instituted intricate rituals, and indulged in all kinds of luxuries such as meat, fish, wine, women [*sic*] which are specifically prohibited by the eight precepts. All of their rituals were for the purpose of fulfilling their selfish ends and are totally opposed to the fundamental principles of Buddhism. . . . Read and recite this mantra to this god or goddess and you will get all of these benefits, but reciting this secret mantra or showing the image to others in initiation and such and such bad things will befall you, saying such things to the innocent and ignorant believers is nothing more than casting dust in their eyes. (Dharmaloka 1959)

But by the 1960s confrontational incidents and anti-Vajrayāna publications subsided. The modernist Theravāda tradition has made *vipassanā* meditation a widespread experience in Newar society; but negative perceptions of the Theravādin movement as it has developed have also hindered its acceptance.[122] For different reasons, the expansion of Tibetan Buddhist monasticism in the Valley during this same period[123] has not reached many more Newar Buddhists. Here, again, there are social and cultural obstacles, not the least of which is language. Despite intermittent attempts to connect Newar Buddhists with prominent Tibetan teachers, this tradition remains outside the purview of most.

What is now clear is that the deep attachment Newars feel for their distinctive and venerable cultural traditions (festivals, life cycle rites, etc.)—which require the performance of Mahāyāna–Vajrayāna rituals and the presence of *Bajrācārya* ritualists—has also worked to preserve the older Buddhist tradition. Thus, the displacement of the older tradition by a successful missionary Theravāda movement has not played out as its exponents (or the scholars tracking its development) had projected.

Perhaps in response to the leadership of women in the Theravāda movement, or a result of growing education and awareness of the demands women are making globally for greater participation in public life, Newar women have sought and won acceptance in Newar Buddhist ritual life in areas that hitherto had been closed to them. Young unmarried girls in castes with traditional processional music groups (*bājans*), playing drums and accompanying percussion instruments, now commonly take part side by side with the boys, some as prominent members. A more surprising innovation has been the formation of recitation groups consisting of the wives of *Bajrācāyas* (*guru-mā*), who began training in 2005; 108 now gather to do public recitations of the *Pañcarakṣā*. A third marker of a growing assertiveness among Newar Buddhist women is a trend for individual women to take the tantric initiations (von Rospatt 2011a).

A number of new Buddhist organizations are endeavoring to conserve, promote, and reform Newar Mahāyāna–Vajrayāna Buddhism: The Nagarjuna Institute of Exact Methods was founded in 1980 as a center of Buddhist learning intended to serve the needs of and promote the traditional Buddhism that is indigenous to the Kathmandu Valley's Buddhist communities. Its founder, Min Bahadur Shakya, forged ties between Himalayan Buddhists, bringing together both Newar and Tibetan tradition lineages. As one of its early pamphlets stated, "For reinstatement of the glorious traditions and lineage of Nepalese Buddhism we have to seek the support from the four major schools of Tibetan Buddhism."[124] Accordingly, and with the initial support of Taiwanese Buddhist organizations, the Institute organizes a variety of meditation courses led by Nepalese and Tibetan Masters who have taught Mārgakrama *(Lam Rim)*, *Pūrvagata Caryā* (*Ngondro* Practice), Avalokiteśvara *Sādhana, Bodhicitta Bhāvana*, and *Nirvikalpa Samādhi*. The Institute conducts classes on Buddhist doctrine, engages in translation projects, and publishes texts in Nepali, English, Sanskrit, Nepal Bhasa, and Tibetan. It periodically hosts seminars and symposiums on Tibetology and Nepalese Buddhist studies.

Founded in Patan in 1988 with support by members of the Shishin-kai Organization of Japan, the Lotus Research Center has sought, as its website states, "to preserve and promote Buddhist culture of Nepal Mandal,"[125] through programs bringing together Nepali intellectuals, "local gentry," and both national and international scholars to promote research, seminars, conferences, and educational training. It regularly publishes a journal, prints new editions of sacred Buddhist scriptures, and is building a digital archive of resources on the cultural heritage of the Nepal Mandala. The Lotus Research Center launched Lotus Academic College for Buddhist Studies in 2007, providing postgraduate courses on Buddhist Studies. It has received support from patrons from Taiwan and Korea.

In Patan, the training of informed *Bajrācāryas* has been undertaken by a new group, the *Bajrācārya-pūjāvidhi-adhyayana Samhiti* (Committee for the Study of the Bajrācārya Rituals), and led by Buddha Ratna Bajracarya of the great monastery Kvā Bāhā. The Committee offers periodic ritual training courses to young men, as well as training to young Bajrācārya women, regarding their role as ritual assistants. It has been active as well in organizing large *vrata* gatherings, as elsewhere, in series at important holy sites.

In Kathmandu, two Bajrācāryas have emerged as leaders in revitalization efforts. The first is Yagyamanpati Bajracarya, who has since 2004 offered classes to householders on Vajrayāna tradition, discussing the purposes and philosophical meanings underlying the rituals, taught from his home in Iku Bāhā classes in tantric yoga practice based on Cakrasaṃvara visualization, and the chanting of tantric songs. His students, primarily educated Śākyas, Bajrācāryas, and Urāy, formally organized the *Bauddhadarshana-dhyayana-puca* ("Buddhist Teachings Study Group") that holds regular classes on these subjects.

The second Kathmandu center of revitalization in Kathmandu was initiated by Naresh Man Bajracharya (co-author of this chapter), the first Newar Bajrācārya to also complete a PhD degree in Buddhist Studies, who has established several organizations to address different needs in the local Buddhist community. The Tri-Ratna Kosha ("Triratna Fund") provides scholarships to students studying Buddhism and recognizes the great past Newar masters (discussed earlier). He also established, with Korean support, the Nepalko Bauddha Dharma Samgha in 1996 to organize Bare Chuyegu initiation programs for the hitherto excluded male children of inter-caste marriages in Kathmandu and Narayanghat. The concomitant founding of a new Newar saṅgha, a "Jina-saṅgha," and the dedication of a building as its own *vihāra* have not resulted in an active monastic center or meritorious offerings by the community. Dr. Bajracharya also founded the Traditional Nepalese Buddhist Association,[126] the first international Newar organization, with branches in Kathmandu, Bhaktapur, Kirtipur, and Maryland (USA). It has organized lectures on Vajrayāna belief and practice as well as retreats dedicated to *Saptavidhānuttara* Meditation, *Acala abhiṣeka,* and *trisamādhi* yoga, *Cakrasaṃvara-Vajravārāhī abhiṣeka,* and *Caṇḍālī-yoga.* Programs—open to all individuals, irrespective of their caste—that have offered lesser forms of tantric initiation, such as the six-syllable Avalokiteśvara *abhiṣeka,* and have attracted hundreds of Newars from across the Valley, as well as Westerners.[127] Its branch in the United

States has begun to schedule *vratas*, *caitya* making, and other rituals to coincide with visits by Naresh Man Bajracharya, for the first time internationalizing Newar Buddhism. Seeking to demonstrate the bodhisattva ideal, this organization also collects funds to hold periodic free health clinics, and the distribution of medicine, food, and clothing. Since 2011, Dr. Bajracharya has also focused on building a distinctively Newar monastery in the international monastic park in Lumbini.[128]

Perhaps the most surprising development to emerge in recent years is a resurgent interest in the priestly performance of, and householder participation in, common Vajrayāna rituals. The attempts by prominent *Bajrācārya* ritualists in Patan and Kathmandu to make accessible authoritative ritual guidebooks for their entire communities was brought out of the medieval hand-copying era by the technology of the printing press after the Shah restoration of 1951. Many of the leading *Bajrācārya* whose lives were sketched in the preceding section quickly took advantage of the new technology. With the revolution of 1991, among the cultural changes that ensued was opening the former Hindu/brahmanical monopoly on personnel and content at Mahendra Sanskrit College to Buddhist thought and ritual study, leading to a surge in young students and the publication of new textbooks to standardize their educations. These efforts represented an attempt to meet the increasing criticism by Newar householders who regard the venerable, ritually dominated Newar Buddhism as poorly presented, philosophically opaque, and spiritually lacking. Especially in Kathmandu,[129] the younger *Bajrācāryas*, aware of these complaints and infused with a sense of Newar cultural restoration, have sought to reform the traditional status quo by upgrading and highlighting the Buddhist elements in the life-cycle rites, stressing a "revised standard edition" of the major rituals in their repertoire.[130] The press and expectation is that instead of mumbling mantras carelessly or passing over ritual text instruction to "explain the Dharma" at certain points in the *pūjā*, the *Bajrācārya* take the time to utter precise *stotras* and instruct the disciples on why—philosophically, morally, and spiritually—they are doing the ritual. This has carried over into tantric initiations as well, in consecrations that were often done for the raw sense of empowerment, but conveyed little of the purpose or deeper Buddhist meanings.

Certain venerable traditions have been revived for renewed attention by householders led by activist *Bajrācāryas*. The practice of the *sapta-vidhānuttara* ritual, detailed earolier, performed at prominent holy

Buddhist locations in the Valley, has grown dramatically in all the above-mentioned revitalization groups; several sponsors have even organized this ritual as part of a pilgrimage to sacred sites such as Lumbini, and in India. Naresh Man Bajracharya and his association have introduced new forms of traditional practice uniting Buddhists across the Kathmandu Valley: a *Nāmasaṅgīti* festival and a restructured Pañcadāna Festival to reinvigorate the day of donations made to the Newar saṅgha held during the holy month of Gumlā. The division between the major cities in the Valley that once led to their isolation from one another culturally and in the work of Vajrayāna Buddhist teachers has declined as well.[131]

The underlying strength of the older Mahāyāna–Vajrayāna tradition is its thorough integration into Newar lifestyle, urban space, and family life. The cultural nationalism that pervades Newar communities in the Valley—the expression of which has risen since the 1991 revolution—finds its ongoing expression in remaining faithful to the venerable and distinctly Newar traditions. The vibrancy of the centripetal draw of Newar Buddhist identity has led, in recent years, to an increase in the number of upper-caste Newar individuals who are eligible and eager to take Newar tantric initiation. This interest, though found in only a small part of the Buddhist population, reflects the interest to connect on a deep level with the traditions of spiritual practice created centuries ago by Newar *Bajrācārya* masters.

What is certain is that, as the Buddha taught, life is always in transition, and so is the Newar tradition of Vajrayāna Buddhism today. The Theravāda and Tibetan competitors, the traditions they have introduced, and the passing from the scene of the *Bajrācārya* elders who resisted modernization have all opened up space for younger Newar Buddhist religious leaders—among Bajrācāryas and Śākyas—to adapt their Mahāyāna–Vajrayāna tradition to the rapidly changing world around them. Their number is relatively small, but they are attracting disciples and wealthy patrons from their own community. Newar Vajrayāna revitalizers are discovering for themselves the great richness in texts and ritual found in their venerable traditions; and they are finding that the educated, prosperous householders in their cities are eager to both explore their Buddhist heritage and support initiatives to recover its vibrancy. Less conservative in regard to gender roles and caste ideology, groups in the Newar Buddhist community today are seeking to find compelling new interpretations of Vajrayāna tradition as a foundation on which to center their lives.

APPENDIX I

Dated Buddhist Texts from Medieval Nepal

Date	Text	Other Information	Source
998	1,008 verse pp	Skt Text in Sakya Tibet, from Patan	Petech Medieval Hist Nepal, 40
1008	1,008 pp		"
1015	1,008 pp		"
1036	Lalitavistara		"
1039	Saddharmapuṇḍarīka		
1045	Catuṣpīṭhanibandha	Padmacakramaha-vihara?	p 41
1056	Saddharmapuṇḍarīka	Skt Text in Sakya, Tibet	43
1063	Pañcarakṣā	Copied in Patan	44
1065	Saddharmapuṇḍarīka	Cambridge Lib, copied?	"
1066	Saddharmapuṇḍarīka	Cambridge Lib, copied?	"
1069	1,008 pp	Skt text in Nor, Tibet	"
1071	1,008 pp	Asiatic Soc of Bengal	"
1078	Bodhicaryāvatāra-pañjikā	Patan	"
1082	Saddharmapuṇḍarīka	Cakavati Mahavihara?	46
1084	Sekanirdeśapañjikā	Buddhist? "Śrī Vajra" in colophon	48
1093	Saddharmapuṇḍarīka	Patan copy	
1093	1,008 Pp	Patan copy	
1099	Ārya-Uṣṇīṣavijaya Nāma-Dhāraṇī	Dhulikhel	
1123	Vasundhārā- Dhāraṇī	?	55
1120	1,008 pp	Patan	
1121	Nāmasaṅgīti	?	
1138	Pañcarakṣā	found in Sakya, Tibet/c=?	60
1140	Pañcarakṣā	Patab	61
1141	Mitapadāpañjikā	Dakshina-Vihara, Patan	
1143	Nāmasaṅgīti	Sakya, Tibet, copied in KTM	
1148	1008 pp	?	63
1155	Pañcarakṣā	Ananda Mahavihara/ c=?	
1164	1,008 pp	?	
1165	1,008 pp	"Gandigulma"	64
1165	1,008 pp	KTM	65
1166	1,008 pp	?	66

(continued)

Date	Text	Other Information	Source
1166	Gaṇḍavyūha	?	66
1173	Dharma-samuccaya	Citra-Vihara c=?	67
1180	Śrī Mahāmanthāna Mahābhairava Tantra	?	71
1184	Manthāna Bhairava Tantra	?	73
1192	Pañcarakṣā	?	75
1196	Kāraṇḍavyūha	Patan	76
MALLA ERA			
1200	1,008 pp	Nor, Tibet	
1216	Sādhanasamuccaya	?	84
1216	Kriyāsaṃgraha		
1217	Kriyāsaṃgraha	?	
1219	Vasundhārā Ṣoḍaśakalpa		
1220	Bajrāvalī-Nāmamaṇḍopāyika		
1246	1,008 pp	Patan	87
1247	Pañcarakṣā	?	88
1252	Kriyāsaṃgraha-pañjikā	?	
1253	1,008 pp	?	88
1257	Kāraṇḍavyūha	?	90
1282	Pañcarakṣā	fr Zva-lu, Tibet	96
1282	Gaṇḍavyūha Sūtra	Sakya, Tibet	96
1283	8,000 pp	Sakya, Tibet/ c=KTM	96
1284	1,008 pp	Sakya, Tibet/ c=Patan	97
1297	Caṇḍamahāroṣaṇa Tantra-pañjikā	?	98
1302	Avadānakalpalatā	?	"
1360	Ārya-Amoghapāśa-Sūtra	?	125
1371	Mudrārākṣasa	Patan	125
1374	Pañcarakṣā	Patan	
1375	Mudrārākṣasa	Patan	126
1384	Pañcarakṣā	?	132
1386	Pañcarakṣā	?	
1389	Pañcarakṣā	Vacca Vihara	134
1391	Kāraṇḍavyūha	?	
1395	? pp	Bktpur	137
1392	Nāmasaṅgītiṭippanī	Navakot	139r
1410	Mahākarmavibhaṅga	KTM	155
1429	Bajrāvalī	Patan	
1470	Pañcarakṣā	?	
1476	Pañcarakṣā	KTM	
1479	Pañcarakṣā	Ktm	165
--	----------------------------	----------------------------------	-------------------

Summaries of Texts copied in Nepal (998–1479 CE)

Pañcarakṣā: 14
Saddharmapuṇḍarīka: 6 early
Kāraṇḍavyūha: 3
Nāmasaṅgīti: 3
Tantras:
Mahāmanthāna [Mahā]bhairava Tantra (1180)
Sādhanasamuccaya (1216)
Bajrāvalī (1220)
Caṇḍamahāroṣaṇa Tantra-pañjikā (1297)
Ritual Texts:
Kriyāsaṃgraha: 3
Dharani Texts:
Ārya-Uṣṇīṣavijaya Nāma-Dhāraṇī (1099)
Vasundhārā- Dhāraṇī (1123, 1429): 2
Narratives:
Lalitavistara (1036)
Saddharmapuṇḍarīka (1039)
Gaṇḍavyūha (1166)
Kāraṇḍavyūha (1196)
Avadānakalpalatā (1302)

Notes

1. In this chapter, we use the locally standard "Bajrācārya" (Sanskrit *vajrācārya*) to refer both to the caste name of the Newar Buddhist sangha priests as well as their religious role.
2. A larger, more comprehensive co-authored book on the history and practices of Newar Buddhist traditions is in preparation by the authors.
3. Due to a variety of reasons—the country's limited access to Westerners until 1951, the impact of the negative impressions expressed by noted scholars, the sociology of Western Buddhist Studies toward canonical traditions, and the resulting academic preference for Tibetan studies over all Himalayan traditions—progress in the study of Buddhism in the Kathmandu Valley has been very slow.
4. Numerous textual accounts assert that Tibetan monks began visiting the Valley after the first missionization of Tibet by monks from the Gangetic Plains. *The Blue Annals* (Roerich 1996, 41–42) record that the monk gSal-snan, an emissary to King Khri-Sron-lde-btsan, visited Nepal in 755.

5. For copying these works, Newar literati devised over ten calligraphic scripts, especially for manuscripts used for ritual "book *pūjā*" purposes: *Newā Lipi* since the ninth century, and *Rañjana* since the fourteenth century.
6. An inscribed sculptural fragment of a more recently discovered image has been assigned an earlier date by Tamot and Alsop (2001), back to the Kushan era. They assume it to be of local production. An accidental find lacking in archaeological context or scientific dating, this sole artifact is insufficient for assuming direct ties with the Kushans.
7. Newar society still is ordered by these institutions called *guthi* in local parlance (Toffin 1975).
8. Located on a pillar in a village outside Patan, and composed by a poet named Anuparamena who is addressing the *Mahābhārata*, it reads: "Repudiated by false thinkers and logicians as well as the Saugatas, who are surrounded by evil, the three Vedas find in you, the Lord of the widespread word, refuge as a river finds refuge in the ocean" (Riccardi 1980, 272). This represents, of course, only one data point, the view of one person.
9. There is one instance of the term *bhoṭṭa* used that could mean Tibet or any people of the Himalayan highlands. Newar trade and artistic ties with Tibet are asserted in certain historical records only as early as 1000 CE (Lewis 1997). Chinese records report an imperial expedition sent to the Gangetic Plains in 648 to avenge a diplomat's mistreatment, but there is nothing in the Licchavi inscriptions mentioning the Chinese in the Kathmandu Valley.
10. Riccardi (1980, 280n65).
11. Examples of similar duties are also assigned to residents of Hindu temples called *maṇḍalis*.
12. Riccardi (1980, 272). The name of this *vihāra* is both peculiar and puzzling.
13. Schopen (1979, 2000).
14. Riccardi (1980, 273).
15. Acharya's study (2008) represents a useful, critical re-evaluation of the key epigraphic sources for ancient society in the Nepal Valley, and on its earliest records of Buddhism there. What undermines this new consideration of primary data, however, is a series of tendentious analytical positions taken on the basis of a single data point in the service of this revisionist conclusion. Examples of this practice include the conclusion that there was a "Mahāmuni cult" implied in one inscription or that the teaching of the *pāramitās* was present, although the term is not, in fact, found. Most problematic is the uncritical, undefined use of the word "cult." It is especially questionable historiographical method to move from one epigraphic reference to Sukhāvatī—that includes only a single, simple mention to attendant celestial bodhisattvas—and then link this to the extant texts found many centuries later in Nepal's Buddhist archives. Together these cannot establish the historical presence of the "Sukhāvatī cult" in ancient Nepal. This is so not least because one cannot assume that the mere existence of a text found in

the library proves that it was a working text or the basis of a "cult" in a Buddhist community.

16. There have been only three archaeological research programs ever undertaken in the Kathmandu Valley: in 1965 (S. B. Deo 1968), 1984–1986 (Silvi and Verardi 1984, 1986, 1989), and 1987–1988 (Khanal and Riccardi 2007). Finds in the last include objects of pre-Licchavi material culture similar to Kushan finds to the south and west. One terracotta seal closely resembles those found across south Asia; it shows a large stūpa surrounded by four smaller ones, and with the standard "*Hetu* . . ." couplet summary of the Buddhist Dharma.
17. Preliminary inquiries into the impact of Tibetan sources, teachers, and institutions on Newar Buddhism are found in Decleer (1994–1995), Lewis and Jamspal (1988), and Lewis (1989, 1996). The paucity of systematic or published studies in the Tibetan sources still make any firm conclusions on this issue little more than conjecture.
18. Decleer's article on this subject (1994–1995) does not match Davidson's, especially in providing the detailed information about the Newar teacher.
19. These are important data points, highlighting both John Locke's (1985, 187–188) and Theodore Riccardi's (1980) insistence that householder monk monasteries might go far back in Newar Buddhism's history, just as they were known in ancient Kashmir at the time of the writer Kalhana (1148 CE), as reported in his historical work, *The Rājataraṅgiṇī* (Stein 1979, 73–74). The recent study on family matters in Indian monasticism by Shayne Clarke (2014) casts doubt on many assumed historical patterns in South Asian Buddhist history. In one place in this ground-breaking monograph he writes, ". . . mainstream Buddhism itself is starting to look surprisingly and increasingly like what we see in later Mahayana Buddhism in Nepal, for instance" (155).
20. Dan Martin has discussed a text by Sakya Pandita, who wrote around 1232 CE about a Newar *siddha* named "Ka-ru-dzin" who "had his *siddha*-hood dissolve" (1996, 26); a story collection from about 1260 CE recounts that a *siddha* of this name was bested in a display of *siddhi* powers by Rinchen Zang-po; yet a third source, Chag-Lotsaba, writing in 1260, has the same Newar become possessed, "put a meditation hat on his head, stuck some bird feathers in it, dressed in fur, and made the announcement at Bsamyas, 'I am Padma [Sambhava],' and taught innumerable wrong teachings" (26–29).
21. Hindu tantras appearing in this assembly are the *Niśvāsākhya Mahā-Tantra* (extant 1056), *Tattvasadbhāva Tantra* (1097), *Pratiṣtha Tantra* (1134), *Kālottara Tantra* (1168), *Vāmakeśvara Tantra* (1388), the *Gupta-Kāli Tantra* (1400), a *Guhya-Kāli Tantra* (1406), and the *Netrajñānārṇava-Mahātantra* (1419).
22. There are questions about the "Buddhist" versus "Hindu" identity of many tantras and the problem of overlapping genres (i.e., many ritual texts have narratives in them, and then narrative texts can in places introduce ritual practices; see, for example, Wedemeyer 2012). The question still remains, of course, of

what a "working text" did in society or what it was used for in context. The two most numerous attested works here are cases in point: the *Prajñāpāramitā* was used, and copied, not to be read for meaning so much as to be the object of *pusta pūjā* ("book ritual"), an Indic practice still extant in the Valley to this day. Similarly, with the *Pañcarakṣā*, Buddhists place a copy inside their houses for the protection its mere presence offered to the building and its inhabitants.

23. The lack of many monuments definitively attested to being in existence before the fourteenth century can be attributed to the profound destructiveness of this invasion, about which the *Gopālarājavaṃśāvalī* reports that the invaders lit and kept fires going for five straight days.
24. While the work on the text itself makes an important contribution to Newar Buddhist studies, Tuladhar-Douglas's treatment of its era of composition, and many other historical conclusions, are too often insufficiently documented to be convincing. The proposition that the composition and acceptance of a single text, or group of texts, are sufficient to explain the changes in any Buddhist tradition in history is simply not tenable. "Tradition" includes much more than texts that few can read, and the historical imagination of change cannot ignore the scope of ritual, institutional economics, and patrons. In the case of Nepal, all attempts to reach a clear understanding of Buddhism in the Malla era are highly speculative until the large corpus of inscriptions from the Valley are analyzed. One attempt to define the breadth of variables in a Buddhist anthropology of a given society is found in Lewis (1997).
25. The summary depends on the synopsis in Tuladhar-Douglas (2006). One looks forward to his fulfilling his intention (36n6) to publish a scholarly translation of this work.
26. Curiously, Tuladhar-Douglas's summary of Chapter XVI has this mantra bestowed by what he characterizes, without clarification, as "an *upāsaka Buddha*" (2006, 24).
27. On these traditions in general, see Lewis (2000). On the modern practice of the *uposatha vrata*, see Locke (1989).
28. But even this text does not capture the full richness of the Avalokiteśvara traditions extant in the Kathmandu Valley.
29. This is an image displayed in Nepal from the time of the Patan king Shrīnivāsa Malla (c. 1670). In Chapter XVI, the cosmological totality of Avalokiteśvara is conveyed by the claim that there is a world system in each pore of his skin.
30. The term "*Svayambhū Purāṇa*" is found only in the first folio of most extant mss. The term is not found in the earliest archived text and even in the last colophon, where usually a text's title is usually mentioned. In the *Svayambhū Purāṇa*, in fact, each chapter ends with as follows: "*Svayambhūbhattarakoddese* . . . such and such . . . *patala samāptam.*" If the *Purāṇa* title is a later imposition, it is consistent with the pattern of Newar Buddhist sites and texts being marked by Hindu-devoted elites as in fact Hindu in essence. The cultural influences

of the brahmanical literary traditions in Malla Nepal remain almost completely unexamined in modern scholarship.

31. According to preliminary studies, there are five different recensions in Sanskrit (Levi 1905, 1: 210), three in Newari (Shakya 1977; Brinkhaus 1987). The eight-chapter version was translated into Tibetan. A useful, recent publication based on a Newari version, with English introduction and chapter summary, is found in Shakya and Bajracharya (2010).
32. Most manuscripts of the text call this figure "*mañjudevācārya*" who in some texts is the *nirmāṇakāya* incarnation of Mañjuśrī.
33. This account states that Mañjuśrī came to Nepal from "Mahā-Cīna," that is, China. This clearly reflects the Nepal Valley Buddhist elite's assimilation of the remarkable pan-Asian awareness of the cult of Mañjuśrī that formed and was associated with the northern Chinese holy mountain Wutai Shan. So strong was this recognition, and the pursuit of visionary experiences there, that monks from across India undertook the arduous journey on the silk routes to make their pilgrimages to this mountain in Shanxi Province. Recent accounts highlight this trans-regional connection between India and China (Sen 2004). The same paradigm of Buddhist territorial definition in this form is found in Khotan, which led Brough (1948) to speculate about a connection between these two centers. Decleer (1998) more cogently argues that both Nepal's and Khotan's accounts were likely based upon common Indic narratives.
34. The summary that follows is based on Shakya and Bajracharya (2010, 33–50).
35. Using Tibetan sources skillfully to decode the identity of the *siddhas* cited in the *Svayambhū Purāṇa*, Hubert Decleer (1998) has connected the Dharmaśrīmitra narrative, his revelation of the *Nāmasaṅgīti* text, and its related tantra to propose a new understanding of the text's historical composition. A well-known *siddha* by the name of Buddhaśrījñāna undergoes a similar experience to that found in Nepalese text, an episode demonstrating how tantric meditation is infinitely more valuable spiritually than scholarship. He found a master and gained initiation in the *Guhyasamāja Tantra*, and the maṇḍala of Mañjuśrī. So this story in the text is really about "the introduction of Vajrayana tradition into the Kathmandu Valley, and of the Yoga Tantras and Anuttara Father Tantra in particular" (1998, 17). Decleer then turns to the second major figure, Śāntaśrī or Śāntikara. Again he finds a congruent story in Tāranātha's history concerned with Vāgīśvara-kīrti, a noted Bajrācārya master who was an accomplished resident at Nālanda and Vikramaśīla, and a specialist in the *Cakrasaṃvara Tantra*. Hubert Decleer's conclusion untangles many of the knots for interpreting of the *Svayambhū Purāṇa*, noting that its chief task was to authenticate the central Vajrayāna lineages in their formulation before their arrival in Nepal. It does so, he concludes, "by establishing the source of the transmission for the chief Vajrayana lineages of Father Tantra and Mother Tantra, i.e. by pointing in the direction of their common origin: the prestigious Buddhist University of Vikrama-shila, where

both Dharma-shri-mitra (alias Buddha-shri-jnana) and Shantikara Acarya (alias Vagishvara-kirti) hailed from" (1998, 18).

36. The study of Newar Buddhism has been vexed with the failure of several generations of scholars to publish reputed inscription collections from Nepal, critical editions or translations of this and other texts, and many other materials related to these central sources for studying the history of this tradition.

37. Groundbreaking work on the sociocultural and political context of tantric traditions in post-Gupta India by Ron Davidson (2002) has greatly advanced scholarly imagination of this era and of the Vajrayāna tradition's formation. As he notes frequently in this monograph, however, much remains to be discovered to enable confident historical assertions. As Gellner noted after this work's publication (2004), *Indian Esoteric Buddhism: A Social History of the Tantric Movement* omits the Kathmandu Valley from his case studies or analysis. Some discussion of Newar Buddhism is found in Davidson's subsequent volume, *The Tibetan Renaissance: Tantric Buddhism in the Rebirth of Tibetan Culture* (2005). The lack of an as yet clear understanding of Vajrayāna tradition in the Gangetic Plains makes it impossible to analyze the Newar domestication of this tradition with certainty.

38. As Robert Miller noted, "This responsibility may he thought of as community service. Thus, (the [Mahāyāna] monk) rejects complete release from the cycle of existence, choosing instead to return again and again in the world in order to aid others in attaining release.... Since the layman is unable to pursue enlightenment directly, the sangha ... is obliged to find a means by which he can pursue it indirectly" (1961, 430).

39. By far, the most common manuscript genres in Newar Buddhist literature created from this era onward were the popular narratives (*jātakas* and *avadānas*) and ritual texts. "Folklorists" in the Newar *sangha* collected, redacted, and "transcreated" (to use Kamal Prakash Malla's apt term) the classical tales from the *Jātakamālā, Avadānaśataka,* and *Mahāvastu.* Some were extracted to stand alone due to their popularity such as the *Siṃhalasārthabāhu Avadāna,* the *Maṇicūḍa Avadāna,* and the *Vīrakūśa Avadāna;* such texts have been used up to the present day by *pandit*-storytellers who attract audiences for evening tellings during the Newar Buddhist monsoon holy month, *Gumlā.*

40. The new English translation of Burnouf's (2010) work is a major contribution to Newar Buddhist studies. While the excellent French scholar worked on what he thought was the texts' pertinence to Indian Buddhism, his translations and analyses are valuable for their insights on the Newar Buddhist tradition.

41. One indication of the spread of the importance of this textual culture, and of Rāma as a ruling idea, is the number of sculptures of Agastya in the Valley dating to the Malla period, This archetypal *ṛṣi* and sage is found in the *Rāmāyaṇa* and is associated with the expansion of Hindu tradition (e.g., Bolon 1991).

42. Only in Patan did Buddhist leaders consistently secure strong political power. Even there, however, its later Malla kings built impressive new temples to Hindu gods such as Viṣṇu and Kṛṣṇa.
43. Brinkhaus (1987, 113ff).
44. If the required duties that endured into the twentieth century for the royal cult of Taleju date back until this period, two Buddhist merchant castes, the Tulādhars and Kansakārs, had to supply ritual dancers and horn players (respectively) when the annual rituals for Talegu were being performed in the palace (see Lewis 1995, 52–53, 69–70).
45. It is far beyond the scope of this chapter to expand on the treatment of this complex Newar tradition. In modern times, Newar *śākta* priests, Karmācāryas, do the main rituals associated involving the royal *kumārī* with the cult of Durgā-Taleju; but there are also Buddhist *Bajrācāryas* associated with the palace that perform exoteric and esoteric rituals involving her. The antiquity of these connections remains uncertain. There is also a Newar Buddhist tradition of having virgin girls, also called *kumārīs*, selected from saṅgha families, and they take part in Newar monastic rituals. Here, the girls are considered the human representation of *prajñā*, just as Mahāyāna scriptures symbolized this salvific insight, or wisdom, anthropomorphically as the goddess Prajñāpāramitā. There are only a few Newar monasteries that still have an affiliated *kumārī* today. Their presence is part of the *thasihna-pūjā* and the secret esoteric *ahoratra homa* ritual. As part of the latter, the *kumārī* is expected to make predictions about the future.
46. Even the often copied, Nepal-composed *Śrīmat-Paśupati Purāṇa*, a text that is primarily dedicated to the narrative of how Śiva as Paśupati came to the KTM Valley, contains this account (Brinkhaus 1987, 7).
47. Major figures from the Sanskrit *purāṇas* written in India are found in these stories, as brahman authors in the Valley composed texts that drew from the classical tradition: the sage Nārada is described as coming to Nepal, narrating previous events and coaching the gods to victory over the demon; Garuda appears to render help in ensuring the success of the Valley creation; and Kṛṣṇa establishes and worships liṅgas in the Valley. The texts describe the Himalayan foothills landscape, and that the ancient mountain and temple at Chāngu Nārayan is Kṛṣṇa's abode.
48. The Buddhist version of this formula is found in the texts discussed earlier, and is a subject to be revisited in the next section.
49. They are mentioned in chapters XV, XVI, and XXVI of this work.
50. This text engages with the *Svayambhū Purāṇa*, noting that "the *deva*" Buddha came from Mahācīna and that the site is to be visited. In this case, there is no attempt at enfolding this site into the Śaiva sacred order.
51. The accounts have him come from Kāmarūpa, Assam, to save the Valley from a famine induced by a drought caused by Gorakhnātha, who had captured the Valley's rainmaking *nāgas*. The establishment of a temple in Patan, and the

annual celebration of the yearly festival in that Malla capital, is likely part of this innovation (see Slusser 1982, 365–380).

52. Shakya (1993) has published a *caryagita* dedicated to this form of Avalokiteśvara, noting that it is attributed to the composition of a *siddha* named Advayavajra (978–1053 CE) in Nepal.
53. *Gopālarājavaṃśāvali* (Vajracarya and Malla 1985, 145). Interestingly, the royal patron was the invading Malla king from the Western Nepal, who also made offerings to Bunga-dya, the Avalokiteśvara of Patan and Bungamati, as well as Śiva-Paśupati.
54. Though in twentieth-century Kathmandu, records indicate that the celebration has been done only once every twelve years. The royal participation in this Newar Buddhist event was continued by the Shahs until the demise of King Birendra in 2001.
55. The elegant translation is found in Bledsoe (2004, 238).
56. The data is all derived from Locke (1985). A systematic culling all of his work, with that in other sources—primarily the Malla inscriptions—is an obvious desideratum for starting to discern the institutional history of Newar Buddhism.
57. A comparative study of "married monks" is especially need for Buddhist historiography. Recent studies by Shayne Clarke (2009a, 2009b, 2014) on Vinaya passages concerned with monastic celibacy have indicated that the early saṅgha's boundaries were more complex that hitherto imagined. The modern Japanese saṅgha's transformation into a married patrilineage community is well documented, the result of nineteenth-century political dictates. A more proximate comparison might be with the married Nyingma-pa Tibetan lineages still present across the rural Himalayan peoples. It may of course be the case that the Newar transition to a married saṅgha is *sui generis*.
58. The term *bare* derives from the Sanskrit term *vande* or *vandanā*, an ancient Indic term of respect for monks.
59. Locke (1985, 317) once noted a case of a brahman, Dhanajaya Upādhyāya, who was ordained in Lagan Bāhā "five generations ago," during the Shah era.
60. While the term "Buddhist Brahmins," coined long ago by Stephen Greenwold (1974) for their modern successors, neglects some crucial portions of their identity, when considering Newar Buddhist rituals, their service today is indeed brahman-like.
61. Richard Widdess, in a study of Newar tantric dance tradition (*cacā*; Skt *caryā*), has identified what is likely the general pattern across various cultural elements in Kathmandu Valley Vajrayāna Buddhism: "The assumption that Newar *cacā* is a living continuation of the Indian *caryā* . . . can be reconstructed, three phases can be distinguished: Phase I: the 'Indian Buddhism phase,' during which the *caryā* genre developed in India, and which came to an end with the disappearance of Buddhism from North India around the fourteenth century. Phase II: the 'Newar Buddhism' phase, where *caryā*/*cacā* became absorbed into the ritual

practice of a priestly caste . . . Phase III: the 'revival' phase, in progress at the present day, where *caryā/cacā* has also become a non-ritual art-form" (2004, 8).

62. On this ritual, see Lewis and Emmrich (2012)
63. See extensive treatment in Lewis (1995).
64. Newar writers were arrested for publishing in any language other than Nepali, the national language. Chittadhar Hridaya, while imprisoned for publishing a short poem on his mother's death, composed his greatest work, *Sugata Saurabha*. See Lewis and Tuladhar (2011).
65. The most important study on this movement is found in Levine and Gellner (2005). The authors' prediction that the Theravada reform movement would eclipse traditional Newar Mahāyā-Vajrayāna Buddhism has yet to be seen.
66. One old and important specialization the Newar sangha of Shākyas and Bajrācārya has long undertaken is fashioning jewelry, ornaments, and Buddhist images.
67. In the Newar Buddhist geography, there are no special ritual ties accorded to the Bauddha stūpa that towers over the north-central Kathmandu Valley, and which for the last 600 years has been recognized in the Tibetan religious world as a pilgrimage destination of great power (Dowman 1982; Ehrhard 1990). Reputed to be a Licchavi monument originally founded by King Manadeva, Newars have their own term for this site—Khasti—but neither Kathmandu nor Patan Buddhists visit it as part of any of their extant traditional community practices.
68. What is striking, especially amidst all the texts stored and copied in the Kathmandu Valley, is the near total absence of Vinaya texts in the Newar archives, a striking contrast with their presence in the Tibetan textual tradition. As Funayama Tōru of Kyoto University has noted (in a talk at the Harvard Buddhist Studies forum, December 9, 2011), we usually understand that Mahāyāna Buddhists did not have their own monastic code (*vinaya*) throughout the history of Indian Buddhism. On the other hand, medieval Chinese Buddhists widely held the idea of Mahāyānavinaya (*dasheng lü* 大乘律) in the sense of a text/texts based on bodhisattva precepts (*bodhisattvaśīla, pusa jie* 菩薩戒), as is clearly evident from Chinese Buddhist catalogs. Is this idea a result of a Chinese misunderstanding? Naturally this question is also concerned with the Sinification of Buddhism. In this talk, Dr. Funayama explored the significance of Mahāyāna precepts with a special focus on the *Scripture of Brahma's Net* (*Fanwang jing* 梵網經) and pointed out that this well-known apocryphal sutra played a critical role for the establishment of the term *dasheng lü* in China. Further, he wanted to verify that basically the same idea, if not entirely identical, is found in the Skt. *Bodhisattvabhūmi*, the most significant text for bodhisattva precepts in India. It seems true that early Yogācārins in India had strong aspirations for the composition of a special vinaya for bodhisattvas—the book of bodhisattva precepts—as an equivalent of the orthodox vinaya and that such an intention was more emphasized by the composition of the *Scripture of Brahma's Net* in China.

69. NMB prefers not to see Buddhist rites as "versions of Hindu *saṃskāras.*" In his view, "*saṃskāras* are natural phenomena; both Hindu and Buddhist practitioners have accepted them and developed ritual in their own mode."
70. On this topic in late Indic Buddhism in NE India and Nepal, see the new study of illustrated manuscripts by Jinah Kim (2013).
71. Claims that "Indian Buddhism died out" defy geography and ignore the unbroken and ongoing survival of Newar Buddhism.
72. Śrī Ratnaketu Mahāvihāra is a Sanskrit name of a *vihāra* that is located in a northeastern neighborhood in Kathmandu city. It is popularly known as Jhwā Bāhā in local (Newari) language, but this name is not a translation of the Sanskrit.
73. This second type of monastery, most of which are located outside the city limits of the major settlements, doubtless points to a formerly important division in the history of Newar Buddhism. Several theories have been proposed, but nothing definitive has been determined.
74. For example: a *mu-bāhā*: "Śrī Ratnaketu Mahāvihāra;" a *bāhā*: "Śrī Śantighat Caitya Mahāvihāra;" a *bāhi:* "Sthavirapatra Mahāvihāra;" a branch *bāhā*: "Gunakara Mahāvihāra." For a comprehensive listing, see Locke (1985); follow-up observations are found in a recent study by Owens (2014).
75. See Lewis and Shakya (1989).
76. Most have directional Buddhas, but there are great, creative variations in the Valley's sculptural tradition. On this topic, see the exhaustive documentation by Neils Gutschow (1997).
77. Two different family lineages of the same monastery can also marry each other. In recent decades, it has been accepted that Bajrācāryas and Shākya-Bhiksuṇīs can intermarry.
78. In most Newar *vihāras*, it is mandatory for the male children of Bajrācārya men to take *ācārya abhiṣeka.* (In some *vihāras* it is optional.) A Bajrācārya man who receives *pravajya* ordination but does not take the *ācārya abhiṣeka* falls to the rank of Shākya-bhikṣu.
79. New *Bajrācāryas* begin their *ācārya* career performing *maṃsa ahuti homa* at *piṭhas*, where a temple to the one of the *aṣṭamātṛka* is found.
80. This breakdown was precipitated due to community disagreements and feuds dating back to the 1920s. On this, see Rosser (1966) and Lewis (1995).
81. For a thorough documentation of this ritual tradition, see Sharkey (2001).
82. Nowadays only a very few monasteries are following the traditions.
83. The usage until today reflects the state of the Valley's polities in the late Malla period: each major city was a separate country (Skt. *deśa*; New. *de*).
84. This tradition certainly suggests historical ties between the Newar Buddhist saṅgha and the Tibetan Buddhist world. While there is no reported memory of what this relationship was among the Newar saṅgha members living today, it is interesting to note that in the eighteenth- and nineteenth-century European accounts of the Kathmandu Valley, the authors report this tea custom, as well as

what they understand to be Newar Buddhist monks wearing red woolen robes. Tibetan accounts of the lives of eminent lamas include their receiving great veneration by local householders and even kings; some give initiations to local Newars. On this nascent field of study, see Lewis (1988, 1999), and Bogin (2013, 54–57, 100–103).

85. The musical analogy is useful here: with the complete change in ritual paraphernalia, ritual utterances, shrine focal points, and esoteric symbolisms, the pre-modern *Bajrācārya* masters of ritual changed the "key" of the brahmanical score to express their Buddhist identity, while allowing their disciples to conform outwardly with high caste practices.
86. In the context of the Newar *guru-maṇḍala-arcana*, the term *guru* denotes all the Buddhist teachers in the broadest sense: the Buddhas, the Dharma (Buddha's teachings), and the saṅgha (Buddhist monks, nuns, and priests). It also acknowledges Vajradhara, the Buddha who symbolizes the *dharmakāya* ("doctrinal body") of all past, present, and future Buddhas. The term *maṇḍala* specifically refers to the body, speech, and mind of oneself. The term *arcana* means sacrifice. So it can be said that the *gurumaṇḍala-arcana* means sacrificing one's own body, speech, and mind to the totality of teachers—the Buddha, Dharma, saṅgha, and Vajradhāra—with the ultimate objective of the attainment of enlightenment.
87. Regarding the sense organs, ears and their object sound cannot be represented by any visible object, so a bell represents the sense organ ears, the object sound, and relation between the two.
88. Thirdly, the bell and *vajra* symbolize skillful means and wisdom, and also, respectively, compassion and wisdom. The holding the bell in the left hand and the *vajra* in the right hand symbolizes that one should employ both compassion and wisdom. Finally, crossing both hands in the cross-hand gesture holding each symbolizes the union of compassion and wisdom. Ultimately, the union of compassion with wisdom produces the thought of enlightenment (*bodhicitta*).
89. There are levels of air, fire, water; seven types of sea; and four great/primary islands (Skt. *mahādvīpa*) in the four directions, as well as four small/secondary islands (Skt. *upadvīpa*) in the four intermediate directions; three main mountains at the center, surrounded by seven mountains; also eight types of jewels in the eight directions. It also includes the moon on the right and the sun on the left.
90. This early Mahāyāna ritual is mentioned in chapter 2 of Shantideva's *Bodhicaryāvatāra*.
91. Confession is nuanced in its listing: first are the ten non-virtuous deeds committed by oneself. But one also confesses the ten non-virtuous deeds committed by others that one might have encouraged or approved.
92. Benefits of all above-mentioned practice, as mentioned in a Newar commentary: Doing this visualization will gradually minimize committing sinful acts. Faced with engaging in misconduct, the individual will remember that one's

sensual organs and sensual objects have been sacrificed often in daily practice, and so one can be detached from them, the root-causes for attachment (*trene*) and hatred (*ghrina*). The effect is gradually to lose individualistic thoughts, self-centered ideas, and to promote focus on life's duties, and dedication to others. You will not forget your ultimate aim of your life (i.e., to be a Buddha, the enlightened one).

93. The *Bajrācārya* accomplishes this through visualization on the air-maṇḍala, likewise fire-maṇḍala: visualize three skinless skulls situated on an oven; upon the oven, is a skinless skull like a bowl. Imagine that you have put your sensual organs and the respective sensual objects inside the skinless skull and then boil them up completely. Now the skull is full of foods transformed to be ambrosia, though made of each of the five sensual organs and their respective objects. After this, invite all the guardian deities, along with their kin from all directions, and ask that they partake in this "food," and so become satisfied and happy.
94. This may well represent the Newar saṅgha's economic adaptation in parallel with the patterns of Newar brahman ritualists who subsist mainly through death-time gift giving. It is important to note that *śrāddha* rituals are one of the chief occasions for laymen presenting *dāna* to the *Bajrācārya* saṅgha.
95. Newar *śrāddha* is consistent with the trans-regional tradition of cultural adaptation that characterizes Buddhism tradition from its origins. In East Asia, Buddhist ritualists designed rites to satisfy families and monastics who wished to keep faith with their Confucian ancestor veneration obligations. They papered over the inevitable contradiction between ancestral spirits residing in graves and altars, and the Buddhist doctrine that holds that rebirth is inevitable, and occurs after no more than 49 days after death. Buddhism could not have survived opposing this central part of the diffuse tradition of popular East Asian religion, and made their grounds available to families to establish their ancestral shrines. The Newar Buddhist inter-cultural milieu in South Asia has been, in some ways, different: ancestor afterlife tradition was defined by brahmans, not Confucians. But the same traditional ethos informed this adaptation by the Nepalese Bajrācāryas from Malla times onward—skillful means, compassion, doing the needful to preserve the Buddhist Dharma—and is clearly discerned below the surface of conformity. It need not obscure that fact that it may well have been in the economic interest of the Newar "householder monks" to compose an elaborate program of tantric Buddhist *śrāddha*, since they have enjoyed, until today, regular employment in the performance of these rites.
96. See Lewis (1994) and chapters of Lewis (2000) for a fuller treatment of this popular Newar Buddhist devotional practice.
97. As usually depicted in Newar paintings, these are Gaganaganja, Khagarbha, Kṣitigarbha, Maitreya, Mañjughoṣa, Samantabhadra, Vajrapāṇi, and Viṣkambhin.
98. The authors are preparing a documentary and analytical study of Newar Buddhist *homa* ritual (Bajracharya and Lewis, forthcoming)

99. The term *hnikam* means "daily" and "regular."
100. The senior woman greets the honored guests at a place where the floor/ground has been marked with a *svāstika*. At the entry point, she pours onto each person's head a small assortment of auspicious items (flowers, rice, small fruit), dropping the mix from a large container. Each individual has this done three times, then the women of the house lead them in, with the first guest grasping a proffered key and other objects as they move into the now auspicious space.
101. Couples share one maṇḍala plate; individuals have their own. This is a special plate called *thayebhu or kayembhu.*
102. Lit: *go* = cow, *ku* = dog, *da* = elephant, *ha* = horse, *na* = human meat. This tradition derives from the *Guhyasamāja Tantra.*
103. NMB has speculated on the meaning: "The idea behind the returning the *hnikam* is that as the distillation of *prajñā*, the mantra is eternal like the Adi Buddha, and should not therefore go to immolation with the dead body."
104. William Stablein's memoir (1993) includes an account of his initiation in this tantra back in 1973, with noted Kathmandu *Bajrācārya* Jog Muni Bajrācārya. Information on the general principles and practices of Newar tantric initiation is found in Gellner (1993).
105. As summarized by Wallis, "Both *puraścaraṇa* and *ādikarma* denote a series of ritualized activities performed at the initial stage of a formalized practice. Though activities vary somewhat from community to community, they generally involve such exercises as mantra recitation (*jāpa*), daily ablutions (*snāna*), oblations (*homa*), meditation (*dhyāna*), devotional worship of *buddhas* and *bodhisattvas* (*pūjā*), maṇḍala offerings, and occasional alms begging. These are carried out under a vow (*vrata*), during an extended period of training. The execution of both the *ādikarma* and the *puraścaraṇa* follows formal initiation into a cult, but precedes the performance of advanced ritual practice" (2003, 7–8).
106. Women cannot undertake the *puraścaraṇa* retreats.
107. It is practiced after the *ksama-pūjā* and before the *nyāsa-likāyegu-pūjā*. These rituals are the Vajrayāna practice that involves taking out the *nyāsa* (life) and transmitting it into a jar that contains water and other materials required for the purpose.
108. NMB writes, "I had played a role as the *karmācārya* in the renovation of the massive vajra and the *dharmadhātu* maṇḍala constructed at Svayamabhū in the 1990s. At that time we practiced *puruśan* in the tantric Santipur cave shrine on the north side of Svayambhū hill."
109. NMB notes, "After finishing my PhD, I practiced *puruśan* for a week under the guidance of Badri Guruju in the *āgam* of the Bijyeśvari Temple and completed it with *maṃsāhuti homa*."
110. The identity of this legendary figure in the Kathmandu Buddhist tradition could possibly be related a Śāśvatavajra, a famous tantric scholar practitioner (active in the twelfth century) who wrote one of the Cakrasaṃvara commentaries preserved in the Tibetan canon.

111. Translation from B. Bajracarya (1979).
112. This story implying the superiority of the Newar master is contradicted by another story told by Hodgson's *Bajrācārya* pandit Amṛtānanda implying the opposite: "It is said that Shankara, a Śivamārgī, having destroyed the worship of the Buddha and the scriptures concerning his doctrine in Hindustan, came to Nepal, where he also effected much mischief; and then he proceeded to Bhot. There he had a conference with the grand Lama. The Lama, who never bathes and . . . disgusted him to the degree that he started to revile the Lama. The Lama replied, 'I keep my inside pure, although my outside be impure; while you carefully purify yourself without, but you are filthy within'; then he drew out his whole entrails, and showed them to Shankara, then replaced them. He then demanded a reply . . . Shankara, by virtue of his yoga, ascended to the heavens; the lama perceiving the shadow of Shankara's body on the ground, fixed a knife in the place of the shadow; Shankara then fell on the knife, which pierced his throat and killed him instantly. Such is the legend or tale that prevails, and thus we account for the fact the Buddhamārgī practice of Tibet is purer, and its scriptures more numerous, than ours" (Hodgson 1874, 48).
113. As summarized by Lall (1968, 55–59), and adapted from informant retellings.
114. A pilgrimage place in the southwest of the Kathmandu Valley is also called "Dāman" (Manandhar 1986, 85).
115. That is, from full moon day of the month of Phalguna to full moon day of Chaitra.
116. On *Gumlā*, see Lewis (1993a).
117. Also called the *Navavaipulya Sūtras*. These are the texts that form the nine texts in the *Dharma maṇḍala* for many Newar rituals, with the *Guhyasamāja Tantra* in the central position (Locke 1989).
118. Oral recollection by Badri Baajracarya, August 2011.
119. TL interview with Divya Bajrācārya, May 1, 1994.
120. Note that what the "Buddhist monastic community" in this era means is far from certain, as Shayne Clarke has made clear. His comments about how the Newar "married sangha" tradition may be less out of the Indic monastic mainstream than once thought are pertinent to attempts to imagine the social locations of tantric Buddhism: ". . . mainstream Buddhism itself is starting to look surprisingly and increasingly like what we see in later Mahāyāna Buddhism in Nepal, for instance" (Clarke 2014, 155).
121. It is important to be clear in this discussion that "Newar" derives from the name of the Valley, also known as "Nepal"; anyone who settled and assimilated in this region—from north, south, or elsewhere in the montaine region—could become "a Newar." Just as many individuals over the centuries were drawn to this idyllic Valley, and who "stayed on" to learn the language, marry into the established society, and participate in the local culture, so was "Newar Buddhism," especially in this era, shaped by a variety of religious teachers,

meditation practitioners, scholars, and others who set down roots, found patrons, and built institutions. Some like Atiśa and Dharmasvamin are well known; but doubtless many others are yet to be identified, especially those from Tibet in later centuries.

122. On this movement, see Levine and Gellner (2005). The Theravāda movement itself has been divided due to scandals involving the early generations of ordained monks, the separation of prominent monks seeking their own set of outside donors, dominance of the movement by high-caste Newars, and the tensions between the monks and the respected *anāgārikas*.
123. Since 1980, there has been a vast increase in the building of Tibetan monasteries throughout the Kathmandu Valley. This has been driven, in large part, by the in-migration of Tibetan and Tibeto-Burman adherents (Sherpa, Manangi, Tamang, Gurung, etc.) from across Nepal resulting from the Maoist civil war. Wealthy individuals have pulled their wealth into the Valley and constructed upward of 100 new monasteries in the last two decades.
124. Pamphlet, The Nagarjuna Institute of Exact Methods (1993).
125. See http://www.lrcnepal.org. Accessed February 27, 2015.
126. In Newari: *Nepal Paramparagar Bauddha Dharma Sangha*
127. These initiatives to open up have been cautious, only moving the caste exclusiveness of Newar Vajrayāna to be slightly less hierarchical.
128. See http://vajrayanivihar.org.np/index.php?page=static&sid=2. Accessed March 4, 2015.
129. It should be noted that the rituals of Patan and Kathmandu do have enduring differences. The pre-modern variations between monasteries and ritualists within cities reveal how independent the Malla era traditions were, a pattern of autonomy in the saṅgha that has characterized Buddhist from its earliest days.
130. There have been hundreds of new ritual manuals and philosophical booklets published over the last decade, many adopting the traditional practice of having mourning families support the costs of publication as a meritorious act in memory of their loved one.
131. As von Rospatt has noted (2011a, 22), Naresh Man Bajracharya has begun to offer initiation to the practice of the *Caṇḍamahāroṣaṇa Tantra* in Patan and Bhaktapur, cities where a lineage of practitioners had apparently ceased.

Further Reading

Akaster, Matthew. 2000. "A Black Demon Peering from the West: The Crystal Cave of Suratabajra in Tibetan Perspective." *Buddhist Himalaya* 10: 20–28.

Anderson, Mary M. 1971. *The Festivals of Nepal.* London: Allen and Unwin.

Bays, Gwendolyn, trans. 1983. *The Lalitavistara Sutra: The Voice of the Buddha, the Beauty of Compassion.* 2 vols. Berkeley: Dharma Publications.

Cowell, E. B. 1969. "The *Buddhacarita*." In *Buddhist Mahayana Texts*, edited by F. Max Muller. New York: Dover Reprint.

Edgerton, Franklin. 1993. *Buddhist Hybrid Sanskrit Dictionary*. Delhi: Motilal Banarsidass.

Gomez, Luis O. 1995. "Unspoken Paradigms: Meanderings through the Metaphors of a Field." *Journal of the International Association of Buddhist Studies* 18: 183–230.

Grandin, Igemar. 1989. *Music and Media in Local Life: Music Practice in a Newar Neighborhood in Nepal*. Sweden: Linkoping University Press.

Hofer, Andras. 1979. *The Caste Hierarchy and the State of Nepal, A Study of the Muluki Ain of 1854*. Innsbruck: Universitätsverlag Wagner.

Hutt, Michael. 1991. *Himalayan Voices*. Berkeley: University of California Press.

Hutt, Michael. 1994. *Nepal: A Guide to the Art and Architecture of the Kathmandu Valley*. Boston: Shambhala.

Ingalls, Daniel H. H. 1968. *Sanskrit Poetry*. Cambridge, MA: Harvard University Press.

Jones, J. J. 1949–1956. *The Mahavastu*. 3 vols. London: Pali Text Society.

Kolver, Bernhard. 1985. "Stages in the Evolution of a World Picture." *Numen* 32 (2): 131–168.

Kolver, Ulrike, and Iswarananda Shresthacarya. 1994. *A Dictionary of Contemporary Newari, Newari-English*. Bonn: VGH Wissenschaftsverlag.

Korn, Wolfgang. 1979. *The Traditional Architecture of the Kathmandu Valley*. Kathmandu: Ratna Pustak Bhandar.

Lévi, Sylvain. 1905–8. *Le Népal*. 3 vols. Paris: Leroux.

Levy, Robert. 1990. *Mesocosm*. Berkeley: University of California Press.

Macdonald, Alexander W., and Anne Vergati Stahl. 1979. *Newar Art*. Warminster: Aris and Phillips.

Pollock, Sheldon. 2003. "Sanskrit Literary Culture from the Inside Out." In *Literary Cultures in History: Reconstructions from South Asia*, edited by Sheldon Pollock, 39–130. Berkeley: University of California Press.

Regmi, Mahesh Chandra. 1971. *A Study of Nepali Economic History 1768–1846*. New Delhi: Manjushri Publishing House.

Regmi, Mahesh Chandra. 1976. *Landownership in Nepal*. Berkeley: University of California Press.

Shrestha, Bal Gopal and Bert van der Hoek. 1995. "Education in the Mother Tongue: The Case of Nepalabhasa (Newari)." *Contributions to Nepalese Studies* 22: 73–86.

Silvi, Antonini Chiara, and G. Verardi 1984. "Excavations in the Kathmandu Valley." *East and West* 34: 535–545.

Silvi, Antonini Chiara, G. Verardi, and O. Volpicelli. 1986. "Archaeological Activity in the Kathmandu Valley, 1986." *East and West* 36: 530–540.

Silvi, Antonini Chiara, and G. Verardi. 1989. "Excavations in Kathmandu." In *South Asian Archaeology 1985*, edited by Karen Frifelt and Per Sorensen, 449–458. London: Curzon.

Sthavir, Dharmalok. 1959. *Nama Rupa Nirodha: Buddhako Panca Jnanamurti.* Kathmandu: Vagisvara Press.

Stiller, L. F. 1973. *The Rise of the House of Gorkha.* New Delhi: Manjusri Publishing House.

Takaoka, Hidenobu. 1981. *A Microfilm Catalogue of the Buddhist Manuscripts in Nepal.* Nagoya, Japan: Buddhist Library.

Tambiah, Stanley J. 1973. "Buddhism and This-Worldly Activity." *Modern Asian Studies* 7 (1): 1–20.

Tambiah, Stanley J. 1984. *The Buddhist Saints of the Forest and the Cult of Amulets.* Cambridge: Cambridge University Press.

Tatelman, Joel. 1999. "The Trials of Yasodharā: The Legends of the Buddha's Wife in the Bhadrakalpāvadāna." *Buddhist Literature* 1: 176–261.

Tatelman, Joel. 2000. *The Glorious Deeds of Pūrnā: A Translation and Study of the Pūrnāvadāna.* London: Curzon Press.

Vergati, Anne. 1995. *Gods, Men and Territory: Society and Culture in the Kathmandu Valley.* New Delhi: Manohar.

Witzel, Michael. 1976. "On the History and Present State of Vedic Tradition in Nepal." *Vasudha* 15: 17–39.

Witzel, Michael. 1980. "On the Location of the Licchavi Capital of Nepal." *Studien zur Indologie und Iranistik* 5/6: 311–337.

Witzel, Michael. 1992. "Meaningful Ritual: Vedic, Medieval, and Contemporary Concepts in the Nepalese Agnihotra Ritual." In *Ritual, State, and History in South Asia,* edited by A.W. van den Hoek et al., 774–825. Leiden: E. J. Brill.

References

Acharya, Diwakar. 2008. "Evidence for Mahayana Buddhism and Sukhavati Cult in India in the Middle Period: Early fifth to late sixth century Nepalese Inscriptions." *Journal of the International Association of Buddhist Studies* 31 (1–2): 23–78.

Allen, Michael. 1973. "Buddhism Without Monks: The Vajrayana Religion of the Newars of the Kathmandu Valley." *South Asia* 3: 1–14.

Bajracarya, Nisthananda. 1914. *Lalitavistara Sutra.* Kathmandu.

Bajracharya, Naresh Man. 1998. *Buddhism in Nepal.* Delhi: Eastern Book Linkers.

Bledsoe, Bronwen. 2004. "Written in Stone: Inscriptions of the Kathmandu Valley's Three Kingdoms." PhD dissertation, University of Chicago.

Bogin, Benjamin. 2013. *The Illuminated Life of the Great Yolmowa.* Chicago: Serindia.

Brinkhaus, Horst. 1980. "References to Buddhism in the Nepalamahatmya." *Journal of the Nepal Research Center* 4: 273–286.

Brinkhaus, Horst. 1987. *The* Pradyumna-Prabhavati *Legend in Nepal.* Stuttgart: Franz Steiner Verlag.

Brinkhaus, Horst. 1991. "The Descent of the Nepalese Malla Dynasty as Reflected by Local Chronicles." *Journal of the American Oriental Society* 111: 118–122.

Brough, John. 1948. "Legends of Khotan and Nepal." *Bulletin of the School of Oriental and African Studies* 12: 333–339.

Burnouf, Eugene. 2010. *Introduction to the History of Indian Buddhism*, translated by Katia Buffetrille and Donald Lopez, Jr. Chicago: University of Chicago Press.

Clarke, Shayne. 2009a. "When and Where Is a Monk No Longer a Monk? On Communion and Communities in Indian Buddhist Monastic Law Codes." *Indo-Iranian Journal* 52: 115–141.

Clarke, Shayne. 2009b. "Monks Who Have Sex: Pārājika Penance in Indian Buddhist Monasticisms." *Journal of Indian Philosophy* 37 (1): 1–43.

Clarke, Shayne. 2014. *Family Matters in Indian Buddhist Monasticisms*. Honolulu: University of Hawai'i Press.

Davidson, Ronald. 2002. *Indian Esoteric Buddhism: A Social History of the Tantric Movement*. New York: Columbia University Press.

Davidson, Ronald. 2005. *Tibetan Renaissance: Tantric Buddhism in the Rebirth of Tibetan Culture*. New York: Columbia University Press.

Decleer, Hubert. 1994–1995. "Bajracarya Transmission in XIth Century Chobar: Bharo 'Maimed Hand's Main Disciple Vajrakirti, the Translator from Rwa." *Buddhist Himalaya* 6 (1–2): 1–17.

Decleer, Hubert. 1998. "Two Topics from the *Svayambhu Purana*: Who was Dharma-shri-mitra? Who was Shantikara Acharya?" Paper presented at the Conference on the Buddhist Heritage of Nepal Mandala in 1998. http://www.aioiyama.net/lrc/papers/cbhnm-ppr-2.htm. Accessed February 13, 2015.

Decleer, Hubert. 2001–2002. "Another Newar Link with Surata-bajra and Lhasa's White Crystal Cave? Zhing-po-lingpa's meditation scenario on the Five Arya Images." *Buddhist Himalaya* 11: 1–7.

Deo, S. B. 1968. *Archaeological Excavation in Kathmandu, 1965*. Kathmandu: HMG.

Dowman, Keith. 1982. "A Buddhist Guide to the Power Places of the Kathmandu Valley." *Kailash* 8 (3–4): 183–291.

Dutt, Sukumar. 1962. *Buddhist Monks and Monasteries of India*. London: George Allen and Unwin.

Ehrhard, Franz-Karl. 1989. "A Renovation of Svayambhunath Stupa in the 18th Century and Its History." *Ancient Nepal* 114: 1–9.

Ehrhard, Franz-Karl. 1990. "The Stupa of Bodhnath: A Preliminary Analysis of the Written Sources." *Ancient Nepal* 120: 1–9.

Ehrhard, Franz-Karl. 1991. "Further Renovations of Svayambhūnāth Stūpa (from the 13th to the 17th Centuries)." *Ancient Nepal* 123–125: 10–20.

Ehrhard, Franz-Karl. 2004. "Spiritual Relationships Between Rulers and Preceptors: The Three Journeys of Vanaratna (1384–1468) to Tibet." In *The Relationship Between Religion and State in Traditional Tibet*, edited by Christoph Cuppers, 245–266. Kathmandu: Lumbini International Research Center.

Gellner, David N. 1986. "Language, Caste, Religion and Territory: Newar Identity Ancient & Modern." *European Journal of Sociology* 27: 102–148.

Gellner, David N. 1989. "Buddhist Monks or Kinsmen of the Buddha? Reflections on the Titles Traditionally Used by Shakyas in the Kathmandu Valley," *Kailash* 15 (1–2): 5–25.

Gellner, David N. 1992. *Monk, Householder and Tantric Priest: Newar Buddhism and Its Hierarchy of Ritual.* Cambridge: Cambridge University Press.

Gellner, David N. 2001. *The Anthropology of Hinduism and Buddhism: Weberian Themes.* Delhi: Oxford University Press.

Gellner, David N. 2004. "Himalayan Conundrum? A Puzzling Absence in Ronald M. Davidson's *Indian Esoteric Buddhism.*" *Journal of the International Association of Buddhist Studies* 27 (2): 411–417.

Gellner, David N., and Declan Quigley, eds. 1995. *Contested Hierarchies: A Collaborative Ethnography of Caste among the Newars of the Kathmandu Valley, Nepal.* Oxford: Oxford University Press.

Greenwold, Stephen. 1974. "Buddhist Brahmins." *Archives Europeennes de Sociologie* 15: 483–503.

Gutschow, Neils. 1997. *The Nepalese Caitya.* Stuttgart: Edition Axel Menges.

Gutschow, Neils, and Manabajra Bajracharya. 1977. "Ritual as Mediator of Space in Kathmandu." *Journal of the Nepal Research Centre* 1: 1–10.

Gutschow, Neils, Bernhard Kolver, and Ishwaranand Shresthacarya. 1987. *Newar Towns and Buildings: An Illustrated Dictionary.* Sankt Augustin: VGH Wissenschaftsverlag.

Hodgson, Brian H. [1874] 1972. *Essays on the Languages, Literature, and Religion of Nepal and Tibet.* Reprint, New Delhi: Manjusri.

Kaji, Vaidya Asha. 2010. *The Dashakarma Vidhi: Fundamental Knowledge on the Traditional Customs of the Ten Rites of Passage among the Buddhist Newars.* Kathmandu: Mandala Book Point.

Khanal, M. P., and Theodore Riccardi, Jr. 2007. *Archaeological Excavations in the Kathmandu Valley.* Opera Minora 5. Cambridge, MA: Harvard Oriental Series.

Kim, Jinah. 2013. *Receptacle of the Sacred: Illustrated Manuscripts and the Buddhist Book Cult in South Asia.* Berkeley: University of California Press.

Levine, Sarah, and David Gellner. 2005. *Rebuilding Buddhism: The Theravada Movement in Twentieth-Century Nepal.* Cambridge, MA: Harvard University Press.

Lewis, Todd. 1989. "Newars and Tibetans in the Kathmandu Valley: Ethnic Boundarics and Religious History." *Journal of Asian and African Studies* 38: 31–57.

Lewis, Todd. 1993. "Contributions to the Study of Popular Buddhism: The Newar Buddhist Festival of *Gumlā Dharma.*" *Journal of the International Association of Buddhist Studies* 16: 7–52.

Lewis, Todd. 1994. "The *Nepāl Jana Jīvan Kriyā Paddhati,* a Modern Newar Guide for Vajrayāna Life-Cycle Rites." *Indo-Iranian Journal* 37: 1–46.

Lewis, Todd. 1995. "Buddhist Merchants in Kathmandu: The Asan Twāḥ Market and Urāy Social Organization." In *Contested Hierarchies: A Collaborative Ethnography of Caste among the Newars of the Kathmandu Valley, Nepal*, edited by David Gellner and Declan Quigley, 38–79. Oxford: Oxford University Press.

Lewis, Todd. 1996. "A Chronology of Newar-Tibetan Relations in the Kathmandu Valley." In *Change and Continuity: Studies in the Nepalese Culture of the Kathmandu Valley*, edited by Siegfried Lienhard, 149–166. Torino: Edizioni Dell'orso.

Lewis, Todd. 1997. "The Anthropological Study of Buddhist Communities: Historical Precedents and Ethnographic Paradigms." In *Anthropology of Religion: A Handbook*, edited by Steven Glazier, 319–367. Westport, CT: Greenwood Press.

Lewis, Todd. 1998. "Growing Up Newar Buddhist: Chittadhar Hridaya's *Jhī Macā* and Its Context." In *Selves in Time and Place: Identities, Experience, and History in Nepal*, edited by Al Pach and Debra Skinner, 301–318. Boulder, CO: Rowman and Littlefield Press.

Lewis, Todd. 2000. *Popular Buddhist Texts from Nepal: Narratives and Rituals of Newar Buddhism*. Albany: State University of New York Press.

Lewis, Todd. 2003. "From Generalized Goal to Tantric Subordination: *Sukhāvatī* in the Indic Buddhist Traditions of Nepal." In *Approaching the Land of Bliss: Religious Praxis in the Cult of Amitābha*, edited by Richard K. Payne and Kenneth K. Tanaka, 236–263. Honolulu: University of Hawai'i Press.

Lewis, Todd, and Emmrich, Christoph. 2012. "Marrying the 'Thought of Enlightenment': The Multivalence of Girls' Symbolic Marriage Rites in the Newar Buddhist Community of Kathmandu, Nepal." In *Little Buddhas: Children and Childhoods in Buddhist Texts and Traditions*, edited by Vanessa Sassoon, 347–373. New York: Oxford University Press.

Lewis, Todd, and Lozang Jamspal. 1988. "Newars and Tibetans in the Kathmandu Valley: Three New Translations from Tibetan Sources." *Journal of Asian and African Studies* 36: 187–211.

Lewis, Todd, and Daya Ratna Shakya. 1988. "Contributions to the History of Nepal: Eastern Newar Diaspora Settlements." *Contributions to Nepalese Studies* 15 (1): 25–65.

Lewis, Todd, and Subarna Man Tuladhar. 2011. *Sugata Saurabha: A Poem on the Life of the Buddha by Chittadhar Hridaya of Nepal*. New York: Oxford University Press.

Lienhard, Siegfried. 1963. *Manicudāvadānoddhrita*. Stockholm: Almquist and Wiksell.

Lienhard, Siegfried. 1984a. "Nepal: The Survival of Indian Buddhism in a Himalayan Kingdom." In *The World of Buddhism*, edited by Heinz Bechert, 108–114. New York: Facts on File.

Lienhard, Siegfried. 1984b. *Songs of Nepal*. Honolulu: University of Hawai'i Press.

Lienhard, Siegfried. 1988. *Nepalese Manuscripts: Part 1: Nevari and Sanskrit*. Stuttgart: Franz Steiner Verlag.

Lo Bue, Eberto. 1985. "Newar Artists of the Nepal Valley: An Historical Account of their Activities in Neighbouring Areas with Particular Reference to Tibet-I." *Oriental Art* 31 (3): 265–277.

Lo Bue, Eberto. 1988. "Cultural Exchange and Social Interaction Between Tibetans and Newars from the Seventh to the Twentieth Century." *International Folklore Review* 6: 86–114.

Lo Bue, Eberto, and F. Ricci. 1993. *The Great Stupa of Gyantse*. London: Serindia.

Locke, John K. 1980. *Karunamaya*. Kathmandu: Sahiyogi.

Locke, John K. 1985. *Buddhist Monasteries of Nepal*. Kathmandu: Sahiyogi.

Locke, John K. 1986. "The Vajrayāna Buddhism in the Kathmandu Valley." In *The Buddhist Heritage of Nepal*. Kathmandu: Dharmodaya Sabba.

Locke, John K. 1989. "The *Uposadha Vrata* of Amoghapāsha Lokeśvara." *L'Ethnographie* 83: 109–138.

Malla, Kamal P. 1981. *Classical Newari Literature: A Sketch*. Kathmandu: Nepal Study Centre.

Malla, Kamal P. 1990. "The Earliest Dated Document in Newari: The Palm leaf from Uku Bahah NS 235/AD 1114." *Kailash* 16 (1–2): 15–25.

Manandhar, Thakur Lal. 1977. "Nepal in the Early Medieval Period: Gleanings from the Bendall Vamshavali." *Journal of the Nepal Research Center* 1: 83–88.

Manandhar, Thakur Lal. 1986. *Newari-English Dictionary*. Delhi: Agam Kala Prakashan.

Martin, Dan. 1996. "Lay Religious Movements in 11th and 12th Century Tibet: A Survey of Sources." *Kailash* 18 (3–4): 23–56.

Mitra, Rajendralala. [1882] 1971. *The Buddhist Sanskrit Literature of Nepal*. Reprint, Calcutta: Sanskrit Pustak Bhandar.

Monier-Williams, M. 1899. *A Sanskrit-English Dictionary*. Oxford: Oxford University Press.

Nattier, Jan. 1990. "Church Language and Vernacular Language in Central Asian Buddhism." *Numen* 37 (2): 195–219.

Nepal Bhasa Dictionary Committee. 2000. *A Dictionary of Classical Newari*. Kathmandu: Cwasa Pasa.

Nepal Rajkiya-Pratisthan. 1977. *Musical Instruments of Nepal*. Kathmandu: Royal Nepal Academy.

Owens, Bruce. 1989. "The Politics of Divinity in the Kathmandu Valley: The Festival of Bunga Dya/Rato Matsyendranath." PhD dissertation, Columbia University.

Owens, Bruce. 2014. "Innovation in Traditions of Transformation: A Preliminary Survey of a Quarter Century of Change in the Bāhāḥs and Bahīs of the Kathmandu Valley." *South Asia: Journal of South Asian Studies* 37: 130–155.

Pal, Pratapaditya. 1974. *Buddhist Art in Licchavi Nepal*. Bombay: Marg Publications.

Petech, Luciano. 1984. *Mediaeval History of Nepal (c. 750–1480)*. 2nd edition. Rome: Istituto italiano per il Medio ed Estremo Oriente.

Riccardi, Theodore, Jr. 1979. "The Inscriptions of King Manadeva at Changu Narayan." *Journal of the American Oriental Society* 109: 611–620.

Riccardi, Theodore, Jr. 1980. "Buddhism in Ancient and Early Medieval Nepal." In *Studies in the History of Buddhism*, edited by A. K. Narain, 265–281. New Delhi: B. R. Publishing.

Roerich, George N. [1949] 1996. *The Blue Annals.* Reprint, New Delhi: Motilal Banarsidass.

Rose, Leo. 1970. *The Politics of Nepal.* Ithaca, NY: Cornell University Press.

Rosser, Colin. 1966. "Social Mobility in the Newar Caste System." In *Caste and Kin in Nepal, India and Ceylon,* edited by C. von Furer-Haimendorf, 68–139. Bombay: Asian Publishing House.

Schopen, Gregory. 1979. "Mahayana in Indian Inscriptions." *Indo-Iranian Journal* 21: 1–19.

Schopen, Gregory. 1988–1989. "On Monks, Nuns, and 'Vulgar' Practices: The Introduction of the Image Cult into Indian Buddhism." *Artibus Asiae* 49: 153–168.

Schopen, Gregory. 1991. "Archaeology and Protestant Presuppositions in the Study of Indian Buddhism." *History of Religions* 31 (1): 1–23.

Schopen, Gregory. 2000. "The Mahayana and the Middle Period in Indian Buddhism: Through a Chinese Looking Glass." *The Eastern Buddhist* 32: 1–25.

Schopen, Gregory. 2004. "If You Can't Remember, How to Make it Up: Some Monastic Rules for Redacting Canonical Texts." In *Buddhist Monks and Business Matters,* edited by Gregory Schopen, 395–408. Honolulu: University of Hawai'i Press.

Shakya, Hem Raj. 1977. *Shri Svayambhu Mahacaitya.* Kathmandu: Nepal Press.

Shakya, Hem Raj. 1979. *Samyak Mahādāna Guthi.* Kathmandu: Samkata Press.

Shakya, Min Bahadur. 1986. *A Short History of Buddhism in Nepal.* 2nd edition. Patan: Young Men's Buddhist Association.

Shakya, Min Bahadur. 1993. "Life and Teaching of Nepalese Siddha Advayavajra." *Buddhist Himalaya* 5 (1–2). http://buddhism.lib.ntu.edu.tw/FULLTEXT/JR-BH/bh117517.htm. Accessed February 16, 2015.

Shakya, Min Bahadur, ed. 1997. *Lalitavistara Sutra as Translated by Pt. Nisthananda Vajracarya.* Lalitpur: Young Men's Buddhist Association.

Shakya, Min Bahadur. 2004. *Hiranyavarna Mahavihara.* Patan: Nagarjuna Publications.

Shakya, Min Bahadur, and Shanta Harsha Bajracharya. 2010. *Svayambhū Purāṇa.* Nepal: Nagarjuna Institute of Exact Methods.

Shakya, Miroj. 2010. *Catalogue of Digitized Rare Sanskrit Buddhist Manuscripts* I. Rosemead, CA: University of the West.

Sharkey, Gregory. 2001. *Buddhist Daily Ritual: The Nitya Puja in Kathmandu Valley Shrines.* Bangkok: Orchid Press.

Slusser, Mary. 1982. *Nepal Mandala.* Princeton, NJ: Princeton University Press.

Snellgrove, David. 1987. "Buddhism in Nepal." In *Indo-Tibetan Buddhism,* by David Snellgrove, 2:362–380. Boston: Shambhala Publications.

Stablein, William. 1976. "A Descriptive Analysis of the Content of Nepalese Buddhist Pujas, with Reference to Tibetan Parallels." In *In the Realm of the Extra-Human: Ideas and Actions,* edited by Agehananda Bharati, 165–173. The Hague: Mouton.

Stablein, William. 1991. *Healing Image of the Great Black One*. Berkeley: SLG Books.

Stein, M. A. [1900] 1979. *Kalhana's Rajatarangini*. Reprint, Delhi: Motilal Banarsidass.

Toffin, Gerard. 1975. "Études sur les Newars de la vallée de Kathmandou: Guthi, Funerailles et Castes." *l'Ethnographie* 2: 206–225.

Toffin, Gerard. 1984. *Société et religion chez les Néwar du Népal*. Paris: Centre national de la recherche scientifique.

Tuladhar-Douglas, Will. 2006. *Remaking Buddhism for Medieval Nepal: The Fifteenth Century Reformation of Newar Buddhism*. London: Routledge.

Uebach, Helga. 1970. *Das Nepālamāhātmyam des Skandhapurānam: Legenden um die hinduistischen Heiligtümer Nepals*. Munich: W. Fink.

Vaidya, Janak Lal, and Prem Bahadur Kamsakar. 1991. *A Descriptive Catalogue of Selected Manuscripts at the Asha Saphu Kuthi Archives*. Kathmandu: Cvasapasa.

Vajracarya, Badriratna. 1982. *Shri Svayambhu Mahapurana*. Kathmandu: Nepal Printing Press.

Vajracarya, Dhanavajra. 1987. "The Development of Early and Medieval Settlements in the Kathmandu Valley." In *Heritage of the Kathmandu Valley: Proceedings of an International Conference in Lübeck, June 1985*, edited by Niels Gutschow and Axel Michaels, 357–364. Nepalica vol. 4. Sankt Augustin: VGH Wissenschaftsverlag.

Vajracarya, Dhanavajra, and Kamal P. Malla. 1985. *The Gopālarājavaṃśāvalī*. Wiesbaden: Franz Steiner Verlag.

Vajracarya, Gautam. 1973. "Recently Discovered Inscriptions of Licchavi Nepal." *Kailash* 1 (2): 117–133.

Vajracarya, Gautam. 1974. "Yangala, Yambu." *Contributions to Nepalese Studies* 1: 90–98.

Vajracarya, Ratna Kaji. 1980. *Yen Deyā Bauddha Pūjā Kriyāyā Halan-Jvalam*. Kathmandu: Sankata Printing Press.

Van de Hoek, Bert. 1996. "Gender and Caste in the Perfect Buddhist Gift, the Samyak Mahadana in Kathmandu, Nepal." *Journal of the Center for Nepal and Asian Studies* 23: 195–211.

Van Kooji, Karel Rijk. 1977. "The Iconography of the Buddhist Wood-carvings in a Newar Monastery in Kathmandu (*Chusya-Baha*)." *Journal of the Nepal Research Centre* 1: 39–82.

von Rospatt, Alexander. 2005. "The Transformation of the Monastic Ordination (*pravrajyā*) into a Rite of Passage in Newar Buddhism." In *Words and Deeds: Hindu and Buddhist Rituals in South Asia*, edited by Jorg Gengnagel et al., 199–234. Wiesbaden: Harrassowitz Verlag.

von Rospatt, Alexander. 2009. "The Sacred Origins of the Svayambhucaitya and the Nepal Valley: Foreign Speculation and Local Myth." *Journal of the Nepal Research Centre* 13: 33–39.

von Rospatt, Alexander. 2010. "The Consecration Ceremony in the *Kriyāsaṃgraha* and Newar Buddhism." In *Hindu and Buddhist Initiations in India and Nepal*, edited by Astrid Zotter and Christof Zotter, 197–260. Wiesbaden: Harrassowitz.

von Rospatt, Alexander. 2011a. "A Short Portrayal of Itum Baha as a Monastic Institution." *Newah Vijnana* 7: 25–34.

von Rospatt, Alexander. 2011b. "The Past Renovations of the Svayambhūcaitya." *In Light of the Valley. Renewing the Sacred Art and Traditions of Svayambhu*, edited by Tsering Palmo Gellek and Padma Dorje Maitland, 157–206. Cazadero, CA: Dharma Publishing.

von Rospatt, Alexander. 2012. "Past Continuity and Recent Changes in the Ritual Practice of Newar Buddhism: Reflections on the impact of Tibetan Buddhism and the Advent of Modernity." In *Revisiting Rituals in an Changing Tibetan World*, edited by Katia Buffetrille, 209–240. Leiden; Boston: Brill.

Wallis, Glenn. 2002. *Mediating the Power of the Buddhas: Ritual in the Mañjuśrīmūlakalpa*. Albany: State University of New York Press.

Wallis, Glenn. 2003. "Advayavajra's Instructions on the *Ādikarma*." *Pacific World* 3 (5): 203–230.

Wedemeyer, Christian K. 2012. "Locating Tantric Antinomianism: An Essay toward an Intellectual History of the 'Practices/Practice Observance' (*caryā/caryāvrata*)." *Journal of the International Association of Buddhist Studies* 34 (1–2): 349–419.

Whelpton, John. 2005. *A History of Nepal*. Cambridge: Cambridge University Press.

White, David Gordon. 1998. *The Alchemical Body: Siddha Traditions in Medieval India*. Chicago: University of Chicago Press.

Widdess, Richard. 2004. "*Caryā* and *Cacā*: Change and Continuity in Newar Buddhist Ritual Song." *Asian Music* 35 (2): 7–41.

4

How Dhāraṇīs *WERE Proto-Tantric*

LITURGIES, RITUAL MANUALS, AND THE ORIGINS OF THE TANTRAS

Jacob P. Dalton

THERE IS AN ongoing debate among Buddhologists over the role that *dhāraṇīs* may have played in the rise of the Buddhist tantras. In his 1996 book, *Mantras et mandarins,* Michel Strickmann coined the term "proto-tantric" to describe the literature and practices of Buddhist *dhāraṇī,* that is, the ill-defined genre of Mahāyāna sūtras that focus on one or more *dhāraṇī*-spells.[1] Since Strickmann first made his suggestion, the term "proto-tantric" has been adopted by some and, particularly in more recent years, rejected by others. In a series of articles on the subject, for example, Richard McBride has criticized the term for being part of a wider misunderstanding that plagued scholars through most of the twentieth century, namely a "teleological position that 'dhāraṇī represent the kernel from which the first tantras developed.' "[2] Ronald Davidson, too, in his groundbreaking study of 2002, has referred to Strickmann's term as "somewhat misleading," and again for similar reasons.[3] Here I do not intend to contradict McBride, Davidson, and others who have argued in this vein. Indeed—and I want to emphasize this point—I largely agree with them that the *dhāraṇī*-sūtras are best seen merely as Mahāyāna sūtras and as distinct from the generally (though not always) later tantras. With this chapter I would, however, like to refine somewhat our understanding of the historical relationship between *dhāraṇīs* and tantras by looking more closely at the ritual uses of *dhāraṇīs*.

When past scholars have studied *dhāraṇīs*, their focus has usually been the *dhāraṇī* spells that lie at the heart of the genre. From Burnouf's 1844 *Introduction to Buddhism*, to Lamotte's oft-cited survey, to Janet Gyatso, and even Ronald Davidson's more recent work on *dhāraṇī* and memory, the *spell* has been the chief aspect of the genre to draw scholarly attention.[4] The *dhāraṇī* spell is undoubtedly a fascinating concept, but we should remember that it functioned within a wider ritual context, embedded within larger *dhāraṇī*-sūtras, liturgical collections, or ritual manuals. Relatively little has been written on how *dhāraṇīs* were actually performed.[5]

This distinction, between the contents of *dhāraṇīs* and their ritual uses, is crucial for understanding this perplexing genre of Buddhist literature. *Dhāraṇīs* were, after all, rarely read for their content. Their reading was largely liturgical and generally a ritual affair. *Dhāraṇīs* were read less for their deep philosophical insights than for the meritorious ritual of reading's own sake. In this sense, how *dhāraṇīs* were *used* was often more important than the significance of their content.

Given that the formal uses of *dhāraṇīs* are of such historical significance, the manuscript cultures that surround them are particularly illuminating. By considering the practices of writing, reading, and performing *dhāraṇīs*, we can gain a better understanding of this intriguing genre of Buddhist literature. And what better place to explore Buddhist manuscript culture than the Dunhuang archive? Here I would like to offer some observations on what the Tibetan Dunhuang manuscripts can tell us about how *dhāraṇīs* were used and what these uses, in turn, might tell us about the role of *dhāraṇīs* in the historical development of Buddhist ritual practice.

What the Dunhuang Manuscripts Can Offer

So we begin with the Tibetan manuscripts that were discovered a century ago outside the city of Dunhuang, in present-day northwestern China. The Dunhuang manuscripts provide a rare window onto the early history of tantric Buddhism, reflecting as they do a crucial period of Indian creativity. Precisely which period they reflect is a matter of some possible confusion. Until recently, it was commonly assumed that the bulk of the Tibetan manuscripts dated from the Tibetan occupation of Dunhuang, that is, from between 786 and 848 CE, the height of the Pugyal dynasty, when Tibetans controlled Dunhuang and indeed most of Central Asia. However, it is increasingly clear that this common preconception was wrong. Closer examination reveals that much of the collection actually dates from the tenth century, and this holds particularly true of the tantric materials.[6]

Despite their mostly tenth-century dates, however, the tantric Dunhuang manuscripts reflect a significantly earlier stage in the development of Buddhism in India. The kinds of rituals described and the texts quoted correspond to the state of Indian tantric ritual as it stood around the end of the eighth century. So, for example, only the first two of the four standard tantric initiations appear; no mention is made of the early ninth-century Jñānapāda- and Ārya-school writings on the *Guhyasamāja*; nor do we see any mention of the *Cakrasaṃvara* and *Hevajra* tantras, the two principal "Yoginī" tantras of the later Mahāyoga period. Thus these tenth-century manuscripts from Dunhuang reflect a late eighth-century stage of Indian ritual development.

Why don't they reflect a period of development *closer* to their own tenth-century dates? It seems there was some kind of an interruption in the transmission of Buddhism from India to Tibet. And indeed, Tibetan historians describe precisely such a break beginning around 842 CE, when the Pugyal dynasty and imperial support for Buddhist monastic institutions and translation efforts collapsed. Still, though, this doesn't explain why the manuscripts reflect an even earlier break of around 800 CE. Lacking further evidence, the remaining difference of roughly forty years perhaps may be attributed to a somewhat to-be-expected time lag between when tantric texts began to circulate in India and when they would actually arrive and be translated in Tibet. In any case, for now we can simply note that the Dunhuang documents generally seem to reflect a point in the development of tantric ritual right around the late eighth or turn of the ninth century.[7]

But the Dunhuang materials are valuable not only for the earliness of their dates. Equally crucial is the fact that so many of them are ritual works (and by this I mean generally liturgical texts, *vidhis*, *kalpas*, and *sādhanas*). Such ritual works are by nature extra-canonical (i.e., not the word of the Buddha [*buddhavacana*]). As such, they do not belong to the class of texts that came to be included in the later Tibetan *bka' 'gyur* collections. Some ritual manuals (and tantric commentaries) were included in the later *bstan 'gyur*, but many of those reflect a later period of Indian ritual development (i.e., from the eleventh century onward) and are therefore less useful for understanding the early history of tantric Buddhism. Thus, generally speaking, while most tantras were preserved in the Tibetan *bka' 'gyur*, innumerable ritual manuals were lost. And this loss is highly significant, for ritual manuals, the present chapter argues, were a major driving force behind the development of early tantric Buddhism.

It is commonly assumed, by the Buddhist tradition and modern scholars alike, that tantras come first and the associated ritual manuals follow, as extractions from, or ritual distillations of, the material found in the canonical tantras. Accordingly, the tantras are regularly presented as the original teachings, as accounts of the mythic first performances of primordial rites upon which all later manuals should be based.[8] Historically, however, precisely the opposite often seems to have been the case.[9] Ritual manuals were in fact the principal creative source of early tantric innovation, and the tantras were written, and rewritten, to encapsulate and canonize these ritual changes. Ritual manuals were, and to a lesser degree still remain,[10] a particularly creative source of innovation, thanks to their extraordinary flexibility. They could be composed or altered by anyone claiming the necessary qualifications (or, more specifically, who had received the *ācārya* initiation that consecrated one as a teacher). They could declare allegiance to any given tantra, and they could easily be updated to include the very latest ritual techniques.

The importance of ritual manuals to the early development of tantric Buddhism cannot be overestimated, yet so far this crucial genre has for the most part been ignored.[11] Ronald Davidson's recent study on *Indian Esoteric Buddhism*, for example, mostly leaves aside questions of ritual, choosing instead to highlight the influence of sociopolitical forces, ideology, and the power of the "royal metaphor." I would suggest that his conclusions may to some extent be tied to his reliance on both canonical sources and the Indian archaeological remains left behind by those rich and powerful enough to afford such grand projects. But ritual manuals were something different; they could be produced by anyone and in much greater numbers, anywhere and anytime, only to die off and disappear from view soon afterward. Using an evolutionary model, we might describe ritual manuals as the DNA of early tantric Buddhism, the quickly mutating substance that shaped the larger canonical tradition. The various species that finally emerged in the form of tantras, and the fossilized archaeological remains they left behind, tell some of the story, but by looking to ritual manuals such as those preserved at Dunhuang we can recover a different perspective on the early evolution of tantric ritual.

The present chapter further suggests that the rise of ritual manuals as a literary genre should be recognized as a significant turning point in Buddhist religious history. Before the late fifth century, ritual manuals were comparatively absent from Buddhism. Their sudden proliferation in the second half of the fifth and sixth centuries marked the dawn of a new era, and they were soon followed by the introduction of the tantras themselves. Of course, the appearance of ritual manuals was just one part of a much wider revolution that Indian religions were undergoing at the time (other parts of which Davidson and others have ably explored). By focusing on ritual manuals I do not mean to ignore these other, often quite radical, changes that accompanied their sudden proliferation. However, in light of the fact that the term "tantra" did, after all, originally refer to a type of *text*, we should perhaps look to ritual manuals as the literary precursors to the tantras.

A Tibetan Tantric Reading of the Dhāraṇīsaṃgraha*: IOL Tib J 711*

Before proceeding, I should clarify my use of the terms "liturgy" and "ritual manual" vis-à-vis *dhāraṇīs*. Within this limited context, I take "liturgies" to include primarily the liturgical collections of *dhāraṇī*-sūtras or *dhāraṇī*-spells known as the *dhāraṇīsaṃgraha* (Tib. *gzungs 'dus*). Other *dhāraṇī*-related liturgical formats might also be included, the *tridaṇḍaka* (Tib. *rgyud/rgyun chags gsum pa*) discussed later in this chapter being a prime example that does appear among the Dunhuang documents. By "ritual manuals" I mean those Buddhist texts known as *vidhi*s or *kalpa*s that were often appended to, or circulated alongside, the *dhāraṇī*-sūtras themselves. As we shall see, the line between liturgy and ritual manual was sometimes less than clear, as when ritual instructions were added to liturgies or liturgical commentaries (see my discussion later of IOL Tib J 711 for an example of the latter). Indeed, the fluidity of these genres was precisely what made them so creative. Nonetheless, for analyzing *dhāraṇī*-based practices, I find the liturgy–ritual manual distinction a helpful one to maintain. While these two kinds of texts share much in common in terms of their uses, adaptability, and extra-canonical status, ultimately it was the genre of ritual manuals (i.e., *vidhi, kalpa,* and the like) that had such a particularly strong impact on the development of Buddhist ritual practice. That said, I begin with a review of what I am calling *dhāraṇī* liturgies, to provide some sense of the ritual context within which *dhāraṇīs* were embedded in Dunhuang.

The *dhāraṇī*-sūtras from Dunhuang often appear as part of a collection. When found in this form, they generally lack the scribal dedications seen at the end of some of the individual *dhāraṇī*-sūtras that seem to have been copied for more apotropaic purposes. Individual spells or sūtras could be copied for merit making, but the *dhāraṇīsaṃgraha* more often functioned as liturgical texts, to be read in one's ritual practice. (The best-known exception to this rule is certainly the *Pañcarakṣā*, a collection that may have been both liturgical and apotropaic.)[12] In any case, I turn to these *dhāraṇīsaṃgraha* now, to see more precisely what their formats can tell us about how they were used in practice.

For the most part, the contents of the *dhāraṇīsaṃgraha* collections seem to have been fairly arbitrary; which *dhāraṇīs* were to be included was apparently left up to the interests of the individual compiler. Some of the collections do, however, share some formal features, and it is here in their structures that we begin to discern the ritual function of the *dhāraṇī* collections. The typical collection includes a number of short ancillary works. It often opens with an invitation to the mundane gods and spirits, which is followed by the *dhāraṇīs* themselves, and finally the collection closes with a series of praises and prayers.[13] Peter Skilling (in his work on "The Rakṣā Literature") has noted a similar pattern in the *paritta* texts: "In all of these collections," he writes, "the canonical *paritta* texts are set within ancillary opening and closing verses (*paritta-parikamma*, etc.)" (1992, 122).[14]

The full significance of this basic triadic structure of opening invitation-*dhāraṇīs*-closing prayers becomes apparent when one sees that it also shapes the *dhāraṇī* section (*gzungs 'dus*; i.e., *dhāraṇīsaṃgraha*) of the later Tibetan canons. There too, we see the same invitation prayer (Q. 470–471), followed by all the *dhāraṇī*-sūtras, then a closing series of praises and prayers (Q. 710–729).[15] These clear parallels suggest that the early *dhāraṇī* collections may have served as formal models for the later canons.[16]

The invitation prayer that sometimes opens the collections was clearly popular, as a number of recensions appear in both the Dunhuang manuscripts and the later canons. The Dunhuang versions bear the title, *An Invitation to the Great Gods and Nāgas* (*Lha klu chen po rnams spyan drang ba*), or sometimes just the *Rgyud gsum pa*, which I will not hazard to translate. As the title suggests, the invitations are directed at the mundane gods and spirits of the Indian pantheon, from Indra to the *saptamātaraḥ*, to come and observe the recitations of the *dhāraṇī* that will follow. Thus the closing line of the prayer reads, "Listen all [of you] to these words of the profound conqueror."[17]

After the mundane gods had been invited, the *dhāraṇī* would be recited. This liturgical order is made explicit in one version of the

Invitation prayer, Pelliot tibétain 25, where immediately following the final line, "listen all [of you] to these words of the profound conqueror," come some additional instructions: "At this point," it says, "one reads the sūtra, ... those verses that were spoken [by the Buddha]."[18] Thus these formal *dhāraṇī* collections were not simply canonical anthologies. They functioned as liturgies, created for recitation in a prescribed ritual order.

Further information on the ritual function of these *dhāraṇī* collections can be gleaned from a detailed and unique commentary on the invitation prayer that is also found among the Stein manuscripts. IOL Tib J 711 situates the *Invitation* prayer within a familiar tantric narrative: In Vaiśālī there was once a prince, we are told, who accomplished seven *samādhi*s over the course of seven days.[19] Having gained all the *siddhi*s, he prostrated to the supreme nondual buddha and caused all the gods and demons of the universe to tremble in fear. Now a wrathful *heruka*-buddha, the prince rained down blazing vajras on the demons and bound them all to serve the Buddhist teachings.

So here we have a full-blown tantric commentary on a prayer that is more commonly associated with the ritual recitation of *dhāraṇī*-sūtras. Used here, the myth of the mundane gods' subjugation implies that by reciting the *Invitation* prayers, the early Tibetan understood him- or herself to be calling upon the mundane gods and spirits to witness his or her recitations of the *dhāraṇī*. The summoned gods were then bound to serve the reciter, thanks to their earlier subjugation by this mythic Vaiśālī prince.

From this point, the rest of the commentary proceeds through the *Invitation* prayer, discussing each god and demon that is named, until the end, where it returns us to the ritual setting within which the invitations are to be read. Final advice is dispersed on which substances are to be offered, depending on which particular gods or demons the reader seeks to invoke. And special attention is given to the *nāgas*, whom we might conclude were of particular concern for these early Tibetans.

Given the detailed discussions found in IOL TIB J 711, it is clear that the Tibetans of Dunhuang were well aware of the liturgical significance of the *Invitation* prayer that opened so many of the *dhāraṇī* collections. We can further suggest that some *dhāraṇī* reciters may even have directed their recitations at specific types of beings (such as *nāgas*), using the appropriate offerings depending on which effect they desired.

Given the present chapter's focus on the historical relationships between *dhāraṇī*s and tantras, it is relevant here that the ritualized recitation of *dhāraṇīs* was a practice into which early Tibetans interpolated their tantric interests. The story of the *heruka*-buddha taming the demon Rudra is the tantric myth par excellence. Here in IOL Tib J 711, it is used to explain the power of the *dhāraṇīs* over the gods and demons of the mundane (*laukika*) world. Tantric myth is used to explain *dhāraṇī* ritual. As seen in this manuscript (IOL Tib J 711), some early Tibetans, at least, understood their liturgical *dhāraṇī* collections within a tantric mythological context. The extraordinary flexibility of liturgies, like ritual manuals (as we shall see), facilitated considerable creativity. In such extra-canonical writings, authors could insert new elements, engage in intersectarian borrowing, and blur the lines between sūtra and tantra.

A Tibetan Tantric Reading of the Tridaṇḍaka *Liturgy*

Another place where we see tantric deities being interpolated into a typically sūtric *dhāraṇī*-related liturgy is IOL TIB J 466. IOL TIB J 466 is an interesting manuscript for a number of reasons. First, we can observe that it reads horizontally, a fact that suggests a possibly early date. Its horizontal format makes it unlike the generally later scrolls that read vertically and often contain tantric or historical texts, and *like* the professionally scribed ninth-century copies of the *Aparimitāyurnāma-mahāyāna-sūtra* that were found in such great numbers in Dunhuang. It is also perhaps relevant here that there is no Chinese on the verso, suggesting again that this collection may date to the ninth century, when Tibetans had greater access to paper scrolls.[20]

In terms of content, IOL TIB J 466 includes a copy of the *Invitation to the Great Gods and Nāgas*, as well as the *Uṣṇīṣavijāya dhāraṇī*-spell, extracted from the sūtra, and several other liturgical and *dhāraṇī*-related works. But here I want to focus on the third item in the manuscript, the so-called *Rgyud chags gsum pa*, also known elsewhere as the *Rgyun chags gsum pa*, and in Sanskrit as the *Tridaṇḍaka*. The *Tridaṇḍaka* is a three-part liturgical sequence that was well known in India. It is referred to multiple times in the *Mūlasarvāstivāda Vinaya*, and appears to have been used in a variety of ritual contexts, from funerary rites, to *caitya* worship, to offering rites performed for a tree spirit before cutting down its tree.[21] In his late seventh-century *Record of the Buddhist Religion*, the Chinese master Yixing (635–713) attributes at least one version of the *Tridaṇḍaka* to Aśvaghoṣa and describes its threefold structure as consisting of (i) ten verses exalting the three jewels, followed by (ii) an unidentified work of *buddhavacana* that is to be recited, and finally (iii) ten more lines of closing prayers and dedications.[22] Precisely which work is meant to be recited as the central text of the liturgy appears to be flexible. As Schopen (1997) has observed, T. 801 represents a version of the *Tridaṇḍaka* that centers on a short sūtra on impermanence, perhaps making it well suited for a funerary context. In IOL TIB J 466 it seems we have another version, this one compiled in early Tibet, possibly (given the format of the manuscript) even dating from the late Tibetan imperial period of the first half of the ninth century.

The three parts of this Tibetan *Tridaṇḍaka* follow an order very similar to that described by Yixing. There are, however, some significant differences. The first part does indeed contain a series of praises to the three jewels, but here it follows the structure of the "seven-limbed worship," or *sapta-pūjā* (a.k.a. *anuttara-pūjā*). Also different is the fact that this first *daṇḍaka* culminates in a recitation of the *Pūjā-megha-dhāraṇī*, thereby affecting the offerings promised in the preceding prayers. This first part is then followed by the central text to be recited, again just as Yixing describes, and the manuscript ends with a final section of closing prayers and dedications. Notably, each of the three parts begins with an instruction on how it should be recited; the first and last parts should be recited without a melody, while the middle one should be accompanied by a melody (*dbyangs dang sbyar ba*).[23]

This second of the three parts, which in Yixing's description is open to ritual interpretation, here consists of a long series of praises. Praises are offered to an assortment of deities, teachers, and Buddhist patrons of the past, as well as "the teachers of our own Tibet," and even "the great king Khri srong lde brtsan," who is described here as a "magically emanated lord . . . who has mastered the royal methods of fortune (*phywa*) and [rules] the kingdom with the sword of the sky-gods."[24] This early Tibetan king is placed alongside some of the best-known Indian Buddhist kings, including Aśoka, Kaniṣka, and Harṣa Śīlāditya. Clearly, then, this text was written, or at least supplemented significantly, inside Tibet.

But perhaps even more interesting for our present purposes is the fact that this central text includes some tantric deities in its praises. From the wrathful buddhas Trailokyavijaya and Yamāntaka, to the female deities Māmakī and Mahāmāyūrī, "all the deities of the secret maṇḍala" are named and venerated. And to these are also added the local gods of Tibet. Here I suggest we view this *Tridaṇḍaka* liturgy as similar in this regard to the commentary on the *Invitation* prayers examined earlier. In both cases, tantric elements are read into well-known and non-tantric Indian ritual procedures. It seems that liturgical manuals served as a doorway through which *dhāraṇīs* could be put into conversation with tantras. Liturgical works of this sort were extra-canonical and for just this reason were open to local innovations. They were linked to more canonical works that were closed to such innovations, yet they provided a forum for new liturgical and ritual forms to be tested, and kept or discarded. With this insight in mind, I turn to a related genre of Buddhist texts, one that also seems to have been a means for great innovation for Buddhists of the sixth to tenth centuries and beyond.

Dhāraṇī-vidhi: *The Rise of Buddhist Ritual Manuals*

Having examined the liturgical formats in which the *dhāraṇī* sūtras were transmitted, I'd like to turn to the ritual manuals (Skt. *vidhi*; Tib. *cho ga*) that accompanied many of the *dhāraṇī* sūtras. It is here that we see a most interesting connection between the ritual practices of the *dhāraṇīs* and the tantras.

A *dhāraṇī*-sūtra typically consists of two parts—(i) the spell and (ii) the narrative dealing with both the setting (*nidāna*) and the various benefits to be derived from the spell. In addition, however, in some *dhāraṇī*-sūtras we find a third part, a ritual section that described the rites associated with that particular *dhāraṇī*. The ritual section is often found marked off from the rest of the text in some way. In the *Mahāśītavana-sūtra*, for example, a short *vidhi* is tacked on at the end of the text, following the final praises and a small gap in the writing (Figure 4.1). In the *Mahāpratisara-vidyarājñī*, the *vidhi* is located in the middle of the text, but it closes with its own "the end," or "*rdzogs so*," ending (Figure 4.2). And in the *Amoghapāśahṛdaya-dhāraṇī*, the final title in the Dunhuang manuscript makes it explicit that the *vidhi* is an addendum of sorts (Figure 4.3).

The odd textual arrangements of these *dhāraṇī vidhi* first caught my attention when I was studying a relatively well-known Chinese altar diagram from Dunhuang (Figure 4.4).[25] The Chinese writing above the diagram specifies that the altar depicted is for the worship of the *Uṣṇīṣavijayā-dhāraṇī*. Around the central image are arranged votive oil lamps, flower offerings, incense, and containers of water. On reading

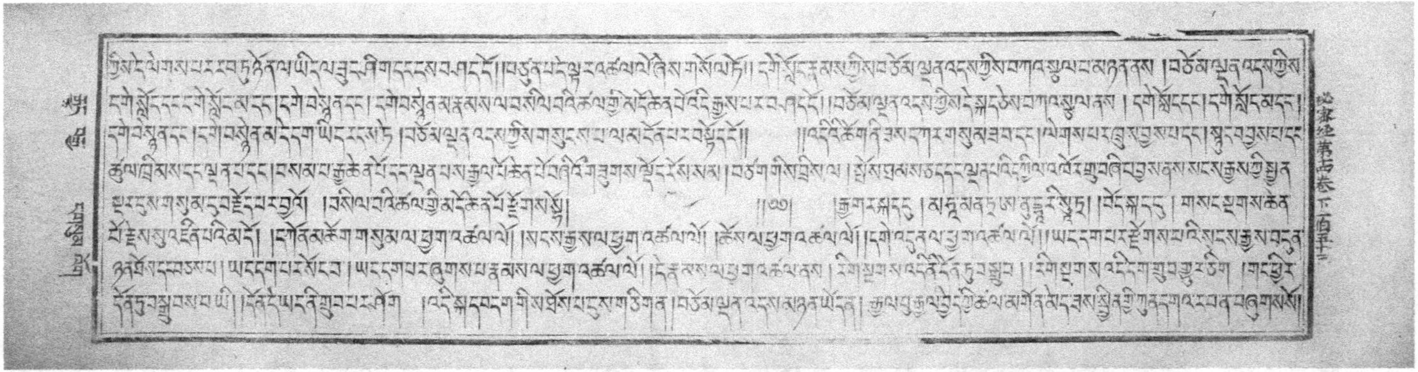

FIGURE 4.1 Final page of the *Mahāśītavana-sūtra* from the Peking *bka' 'gyur* (Q. 180, 153b), with appended *vidhi*.
Courtesy of the Tibetan Buddhist Resource Center.

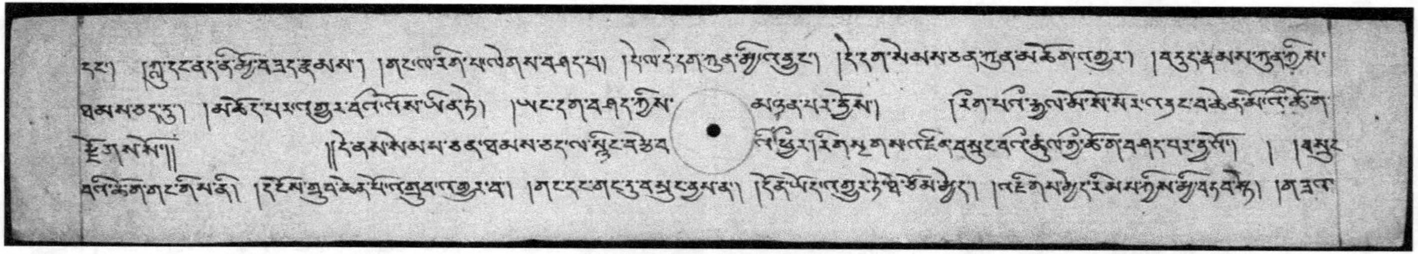

FIGURE 4.2 Page from the *Mahāpratisara-vidyarājñī* from Dunhuang (IOL Tib J 388, 4v), with inserted *vidhi*.

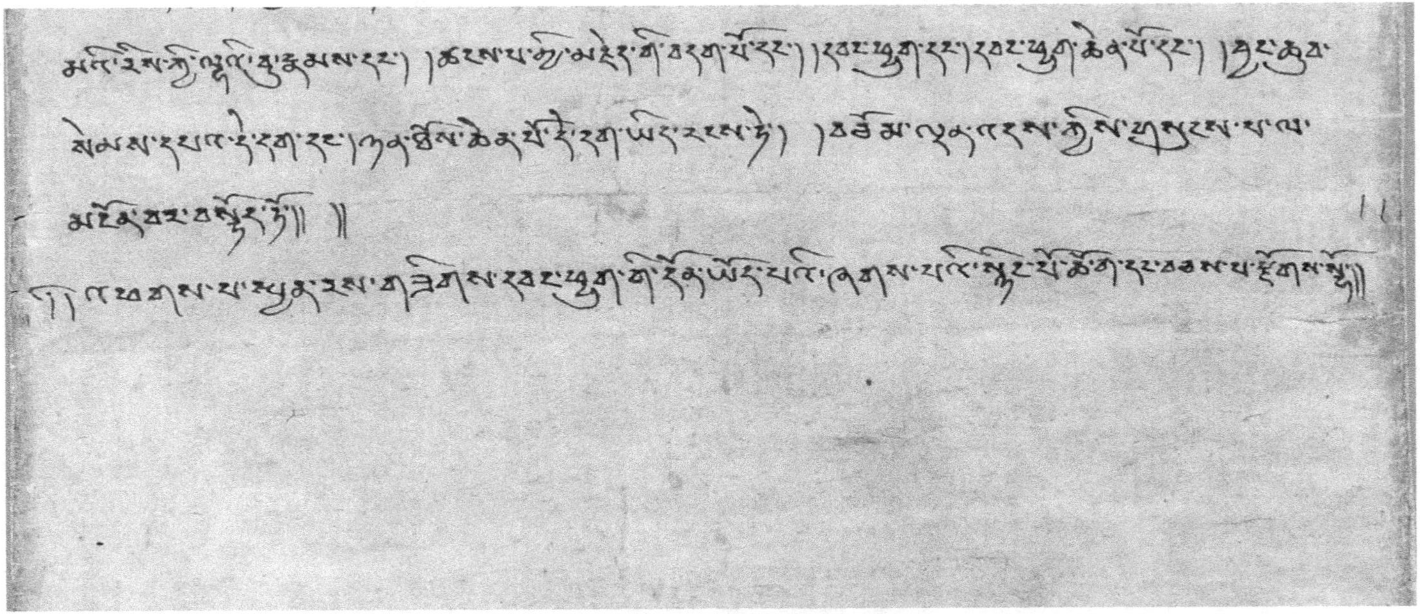

FIGURE 4.3 Final lines of the *Amoghapāśahṛdaya* from Dunhuang (Pelliot tibétain 49/4), with title shown.
Courtesy of the Bibliothèque nationale de France.

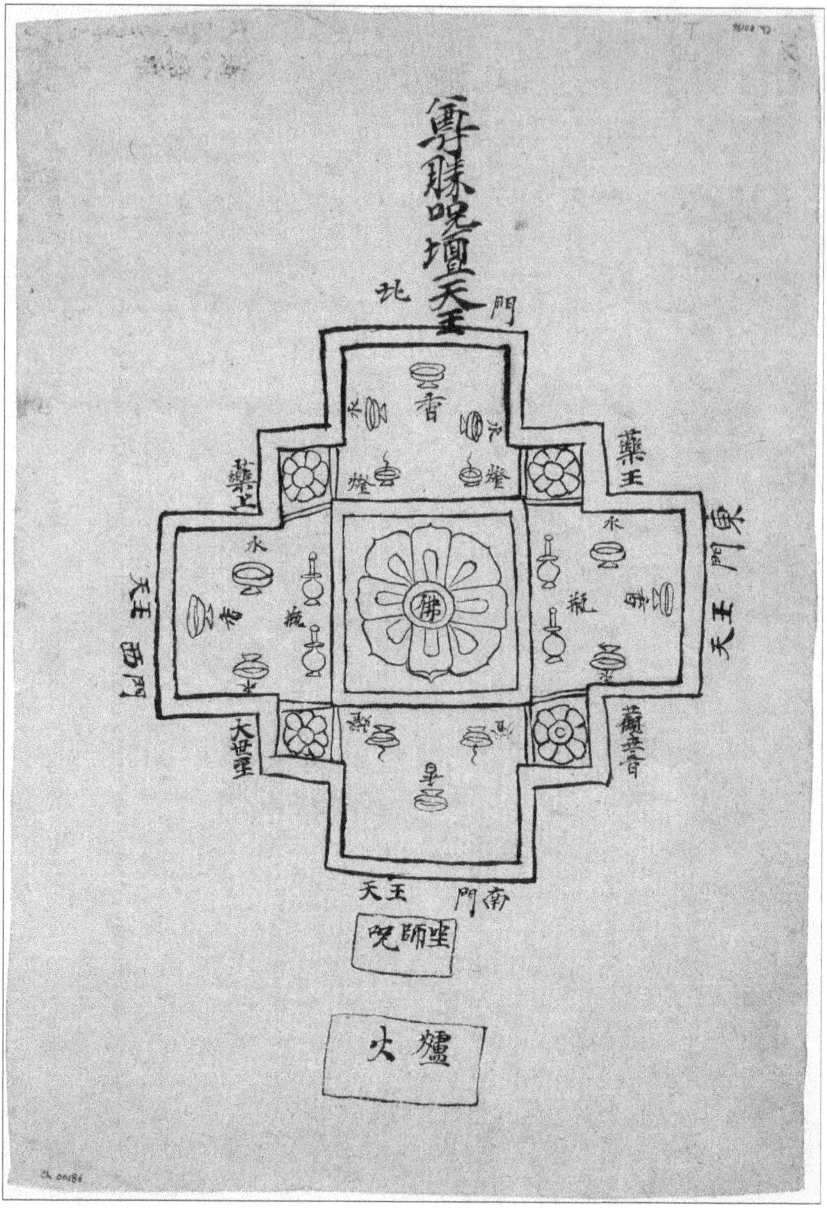

FIGURE 4.4 *Uṣṇīṣavijayā* altar diagram from Dunhuang (Stein Ch. 00186). Courtesy of the British Museum.

the *Uṣṇīṣavijayā-dhāraṇī*, however, I was surprised to discover no discussion of any such ritual. However, in the Tibetan canon we do find a second *Uṣṇīṣavijayā-dhāraṇī* that is not in the Chinese canon. Titled the *Sarvatathāgatoṣṇīṣavijāya-nāma-dhāraṇī-kalpasaṃhitā*,[26] the work deals with the same *dhāraṇī* spell, and here (as the title suggests) we find the *vidhi* (or *kalpa*) section that begins as follows:

> With cow dung make a square maṇḍala and scatter it with white flowers. Place oil lamps with melted butter in the four corners. Make an incense of aloe and fir. Adorn with flowers vessels filled with water that has been similarly perfumed. In the center, place a *stūpa* or a statue containing the *hṛdaya* of the *dhāraṇī*. While touching it with your left hand and holding a rosary in your right, recite the *dhāraṇī* three times each day for twenty-one days. Then, if you drink the offering waters in three sips from cupped hands, you will have no illness, your life will be long, your enemies will fade, your intellect will be sharp, and your speech noble. If you sprinkle those waters around a barn or stables, or around a royal palace, there will be no fear of thieves, snakes, spirits or demons, and there will be no afflictions from illness. If you sprinkle them over someone's head, that person will be cured of any illness.[27]

The correspondences between this passage and our Dunhuang diagram are obvious enough. A ritual manual resembling this Tibetan *Kalpasaṃhitā dhāraṇī* must have been known to the Chinese Buddhists around Dunhuang. A variety of manuals were apparently circulating alongside the main *dhāraṇī*-sūtra.[28] Eventually, one such manual came to be formulated as an independent sūtra that was included in the Tibetan canon.

A similar situation, again with one *dhāraṇī*-sūtra focusing on the narrative parts and another on the ritual parts, has been observed by Gregory Schopen. In a 1985 article, Schopen notes that the *Samantamukha-praveśa*[29] and the *Sarvaprajñā-dhāraṇīs*[30] both deal with the same *dhāraṇī* spell, but that the former is "almost entirely made up of narrative and lacks the detailed descriptions of the necessary ritual procedures. It does not have a *vidhi* section. What appears to be the *vidhi* section, however, is found in the *Śes pas thams cad* [= **Sarvaprajñā*], which—not surprisingly—contains very little narrative."[31] Schopen goes on to argue—on the basis of a scribal error in the copying of the spell—that the ritual text was probably written *after* the narrative *Samantamukha-praveśa*, and probably between the sixth and ninth centuries.[32]

When we combine the evidence on the *Uṣṇīṣavijayā-dhāraṇī* with Schopen's observations on his two *dhāraṇī*, and the awkward format of the *vidhi* sections in so many other *dhāraṇī*, a pattern begins to emerge.[33]

It seems that the ritual sections of many *dhāraṇī*-sūtras may have been added later, at some point after the earlier recensions—containing just the spell couched in a narrative setting—had already been circulating. Of course, many other *dhāraṇī*-sūtras were composed in one go with *vidhi* sections already present, but these tend to be later works, composed after the sixth century.

Finally, we may also note that in the *'Phang thang ma*, a mid-ninth century Tibetan catalogue of Buddhist translations, the *dhāraṇī* lists are divided into those with *vidhi* attached and those without. Some thirteen *dhāraṇī*-sūtras with *vidhi* sections are listed.[34] That the early Tibetan translators themselves distinguished the *vidhi*-bearing sūtras from the rest seems to indicate that they, too, recognized the significance of the addition of the ritual manual to these works.

Dating the Spread of Ritual Manuals

All this leads us to a further question: When exactly did these Buddhist manuals begin to appear? Certainly there were rituals in Buddhism right from the beginning, the monastic ordination rites being one good example. The principal source for the ordination rites, however, seems to have been the canonical Vinaya, and, to my knowledge at least, not distinct manuals.[35] Today's Theravāda ordinations do include the use of *kammavaca*, or manuals, which consist of passages from the Vinaya, but there is little evidence of their use in early Buddhism.[36] Another place to look for early ritual manuals might be in connection with the Mahāyāna liturgical format of the "seven-limbed worship." However, Dan Stevenson has spent some time exploring the Indian roots of this ubiquitous seven-part liturgical sequence, and has himself remarked on the peculiar lack of any related manuals. "As a quick glance should show," he writes, "the Indian sources are noticeably thin in liturgical content (rarely do we find what could be considered a full description of liturgical procedure)."[37] Nonetheless, we must maintain the possibility that scattered ritual notes or even short manuals may well have existed in Buddhism to some limited extent prior to the sudden and dramatic proliferation we see around the later *dhāraṇī* literature.

In order to determine when Buddhist ritual manuals really began to spread, one can look to the Chinese translations of the relevant *dhāraṇī-sūtras*. Toward this end, I have conducted a preliminary survey of *dhāraṇī vidhi* sections. Certainly more work is still necessary, but it seems that such ritual sections first started to appear around the second half of the fifth century. Michel Strickmann has noted the anomalously early ritual techniques described in the Chinese apocryphal *Consecration Sūtra* (*Guanding jing* 灌頂經), which dates from the second half of the fifth century,[38] and a few similar ritual discussions dating from the same period may also exist.[39] Stephen Hodge has noted what appears to be an *extremely* early *vidhi* section appended, he claims, to a 342 CE translation of the *Mahāmāyūri-vidyā-rāja Sūtra.*[40] Unfortunately, there seems to be some confusion here, as no such appendix is to be found in that location.[41] Instead, a *vidhi* section containing precisely the same ritual procedures Hodge describes *is* found, as an appendix, to a significantly later, early sixth-century translation of the *Mahāmāyūrī.*[42] As an interesting aside, a Taishō footnote to the latter text notes that the *vidhi* appendix in question does not appear in all Chinese versions of the text, so here again we have yet another *vidhi* that circulated separately at first and was appended only later to its parent *dhāraṇī sūtra*.

In short, all indications suggest that ritual manuals began to appear in Buddhism around the mid-fifth century. They continued to gain increasing popularity through the next decades, and by the middle of the sixth century Buddhist *vidhi*s were proliferating rapidly throughout India. Despite the possible existence of early manuals in connection with ordination rites or the seven-limbed worship, this sudden proliferation of ritual manuals in the late fifth and sixth centuries was unprecedented. Never before had such a number of locally produced manuals played such a central role in orthodox Buddhist practice. And compared to the earlier seven-limbed worship, the new rites described in the manuals were far more complex and of a completely different order. No longer just liturgies, the early *dhāraṇī vidhi*s described rites that placed a greater emphasis on arranging the ritual space and the practitioner's own physical activities. Now the reader prepared the ritual ground, constructed an altar, scattered flowers, sprinkled waters, and worshipped the central image while reciting the appropriate spells. Before long, these basic ritual forms were being varied according to the practitioner's desired results, so that the *Amoghapāśa-hṛdaya*'s *vidhi* section, for example, describes a number of ritual variations that could be performed: you practice it like this for curing disease, like that for turning back curses, and so forth. And from these kinds of variable rites it was a short step to the full-blown tantric rituals we see in the early tantras.

A proliferation of ritual manuals in the sixth century is of great significance for the history of tantric Buddhism, of course, for within a hundred years of this date we see the first tantras beginning to appear. By the early seventh century the first retroactively labeled "Kriyā tantras" were emerging in India, and by around 650 the seminal *Mahāvairocana-abhisaṃbodhi* was in circulation.[43] These initial tantras were the direct descendants of the earlier ritual manuals. The eighth-century scholar Buddhaguhya provides one of our earliest significant Indian discussions of the tantras as a whole. Having differentiated the Kriyā tantras from the slightly later Yoga tantras, he distinguishes two subclasses within the typically earlier Kriyā category: the "general tantras that are compilations of ritual manuals" (*spyi'i cho ga bsdus pa'i rgyud*), and the "distinct tantras" (*bye brag gi rgyud*).[44] Under the former type he lists the classic Kriyā sources such as the *Susiddhikāra*, the *Subāhuparipṛcchā*, and the *Kalpa-laghu*, and indeed these are all essentially compilations of ritual manuals.[45] Thus by seeing ritual manuals as a key developmental bridge between the earlier *dhāraṇīs* and the later tantras, we are simply following Buddhaguhya's lead. Many of the earliest Kriyā tantras were simply collections of these new ritual manuals.[46]

Matsunaga, Skilling, and many others have demonstrated the difficulties inherent in trying to identify tantric Buddhism with the advent of any one ritual practice, be it visualization, chanting mantras, or whatever.[47] They point out that the accumulation of such supposedly "tantric" ritual techniques was really an extremely gradual process that unfolded over many centuries. Yet only with the sixth century do we begin to see the rapid proliferation of ritual manuals as a distinct genre. This new body of literature facilitated more complex ritual sequences, but it also required a new place in the Buddhist systems of canonical classification, and so were born the tantras. Here we may remind ourselves again that tantras were *texts*, and as such their literary forebears were the new ritual manuals. In this sense, *dhāraṇīs* may not have been "proto-tantric," but ritual manuals truly were.[48]

Case Study: The Uṣṇīṣavijayā-dhāraṇī *and the* Sarvadurgatipariśodhana-tantra

For some further speculation on how more precisely ritual manuals may have contributed to the rise of the tantras, I return to the Chinese altar diagram that began my own interest in *dhāraṇīs*. In fact, we still have no clear textual source for this particular altar as it is depicted in the diagram. The Tibetan "*kalpasaṃhitā*" manual that I quoted earlier describes a similar altar, also for the worship of Uṣṇīṣavijayā, but it does not mention the various other deities that appear in our diagram in the various directions. The Chinese ritual manuals available in the Taishō do place other deities on the altar, but not the same ones. The closest match seems to be the manual attributed to Amoghavajra, which dates to 764. He too describes an altar in a 3 x 3 arrangement of nine squares, but in place of the buddhas and bodhisattvas that surround the central buddha image on our diagram, he has the well-known set of eight bodhisattvas.

In terms of ritual, Amoghavajra describes rites that are drawn more from the greatly influential system of the *Vajroṣṇīṣa* (sometimes called the *Vajraśekhara* by modern scholars), the so-called "root tantra" of the Yoga class. So it is clear that here Amoghavajra was reading his beloved later tantric ritual techniques back into the *Uṣṇīṣavijayā dhāraṇī*. Indeed, he seems to make explicit the Yoga-tantra versus more strictly *dhāraṇī*-based hermeneutic distinction when, in the context of determining the proper time for the performance, he writes, "Regarding fixing the time: [It may be performed] either twice a day, namely at dawn and dusk, or three times, in which case you add noon, or four times as in the Yoga system, in which case you add midnight. If you are following the original teaching of the *Vijayā Dhāraṇī* and reciting on the fifteenth day of the brightening moon [i.e., of the first half of the month] in order to remove the karmic hindrances, increase merit, and prolong life, then it is important to recite 1,000 times."[49]

Another interesting manual for the worship of the same *dhāraṇī* is the one attributed to the Indian master Śubhākarasiṃha, who was active in China in the early eighth century, a few decades before Amoghavajra. Being as early as they are, the writings of Śubhākarasiṃha provide many valuable insights into the early formation of the Yoga tantras and tantric Buddhism more generally. Śubhākarasiṃha's *Uṣṇīṣavijayā* manual also reads later developments into the rite, but unlike Amoghavajra's, they are less drawn from another ritual system; *these* later developments seem more native to the *Uṣṇīṣavijayā* ritual system itself. Where Amoghavajra surrounds the central buddha with the eight great bodhisattvas, Śubhākarasiṃha has a set of eight *uṣṇīṣa-buddhas*, with Mahāvairocana at the center, Sitātapatra-Buddhoṣṇīṣa to the north, Vijayā- Buddhoṣṇīṣa to the east, Cakravartin-Buddhoṣṇīṣa to the south, Tejorāśi-Buddhoṣṇīṣa to the west, and four others in the intermediate directions.[50]

The full significance of these ritual developments becomes clear when we turn to the full-fledged tantras, and specifically to the *Sarvadurgatipariśodhana-tantra*. The *Sarvadurgati* is an influential member of the Yoga-tantra class, and it probably developed around the early eighth century. While clearly influenced by the Vajroṣṇīṣa corpus, it represents a distinct line of development within the Yoga tantras, a line that appears to have connected the *Sarvadurgati-pariśodhana-tantra* to the *Uṣṇīṣavijayā-dhāraṇī*.[51] Several clues point to their developmentally close relationship. For starters, the latter's full title is in fact the *Sarvadurgati-pariśodhana-uṣṇīṣavijayā-dhāraṇī*. Both works, moreover, open with similar narratives in which a *devaputra* dwelling in the god-realms either dies or learns that he is soon to die and that he will then plunge into the hells for an eon of terrible sufferings. Greatly distressed, he (or his god friends) goes to the Buddha to plead for help. The Buddha is moved by compassion and teaches the saving techniques of the *dhāraṇī*, or of the tantra, as the case may be. The *Sarvadurgati-pariśodhana-tantra* and the *Uṣṇīṣavijayā-dhāraṇī* tell quite different versions of this story, but the basic plot is the same.[52]

The nature of this relationship may become clearer when we look at the iconography of the tantra's *Sarvadurgati-pariśodhana* maṇḍala, for here we find a ritual altar (i.e., maṇḍala) with the Buddha at the center and the now familiar eight *uṣṇīṣa-buddhas* surrounding him, seated in a slightly different arrangement from that seen in Śubhākarasiṃha's Chinese *Uṣṇīṣavijayā* ritual manual.[53] We are left with a striking possibility, that the *Uṣṇīṣavijayā-dhāraṇī* and the *Sarvadurgati-pariśodhana-tantra* were developmentally related in more ways than one, and that the bridges that linked them were the multiple ritual manuals that grew up around this tradition, bridges most clearly represented by Śubhākarasiṃha's early eighth-century manual. The original *Uṣṇīṣavijayā-dhāraṇī* spawned numerous manuals, then, that continued to develop over the century that followed its appearance. By the early eighth century, the developments had reached a critical mass, and the new *Sarvadurgati-pariśodhana-tantra* was compiled to re-encapsulate the tradition.

Conclusions

I want to end with some thoughts on how a greater appreciation of ritual manuals might add to present-day theories on the rise of tantric Buddhism. In his 2002 book, *Indian Esoteric Buddhism*, Ronald Davidson traces the general outlines of the political sea changes that early medieval India underwent. Building on earlier Indian historians like R. N. Nandi, R. S. Sharma, and B. D. Chattopadhyaya, he argues that the political fragmentation and the socioeconomic regionalism of the period forced Buddhists to adopt new ritual strategies that mirrored the political models at work in the surrounding society. Thus the tantric maṇḍala replicated the organization of the Indian state, with the king at the center, surrounded by his ministers and vassals. Of course, ritual manuals played a necessary role in the Buddhist developments of Davidson's model as well; manuals were needed, for example, to conduct the complex new coronation-style initiation ceremonies. And in this sense, shifting our focus to ritual manuals does not have to contradict Davidson's model. Rather, the new manuals can be seen as just another part of the wider ritual changes Davidson so ably describes.

But there is more. A close examination of Davidson's model reveals that he is really talking about a somewhat later period than is the present chapter. For Davidson, "It is only in the second half of the seventh century that the definitive esoteric system emerges,"[54] whereas our ritual manuals began to appear in the second half of the fifth and especially the sixth centuries. Again, the present chapter does not refute Davidson, but adds another perspective and some further nuance. I agree that "definitive" tantric Buddhism did not appear until the seventh century. However, when Davidson defines his "definitive esoteric system" exclusively in terms of a royal metaphor, he limits his narrative to no earlier than the second half of the seventh century. For only when the Yoga tantras began to appear did the royal rites and imagery really take center stage. Ritual manuals, however, started to spread well before this. The earlier *dhāraṇī*-based materials, and the so-called Kriyā-tantras, exhibit far less interest in the kinds of politically inspired rites that Davidson emphasizes. Instead, the earliest Buddhist manuals describe rites for image worship, for preparing the ritual space, for bodily purification, blessing buildings, curing diseases, and so on. Clearly a more nuanced explanation is required for the appearance of these "proto-tantras," these early ritual manuals that appeared a century or more before the first Yoga tantras.[55]

Thus by placing our focus on ritual manuals, the emergence of esoteric Buddhism becomes a much more gradual affair than Davidson describes. The rise of Davidson's esoteric Buddhism is a surprisingly sudden phenomenon that "was effected in decades, not centuries."[56] Because of his focus on tantric ideology, Davidson concludes that "[i]n the course of a few decades in the mid-seventh century, the most effective strategies for

Buddhist support had come unraveled. . . ."[57] Such a sudden socioeconomic shift seems to me improbable. Indeed, Davidson himself traces the causes for this shift to the fall of the Gupta Empire, an event that occurred much earlier, in the late fifth and early sixth centuries. And certainly the rise of India's early medieval feudalism, of which Davidson makes much, was a far more gradual affair that began well before the mid-seventh century, having roots even already in the Gupta period.[58] Surely we would do better to understand the appearance of the Buddhist tantras as the culmination of a much longer and more gradual process. By highlighting the role of ritual manuals, a more nuanced story is revealed, one that unfolds over a period of two hundred years, from the mid-fifth to the mid-seventh centuries.

The genre of *dhāraṇī-vidhis* thus offers an invaluable window onto the development of early tantric Buddhist ritual techniques. Through these texts we can catch a glimpse of a formative period, when Buddhist ritual was in full flux. These long-lost literary treasures attest to the powerful influence of local innovation and individual practice upon the development of the Tibetan Buddhist tradition. Only the *dhāraṇī-vidhis* and liturgical collections, thanks to their fluid and individualizable character, could allow for the innumerable creative mutations that were necessary for the tantras to evolve.

Notes

1. See Strickmann (1996, 130, and 2002, 103–109). For Strickmann, the main point of similarity between *dhāraṇīs* and tantras is their shared emphasis on worldly gods and demons. Such an emphasis, however, is by no means specific to *dhāraṇīs*. Indeed, as Gregory Schopen (1997), Peter Skilling (1992), Robert Decaroli (2004), and others have noted, Buddhists were widely concerned with ghosts and worldly gods from early on.
2. McBride (2005, 86, citing Waddell 1912–1913, 160–165, 169–178). See also McBride (2004) and Sharf 2002, 263–278.
3. Davidson (2002, 117). For his reasons, see p. 368n12.
4. See Burnouf (1844, 540–541); Lamotte (1976, 4:1855–1877); Gyatso (1992); Davidson (2009, 2014).
5. Two significant exceptions are Schopen (1985) and Skilling (1992). More recently Paul Copp, who works on the Chinese cultural context, has been drawing attention to the material uses of *dhāraṇīs*; see Copp (2008a, 2008b).
6. In my own research, I have yet to see a single Mahāyoga tantric manuscript that can be dated before the tenth century. On the basis of handwriting, I have argued

elsewhere that some of the Yoga-tantra materials, and particularly those based on the *Sarvatathāgata-tattvasaṃgraha*, may date from slightly earlier, perhaps as early as the mid-ninth century. On dating the Tibetan Dunhuang manuscripts according to handwriting style, see van Schaik (2013).

7. PT849 represents an exception to this rule, and others may yet be found; as Kapstein (2006) has suggested, PT849 appears to reflect a stage of Indian development closer to the manuscript's own tenth-century date.
8. The eighth-century scholar Buddhaguhya, for example, writes that, "The Bhagavat Vairocana is to be viewed as the accomplishing practitioner.... This also indicates to future disciples that they should make themselves appear in the body-image of their own deity ..." (*Mahāvairocana Vṛtti*, 157b.1–3: *rnam par snang mdzad ni sgrub pa po lta bur blta la/... rang gi lha'i sku'i gzugs su snang bar 'gyur ro zhes ma 'ongs pa'i gdul ba'i 'gro ba rnams la bstan pa yin no*). For an English translation of the relevant passage, see Hodge (2003, 257).
9. This was particularly true of the crucial first few centuries of tantric ritual development, from around the seventh to the eleventh centuries, after which new tantras largely stopped being written.
10. Think only of the recent proliferation of new tantric ritual manuals in the West, written by Tibetan teachers for a Western audience.
11. A similar trend may be seen in research on tantric Śaivisim, too, where scriptural works have received the bulk of scholarly attention, though mention should be made of the work of Hélène Brunner, who has done some pioneering work on the mid-eleventh-century *Somaśambhu-paddhati*; see Brunner (1963, 1968, 1977, 1998).
12. On the most complete Tibetan copy of the *Pañcarakṣā* from Dunhuang, see my notes to IOL Tib J 399 in Dalton and van Schaik (2006, 80–81).
13. Many of the Dunhuang *dhāraṇī* collections are incomplete and thus their order is difficult to discern, but for some particularly clear examples of this order, see IOL Tib J 316 and 366 and Pelliot tibétain 22, 23, 24. Cases of the invitation appearing in the middle of the collection also do occur; see IOL Tib J 466 (discussed later) for an example.
14. In another comment that is relevant to the present chapter, Skilling (1992) points out that "[i]f a collection of Sri Lankan *parittas* were published along with all such preliminaries, admonitions, ceremonies, and rites, in both contents and length it would resemble one of the composite *Pañcarakṣā* texts, minus, of course, the *mantras*" (144).
15. For a discussion of these final *gāthās*, see Skilling (1992, 129–137), where Skilling demonstrates how many of them are extracted from earlier sūtras. Skilling also translates an explanation for the inclusion of the closing *gāthās* from the index (*dkar chag*) to the *Golden Tanjur* as follows: "In order to make fruitful the work that has [just been] completed [the copying of the *Tanjur*], the dedications (*bsngo ba* = *pariṇamanā*), aspirations (*smon lam* = *praṇidhāna*), and blessings

(*bkra śis* = *maṅgala*) [follow] . . ." (Skilling 1992, 131). It is unclear from this passage alone whether Skilling's interpolations are correct, that is, whether the "completed work" was that of compiling the canon, or of reciting the *dhāraṇī*. If Skilling is right, however, we can conclude that the liturgical function of these closing sections may have been forgotten by the time of the later canons' compilation.

16. The separate *dhāraṇī* section appears only in those *bka' 'gyur* collections stemming from the *Tshal pa* edition (see Eimer 1989, 40n7).
17. Pelliot tibétain 22, R1.8: *zab mo rgyal ba'i bka' la kun gson cig.* While several Dunhuang versions share this ending (e.g., Pelliot tibétain 24, r4.4 and Pelliot tibétain 26, r2.3–4), others end differently, though with a similar sentiment; see, for example, IOL Tib J 316, v3.3–4.1. Further work is necessary to determine the relationships between the multiple versions of this much-varied work. My comments here are only meant to represent the general form and ritual purpose of the work.
18. Pelliot tibétain 25, 1v.4: *skabs 'dir mdo sde 'am zhal . . . gsungs pa'i tshigs bcad klag.* Unfortunately, the folio is damaged in the middle of the line. Note that while this line does not appear in the canonical versions, what follows it is present (compare Q. 471, 3b.4). Lalou mistook these final lines for the beginning of a new text (see Lalou 1939–1961, 1:9).
19. The standard *Rnying ma pa* narrative of the origin of the tantras begins with a King Dza who receives the teachings after a series of seven dreams over the course of seven nights. That narrative, in turn, is closely connected to the legend of how the *Karaṇḍavyūha Sūtra* first arrived in Tibet by descending down to the king Lha tho tho ri. (On these early myths see Stein 1972, 51; Karmay 1981; Dudjom Rinpoche 1991, 1:508.) The narrative in IOL Tib J 711 appears to have emerged from this same narrative mix that was circulating in the early centuries of Tibetan Buddhist history. For more on IOL Tib J 711, see Dalton (2011, 62–64).
20. In discussing the same manuscript for its mention of King Khri srong lde brtsan, Van Schaik and Doney (2007, 195–196), have made similar observations regarding its format and possible date.
21. On the former contexts, see Schopen (1997, 207–208 and 231–233). On the latter, see Silk (2008, 80–81).
22. For a translation of the relevant passage, see Lévi (1915, 432–434), and Takakusu (1896, 152–153). (References drawn from Schopen 1992, 232.)
23. IOL Tib J 466, 2r.20.
24. Translation following that of Sam van Schaik on his blog, "EarlyTibet.com"; see "Buddhism and Empire III: The Dharma King" (August 21, 2008).
25. Earlier studies of this diagram include Whitfield (2004, 274); Fraser (2004, 154–155, fig. 415); Zwalf (1985, no. 324); Whitfield (1982–1985, vol. 2, fig. 81); Waley (1931, no. 74); Stein (1921, 893, 974).

26. The back-formation of the Sanskrit for this title in the Peking edition I am citing here actually reads *kalpa-sahita*, but I am following the more preferable *kalpasaṃhitā* that appears in the Cone edition.
27. Q. 197, 223a.5–223b.1: *lci bas maṇ ḍal gru bzhir byas la me tod dkar po bkram ste/ mtshams bzhir zhun mar gyi mar me bzhi bzhag la/ a ka ru dan du ru ka'i bdrug pa byas la de bzhin du dri'i chus gang ba'i snod me tod dkar pos brgyan te/ gzungs kyi snying po can gyi mchod rten nam sku gzugs dbus su bzhugs su gsol la/ de la g.yon pa'i lag pas reg ste/ g.yas pa'i lag pa phreng ba 'dzin pas/ nyi ma re re zhing nyi shu rtsa gcig rtsa gcig dus gsum du bzlas pa byas la de'i chu khyor ba gsum 'thungs na nad med pa dang/ tshe ring ba dang dag yongs su nyams pa dang/ 'dzin blo rno ba dang ngag btsun par 'gyur ro/ skye ba nas skye bar skye ba dran par 'gyur ro/ de'i chus khang pa dang phyugs kyi ra ba 'am rta'i ra ba 'am/ rgyal po'i khab tu gtor na rkun mo dang/ sbrul dang gnod sbyin dang/ srin po la sogs pa'i 'jigs pa mi 'byung zhing nad kyis yongs su gdungs par mi 'gyur ro.*
28. Unfortunately, the *Kalpasaṃhitā* has no colophon, making it difficult to tell when it was translated. This, in turn, makes it difficult to determine more precisely the relationship between the *Kalpasaṃhitā* preserved in the Tibetan canon and the hypothetical *vidhi* that circulated around Dunhuang. Note, however, that the *Dkar chag 'phang thang ma*, 23, does include an **Uṣṇīṣavijayā-dhāraṇī-vidhisaṃhitā* (*cho ga dang bcas pa*).
29. Full title: *Ārya-samantamukha-praveśaraśmi-vimaloṣṇīṣaprabhā-sasarvatathāgatahṛdaya-samayavilokate-nāma-dhāraṇī* (Q. 206).
30. Full title: *Sarvaprajñāntapāramitasiddhicaitya-nāma-dhāraṇī* (Q. 219).
31. Schopen (1985, 144). For some additional observations on these texts using the Dunhuang manuscripts, see Scherrer-Schaub (1994).
32. Schopen (1985, 145).
33. Further evidence lies in related observations that have been made in passing by other scholars. Skilling, for example, has noted the ritual "annexes" in the later recensions of the *Mahāsamāja-sūtra*, as well as in the Tibetan *Bhadrakarātrī* and the Central Asian Sanskrit *Nagaropama-sūtra* (Skilling 1994–1997, 2:533–535). In personal correspondence, Skilling also confirms that "[i]n the Theravada lineage the texts—*paritta* and other *rakṣās*—were memorized and also written, but the rites rarely.... It seems the specifics of the rite are transmitted orally and by example." And perhaps in a similar vein, John Kieshnick has observed that "[w]ith the three great Tang ritual specialists Amoghavajra, Vajrabodhi, and Śubakarasiṃha [*sic*] ... it was no longer enough to chant a common spell; spell-casting now required expertise in a vast body of technical, esoteric lore" (Kieschnick 1997, 89–90).
34. *Dkar chag 'phang thang ma*, 23–24.
35. In the Pāli canon, the *Mahāvagga* provides the most detailed descriptions of the ordination ceremony. Today's ordinations do include the use of *kammavaca*, or manuals, which consist of passages from the Vinaya, but there is little evidence

of their use in early Buddhism. For a description and translation of an *upasampada kammavaca*, see Dickson (1874), reprinted in Warren (1896, 393–401). My thanks to Charlie Hallisey for his assistance on these points.

36. My thanks to Peter Skilling for confirming this observation in oral communication, April 2014.
37. Stevenson (1987, 440–441). On the *sapta-pūjā*, see too Crosby and Skilton (1995, 9–13), where the worship is traced to the second century CE.
38. Dating according to Ōmura (1918, 128–133), as cited by Strickmann (1990, 80, 110n12). On this sūtra, see also Davidson (2002, 127–129).
39. Another purportedly fifth-century ritual section appears at the end of the *Dhāraṇī for Great Benefit* (*Da jiyi shenzhou jing* 大吉義神咒經; T. 1335), supposedly translated by Tanyao in 462. Unfortunately this ascription, as is the case with many such Chinese translators (see Strickmann 1990, 79) is not necessarily reliable. Tanyao was a highly reputed monk of the sort that might attract false attributions. The Taishō lists him as the translator of three works in all. For his other two translations he worked as part of a two-man team, whereas for the *Dhāraṇī of Great Benefit* he is said to have worked alone. Moreover, both of his other works are thoroughly exoteric in content. (My thanks to Koichi Shinohara for his generous help on these points.)
40. Hodge (2003, 8).
41. Hodge identifies the text in question with the T. 1331, which is actually the abovementioned *Consecration Sūtra*.
42. T. 984, translation ascribed to Saṅghavarman (460–524).
43. See Hodge (1995, 65).
44. See his *Dhyānottarapaṭala*, 11b.1–3. Nyangral makes a similar distinction; see *Zangs gling ma*, 63.
45. Under "distinct tantras" he lists works like the *Mahāvairocana-abhisaṃbodhi* and the *Vajrapāṇyabhiṣeka*. He also lists the *Vidyādhara-piṭaka* and the *Bodhimaṇḍa*, neither of which has been firmly identified. In his *Piṇḍārtha*, 4a.6, he further adds to this subclass the *Trisamayarāja*, and the *Trikāyauṣṇīṣa*.
46. Note too that around this same time (i.e., the early seventh century), we begin to see a parallel development within the iconographic sphere, there of multiple deities (rather than *vidhis*) being gathered into more complex mandalas (rather than *saṃgrahas* or *tantras*); see, for example, Atikūṭa's mid-seventh-century *Tuoluoni ji jing* 陀羅尼集經 (T. 901), which has been discussed extensively by both Davidson (2012) and Shinohara (2010, 2014).
47. See Matsunaga (1977) and Skilling (1994–1997).
48. The same appears to have been the case for early tantric Śaivism. Discussions of tantric Śaiva material in early works such as the *Niśvāsatattvasaṃhitā*, for example, speak of multiple, no longer extant *kalpas* or *mantrakalpas* that circulated as supplements to tantric literature proper. (I thank Shaman Hatley for his observations on this point.) Richard Davis has similarly noted the proliferation

of *paddhatis* (ritual manuals that "follow in the footprints" of the Śaiva *āgamas*) in the early medieval period; see Davis (1991, 15–16).

49. T. 972, 19:365a6–9. My thanks to Koichi Shinohara for helping me to translate this passage.
50. See T. 973, 19:376a1–27 for the relevant descriptions.
51. For more on this line of ritual development, see Davidson (2012).
52. I plan a more complete translation and study of this narrative and its various tellings in my forthcoming book on tantric ritual development as seen through the lens of the Dunhuang manuscripts.
53. In the tantric maṇḍala, the central Buddha is surrounded by Vajrapāṇi to the east, Jayoṣṇīṣa to the south, Uṣṇīṣacakravartin to the west, and Uṣṇīṣavijayā to the north, with Uṣṇīṣatejorāśi, Uṣṇīṣavidhvaṃsaka, Uṣṇīṣavikiriṇa, and Uṣṇīṣasitātapatra in the intermediate directions, clockwise from southeast to northeast.
54. Davidson (2002, 117).
55. I believe that the spread of image worship played a central role in the development of Buddhist ritual during this same period. Koichi Shinohara (2014) is a study of the chronological development of image worship and early tantric ritual in some early ritual manuals preserved in the Chinese canon. His work adds much to the theories laid out here in the present chapter. Davidson (2012) has also looked at some of the same Chinese texts, and it should be emphasized that his work is increasingly focused on pre-seventh-century ritual developments, all of which promises also to add much to our understanding.
56. Davidson (2002, 118).
57. Davidson (2002, 85; see also 105 et al.).
58. Sharma (1974, 2), writes, "The Gupta period saw a strong feudalization of the state apparatus which is not to be found in Mauryan times." Sharma goes on to trace the feudalization process back to the first century CE, when the practice of making land grants to the *brāhmaṇas* first began, though it should be pointed out that the practice did not become widespread, especially among secular recipients, until somewhat later; see Chattopadhyaya (1994, 11).

References

PRIMARY SOURCES

Dhyānottarapaṭalaṭīkā. Buddhaguhya. Q. 3495.

Dkar chag 'phang thang ma. Full title: *Dkar chag 'phang thang ma/ Sgra sbyor bam po gnyis pa*. Beijing: Mi rigs dpe skrun khang, 2003.

Foding zunsheng tuoluoni niansong yigui fa 佛頂尊勝陀羅尼念誦儀軌法. Amoghovajra. T. 972.

Mahāvairocana Vṛtti. Full title: *Vairocanābhisambodhivikurvitādhiṣṭānamahātantravṛtti*. Buddhaguhya. Q. 3490.

Piṇḍārtha. Full title: *Vairocanābhisambodhitantrapiṇḍārtha*. Buddhaguhya. Q. 3486.

Zangs gling ma. Nyang nyi ma 'od zer gyis gter nas bton. Full title: *Slob dpon padma'i rnam thar zangs gling ma bzhugs*. Chengdu, China: Si khron mi rigs dpe skrun khang, 1989.

Zunsheng Foding xiu yujia fa guiyi 尊勝佛頂脩瑜伽法軌儀. Śubhākarasiṃha. T. 973.

SECONDARY SOURCES

Brunner, Hélène. 1963. *Somaśambhupaddhati. Première partie: Le rituel quotidien dans la tradition śivaïte de l'Inde du Sud. Introduction, text, et notes*. Publications de l'Institut Fraņcais d'Indologie 25.1. Pondicherry: Institut Fraņcais d'Indologie.

Brunner, Hélène. 1968. *Somaśambhupaddhati. Deuxième partie: Rituels Occasionnels dans la tradition śivaïte de l'Inde du Sud selon Somaśambhu. I: pavitrārohaṇa, damanapūjā et prāyaścitta. Texte, traduction et notes*. Publications de l'Institut Fraņcais d'Indologie 25.2. Pondicherry: Institut Fraņcais d'Indologie.

Brunner, Hélène. 1977. *Somaśambhupaddhati. Troisième partie: Rituels Occasionnels dans la tradition śivaïte de l'Inde du Sud selon Somaśambhu. II: dīkṣā, abhiṣeka, vratoddhāra, antyeṣṭi, śrāddha. Texte, traduction, et notes*. Publications de l'Institut Fraņcais d'Indologie 25.3. Pondicherry: Institut Fraņcais d'Indologie.

Brunner, Hélène. 1998. *Somaśambhupaddhati: rituels dans la tradition sivaïte selon Somaśambhu. Quatrième partie: rituels optionnels: pratiṣṭhā. Texte, traduction, et notes*. Publications de l'Institut Fraņcais d'Indologie 25.4. Pondicherry: Institut Fraņcais d'Indologie.

Burnouf, Eugene. 1844. *Introduction a l'Histoire du Buddhism Indien*. Paris: Imprimerie Royale.

Chattopadhyaya, Brajadulal. 1994. *The Making of Early Medieval India*. Delhi and New York: Oxford University Press.

Copp, Paul. 2008a. "Notes on the Term 'Dhāraṇī' in Medieval Chinese Buddhist Thought." *Bulletin of the School of Oriental and African Studies* 71 (3): 493–508.

Copp, Paul. 2008b. "Altar, Amulet, Icon: Transformations in Dhāraṇī Amulet Culture, 740–980." *Cahiers d'Extrême-Asie* 17: 239–264.

Crosby, Kate, and Andrew Skilton, trans. 1995. *Śāntideva: The Bodhicaryāvatāra*. Oxford: Oxford University Press.

Dalton, Jacob P. 2011. *The Taming of the Demons: Violence and Liberation in Tibetan Buddhism*. New Haven, CT: Yale University Press.

Dalton, Jacob P., and Sam van Schaik. 2006. *Tibetan Tantric Manuscripts from Dunhuang: A Descriptive Catalogue of the Stein Collection at the British Library*. Leiden: Brill.

Davidson, Ronald. 2002. *Indian Esoteric Buddhism: A Social History of the Tantric Movement*. New York: Columbia University Press.

Davidson, Ronald. 2009. "Studies in Dhāraṇī Literature I: Revisiting the Meaning of the Term *Dhāraṇī*." *Journal of Indian Philosophy* 37: 97–147.

Davidson, Ronald. 2012. "Some Observations on an Uṣṇīṣa Abhiṣeka Rite in Atikūṭa's *Dhāraṇīsaṃgraha*." In *Transformation and Transfer of Tantra/Tantrism in Asia and Beyond*, edited by István Keul, 77–97. Berlin: Walter de Gruyter.

Davidson, Ronald. 2014. "Studies in *Dhāraṇī* Literature II: Pragmatics of *Dhāraṇīs*." *Bulletin of SOAS* 77 (1): 5–61.

Davis, Richard. 1991. *Ritual in an Oscillating Universe: Worshiping Śiva in Medieval India*. Princeton, NJ: Princeton University Press.

Dudjom Rinpoche. 1991. *The Nyingma School of Tibetan Buddhism*. 2 vols. Boston: Wisdom Publications.

Eimer, Helmut. 1989. *Der Tantra-Katalog des Bu ston im Verglieich mit der Abteilung Tantra des tibetischen Kanjur*. Bonn: Indica et Tibetica Verlag.

Fraser, Sarah E. 2004. *Performing the Visual: The Practice of Buddhist Wall Painting in China and Central Asia, 618–960*. Stanford, CA: Stanford University Press.

Gyatso, Janet. 1992. "Letter Magic: A Peircean Perspective on the Semiotics of Rdo Grub-chen's Dharani Memory." In *In the Mirror of Memory*, edited by Janet Gyatso, 173–213. Albany: State University of New York Press.

Hodge, Stephen. 1995. "Considerations on the Dating and Geographical Origins of the *Mahāvairocanābhisambodhi-sūtra*." In *The Buddhist Forum*, edited by Tadeusz Skorupski and Ulrich Pagel, 3:57–83. London: School of Oriental and African Studies.

Hodge, Stephen. 2003. *The Mahā-vairocana-abhisaṃbodhi Tantra, with Buddhaguhya's Commentary*. London: Routledge Curzon.

Kapstein, Matthew. 2006. "New Light on an Old Friend: PT 849 Reconsidered." In *Tibetan Buddhist Literature and Praxis*, edited by Ronald Davidson and Christian Wedemeyer, 9–30. Leiden: Brill.

Karmay, Samten. 1981. "King Tsa/Dza and Vajrayāna." In *Tantric and Taoist Studies in Honour of R. A. Stein*, edited by Michel Strickmann, 192–211. *Mélanges chinois et bouddhiques* 20. Louvain: Institut belge des hautes etudes chinoises.

Kieschnick, John. 1997. *The Eminent Monk: Buddhist Ideals in Medieval Chinese Hagiography*. Honolulu: University of Hawai'i Press.

Lalou, Marcelle. 1939–1961. *Inventaire de Manuscrits tibétains de Touen-houang*. 3 vols. Paris: Libraire d'Amérique et d'Orient.

Lamotte, Étienne. 1976. *Le Traité de le Grande Vertu de Sagesse*. 5 vols. Louvain: Institut Orientaliste.

Lévi, Sylvain. 1915. "Sur la récitation primitive des texts bouddhiques." *Journal Asiatique* 11 (6): 401–447.

Matsunaga, Yukei. 1977. "A History of Tantric Buddhism in India, with Reference to Chinese Translations." In *Buddhist Thought and Asian Civilization, Essays in Honor of Herbert V. Guenther on His Sixtieth Birthday*, edited by Leslie S. Kawamura and Keith Scott, 167–181. Emeryville, CA: Dharma Publishing.

McBride, Richard D. 2004. "Is There Really 'Esoteric' Buddhism?" *Journal of the International Association of Buddhist Studies* 27 (2): 329–356.

McBride, Richard D. 2005. "*Dhāraṇī* and Spells in Medieval Sinitic Buddhism." *Journal of the International Association of Buddhist Studies* 28 (1): 85–114.

Ōmura Seigai 大村西崖. 1918. *Mikkyō hattatsu shi* 密教發達志. Tokyo: Bussho Kankōkai Zuzōbu 佛書刋行會図像部.

Scherrer-Schaub, Christina. 1994. "Some Dhāraṇī Written on Paper Functioning as Dharmakāya Relics: A Tentative Approach to PT 350." In *Tibetan Studies: Proceedings of the 6th Seminar of the International Association for Tibetan Studies*, 2: 711–727. Oslo: Insitute for Comparative Research in Human Culture.

Schopen, Gregory. 1985. "The Bodhigarbhālaṅkāralakṣa and Vimaloṣṇīṣa Dhāraṇīs in Indian Inscriptions." *Wiener Zeitschrift für die Kunde Südasiens* 29: 119–149.

Schopen, Gregory. 1997. *Bones, Stones, and Buddhist Monks: Collected Papers on the Archaeology, Epigraphy, and Texts of Monastic Buddhism in India.* Honolulu: University of Hawai'i Press.

Sharf, Robert H. 2002. *Coming to Terms with Chinese Buddhism*. Honolulu: University of Hawai'i Press.

Sharma, Ram Sharan. 1974. *Early Medieval Indian Society: A Study in Feudalisation. Indian Historical Review* 1 (1): 1–9.

Shinohara, Koichi. 2010. "The All-Gathering Maṇḍala Initiation Ceremony in Atikūṭa's Collected Dhāraṇī Scriptures: Reconstructing the Evolution of Esoteric Buddhist Ritual." *Journal Asiatique* 298 (2): 389–420.

Shinohara, Koichi. 2014. *Images, Spells, and Maṇḍalas: Tracing the Evolution of Esoteric Buddhist Rituals*. New York: Columbia University Press.

Silk, Jonathan A. 2008. *Managing Monks: Administrators and Administrative Roles in Indian Buddhist Monasticism*. Oxford; New York: Oxford University Press.

Skilling, Peter. 1992. "The Rakṣā Literature of the Śrāvakayāna." *Journal of the Pali Text Society* 16: 109–182.

Skilling, Peter. 1994–1997. *Mahāsūtras*. 2 vols. Oxford: Pali Text Society.

Stein, Marc Aurel. 1921. *Serindia: Detailed Report of Explorations in Central Asia and Westernmost China*. 5 vols. Oxford: Clarendon Press.

Stein, R. A. 1972. *Tibetan Civilization*. Stanford: Stanford University Press.

Stevenson, Daniel B. 1987. *The T'ien-t'ai Four Fourms of Samādhi and Late North-South Dynasties, Sui, and Early T'ang Buddhist Devotionalism*. Unpublished PhD thesis, Columbia University.

Strickmann, Michel. 1990. "The *Consecration Sūtra:* A Buddhist Book of Spells." In *Chinese Buddhist Apocrypha*, edited by Robert E. Buswell, 75–118. Honolulu: University of Hawai'i Press.

Strickmann, Michel. 1996. *Mantras et mandarins: Le bouddhisme tantrique en Chine.* Paris: Gallimard.

Strickmann, Michel. 2002. *Chinese Magical Medicine.* Stanford, CA: Stanford University Press.

Takakusu, J. 1896. *A Record of the Buddhist Religion as Practiced in India and the Malay Archipelago*. Oxford: Clarendon Press.

van Schaik, Sam. 2013. "Towards a Tibetan Paleography: A Preliminary Typology of Writing Styles in Early Tibet." In *Manuscript Cultures: Mapping the Field*, edited by Jörg Quenzer and Jan-Ulrich Sobisch, 299–337. Berlin: de Gruyter.

van Schaik, Sam, and Lewis Doney. 2007. "The Prayer, The Priest and The Tsenpo: An Early Buddhist Narrative from Dunhuang." *Journal of the International Association of Buddhist Studies* 30 (1–2): 175–217.

Waddell, L. A. 1912–1913. "The 'Dhāraṇī' Cult in Buddhism, Its Origin, Deified Literature and Images." *Ostasiatische Zeitschrift* 1. Berlin: Oesterheld.

Waley, Arthur. 1931. *A Catalogue of Paintings Recovered from Tun-Huang*. London: British Museum.

Warren, H. C. 1896. *Buddhism in Translation*. Cambridge, MA: Harvard University Press.

Whitfield, Roderick. 1982–1985. *The Art of Central Asia*. 3 vols. Tokyo: Kodansha.

Whitfield, Susan, ed. 2004. *The Silk Road: Trade, Travel, War and Faith*. London: The British Library Press.

Zwalf, Vladimir. 1985. *Buddhist Art and Faith*. London: British Museum Publishing.

5

The Purification of Heruka

ON THE TRANSMISSION OF A CONTROVERSIAL BUDDHIST TRADITION TO TIBET

David B. Gray

RELIGIOUS TRADITIONS CHANGE over time.[1] One way that they change is by borrowing and adapting elements of textual discourse and ritual practice from other religious traditions, often while maintaining the ideological stance that they have remained unchanged. Yet despite such claims, traditions that change in this manner are not seamless; rather, they are marked by signs of transformation, which can leave them open to critique from both outsider and, especially, insider critics. Such transformations are particularly pronounced when religious traditions cross cultural boundaries; this makes cultural transmission a particularly fascinating phenomenon. When traditions cross boundaries, not only do they become more open to change and transformation, but their preexisting seams and fissures also become more obvious, leaving them vulnerable to criticism.

This chapter will focus on a particularly interesting moment in the transmission of Indian tantric Buddhist traditions to Tibet. This moment is the late tenth century, the opening of the second or "latter transmission" (*phyi dar*) of Buddhism to Tibet, which continued until Buddhism had largely disappeared from the plains of North India in the fourteenth century.[2] Many traditions of text and practice were transmitted to Tibet during this period, with varying degrees of success. Resistance to this process appears to have been greatest in the beginning, particularly with respect to the Mahāyoga and Yoginītantric traditions that challenged Buddhist identity, either via their apparent advocacy of transgressive practices, or their possession of signs of non-Buddhist identity or origination. Among the more difficult materials for Tibetans to accept were the Yoginītantras associated with the deity Heruka, as they challenged Buddhist identity in both ways.

The Syncretistic Process in South Asian Religions

The question of whether or not a given religious tradition has borrowed or appropriated elements from other religious traditions, whether at its origin or later in its history, is always a politically sensitive question. Here I use the term "appropriation" in the sense suggested by Tony Stewart and Carl Ernst, as a process "wherein the borrowed item is transformed through the process of incorporation, thus fundamentally altering both the appropriated and the appropriator" (2003, 587). It seems evident that all religions have, at varying points in their history, depended upon and drawn from the larger cultural contexts in which they arise and in which they are embedded, and this context very often includes other religious traditions. Yet this is politically charged precisely because most religious traditions do not focus upon such dependence, and often create narratives that work to obscure it, either by ignoring competing religious traditions, or by advancing triumphalist ideologies that reduce rival traditions to subordinate positions. A well-known example in the Western traditions is the supersession argument made, for example, by some advocates of Islam. It holds that Islam, while obviously dependent on the earlier traditions of Judaism and Christianity, "supersedes" them by presenting a fuller revelation of God's law (Sachedina 1996, 2006). In South Asia, the most common strategy was to likewise subordinate competing traditions, typically by advancing cosmologies in which the chief figures of the competing traditions (deities, buddhas, etc.) are relegated to lower positions in the cosmic hierarchy.

Mythology was thus the form of discourse most often used to articulate the relationship envisioned by a given tradition with competing traditions. Buddhists had, from very early in their history, actively engaged in the borrowing and transformation of elements of the preexisting religion, usually called "Brahmanism" or "Hinduism."[3] Yet the Buddhists also deployed mythic discourse to subordinate Vedic Hinduism, by, for example, ridiculing the late Vedic creator deity Brahmā, and portraying him as arrogant and ignorant on the one hand, and a devotee of the Buddha on the other.[4]

Later, in Mahāyāna literature, Buddhists reacted to the growing popularity of theistic Hindu devotional movements by portraying Buddhist deities, such as Avalokiteśvara, as Hindu creator deities, while at the same time disparaging the Hindu rivals that were the objects of appropriation. We see this, for example, in the *Kāraṇḍavyūha Sūtra,* a text probably composed during the fifth century.[5] It is a sūtra that focuses on the Bodhisattva Avalokiteśvara, emphasizing in particular his great compassion, for which he or she is well-known to this day in his or her varied manifestations throughout South, Central, and East Asia. The very figure of Avalokiteśvara, it has been argued, is a Buddhist appropriation and transformation of Śiva. While there has been debate regarding this,[6] it seems to me undeniable that the term *īśvara*, "lord or "god," contained within his name is, to use Norman's classification, an example of a Hindu theological term "taken over by [Buddhists] but used with [a] new [sense]."[7]

In the first major section of this scripture,[8] Śākyamuni Buddha is asked about the excellent qualities of Avalokiteśvara. He replies with the following passage, which he attributes to the Tathāgata Vipaśyin:

> The Blessed Lord said: The sun and moon were born from [Avalokiteśvara's] eyes, Mahādeva from his forehead, Brahmā and so forth from his shoulders, Nārāyaṇa from his heart, and Sarasvatī from his teeth. The wind was born from his mouth, the earth from his feet, and Varuṇa from his belly. When these deities were born from Avalokiteśvara's body, noble Avalokiteśvara Bodhisattva, the Great Hero (*mahāsattva*) said the following to Maheśvara, the divine son: 'When the Kaliyuga arrives you will become Maheśvara. Once you are born from the realm of pernicious beings, you will be called Ādideva, the Creator. All of these beings who speak about [you] to ordinary people will be excluded from the path to Awakening.'[9]

This text highlights a key pattern that is commonly found throughout the history of South Asian religious traditions; as one tradition appropriates elements for another, such as the iconography of a deity and/or elements of its cult practice, they typically attempt to justify this by subordinating the deities that were the objects of the appropriation. In this case, the appropriation of key elements of Hindu theological discourse is particularly striking, which may account for the harsh vituperation placed in the mouth of the Buddha.

This pattern is found in Hindu traditions as well, which likewise borrowed elements from Buddhists during this same period, that is, the mid first millennium CE.[10] The *purāṇas*, which were the very Hindu scriptures that advocated an appropriated and transformed imperial cult practice, in turn advanced myths that belittled Buddhism and other non-Hindu religions, portraying them as "heresies," preached by incarnations of the deities in order to delude the demons, making them vulnerable to conquest by the gods.[11] Well-known examples of such mythology includes the Hindu discourse concerning the avatars of the deity Viṣṇu, the ninth of which was Buddha, who was portrayed in the *purāṇas* as a purveyor of "heresy." Buddhists countered this myth by appropriating and, in turn, subordinating Viṣṇu.[12]

These myths encode taxonomies, cosmic hierarchies by which the deities of one group are correlated to another. As Bruce Lincoln has argued,

> [W]hen a taxonomy is encoded in mythic form, the narrative packages a specific, contingent system of discrimination in a particularly attractive and memorable form. What is more, it naturalizes and legitimates it. Myth, then, is not just taxonomy, but *ideology* in narrative form. (1999, 147)

The South Asian mythic discourses that attempt to subordinate other groups clearly serve this role. A typical Buddhist case involves hierarchical division of deities into a twofold structure. The superior category includes, naturally, the divinities that are specific to Buddhism. This "supramundane" (*lokottara*) class consisted of awakened deities, namely the buddhas and advanced bodhisattvas. All other divinities, including the deities of competing religious traditions, are classified as "mundane" (*laukika*), and are portrayed as being unrealized and trapped within cyclic existence. They are thus incapable of saving other beings. The portrayal of other religions' deities in this fashion has obvious political implications, and represents a form of ideological discourse.

David Ruegg has recently argued for a non-political interpretation of this hierarchy. In so doing, he accepts the Buddhist representation of Hindu deities as "mundane," and thus reproduces Buddhist hegemonic discourse. With respect to the passage from the *Kāraṇḍavyūha Sūtra* passage quoted above, he argues:

> To regard divinities included in such Sūtra-lists . . . as being specifically Hindu ones eclectically borrowed by, or syncretistically

> infiltrated into, Buddhism would be, it seems, to take a much too one-sided view of the matter. They are, rather, deities conceived of as belonging to the mundane level who are worshipped by still immature trainees, but who in fact take their refuge in the infinite compassion of Avalokiteśvara and his six-syllable *vidyā*. (2008, 33)

However, here Ruegg merely accepts as definitive the Buddhist view of Hindu deities; to portray the "ultimate" *lokottara* deities of major Hindu theological traditions, such as Maheśvara and Nārāyaṇa, as "mundane" is so obviously political that little more needs to be said on this point.[13] Ruegg further attempts to support this by arguing that Buddhists have always, since the earliest strata of Buddhist literature, portrayed Hindu deities in this manner (2008, 25–28), but this merely shows that Buddhists have been employing this political strategy from a very early point in their history.[14]

The Synthesis of Heruka

The appropriation and transformation of elements of non-Buddhist discourse and practice by Buddhists continued in the later tantric phase of Buddhist development, which began during the seventh century CE, and continued until the demise of Buddhism in most of South Asia. This era is marked by the continued production of myths that attempt to legitimate this practice by subordinating the Hindu deities closely associated with the objects of appropriation. At this point, the Śaiva traditions were often an inspiration for the developing tantric Buddhist traditions. As a result, we see the chief Śaiva deities, Śiva/Mahādeva/Mahāśvara, and closely related Śaiva deities such as Rudra, Mahākāla, and Bhairava, singled out in the origin myths of many of the Buddhist tantras. The most famous of these narratives was the myth of Vajrapāṇi's subjugation of Maheśvara related in the *Sarvatathāgatatattvasaṃgraha Tantra*, although there are numerous variants of this myth contained in other tantras and commentaries.[15]

This literature often portrays Śaiva deities or their followers as engaging in violent or immoral behavior, which marks them as spiritually inferior. The spiritually superior Buddhist deities, the buddhas and bodhisattvas, observe this, and motivated by compassion, they manifest in the world, often in fierce forms or in Śaiva guise, to subjugate these deities, and often violently.[16] These deities are sometimes rehabilitated, and "awakened," thus turning them into Buddhist deities. But in other cases, their subjugation appears to be permanent, that is, fatal.[17]

Many of these elements are present in the myth of the origin of the Buddhist deity Heruka. Like other narratives of this sort, this myth can be profitably read as a justification for Buddhist appropriation of non-Buddhist texts and practices. In this case, however, the fact that such appropriation had actually occurred has been clearly established.

The deity Heruka is strongly connected with a genre of Buddhist scriptures known as the Yoginītantras. These scriptures, as the name suggests, largely focused on a class of female deities known as *yoginīs* and *ḍākinīs*. They were also notorious for their apparent advocacy[18] of the transgressive conduct called "heteropraxy" (*vāmācāra*), involving sexuality, the consumption of meat, alcohol, and "impure" bodily substances, and, in some scriptures, sacrificial violence. Heruka figured prominently in the earliest known Yoginītantra, the *Sarvabuddhasamāyoga-ḍākinījālasaṃvara Tantra*, which was composed during the late seventh or early eighth century.[19] He is the central deity in both the *Cakrasaṃvara* and *Hevajra* tantras, both of which were composed circa the ninth century.[20]

There is considerable evidence linking this genre of Buddhist scripture with closely related Śaiva scriptures. This is particularly the case with respect to the *Cakrasaṃvara Tantra*, also known as the *Laghusaṃvara* and *Śrīherukābhidhāna*. Alexis Sanderson, in a series of articles (1994, 2001, 2009), has argued persuasively that significant portions of the *Laghusaṃvara Tantra* were borrowed from Śaiva sources. This argument has been further advanced by Shaman Hatley (2007) and Judit Törzsök (1999). My own work on the *Laghusaṃvara Tantra* and its commentaries has uncovered repeated attempts by Buddhists to emend and expand this text, both to erase the names of Śaiva deities and to enrich the presence of Buddhist technical terminology. These attempts likely reflect Indian Buddhist recognition of, and discomfort with, the text's Śaiva elements (2012, 4–22).

I suggested earlier that the appropriation and adaption of elements of other religions is rarely if ever seamless, and that traditions that are so constituted are marked in ways that can leave them open to critique from both insiders and outsiders. This is certainly the case with respect to the deity Heruka and the scriptures that constitute the textual basis of his cult. There is, in fact, considerable evidence that both Heruka and his scriptural corpus were subjected to criticism by other Buddhists, some of whom claimed that they were spoken by Māra, the deceiver, rather than the Buddha (Gray 2005b, 66–68).

The origin myth of the deity Heruka is a narrative that appears to be designed to deflect criticism of the deity and his associated tradition by transferring fault to the very Śaiva tradition that was an initial source for this deity's traditions of scripture and practice. As this myth has already received extensive treatment elsewhere, here I will simply highlight some key points of the narrative.[21]

The Tibetan scholar Bu-ston, in his *Illumination of the General Meaning of the Laghusaṃvara Tantra,* relates that in the distant past Bhairava and his consort, Kālarātri, along with their various divine and demonic followers, began to cause mayhem throughout the world. Bhairava and his consort took control of the axial mountain, Mount Sumeru, and their followers took control of twenty-four other sites located throughout South Asia and the Himalayas. Thence they proceeded to worship Maheśvara, as follows:

> All of them invited and made offerings to the god Maheśvara as they desired to gain control over the three realms of existence. Maheśvara, embracing Umā in love play, did not have time to go, so he emanated as his likeness twenty-four stone liṅga in the likeness of a head, etc., and placed each one in each of the regions as objects of worship. They considered them as such and worshipped them and performed *gaṇacakra* rites there. On account of their preponderance of desire, the behavior of these gods was such that they embraced their wives during the four times [of the day]. Due to their overabundance of anger, they killed many humans and played with their flesh and blood. And because of their preponderance of ignorance they were deluded regarding the cause and effect of their actions and the import of reality. Each of them was surrounded by a retinue of evildoers. They wantonly reveled in the five objects of passion.[22] Having brought all of Jambudvīpa into their control, the spoke haughty boasts. Performing perverse actions themselves, they also caused others to do so.[23]

Mahāvajradhara Buddha, viewing this from the highest heaven, decided to act in order to preserve the cosmic order. He manifested in Bhairava's form, as Heruka, and his host of buddhas and bodhisattvas also manifested in Śaiva guise. They descended to earth in this form, and subdued Bhairava, Kālarātri, and all of their followers, seizing control of Mount

Sumeru and the other twenty-four sites. In the process, they established the Heruka mandala on earth.

Interestingly, the association of "heretical" behavior, such as ritual killing and anthropophagy in order to gain the magical power of flight, with the deities Kālarātri and Bhairava was not limited to Buddhist sources. Somadevabhaṭṭa, in his eleventh-century story collection the *Kathāsaritsāgara*, relates the story of Queen Kuvalayavatī's attainment of the magical power of flight via an initiation bestowed by Kālarātri, the leader of a "witches' circle" (*ḍākinīcakra*) as follows:

> She [Kālarātri] had me bow down and touch her bare feet, bathe, worship Ganésha, remove my clothes and, inside a circle, perform a terrifying worship of Bhairava. After anointing me she gave me various of her spells and some human flesh to eat which had been presented as a sacrificial offering in the worship of the gods. After taking all the spells and eating the human flesh I immediately flew up into the sky, completely naked, in the company of the friends. After playing about I then came down from the sky at the order of my teacher and I went, my lord, to my own ladies' apartments. Thus, even as a girl I came to take part in the witches' circle, and there we met and consumed many men. (Mallinson 2009, 43–45)

It appears that stories about the *ḍākinīs* and their black magic were an object of both anxiety and fascination in India, and not only among Buddhists. These practices were likewise largely attributed to unorthodox Śaiva groups in the Indian cultural context.[24]

The myth of Heruka's origin is apologetic, in that it acknowledges both the organic connection between the cults of Bhairava and Heruka and the historical precedence of the former. But it subordinates the Śaiva cult, representing its appropriation and transformation as an example of the enlightened activity of the buddhas in the distant past, rather than the historical activity of South Asian Buddhist communities. It would be a mistake to deny that narratives such as these are political; indeed, they were viewed as such by Hindu contemporaries, who did not appreciate textual and iconographic depictions of their deities being trampled, and reacted with the composition of counter-mythic narratives (Sanderson 1994, 93–94). That said, this literal reading of the narratives is not the reading privileged by Buddhists, who typically call for a nondual and arguably apologetic reading that erases the sectarian tensions by asserting that the ultimate meaning of these narratives is purely soteriological. That is, they read the violence expressed in this discourse allegorically, in reference to the conquest of inner demons such as anger and so forth, rather than the outer subjugation of rival religions' deities (Davidson 1991, 223–228; Mayer 1998; Ruegg 2008; 77–78). As we shall see, this exegetical strategy played a very important role in Tibet, where the threat posed by Śaiva Hinduism was tenuous at best.

The Heretical Tantras in Tibet

Myths such as this were apparently sufficient to allay the concerns of tantric Buddhists in India. By the tenth century, when Tibetans began to resume the their travels to India to acquire Buddhist teachings, the traditions that focused on Heruka, such as the *Cakrasaṃvara* and *Hevajra* tantras, were quite popular in India. However, the seams present in these traditions were still visible, and they would become apparent again as these traditions were transmitted into the Tibetan cultural world, and their scriptures were translated into Tibet.

The same transgressive "heteroprax" features of the Mahāyoga and Yoginītantras, which likely vexed the monks at Bodhgaya, also perturbed influential Buddhists in Tibet. Apparently, new Tantric practices entered Tibet from India during the tenth century, and some of these were of the "heteropraxic" variety, much like the Yoginītantras, or "Mother Tantras" (*ma rgyud*), as the Tibetans called them. These new teachings greatly concerned the King of Western Tibet, Lha-bla-ma Ye-shes-'od, who in 985 CE wrote an ordinance criticizing these practices, and characterizing them as non-Buddhist, as follows:

> Not being freed from the mire of the five objects of passion and women, what a wonder that [you] say, "[This] is the Reality Body." Engaging in the ten non-virtuous actions[25] and assuming the observance of dogs and pigs, you practice the religion of heretical yelping dogs,[26] yet say, "we are Buddhists."[27]

We might take note of the fact that the king employs the venerable tendency in South Asian discourse to link "heresy" (i.e., other religious traditions) with immoral behavior. He describes as follows the source and symptom of this problem, the "heretical tantras," and the practices in which these self-styled "Buddhists" allegedly indulged:

> Heretical tantras, pretending to be Buddhist, are spreading in Tibet. These have brought harm to the kingdom in the following ways:
>
> As 'deliverance' has become popular goat and sheep are afflicted. As 'sexual rite' has become popular the different classes of people are mixed. . . . As the ritual of sacrifice has become popular it happens that people get delivered alive. As demons who eat flesh are worshipped there is plague among men and animals. (Karmay 1980a, 154)

He continues his critique, explicitly linking ethical behavior and ritual purity with Buddhist identity, as follows: "The conduct of you say 'we are Buddhists' is less compassionate than demons of action . . . what a shame that you will be reborn in the [hell called] Corpse Mire due to making offerings of feces, urine, semen, and menstrual blood to the pure class of deities."[28]

We see here the traditional Buddhist association of transgressive behavior with non-Buddhist identity. Some of the language used to describe these heretical practices—namely, the description of violent and lustful behavior—is evocative of the language used in Indian sources to characterize the non-Buddhist deities and their followers in the myths discussed earlier in this chapter. There is no doubt that the Yoginītantras, with their apparent advocacy of "heteropraxy," seriously challenged traditional Buddhist identity. Perhaps due to doubt whether or not the "heretical tantras" that describe these practices are genuinely Buddhist or not, King Lha-bla-ma Ye-shes-'od is reported to have sent the Tibetan translator-monk Rin-chen bZang-po (958–1055 CE) to India precisely "to find out whether these practices were correct at all" (Karmay 1980, 151).

When Rin-chen bZang-po arrived in Kashmir circa 975 CE, he would soon learn that these scriptures were not deemed heretical by the Buddhists whom he met there, but that they were rather deemed to be among the "highest" teachings. He would thus, with the help of several Kashmiri Buddhist scholars, translate a number of tantras and tantric literature into Tibetan, including the *Laghusaṃvara Tantra,* which is probably one of the Buddhist tantras most open to the charge of being a "heretical tantra, pretending to be Buddhist."[29] And despite Rin-chen bZang-po's enthusiastic embrace of this genre of Tantric Buddhist literature, and the confirmation of its canonical status by the great Indian scholar Atiśa, one of Lha-bla-ma Ye-shes-'od's successors, King Zhi-ba-'od, would write in an ordinance the following in 1092 CE, with obvious resignation: "Although the 'Mother tantras' are excellent, they nevertheless cause many monks to break their monastic vows as a result of not knowing the implications of certain terms. There will not be any contradiction if they are not practiced at all" (Karmay 1980b, 17).

I would suggest that the seams present in this literature—the presence of "non-Buddhist" deities and descriptions of "non-Buddhist" practices, such as animal or human sacrifice—posed a considerable obstacle to its acceptance and dissemination in Tibet. The challenge facing their early advocates, such as Rin-chen bZang-po and his Indian collaborators, was to overcome this resistance by presenting this literature and their associated deities and practices as thoroughly and normatively Buddhist.

The Purification of Heruka

It was in this context, and perhaps in this response to this challenge, that the Kashmiri scholar Śraddhākaravarma wrote, and translated with the help of Rin-chen bZang-po, an intriguing little text entitled the "Purification of Heruka" (*he ru ka'i rnam par dag pa*).[30] This text almost certainly dates to the late tenth century, during the time when these scholars were actively collaborating in Kashmir.[31]

The term "purification" (*rnam par dag pa, viśuddha/viśuddhi*) is in an important technical term in Tantric Buddhist discourse, one which can designate a state of being, the "purified" reality of awakening that is the very nature of reality as we experience it, or the practices that are designed to achieve this realization—the gnosis of nonduality (Sferra 1999). The title of this text evokes an important step in the Tantric meditative traditions focusing on Heruka and related tantric tradition. In these traditions, the practitioner visualizes her- or himself as the deity, in this case Heruka. But in the process of this visualization, she or he is typically instructed to correlate the deity both to the world at large, as well as with "pure" categories, the elements and stages of awakening as conceived by the Mahāyāna tradition such as the bodhisattva grounds, the perfections, and so forth. The deity qua meditator is thus taken as the nexus of a set of interrelations that connect the supposedly impure mundane world with the pure supramundane realm of awakening. The dichotomy is collapsed, and the practitioner's identity as an impure, mundane being in an impure world is hopefully transformed in the process.

A characteristic and relatively early example of this sort of purification occurs in the *Hevajra Tantra,* as follows:

> Cyclic existence (*saṃsāra*) is Heruka's form. He is the Lord Savior of the World. Listen, as I will speak of that form in which he manifested. His eyes are red with compassion, and his body is black due to his loving mind. His four legs refer to the four means of conversion.[32] His eight faces are the eight liberations,[33] and his sixteen arms the [sixteen forms of] emptiness.[34] The five buddhas are [represented] by his [five] insignia,[35] and he is fervent in the subjugation of the wicked.[36]

This passage is a relatively straightforward description of Heruka, yet a fascinating one, in that it begins with language evocative of Hindu theology, but then quickly segues into Buddhist terminology. This early correlation of elements of Heruka's form and iconography to classical Buddhist doctrinal categories was dramatically expanded in later works, such as the *Purification of Heruka.*

Śraddhākaravarma's text begins with a brief introductory passage, which makes it clear that this text employs the term in both senses identified by Sferra—a gnosis of reality, and a practice designed to achieve this. It reads as follows:

> The teaching on the purification of the Reverend Blessed Lord Śrī Heruka has the nature of the purity of true concentration. It is true—that is, unerring—because it is not common to the disciples (*śrāvaka*) and so forth, and because [it teaches that] mind—as [the five gnoses] such as the discerning,[37] in the form of the moon and vajra, the five clans or the single host—is the very nature of consciousness. It is the stage of devotional practice. Devotion refers in particular to the reverential practice of meditating on the deity's form as the embodiment, in a single savor, of all of the aids to awakening (*bodhipakṣikadharma*), because this is the antidote to misknowledge. The purification of each thing is none other than this.[38]

Here we find several important points expressed. Contra the *śrāvakas*, the adherents of the early Buddhist traditions, Heruka and his textual tradition are no mere deception taught by Māra, despite his fierce appearance and similarity to Hindu deities such as Bhairava. He is in fact "pure," and this purity is realized via a devotional practice of meditating upon Heruka as the embodiment of the thirty-seven aids to awakening, that is, all of the factors needed to achieve the complete awakening of a buddha.[39] Meditation on Heruka is thus portrayed in classical Mahāyāna terms, yet in a manner consistent with cutting-edge tantric praxis. However, despite, this initial invocation of praxis, this text is by no means a *sādhana,* and contains no detailed meditation instructions. It is a textual anomaly, for what follows is a description of the central deities of the *Cakrasaṃvara* maṇḍala: Heruka, his consort Vajravārāhī, as well as the Śaiva deities on which they tread, Bhairava and Kālarātri, and the correlation of their iconographical elements to classical Mahāyāna Buddhist categories. It reads like an extended *viśuddhi* contemplation from a *sādhana,* but without the concomitant meditation instructions.

The text continues with what appears to be, on the surface at least, a rather conventional depiction of a tantric Buddhist deity. However, the subtle way in which this text treats Heruka's and his textual tradition's seams is intriguing, given the historical moment in which this text was composed. It thus worth paying careful attention to the signs of violence and non-Buddhist origination present in this iconography that derive from his "origin," as justified by his origin myth. The description begins as follows:

> His four faces have the nature of the four joys,[40] because he is the nature of the joys that arise from contact with the four great elements, and of the fruit, the exalted doors of liberation such as emptiness.[41] The double drum *(ḍamaru)* in the first of his twelve hands is the purification of the perfection of generosity because it continually sounds the teaching of the maṇḍala's wheel of the inseparability of self and other. It is the antidote for the envy that steals the happiness of others. It is the ground of delight,[42] because it gives rise to the enjoyment of the great bliss of the inseparability of self and other.
>
> His axe is the purity of the perfection of moral discipline, as it cuts off with moral discipline the disorder of breaking the commitments of eating and so forth, as well as the non-virtuous actions such as killing. It is the stainless ground,[43] because it turns one away

> from all sins. His curved knife is the purification of the perfection of patience, because it completely cuts away impatience and disturbances of consciousness brought about by being struck with a sword, staff, cudgel and so forth by someone thoroughly agitated. It is the ground of luminosity.[44] This means that one rests one's mind without disturbance, and by thus resting one destroys misknowledge. Lacking that, stainless gnosis *(anāvilajñāna)* shines.[45]

This presents the "inner meaning" of Heruka's iconography, in some cases completely reversing the outer meaning. His curved knife, for example, should not be seen as a weapon, an implement of violence, but rather represents the perfection of patience, the ability to endure, without resorting to violence, the violent conduct of others.

Of particular interest is the description of his axe, which "cuts off with moral discipline the disorder of breaking the commitments of eating and so forth, as well as the non-virtuous actions such as killing." This could very well have been written in response to King Ye-she-'od's concerns about the transgressions that were allegedly being practiced by some tantric practitioners in Tibet. He was particularly concerned about violent sacrifice and the use of impure substances as food and offerings. Buddhists have long opposed the former, and the latter inspired his indignation as a sacrilege (Ruegg 1984, 377–378). This language completely transforms the violence implicit in the iconography, portraying the deity's militaristic demeanor as symbolizing his ardent resistance to moral turpitude.

The text continues in this vein, correlating the other implements held in his hands to the perfections and bodhisattva grounds. While it lacks detailed meditation instructions, some of the comments on the meaning of elements of his iconography hint at practice. For example, Śraddhākaravarma described his skull-bowl as follows:

> His skull bowl is the purification of the perfection of aspiration.[46] It is the promised aspiration through [thinking] "May I become Heruka," etc., when one first gives rise to the spirit of awakening. He is adorned with the ornament of aspiration that flows for the sake of sentient beings.[47]

This passage evokes *sādhana*-type practices, in which one would think or say things such as "May I become Heruka" at certain stages of the contemplative exercise, but the details of this practice are not presented here.

It also describes the other deities present with Heruka at the center of the maṇḍala. But as this text explicitly focuses on Heruka, they are treated much like his other attributes, and are explained as symbols of Mahāyāna categories. His consort, Vajravārāhī, receives the following detailed description:

> The Blessed Lady Vajravārāhī is the purification of the perfection of gnosis.[48] She is the effortlessly realized omniscient gnosis, devoid of signification and signs, inexpressibly the nature of great bliss, the joy of experiential uniformity. She endures serving, without appearing to do so, as the antidote ignorance of conceptions of 'me' or 'mine,' and conceptions of substantial existence, and she eliminates both torpor and agitation. Since she cuts through these things she has a curved knife, and because she experiences the equality of both [extremes] she has a bowl filled with blood. She is the Dharma Cloud ground,[49] since she is the reality which has the nature of being unelaborated, and like a cloud in being moistened with the flow of natural water. This means that she satisfied all realms of sentient beings without exception.[50]

Vajravārāhī's correlation to the perfection of gnosis and her characterization in terms of the "omniscient gnosis" that cuts through cognitive obstacles fit well with the standard Tantric Buddhist correlation of female deities with wisdom, and male deities with compassion, which in Heruka's case is the fierce compassion that assumes a wrathful guise for the purpose of intimidating and subduing the wicked (Gray 2007b, 245–246).

While this is a standard explanation, one should note that it does serve to account for the deity couple's transgressive iconographic appearance. Vajravārāhī, a red goddess, nude, conjoined to the blue/black deity Heruka in sexual embrace, brings to mind the "sexual rite" in which "the different classes of people are mixed," about which King Lha-bla-ma Ye-shes-'od expressed concern. To the South Asian viewer, it would likely evoke the cross-class unions of the transgressive sort, the "against the grain" (*pratiloma*) type in which the male is lower status than the female.[51] This is due to the fact that Heruka is depicted as blue/black, the color commonly associated with the *śūdra* serving class, while Vajravārāhi is colored red, like the *kṣatriya* ruling class.[52] These color associations were definitely known to Buddhists; the ninth-century Indian scholar Kambala specifically correlated Heruka to the *śūdra* class.[53]

Śraddhākaravarma then turns to the Hindu deities subjugated by Heruka, Bhairava, and Kālarātri, whom he describes as follows:

> Bhairava is the essence of Māra of the Afflictions. The afflictions are the root of passion (*kāma*), and passion is Maheśvara. He has the pride of emanating and recollecting out of desire and attachment, and he is the very thing that binds one, namely cyclic existence. He is the lord who terrifies (*bhairava*) with his eyebrows, moustache and so forth, [and produces the terrors] of old age and dilapidation, by means of partiality and impartiality. This is because he is nature of speech which is sound itself such as the sound of thunder and so forth. In order to counteract his pride, he is supine, pressed down with [Heruka's] left foot, playfully, without undue fixation or zeal.
>
> Kālarātri is the essence of Māra Lord of Death. [She represents] the destruction and emptiness of the aggregates. Lacking all mental states of wrath, she has the nature of nirvāṇa, while at the same time appearing as the most important element of cyclic existence, the inner and outer essence of which exists in the three times, the past, future and present. This is because she apprehends the gnosis that manifests as great bliss, which arises from the contact of his right foot with her who is the passionless night, the darkness of unknowing.[54]

Śraddhākaravarma described them in terms of the Buddhist mythology of evil, associating both deities with forms of Māra, the antagonist of Buddhist practitioners.[55] He employs an old Buddhist partisan strategy of identifying Hindu deities with Māra, the classical Buddhist evil one. He demonizes the Hindu deities, but does so in a subtle fashion. He portrays the deities as almost willing participants in the play of awakening. Bhairava is pressed by Heruka's foot, but playfully, not zealously, to counteract his pride, just as a parent might correct a child's misbehavior. And Kālarātri is assigned an ambiguous role, inwardly awakened while outwardly participating in the maintenance of cyclic existence. The text hints at the erotic violence that is present in older versions of the myth, which relates that after the Buddhist deities subjugated their male Śaiva counterparts, they enjoyed their wives sexually (Gray 2007a, 52–53). But it does so in a much milder fashion, eliminating the more troubling elements of the narrative, such as the specter of sexual violence. The Śaiva deities, the allegedly dangerous antagonists portrayed in the origin myth and iconography, become almost willing participants in a Buddhist soteriological drama. The "heresy" that they represent, and with which Heruka was associated by some Buddhists, is thus eliminated, reduced to a subordinate position within the Buddhist cosmic taxonomy, represented by the prone Śaiva deities in the iconography.

What exactly was Śraddhākaravarma and Rin-chen bZang-po attempting to accomplish with this text? These descriptions of the deities' iconography are not in themselves peculiar. The text is a bit anomalous in that it does not attempt to embed these in a framework of practice. This leads me to suspect that it was not intended for practitioners per se. Rather, its fascinating connections with King Lha-bla-ma Ye-shes-'od's ordinance suggest that it was written as a work of rhetoric, calculated to persuade an audience of learned and influential Tibetans that Heruka was in fact a genuine Buddhist deity.

This was necessary because Heruka was actually associated with one of the "heresies" that most deeply concerned King Lha-bla-ma Ye-shes-'od. According to later Tibetan histories, the "heretics" addressed by the king in the ordinance were a religious group known as the *ar tsho bande* or *a ra mo bande*, who were evidently led by an infamous practitioner known as the "Red Ācārya."[56] He is reported to have taught the practice known as "drop of the path of passion" (*chags lam thig le*), and was apparently an advocate of the *Hevajra Tantra*, the chief deity of which is Heruka (Karmay 1980b, 14). Heruka was thus likely suspect, "tainted" by association with heresy. I thus strongly suspect that this text was written to purify *him*, to assure the intended audience, the intelligentsia of Western Tibet, that Heruka was in fact a "pure deity," not a lustful "demon who eats flesh." In other words, he was not a heretic, given the association of heresy with exactly this sort of behavior.

In India, Rin-chen bZang-po would have learned that the transgressive texts about which King Ye-shes-'od was suspicious were popular and were considered to be canonical by the Buddhist scholars he met in Kashmir and Magadha. However, he would also learn that Indian Buddhist scholars developed sophisticated hermeneutical systems for the interpretation of these texts, and that these systems did not usually privilege the literal interpretation of these passages. In other words, the tantras employed language in a radical fashion in order to accelerate the awakening process in properly prepared students, and were not understood as advocating the overturning of the conventional moral order. Indeed, largely for these reasons, the tantras were considered to be highly secret. This secrecy was for the protection of the unprepared, and not for the hoarding of wisdom by an initiated elite.

One might surmise that Śraddhākaravarma wrote this text to assuage doubts that the king's envoy, Rin-chen bZang-po, may have had concerning the deity Heruka and the Yoginītantras that focus on him. These texts, after all, were notorious for their apparent advocacy of practices that violated mainstream Indian behavioral norms, including those dealing with sexuality and violence. Heruka would have been doubly suspect, on account of his obvious connection with a major non-Buddhist deity. By firmly associating Heruka with pivotal Buddhist concepts, the author may have been attempting to assure the reader of his bona-fide Buddhist credentials.

Śraddhākaravarma's association of all of the major iconographic elements of Heruka with normative Mahāyāna concepts appears to have been an attempt to achieve what Robert Thurman called the integration of the *sūtras* within the Tantras (1985, 382). This is a twofold process. Tantric exegetes not only drew upon classical Mahāyāna *sūtric* categories to legitimize the tantras as Buddhist, but these categories were transformed in the process, becoming elements in the edifice of tantric theory and practice. This integration most likely eased Tibetan anxieties concerning the orthodoxy of the tradition.

There is no doubt whatsoever that Śraddhākaravarma was successful in this attempt, for not only was Heruka "purified" in the eyes of most Tibetans, but he also became a preeminent means of purification. His application of what might be called "creative commentary" should not be viewed as simply an apologetic attempt to obscure Heruka's heterodox associations. It was that, but much more; it was also an attempt to reinterpret and reposition Heruka and the Yoginītantras, to recreate them in and for a new cultural context.

Through the efforts of Indian commentators such as Śraddhākaravarma, and the later generations of Tibetan commentators who followed him, Yoginītantras such as the *Hevajra* and *Cakrasaṃvara* became extremely popular in Tibet, and Heruka became one of the most important tantric deities. Tantric practices centering on him became quite widespread. One *sādhana* focusing on Heruka that is very popular among contemporary practitioners of the Geluk tradition today is entitled "The Śrī Cakrasaṃvara Yoga of Triple Purification" (*dpal 'khor lo sdom pa'i dag pa gsum gyi rnal 'byor*). This triple purification is enacted by identifying one's body, speech, and mind with the body, speech, and mind of Heruka and Vajravārāhī. This is effected by visualizing oneself in their forms, reciting their mantras, and contemplating the esoteric significance of the syllables *śrī he ru ka*.[57]

The deity Heruka, in his journey from India to Tibet, underwent tremendous transformation. From his origins as a blood-drinking ghoul in Śiva's entourage, he became a *nirmāṇakāya* buddha in Śaiva garb. While his non-Buddhist persona made him suspect in Indian Buddhist circles, he completely shed the suspicion of heretical origination in Tibet, where Śaivism was not a thriving and threatening competing tradition, but was simply a doctrinal category. In this new terrain, he himself became a source for purification, for tantric Buddhists seeking to put into practice the esoteric teaching that he was believed to have propounded eons ago. He is also a living presence, accessible to the faithful via meditation or pilgrimage to his sacred abode at Mount Kailash. His purification, the *He ru ka'i rnam par dag pa*, was undoubtedly a great success.

Notes

1. This paper originated as a presentation given at the 2008 IABS conference in Atlanta, Georgia, and a revised version of this conference paper was published as "The Purification of Heruka: Reflections on Identity Formation in late Indian Buddhism," in *Pacific World* 3.13 (2011): 81–93. This chapter represents a significant expansion of this earlier exploration of Śraddhākaravarma's work.
2. While most North Indian Buddhist institutions were destroyed by the end of the thirteenth century, there are documented instances of Indian gurus who apparently self-identified as "Buddhist" visiting Tibet as late as the sixteenth century. See Templeman (1997).
3. For a compelling of example of an early Buddhist transformation of Vedic cosmological thought, see Jurewicz (2000).
4. Examples of Buddhist belittlement of Brahmā can be found in the *Brahmajāla* and *Kevaddha Suttas* in the *Dīgha Nikāya*, while the *Janavasabbha Sutta* in the same collection portrays him as a devotee of the Buddha. See Walshe (1987, 75–76, 178–179, and 295–300).
5. Alexander Studholme, contra previous authors who have dated the sūtra much later, argues for its composition by the late fourth or early fifth century (2002, 13–17).
6. Marie Thérèse de Mallman argued in her *Introduction à l'Étude d'Avalokiteçvara* that textual and iconographic analogies between Śiva and Avalokiteśvara do not appear prior to the tenth century (1948, 115). Guiseppe Tucci, however, criticized

her view, noting Xuanzang's report that Buddhists and Hindus alike worshipped, respectively, Avalokiteśvara and Īśvara Deva at Mt. Potala in South India (1951, 186); see Beal (1884) 1981, 2:233. See also Deshpande (1997), which, contra de Mallman, carefully documents Buddhist-Śaiva claims and counterclaims that indicate that these deities were in many ways functionally equivalent or overlapping from an early period. This is also argued convincingly by Studholme (2002, 37ff).

7. See Norman (1991, 194). Norman introduces the class of terms that he titles "Terms taken over by the Buddha but used with new senses." In place of "Buddha" we can more safely read "Buddhists," in the case of the Mahāyāna *sūtras* at least.
8. In the Sanskrit text as preserved in the *Mahāyānasūtrasaṃgraha* this text occurs toward the beginning of the fourth section (*caturthaṃ prakaraṇaṃ*) entitled *candrādyutpattiḥ*. The Tibetan translation is divided differently; there it occurs toward the end of the first section (*bam po dang po*).
9. My translation from the Sanskrit edited in Vaidya (1961, 265). See also the Tibetan translation (To. 116) in *sde-dge mdo-sde* vol. ja, fol. 207a; cf. Deshpande's translation (1997, 458).
10. Ronald Inden (1979) has argued that the developing theistic Hindu cults borrowed heavily from Buddhist ritual practices during this period, most notably the *mahādāna* ceremony.
11. For examples of Hindu mythology of this sort see Wendy Doniger O'Flaherty (1983).
12. Regarding a Buddhist appropriation of the deity Viṣṇu, see John Holt (2004).
13. It should be noted that in this work Ruegg provides an expanded version of an argument that he initially made in his essays "Sur les rapports entre le Bouddhisme et le 'substrat religieux' indien et tibétain" (1964) and "A Note on the Relationship Between Buddhist and 'Hindu' Divinities in Buddhist Literature and Iconology: The *Laukika/Lokottara* Contrast and the Notion of an Indian 'Religious Substratum'" (2001). In these works he argues for a pan-Indian "substratum" of South Asian religious life, and argues that this substratum includes the Hindu deities. On this basis he denies the political implications of these narratives. This argument has been criticized both by Alexis Sanderson (1994, 92–93) and also by Ronald Davidson (2002, 171–172).
14. This indeed has been shown by Joanna Jurewicz (2000). Richard Gombrich has also argued this in several of his essays on early Buddhism, including his "The Buddha's Book of Genesis?" (1992), as well as several of the essays included in his work *How Buddhism Began* (1996).
15. There have been numerous studies published of this literature. For a study of the *Tattvasaṃgraha*'s narrative see Snellgrove (1987, 134–141). For a study of both this and variant versions of this myth, see IYANAGA (1985).
16. Ronald Davidson has argued that the increase of violent rhetoric in Indian religious literature during the latter half of the first millennium CE is linked to the increasingly unstable political situation (2002, esp. ch. 2).

17. Other myths contain even more violent imagery, such as Hayagrīva's violent anal penetration and destruction of Rudra related in one of Padmasambhava's hagiographies, or the *Bhūtaḍamara Tantra*'s narrative of Vajrapāṇi's destruction of all of the gods, followed by their revival. Regarding these see, respectively, Matthew Kapstein (1992), and Davidson (2002, 333). For a fascinating exploration of the influence of the myth of the subjugation of Rudra in Tibet see Dalton (2011).
18. That is, if the texts are interpreted literally. The interpretation of these scriptures was therefore politically charged, as I discuss in my (2005a) essay.
19. This text (To. 366) is datable via its description in Amoghavajra's *Index of the Vajroṣṇīṣa Sūtra Yoga in Eighteen Sections* (*Jīngāngdǐng jīng yújiā shíbā huì zhǐguī* 金剛頂經瑜伽十八會指歸, T. 869), a work he composed following his return to China from South Asia in 746 CE. For an annotated English translation of this important text see Giebel (1995).
20. Regarding the dating of the *Cakrasaṃvara* and *Hevajra* tantras, see Gray (2007a, 11–14, and 71n192), respectively. See also Gray (2012, 6–9).
21. See Davidson (1991, 197–235), for a translation of an early Tibetan version of the myth. See also Gray (2007a, 45–51) for a translation of an eleventh-century Indian version of the myth.
22. These are *pañcakāmaguṇa*, the objects of sight, hearing, smell, taste, and touch.
23. Bu-ston Rin-chen-grub, *bde mchog nyung ngu rgyud kyi spyi rnam don gsal*, 57–58.
24. Regarding contemporary Hindu views concerning the *ḍākinī*s as "witches," see Herrmann-Pfandt (1996) and McDaniel (2004, 85).
25. The ten non-virtuous actions (*daśākuśalakarma, mi dge ba bcu*) are (1) killing, (2) stealing, (3) sexual misconduct, (4) lying, (5) divisive speech, (6) harsh speech, (7) idle speech, (8) covetousness, (9) malice, and (10) wrong views.
26. This is a tentative translation of *'ba' 'ji ba* and *'ba' 'ji*, which Karmay does not translate. It appears to be an archaic insult, and as *'ba'* can mean "bleat" and *'ji* "dog," "yelping dog" seems to be a suitable translation, given the context, and the writer's obvious desire to associate the objects of his invective with lowly animals.
27. My translation from the text edited in Karmay (1980a, 156); cf. Karmay's translation at p. 153.
28. My translation from the text edited in Karmay (1980a, 156–157).
29. For a study of Rin-chen bZang-po's life and a list of the works he translated, see Tucci (1988).
30. Śraddhākaravarma, *he ru ka'i rnam par dag pa* (HN), To. 1481, D rgyud 'grel vol. zha, 125a3–128b4. This text has no transliterated Sanskrit title, which might possibly indicate that it was composed in Tibetan rather than Sanskrit. Possible Sanskrit reconstructions/back-translations would be **herukaviśuddha,* or, perhaps, **herukaviśuddhi.*
31. According to Tucci, Rin-chen bZang-po studied in India in 975–988 CE (1988, 3–4); I believe that Śraddhākaravarma likely composed (orally or in writing) this text during the period when Rin-chen bZang-po was studying with him.

32. The "four means of conversion" (*saṃgrahavastucatuṣka*) are (1) generosity (*dāna*), (2) pleasant speech (*priyavāditā*), (3) altruistic conduct (*arthacaryā*), and (4) having the same interest [as others] (*samānārthatā*). Regarding these see Dayal (1932, 251–259).
33. The eight liberations (*vimokṣa*) are (1) the liberation of the embodied looking at a form, (2) the liberation of the disembodied looking at a form, (3) liberation through beautiful form, (4) liberation of infinite space, (5) liberation of infinite consciousness, (6) liberation of nothingness, (7) liberation of the peak of existence, and (8) liberation of cessation. See Rigzin (1986, 236).
34. These are (1) internal emptiness, (2) external emptiness, (3) emptiness of the internal and external, (4) the emptiness of emptiness, (5) emptiness of the great, (6) emptiness of the ultimate, (7) emptiness of conditioned phenomena, (8) emptiness of unconditioned phenomena, (9) emptiness of the extremes, (10) emptiness of the beginningless and endless, (11) emptiness of the unabandoned, (12) emptiness of nature, (13) emptiness of all phenomena, (14) emptiness of self-characteristics, (15) emptiness of non-apprehension, (16) emptiness of the reality of nonexistence. See Rigzin (1986, 160–161).
35. These are a necklace, crest jewel, earring, choker, and sacred thread.
36. My translation of *Hevajra Tantra* 2.9.10–12, from the Sanskrit edited in Snellgrove (1959, 2:92).
37. The five gnoses (*pañcajñāna*) are (1) mirror-like gnosis (*ādarśajñāna*), (2) gnosis of equality (*samatājñāna*), (3) discerning gnosis (*pratyavekṣaṇājñāna*), (4) accomplishing gnosis (*kṛtyānuṣṭhānajñāna*), and (5) gnosis of reality (*dharmadhātujñāna*). See Rigzin (1986, 384).
38. HN 125a.
39. For a complete list of the 37 *bodhipakṣikadharma* see Thurman (1976, 156).
40. The four joys are (1) joy (*ānanda*), (2) supreme joy (*paramānanda*), (3) the joy of cessation (*viramānanda*), and (4) natural joy (*sahajānanda*). Regarding these see Snellgrove (1959, 1:34–35).
41. The *trivimokṣamukha* are emptiness (*śūnyatā*), signlessness (*animittatā*), and wishlessness (*apraṇihitatā*).
42. That is, *pramūditabhūmi*, the first bodhisattva ground.
43. That is, *vimalabhūmi*, the second bodhisattva ground.
44. That is, *prabhākarībhūmi*, the third bodhisattva ground.
45. HN 125a, b.
46. This perfection, *praṇidhānapāramitā, smon lam gyi pha rol tu phyin pa*, is not one of the well-known sixth perfections. It is the eighth in the longer list of ten perfections, which was produced in order to correlate these with the ten bodhisattva grounds. See Dayal (1932, 168).
47. HN 126a.
48. The *jñānapāramitā, ye shes kyi pha rol tu phyin pa*, is the tenth perfection in the expanded list. See Dayal (1932, 168).

49. The *dharmameghābhūmi,* the tenth bodhisattva ground.
50. HN 126b.
51. The *dharmasūtras* are filled will vitriol concerning *pratiloma* unions in which the male is lower status. The *Dharmasūtra of Āpastamba,* for example, calls for the execution of the male *śūdra* who is guilty of sex with an Ārya woman. See Olivelle (1999, 70).
52. The ancient correlation of the colors white to the brahmins, red to the *kṣatriya,* yellow to the *vaiśya,* and black to the *śūdra* is ubiquitous in premodern South Asian discourse about society. See Naronakar (2003, 69).
53. Despite the apparent resistance to the *varṇa* ideology found in some tantric literature, the invocation of *varṇa* classificatory discourse is relatively common, no doubt due to its ubiquity in South Asia. For example, the late tenth-century *Cakrasaṃvara* commentator Kambala equates the seven yoginī clans in chapter sixteen with buddhas and social groups; he correlates Heruka with the *śūdra* class. See Gray (2007a, 229n19). Alaṃkakalaśa, in his *Vajramālāṭīkā,* likewise correlates the Buddhist tantras to social groupings, and relegates the *Cakrasaṃvara Tantra* to the untouchable *caṇḍāla* caste. See To. 1795, D rgyud 'grel vol. gi, 4a.
54. HN 126b–127a.
55. Māra, literally "Death," is traditionally considered to have four forms. These are (1) Māra of the Aggregates, *skandhamāra,* (2) Māra of the Afflictions, *kleśamāra,* (3) Māra, Lord of Death, *mṛtyupatimāra,* and (4) Māra, Son of God, *devaputramāra.* Concerning the mythology surrounding the Māras, see Ling (1962).
56. Ruegg reports (1984, 376) that the *atsarya dmar po* was identified by the Fifth Dalai Lama with the Paṇḍit gSang-ba-shes-rab, Guhyaprajñā, who was apparently a Kashmiri Śaiva adept who became the student of the Buddhist master Ratnavajra. Karmay reports the name as *shes rab gsang ba,* or Prajñāgupta (1980b, 13).
57. This *sādhana* is entitled *dpal 'khor lo sdom pa'i dag pa gsum gyi rnal 'byor.* It is contained in a popular book of *sādhanas* entitled *bla ma'i rnal 'byor dang yi dam khag gi bdag bskyed sogs zhal 'don gces btus* (Dharamsala: Tibetan Cultural Printing Press, 1994).

References

Alaṃkakalaśa. *Śrīvajramālāmahāyogatantraṭīkā-gambhīrārthdīpaka-nāma.* To. 1795, D rgyud 'grel vol. gi, 1b–220a.

Ārya-kāraṇḍavyūha-nāma-mahāyāna-sūtra, 'phags pa za ma tog bkod pa shes bya ba theg pa chen po'i rgyud. To. 116. D mdo sde vol. ja, 200a–247b.

Beal, Samuel. [1884] 1981. *Si-Yu-Ki: Buddhist Records of the Western World: Translated from the Chinese of Hiuen Tsiang (A.D. 629).* Reprint, Delhi: Motilal Banarsidass.

bla ma'i rnal 'byor dang yi dam khag gi bdag bskyed sogs zhal 'don gces btus. Dharamsala: Tibetan Cultural Printing Press, 1994.

Bu-ston Rin-chen-grub. *bde mchog nyung ngu rgyud kyi spyi rnam don gsal.* In *The Collected Works of Bu-ston*, edited by Lokesh Chandra, vol. cha, 1–118. New Delhi: International Academy of Indian Culture, 1966.

Dalton, Jacob. 2011. *The Taming of the Demons: Violence and Liberation in Tibetan Buddhism.* New Haven, CT: Yale University Press.

Davidson, Ronald. 1991. "Reflections on the Maheśvara Subjugation Myth: Indic Materials, Sa-skya-pa Apologetics, and the Birth of Heruka." *Journal of the International Association of Buddhist Studies* 14 (2): 197–235.

Davidson, Ronald. 2002. *Indian Esoteric Buddhism: A Social History of the Tantric Movement.* New York: Columbia University Press.

Dayal, Har. 1932. *The Bodhisattva Doctrine in Buddhist Sanskrit Literature.* Reprint, Delhi: Motilal Banarsidass, 2004.

Deshpande, Madhav. 1997. "Who Inspired Pāṇini? Reconstructing the Hindu and Buddhist Counter-claims." *Journal of the American Oriental Society* 117 (3): 444–465.

Giebel, Rolf. 1995. "The *Chin-kang-ting ching yü-ch'ieh shih-pa-hui chih-kuei*: An Annotated Translation." *Journal of Naritasan Institute for Buddhist Studies* 18 (1995): 107–201.

Gombrich, Richard. 1992. "The Buddha's Book of Genesis?" *Indo-Iranian Journal* 35: 159–178.

Gombrich, Richard. 1996. *How Buddhism Began: The Conditioned Genesis of the Early Teachings.* London: The Athlone Press, 1996.

Gray, David B. 2005a. "Disclosing the Empty Secret: Textuality and Embodiment in the *Cakrasamvara Tantra.*" *Numen* 52 (4): 417–444.

Gray, David B. 2005b. "Eating the Heart of the Brahmin: Representations of Alterity and the Formation of Identity in Tantric Buddhist Discourse." *History of Religions* 45 (1): 45–69.

Gray, David B. 2007a. *The Cakrasamvara Tantra: A Study and Annotated Translation.* New York: American Institute of Buddhist Studies/Columbia University Press.

Gray, David B. 2007b. "Compassionate Violence? On the Ethical Implications of Tantric Buddhist Ritual." *Journal of Buddhist Ethics* 17: 239–271.

Gray, David B. 2012. *The Cakrasamvara Tantra: Editions of the Sanskrit and Tibetan Texts.* New York: American Institute of Buddhist Studies/Columbia University Press.

Hatley, Shaman. 2007. "The *Brahmayāmalatantra* and Early Śaiva Cult of Yoginīs." PhD dissertation, University of Pennsylvania.

Herrmann-Pfandt, Adelheid. 1996. "The Good Woman's Shadow: Some Aspects of the Dark Nature of Ḍākinīs and Śākinīs in Hinduism." In *Wild Goddesses of India and Nepal: Proceedings of an International Symposium, Berne and Zurich, November 1994*, edited by Axel Michaels et al., 2:39–70. New York: Peter Lang.

Holt, John. 2004. *The Buddhist Viṣṇu: Religious Transformation, Politics, and Culture.* New York: Columbia University Press.

Inden, Ronald. 1979. "The Ceremony of the Great Gift (Mahādāna): Structure and Historical Context in Indian Ritual and Society." In *Asie du Sud: Traditions et changements*, edited by Marc Gaborieau and Alice Thorner, 131–136. Paris: Éditions du centre national de la recherche scientifique.

IYANAGA Nobumi. 1985. "Récits de la soumission de Maheśvara par Trailokyavijaya–d'après les sources chinoises et japonaises." In *Tantric and Taoist Studies in Honour of R. A. Stein*, edited by Michel Strickmann, 633–745. Brussels: Institut belge des hautes études chinoises.

Jurewicz, Joanna. 2000. "Playing with Fire: The *pratītyasamutpāda* from the Perspective of Vedic Thought." *Journal of the Pali Text Society* 26: 77–103.

Kapstein, Matthew. 1992. "Samantabhadhra and Rudra: Innate Enlightenment and Radical Evil in Tibetan Rnying-ma-pa Buddhism." In *Discourse and Practice*, edited by Frank Reynolds and David Tracy, 51–82. Albany: State University of New York Press.

Karmay, Samten. 1980a. "The Ordinance of Lha Bla-ma Ye-shes-'od." In *Tibetan Studies in Honour of Hugh Richardson: Proceedings of the International Seminar of Tibetan Studies, Oxford 1979*, edited by Michael Aris and Aung San Suu Kyi, 150–162. Warminster: Aris & Phillips.

Karmay, Samten. 1980b. "An Open Letter by the Pho-brang Zhi-ba-'od." *The Tibet Journal* 5: 2–28.

Lincoln, Bruce. 1999. *Theorizing Myth: Narrative, Ideology, and Scholarship*. Chicago: University of Chicago Press.

Ling, Trevor. 1962. *Buddhism and the Mythology of Evil*. London: George, Allen and Unwin.

Mallinson, Sir James. 2009. *The Oceans of the Rivers of Story, Volume Two, by Somadeva*. New York: New York University Press.

de Mallman, Marie Thérèse. 1948. *Introduction à l'Étude d'Avalokiteçvara*. Paris: Annales du Musée Guimet.

Mayer, Robert. 1998. "The Figure of Maheśvara/Rudra in the rÑiṅ-ma-pa Tantric Tradition." *Journal of the International Association of Buddhist Studies* 21 (2): 271–310.

McDaniel, June. 2004. *Offering Flowers, Feeding Skulls: Popular Goddess Worship in West Bengal*. New York: Oxford University Press.

Naronakar, A. R. 2003. *Untouchability and Caste System in India*. New Delhi: Anmol Publications.

Norman, K. R. 1991. "Theravāda Buddhism and Brahmanical Hinduism: Brahmanical Terms in a Buddhist Guise." In *The Buddhist Forum*, Volume II, edited by Tadeusz Skorupski, 193–200. New Delhi: Heritage Publishers, 1991.

O'Flaherty, Wendy Doniger. 1983. "Image of the Heretic in the Gupta *Purāṇas*." In *Essays on Gupta Culture*, edited by Bardwell L. Smith, 107–127. Delhi: Motilal Banarsidass.

Olivelle, Patrick. 1999. *Dharmasūtras: The Law Codes of Ancient India*. New York: Oxford University Press.

Rigzin, Tsepak. 1986. *Tibetan-English Dictionary of Buddhist Terminology.* Dharamsala: Library of Tibetan Works and Archives.

Ruegg, David Seyfort. 1964. "Sur les rapports entre le Bouddhisme et le 'substrat religieux' indien et tibétain." *Journal Asiatique* 252: 7–95.

Ruegg, David Seyfort. 1984. "Problems in the Transmission of Vajrayāna Buddhism in the Western Himalaya about the Year 1000." In *Studies of Mysticism in Honor of the 1150th Anniversary of Kobo Daishi's Nirvāṇam, Acta Indologica* (Indo koten kenkyō) 6:369–381. Narita: Naritasan Shinshōji.

Ruegg, David Seyfort. 2001. "A Note on the Relationship Between Buddhist and 'Hindu' Divinities in Buddhist Literature and Iconology: The *Laukika/Lokottara* Contrast and the Notion of an Indian 'Religious Substratum.'" In *Le parole e i Marmi,* edited by R. Torella, 735–742. Roma: Istituto italiano per l'Africa e l'Oriente.

Ruegg, David Seyfort. 2008. *The Symbiosis of Buddhism with Brahmanism/Hinduism in South Asia and of Buddhism with 'Local Cults' in Tibet and the Himalayan Region.* Wien: Verlag der Österreichischen Akademie der Wissenschaften.

Sachedina, Abdulaziz. 1996. "Political Implications of the Islamic Notion of 'Supersession' as Reflected in Islamic Jurisprudence." *Islam and Christian-Muslim Relations* 7 (2): 159–168.

Sachedina, Abdulaziz. 2006. "The Qur'ān and other religions." In *The Qur'ān,* edited by Jane Dammen McAuliffe, 291–309. Cambridge: Cambridge University Press.

Sanderson, Alexis. 1994. "Vajrayāna: Origin and Function." In *Buddhism into the Year 2000: International Conference Proceedings,* 87–102. Los Angeles: Dhammakaya Foundation.

Sanderson, Alexis. 2001. "History Through Textual Criticism in the Study of Śaivism, the Pañcarātra and the Buddhist Yoginītantras." In *Les Source et le temps,* edited by François Grimal, 1–47. Pondicherry: École française d'Extrême Orient.

Sanderson, Alexis. 2009. "The Śaiva Age: The Rise and Dominance of Śaivism during the Early Medieval Period." In *Genesis and Development of Tantrism,* edited by Shingo EINOO, 41–349. Tokyo: Institute of Oriental Culture, University of Tokyo.

Sferra, Francesco. 1999. "The Concept of Purification in Some Texts of Late Indian Buddhism." *Journal of Indian Philosophy* 27 (1–2): 83–103.

Snellgrove, David. 1959. *The Hevajra Tantra: A Critical Study.* 2 vols. London: Oxford University Press.

Snellgrove, David. 1987. *Indo-Tibetan Buddhism.* London: Serindia Publications.

Śraddhākaravarma. *he ru ka'i rnam par dag pa.* To. 1481. D rgyud 'grel vol. zha, 125a3–128b4.

Stewart, Tony K., and Carl W. Ernst. 2003. "Syncretism." In *South Asian Folklore: An Encyclopedia,* edited by Margaret Mills et al., 586–588. New York: Routledge.

Studholme, Alexander. 2002. *The Origins of Oṃ Maṇipadme Hūṃ: A Study of the Kāraṇḍavyūha Sūtra.* Albany: State University of New York Press.

Templeman, David. 1997. "Buddhaguptanātha: A Late Indian *Siddha* in Tibet." In *Tibetan Studies: Proceedings of the 7th Seminar of the International Association for Tibetan Studies, Graz 1995*, edited by Helmut Krasser et al., 2:955–965. Wien: Verlag der Österreichischen Akademie der Wissenschaften.

Thurman, Robert A. F. 1976. *The Holy Teaching of Vimalakīrti, A Mahāyāna Scripture.* University Park: Pennsylvania State University Press.

Thurman, Robert A. F. 1985. "Tsoṅ-kha-pa's Integration of Sūtra and Tantra." In *Soundings in Tibetan Civilization: Proceedings of the 1982 Seminar of the International Association for Tibetan Studies Held at Columbia University*, edited by Barbara Nimri Aziz and Matthew Kapstein, 373–382. New Delhi: Manohar.

Törzsök, Judit. 1999. "The Doctrine of Magic Female Spirits: A Critical Edition of Selected Chapters of the Siddhayogeśvarīmata(tantra) with Annotated Translation and Analysis." PhD dissertation, University of Oxford.

Tucci, Guiseppe. 1951. "A propos Avalokiteçvara." *Mélanges chinois et bouddhique* 9: 174–219.

Tucci, Guiseppe. 1988. *Rin-chen-bzaṅ-po and the Renaissance of Buddhism in Tibet Around the Millennium*, translated by Nancy Kipp Smith and Thomas J. Pritzker, edited by Lokesh Chandra. New Delhi: Aditya Prakashan.

Vaidya, P. L. 1961. *Mahāyāna-sūtra-saṃgrahaḥ, Part I.* Darbhanga: Mithila Institute.

Walshe, Maurice. 1987. *The Long Discourse of the Buddha.* Boston: Wisdom Publications.

6

Vicissitudes of Text and Rite in the Great Peahen Queen of Spells

Ryan Richard Overbey

Introduction

The *Great Peahen Queen of Spells* (*Mahāmāyūrīvidyārājñī*) is a dynamic corpus of scriptures, incantations, and rituals produced and practiced in South, Central, and East Asia from the early centuries CE to the present day.[1,2] The text survives in many versions, including six Chinese translations, a Tibetan translation, in Sanskrit manuscripts, and as part of a later ritual collection called the *Fivefold Protection* (*Pañcarakṣā*).[3] The earliest extant versions are Chinese translations dating to the late fourth century; the text coalesced into its final form by the early sixth century.

This large body of evidence serves as a resource not only for text-critical studies, but also for addressing questions in Buddhist intellectual and ritual history. By closely studying the transmission and transformations of the *Great Peahen*, one can learn more about the interaction of Buddhism with Chinese religions, about the rapid development and flexibility of Buddhist ritual practices, and about the appeal of Buddhist spells in much broader religious and cultural contexts.

On the Character and Classification of the Great Peahen

Characterizing a text like the *Great Peahen* is no easy task. Generally speaking, the versions of the *Great Peahen* contain a narrative frame and a series of spells associated with gods, demons, and assorted numina. Many versions of the text also include ritual instructions as well as appended spells from other scriptures. The text has at least two early recensions, which later coalesced into a stable, expanded version (Sørensen 2006, 91–109). The text thus reads less like a standard Buddhist scripture and more like a grimoire. Sylvain Lévi quipped that the *Great Peahen* "ne doit son importance qu'à sa valeur magique; sa valeur littéraire est nulle" (1915, 25).[4]

Since the scripture is so difficult to characterize, I will begin with a translation of the simplest version, a short spell translated into Chinese in the late fourth century, entitled *The Great Golden Peacock King Spell Scripture* (T. 986):[5]

> The Buddha told Ānanda, "Long ago, south of the king of the snowy mountains, there was a golden peacock king. The Buddha dwelled within him. Using this *Great Peacock King Spell Scripture*, he uttered it in the morning for self-defense, and the day would be peaceful. He uttered it at dusk for self-defense, and the night would be calm." Then he uttered the spell, saying "*Hu hu hu hu hu hu hu hu hu hu, le le le le dumba le le le vima le le huya huya vija vija thusa guru elā melā ili melā tili melā ili me tili ili tili mitte dumbe sudumbe tosu to golā velā capalā velā ca iṭṭiri bhiṭṭiri ṭiri!*"[6]
>
> "Ānanda, now I will utter for you the heart of the Queen of Spells of the Great Peacock King." Then he uttered the spell, saying "*ili kili . . . [&c.]*[7] *may the heavens quickly pour forth rain!*"
>
> "Circumambulate the ritual area seven times and recite." Then he uttered a spell, saying "*nārayaṇa pārayaṇa . . . [&c.]*"
>
> "Ānanda, this Great Peacock Queen of Spells was uttered according to Maitreya Bodhisattva." Then he uttered a spell, saying "*kili kili kili kili . . . [&c.]*"
>
> "Ānanda, this Great Peacock Queen of Spells was uttered according to the god Brahmā, ruler of the Sahā World." Then he uttered a spell, saying "*hili hili hari . . . [&c.]*"
>
> "Ānanda, this Great Peacock Queen of Spells was uttered according to Śākya, king of the gods." Then he uttered a spell, saying "*tala kṣāntali . . . ili ha hi hu, may all calamity and evil submit! Seize their hands, feet, joints, and knuckles! May they never be able to move, even the Trayastriṃśa gods! . . . [&c.]*"
>
> "Ānanda, you should learn the names of the divine seers of yore.[8] Now I will utter the names of those who have accomplished

the end of suffering, who have accomplished the observance of vows, who have accomplished the spell arts, who always practice ascetic practices, who dwell in the mountains and forests, who have potency and sovereignty, whose transformations are formidable, who have the five supernormal knowledges and the powers of accomplishing their wishes, who fly through the sky. They are called: Great Seer Aṣṭamaka, Great Seer Vāmaka, Great Seer Vāmadeva . . . [Here follows a list of Greet Seers; the entire list contains 51 seers in total.]"

"Ānanda, these are the great seers of yore, who created the Four Vedas. Whatever they desire is entirely accomplished through the great power of their ascetic practices and glorious energy. May they also use this *Great Peacock King Spell Scripture* to protect so-and-so, and cause him to live for one hundred years, to get to see one hundred autumns!" Then he uttered a spell, saying "*hari hari hari . . . [&c.]*"

"May the Four Kings of the Gods and the Great Demon Spirit Kings also use the *Peacock Queen of Spells* to protect so-and-so, and cause him to live for one hundred years, to get to see one hundred autumns!" Then he uttered a spell, saying "*akaṭe vikaṭe . . . [&c.] Protect so-and-so, and cause him to live one hundred years, to get to see one hundred autumns!*"

"The *Maṇiratna Scripture* and the **Mahāgandhabhikṣu*[9] rescue from sickness, suffering, and calamity. The *Peacock King Spell* eliminates enemies."

Even with its many layers of later additions and emendations, the *Great Peahen* does not fundamentally deviate from this style of writing. It is a pragmatic text, a whirlwind tour of gods and demons and their associated spells and rituals. The text's relative lack of narrative coherence, its jarring leaps from one spell to the next, make the process of expansion relatively easy. Adding another set of deities, spells, or ritual procedures would not radically change the nature of the scripture.

The *Great Peahen* has been called an "esoteric" or "prototantric" text.[10] Two factors contribute to this classification. First, the text's many versions contain numerous incantations and rituals, which remind scholars of the maṇḍalas, mantras, and *mudrās* of later tantric scriptures.[11] Second, scholars have shown that the *Great Peahen* was an important influence on other early Buddhist texts commonly regarded as prototantric.[12]

In recent years some scholars have argued that words like "esoteric" or "prototantric" are simply not useful in describing Chinese Buddhist literature. The key argument for this position, made by Robert Sharf, is that the very concept of esoteric Buddhism is wholly the invention of late Japanese sectarians. Innovative ritual technologies like mantras and mandalas were coming to China from India, to be sure, but these new technologies did not occasion the formation of a new institution or Buddhist school called "esoteric Buddhism." Discussions of esoteric Buddhism, for Sharf, smack of Japanese triumphalism, a teleological reading of history that regards the work and legacy of Kūkai as the apogee of authentic Buddhist practice, with the early history of Mahayana Buddhism serving as a mere prelude (2002, 263–278). Richard McBride, following Sharf, argued that the *dhāraṇīs* and spells of East Asian Buddhism were quite normal, identified with no particular sectarian affiliation, and that we need not bother with categories like "prototantrism" when dealing with texts like the *Great Peahen* (McBride 2004, 2005).

Scholars should be grateful that these recent debates are shedding new light on the ubiquity and tremendous influence of spells and liturgical manuals for early Chinese Buddhism. However, much of the debate about what constitutes "esoteric" or "prototantric" Buddhism rests on semantic quibbles.[13] In this chapter, I will call the *Great Peahen* "prototantric" because (1) its ritual manuals show a clear trend toward increasing complexity, with many procedures and instructions reminiscent of later, recognizably tantric Buddhist ritual manuals; and (2) the preface to Amoghavajra's translation of the text explicitly calls the *Great Peahen* an "esoteric teaching" (*mìjiào* 密教; T. 982, 19:415a16). This means, at the very minimum, that the earlier versions of the *Great Peahen* furnished raw material from which Amoghavajra could assemble what *he* viewed as an esoteric scripture and ritual manual, complete with a maṇḍala, mantras, and *mudrās*.[14] The labels "prototantric" or "tantric" need not refer to unique institutional identities or monastic lineages—we may instead use them to describe a set of historically and textually related ritual techniques.

Much research on the *Great Peahen* has already been conducted. Since the late version of the text contains long lists of *yakṣas* and the lands they rule, Sylvain Lévi studied the text as a resource for South Asian geography (1915). Lambert Schmithausen studied the spell in the context of Buddhist encounters with dangerous natural phenomena like cobras and famine, and delved into its many precursors, including the *Āṭānāṭiyasutta* of the *Dīghanikāya*, the *Cullavagga* of the *Vinayapiṭaka*, the *Morajātaka*, the *Upasenasūtra* in the *Saṃyuktāgama*, and the *Bhaiṣajyavastu* of the *Mūlasarvāstivādavinaya* (1997, 11–23, 53–57). J. F. Marc DesJardins explored the text's pantheon, its connection to South and East Asian spells more broadly, and its later developments in China and Japan (2002). Most recently, Henrik Sørensen studied the differences between the Chinese versions in detail, situating the text within the broader history of esoteric Buddhism in East Asia (2006).

While scholars have explored the text's South Asian antecedents and its development in East Asia, relatively little has been written on the possible significance of the *Great Peahen*'s vicissitudes. In this chapter I will analyze the ways in which the *Great Peahen* grew and changed, and how these different kinds of change might be usefully interpreted by historians of religion.

Types of Change in the Great Peahen

The wealth of surviving versions of the *Great Peahen* offers scholars rare insight into the complexity of Buddhist textual and ritual change. The growth of the *Great Peahen* was not a simple or linear process. Thinking about textual development as a conjunction of overlapping processes, one can isolate at least four discrete types of textual change: (1) the merging of recensions, (2) a sudden expansion of the pantheon, (3) the addition of spells and passages from Chinese Buddhist texts, and (4) continuous changes in ritual procedures.

Merging Recensions

The extant versions of the *Great Peahen* may be divided into four main recensions, which have been explored in some detail by Henrik Sørensen (2006, 91–109).

1. T. 986. *Dà jīnsè kǒngquè wáng zhòu jīng* 大金色孔雀王呪經 [*Great Golden Peacock King Spell Scripture*]. Attributed to Śrīmitra. Probably late fourth century.
2. T. 987. *Fóshuō dà jīnsè kǒngquè wáng zhòu jīng* 佛說大金色孔雀王呪經 [*Scripture Spoken by the Buddha on the Great Golden Peahen Queen Spell*]. Attributed to Śrīmitra. Early fifth century.
3. T. 988. *Kǒngquè wáng zhòu jīng* 孔雀王呪經. [*Peahen Queen Spell Scripture*]. Attributed to Kumārajīva. Early fifth century.

4. T. 984. *Kǒngquè wáng zhòu jīng* 孔雀王呪經. [*Peahen Queen Spell Scripture*]. Translated by Sēngqiépóluó 僧伽婆羅 [*Saṅghabhara]. Early sixth century.

The text of T. 984 is basically identical to the two later Chinese translations (T. 985, translated in 705 by Yìjìng 義淨, and T. 982, translated in the eighth century by Amoghavajra), to the surviving Sanskrit manuscripts, and to the Tibetan translation (Tōhoku 559, translated ninth–tenth century by Śākyaprabha and Ye shes sde). The two earliest recensions feature the same spells, but have entirely different narrative frames. T. 986, translated earlier in this chapter, is centered on the story of the peacock king named Suvarṇāvabhāsa, who recites a spell to keep him from danger. T. 987 narrates the story of a monk named Svāti who, when bitten by a venomous snake, is healed through the power of the *vidyā*. Both recensions contain a core set of spells: the *hu hu hu* spell, the heart spell, and the spells to Maitreya, Brahmā, Indra, the Great Ṛṣis, and the Devarājas. T. 988, on the other hand, shares the narrative frame of T. 987 but almost none of the spells found in the earliest two recensions. It shares with its predecessors only the spell of the Devarājas.

It is in T. 984 and its later manifestations that one can detect the merging of the earliest two recensions. Not only are the spells of both texts found in T. 984, but both narrative frames of the peacock king and the monk Svāti are found in the text. The unique elements of T. 988 are entirely missing from T. 984 and all later texts. Figure 6.1 shows what a

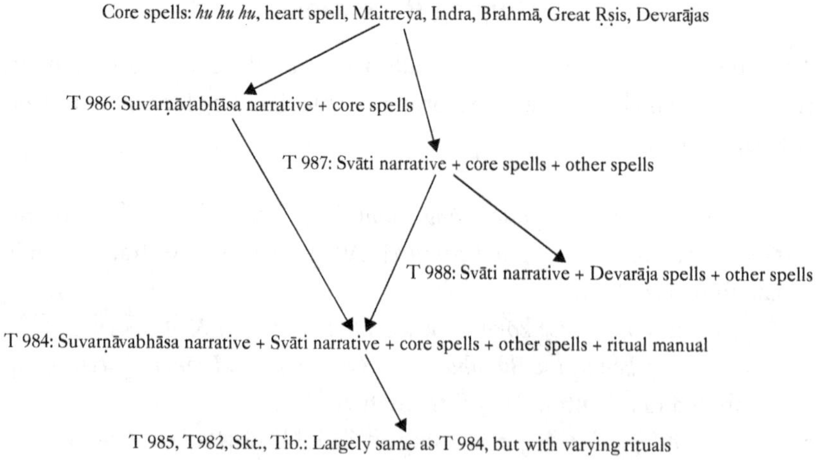

FIGURE 6.1 Relationship of Extant Versions of the *Great Peahen*

provisional stemma based on the surviving versions of the *Great Peahen* would look like. Table 6.1 collates shared material across the earliest versions.

The most striking fact to keep in mind here is the remarkable consistency of what I label the "core spells" across versions, with the exception of the anomalous T. 988. The main recensions of the *Great Peahen* vary mainly in their narrative frames, and by the early sixth century translation these recensions coalesced in the version of *Saṅghabhara, from which all later translations would not substantially diverge.

This recensional history can tell us some important facts. First, even though the text changes a great deal, the *spells* of the *Great Peahen* exhibit remarkable stability given the linguistic and geographic distances that must have been involved in the text's transmission from South to Central and East Asia. One may readily consult the Sanskrit or Tibetan versions for guidance in reconstructing the transcribed spells of T. 986 or T. 987. The remarkable accuracy with which the *vidyā* was transmitted through the centuries testifies to the importance given by this tradition to the proper utterance of spells. Second, the *Great Peahen* gives us at least one way of thinking about what how prototantric literature works: the narrative frames for these texts are secondary to the spells and rituals they transmit. The pragmatic and modular nature of Buddhist prototantrism is thus reflected in the *Great Peahen*'s textual history.[15]

Expanding Pantheon

The core of the *Great Peahen* features spells connected with Maitreya, Brahmā, Indra, the Great Seers, and the Devarājas. Over time, new recensions of the *Great Peahen* expanded the range of featured deities, demons, and numina. The earliest signs of this expansion are found in T. 987, which contains a list of fourteen demonesses (*luóchànǚ* 羅刹女, *rākṣasī*) who are propitiated for protection.[16] In T. 984, the pantheon radically expanded, swelling to include long lists of the past Buddhas, *yakṣas*, demonesses, dragon kings, river queens, mountain queens, constellations, and even poisons. Each section of this expanded version lists the names (and sometimes the locations) of these beings and gives a protective spell.

Sylvain Lévi already showed how useful this was as a resource for early medieval Indian geography. He investigated the long list of *yakṣas* and their domains in detail, and pointed out the relative importance of Pāṭaliputra and the high frequency of locations in the northwest of India

(1915, 116–117). Lévi dated the list to the first few centuries of the Common Era, in the time between the Kuṣāṇa and the Gupta empires.[17]

While Lévi's contribution was immensely valuable, he did not write about the religious and cultural implications of the *Great Peahen*'s long lists of deities, demons, and numina. This necessary work was begun by DesJardins, whose dissertation devoted an entire chapter to the pantheon of the *Great Peahen*, tracing the Indian antecedents of the various deities (2002, 70–157). For DesJardins, the lists allow one to read the *Great Peahen* as a comprehensive inventory or census of the Buddhist spiritual world.[18]

But how might one read the broader meaning of such an inventory? One could see the list of *yakṣas* as the product of Buddhist expansion through the subcontinent and into the northwest, but the exact nature of the relationship between the Buddhist community and the *yakṣas* for this text is ambiguous. Not only do the deities chant the spells of the *Great Peahen*, but the text in turn implores the deities to recite their spells on behalf of the reader, and wishes long life for the deities. This is no simple appropriation or conquest of local cults.[19] The *Great Peahen* reflects a complex interplay of Buddhist accommodation to or incorporation of local cults, as well as an attitude of superiority and conquest over these mundane spirits.[20]

Much as Lévi found the text most useful for thinking about Indian geography, I find the *Great Peahen* useful for thinking about Buddhist cosmology as a practical religious concern. When I teach undergraduates about Buddhist cosmology in the classroom, it is all too easy to think of and teach this system as a simple topographic "map," a spatial model that helps orient the bewildered students as they try to make their way through the confusing details in the *nidāna* of a Buddhist text. But Buddhist cosmology is of course much more than a spatial model—it is a political map as well.

As the *Great Peahen*'s root text develops, we see increasing density and detail in its mapping. The earliest text has a broadly vertical arrangement; Brahmā, Maitreya, Indra, and the Seers all live at different altitudes. The later versions of the *Great Peahen* expand our view horizontally within Jambudvīpa proper, mapping out communities of *rākṣasas* and *yakṣas*, mountains and rivers, poisons and stars, all with great density and detail. This cosmology is less about the broad outlines of spatial organization, and much more about the sociopolitical world of the Buddhist practitioner. The practitioner's immediate concerns are simple: Which agents are responsible for my sickness? Which agents can I petition or coerce for redress? The developments of the *Great Peahen* allow us to trace the growth and increasing density of a Buddhist practical cosmology.

As the text moved from South to East Asia, the reception of these lists must have drastically changed. Chinese monks were surely less familiar with the intricate details of the local numina of the Indian subcontinent. Rather than *reminding* the listener of the deities and places of one's homeland, the *Great Peahen* in Chinese would have likely communicated a vast and largely incomprehensible list of powerful alien beings. But even if the names and locations of the Indian demons were exotic and unfamiliar, the Chinese audience would have seen some resonance with their own practices. The notion of addressing demons by name to cure illness has been a constant feature of Chinese lived religion since at least the Warring States.[21] Any Daoist in the Celestial Master tradition during the fourth or fifth centuries would surely have understood the gist of the *Great Peahen*, as its long lists of demons closely resembled early demonographic literature such as the *Demon Statutes of the Lady Azure* (*Nǚqīng guǐlǜ* 女青鬼律).[22] The similarity of approach would have made it quite easy for Chinese practitioners to adopt the *Great Peahen* and augment it with their own materials.

Incorporation of Chinese Material

While the South Asian material may have been opaque at best to the East Asian readers of the *Great Peahen*, some of the Chinese versions contain lists of deities and excerpts from texts that would have been much more familiar. These Chinese additions reveal the fluidity and flexibility of the early medieval grimoire.

The mention of the *Maṇiratna Scripture* and the **Mahāgandhabhikṣu* at the end of T. 986 is the earliest example of a Chinese intervention into the *Great Peahen*. The **Mahāgandhabhikṣu* is now lost. The *Maṇiratna Scripture*, which survives only in a late fourth-century Chinese translation, is a short catalog of the names of demons (*guǐ* 鬼).[23] T. 986 makes only the briefest reference to these scriptures, noting their ability to "rescue from sickness, suffering, and calamity." The *Great Peahen*, on the other hand, is given an offensive mission: to "eliminate enemies" (T. 986, 19:478c27–28). This is powerful evidence that by the fifth century at the latest, the *Great Peahen* existed within a rich network of Chinese Buddhist ritual texts, and that the circulating copies of these texts contained instructions about their own use.

T. 987 was even more explicit in forging connections between the *Great Peahen* and the growing Chinese corpus of Buddhist spells. The end of the scripture contains verbatim excerpts of Chinese translations of the *dhāraṇīs* of Buddhist texts like the *Bandit Scripture*, the *Lotus Scripture*, and the *Nirvāṇa Scripture*.[24] This appendix of spells shows the reader how *dhāraṇīs* could be detached from their literary context and circulated through Buddhist communities. Spells from the *Lotus Scripture* were separable lemmata from which the redactors of the *Great Peahen* could draw to create their new grimoire. The fact that these spells were taken from Chinese translations shows us that Chinese practitioners were actively engaging with Buddhist texts to build their own scriptures and traditions. T. 987 should be considered not just a distinct "version" or "recension" of the *Great Peahen*; it should be considered a new work—a Chinese liturgy—with the *Great Peahen* as its primary ingredient.[25]

T. 988 takes this trend to its extreme, stripping away many of the *Great Peahen*'s "core spells" and prepending the text with invocations to the Dragon Generals of the five directions, and uttering the "*Mahāprajñāpāramitā* Spell" (T. 988, 19:481c25–482b19). This version closes with the inclusion of a completely different scripture, the *Āṭavaka Spell Scripture*.[26] The radical differences between T. 988 and the other versions of the *Great Peahen* only reinforce the conclusion that the notions of "transmission" and "translation" in prototantric Buddhism are dangerously imprecise. Even while one might identify shared elements in most texts over time, these elements could be tossed out in favor of new texts and new spells. Besides speaking to the flexibility and fluidity of the Buddhist tradition, the *Great Peahen*'s inclusion of explicitly Chinese material shows how much freedom Chinese translators and editors could exert when fashioning their texts. This creativity and continuous innovation was reflected not only in the base text, but in the continuously changing ritual manuals as well.

Changes in Ritual Procedures

Beginning with T. 988, all versions of the *Great Peahen* append ritual manuals. Even as the base text more or less solidified and remained static after the translation of *Saṅghabhara, the ritual manuals continued to expand and transform, often quite radically.

The manual of T. 988 does not outline any specific ritual procedures. Instead, it reads like a shopping list:

> The *Peahen Queen Spell* arena: use cow dung to smear the ground. Use scattered seven-colored flowers, forty-nine pennants, four blades, four mirrors, one hundred arrows, one bow, seven vessels filled with broth, sixty lengths of black wool rope, twenty-five small cakes. Burn seven oil lamps. One dish of cream, one dish of grits, one dish of rice, one dish of small cakes. Set down one dish of honey and one dish of flowers. (T. 988, 19:484c4–8)

Though there is not much to go on here, the ritual undoubtedly would have involved propitiation with food and flowers, as well as decoration of the ritual space with pennants, mirrors, weapons, and lamps.

A ritual along similar lines was more thoroughly elaborated at the end of *Saṅghabhara's translation. T. 984 lists similar ingredients, but also gives explicit instructions for the ritual procedure. The ritual involves the creation of a circular arena, invocation of the guardians of the directions for protection, and the ritual burning and beating of demons. The text even closes with a helpful diagram showing the arrangement of the lamps, swords, mirrors, pennants, and censer (T. 984, 19:458c13ff.) This ritual is strikingly simple. It involves no Buddha images, not even a bodhisattva or other central deity. Instead, the practitioner engages in a direct, violent battle with demonic forces within a delimited, ritually protected space.

The next translation by Yìjìng in the early eighth century features a much more complex ritual repertoire. The end of the text features no fewer than six distinct rituals: (1) a mandala rite involving the propitiation of painted images; (2) a mid-month rite featuring ingested metal beads and a fire ritual; (3) an abbreviated protective ritual for use at crossroads or in cemeteries; (4) emendations to the main ritual in order to care for a sick male child; (5) a heart spell; and (6) instructions on setting up a *Great Peahen* image in one's own household (T. 985, 19:476a10ff.) The mandala rite is the most involved. In the center of Yìjìng's mandala are a Buddha statue and a clay statue, painting, or iconic representation of the Peahen Queen. These figures are flanked by a kneeling Ānanda and an image of Vajrapāṇi. Flowers are scattered; the Buddha and the Peahen Queen are offered food, drink, and sweets; incense is burned; and the guardian deities of the four directions are invoked for protection and are bribed with food and drink. The guardian deities stand on the four continents of the Sumeru world-system: Videha, Jambudvīpa, Godānīya, and Uttarakuru. Finally, the mandala rite prescribes a procedure for protecting the body in which a young virgin girl weaves a rope, enchants it with the spell, knots it 108 times, and ties the spellcaster to herself with the rope.

One striking feature of this rite is the provision of substitute flowers and fruits: if no white *arka* flowers may be found, one may substitute them with lotus flowers. If no oleander flowers are available, one may use white apricot flowers instead (T. 985, 19:476a21–24).

The arena itself takes on a broader cosmological significance when compared with the simple circle in T. 984. While both rituals invoke the directional guardians, Yìjìng places the practitioner explicitly into the center of the Sumeru world system. The presence of the Buddha and Ānanda in the mandala mimics the narrative frame of the scripture itself, as does the inclusion of the Great Peahen and the great *yakṣa* Vajrapāṇi. If the root text of the *Great Peahen* reflects an increasingly dense practical cosmology, we can see in this ritual manual a concrete enactment of that cosmology.

As complex as this mandala might seem, it would become even more intricate in the ritual manual of Amoghavajra. This mandala features the Great Peahen in the center on an eight-petalled lotus blossom, riding a golden peacock. The eight petals of the lotus contain the seven Buddhas of the past and Maitreya, Buddha of the future. Outside the lotus petal are four *pratyekabuddhas* in the four cardinal directions and the four great *śrāvakas* (Ānanda, Rāhula, Śāriputra, and Maudgalyāyana) in the intermediate directions. Outside the inner sanctum are the "Celestial Kings of the Eight Directions" (Indra, Agni, Yama, Rākṣasa King, the Water God, Vāyu, Vaiśravaṇa, and Śiva). The third level contains the twenty-eight *yakṣa* generals, the constellations, planets, and the twelve spirits of the zodiac. All groups of deities in the three levels of the mandala are propitiated with incense, food, and drink, and the practitioner is enjoined to set down a lectern with the scroll of the *Great Peahen*. Making offerings of flowers to the scripture, he and his assistants should read it aloud continuously for days on end. The practitioner smears his hands with incense and forms various *mudrās* while uttering short mantras like "*oṃ samaya sattvam!*" (T. 983a).

Here we see the *Great Peahen* integrated into a recognizably esoteric ritual context. The practitioner is encouraged to supplicate the thirty-seven deities of the Diamond Realm mandala, thus linking the *Great Peahen* to one of the fundamental texts of East Asian esoteric Buddhism.[27] The deities in this mandala stand in clear hierarchical relation to one another. As in the previously discussed rituals, they are given food and drink as a way of establishing and sealing off the ritual boundary. However, instead of violently beating the demons or simply reciting the spell, the practitioner is ordered to read the scripture itself with a team of assistants. While the formation of the *Great Peahen*'s text may have involved the remixing and fluid circulation of various Indian and Chinese spells, by Amoghavajra's time we can see the emergence of the *Great Peahen* as a discrete text, a ritual object with its own particular efficacy. No longer are the practitioners simply repeating oral formulæ; they are reading from a ritually consecrated scroll.

The rapid changes in ritual manuals in every version of the *Great Peahen* is striking, especially given the stability of the base text from the early sixth century forward. Once the text coalesced into its final form, it became a carrier of innovative ritual procedures. It is in these ritual procedures, the detailed instructions for describing the world of gods and demons, propitiating and commanding them, that we can see how rapidly the traditions of prototantric Buddhism were developing in the fifth through the eighth centuries. The ritual manuals show increasing systematization and detail, an expansion of their underlying cosmology, and ultimately an assimilation of the *Great Peahen* into more influential esoteric ritual systems.

Conclusion

> That year [746 CE] the entire summer was exceedingly sunny. The Emperor asked the Great Master to enter the palace and pray for rain. His edict read, "The duration should not be long, and the rain should not be heavy." The Great Master formally requested the mandalic rite of the *Great Peahen Spell Queen Scripture*. Before three days had passed, they were completely drenched with precipitation. The Emperor greatly rejoiced. Personally taking up his treasure chest, he bestowed upon the Great Master a purple *kaṣāya*-robe. The Emperor opened it up for him to put it on. He also bestowed upon him two hundred bolts of silk.[28]

This passage, written by Zhàoqiān 趙遷, a disciple of Amoghavajra, seems at first glance a hagiographic cliché. But we know that Amoghavajra translated the *Great Peahen*. We know that the text instructs the reader to recite the spell in case of famine. We know that some of the Indian spells in the text contain exhortations to the gods to let rain pour forth. We also know that Amoghavajra wrote two appendices to this text, one a list of the spells to be recited in Siddham characters (T. 983b), the other a set of instructions for the images and mandala of the Peahen Queen rite (T. 983a). Given Amoghavajra's interest in this spell, his prominent position in the Táng court, and the spell's clear association with the production of rain, it seems wise not to view the account of Zhàoqiān with excessive suspicion.

The scenario described by Zhàoqiān is even more striking when we turn our gaze southwest, to the great city of Kanyakubja. Here reigned Harṣa, the Indian king who in 641 opened diplomatic ties with the Táng court after his celebrated meeting with the Buddhist pilgrim Xuánzàng 玄奘. In the *Harṣacarita*, an account of the king's deeds by the great poet Bāṇa, the reader finds an amusing tale of Harṣa's father Prabhākaravardhana overcome by a grave illness, and the frantic efforts of his subjects to find a remedy:

> Slowly, the guardians of the gates bowing to him, he entered the palace of the king, whose grievous condition was being discussed by the lords of men who had entered the courtyard. Their minds were aggrieved because they had not seen their master. They learned news from the members of his close retinue who emerged from the palace interior. Bathing, eating, and sleeping had become a mere fiction to them. Their clothes were filthy from rejecting personal hygiene. There were motionless, like drawings in a picture. They were with their outside retinue, who had formed a circle on the terraces, talking day and night of sorrow and misery in whispered discussions. Someone was pointing out the faults of the doctors. Someone was reciting passages concerning the characteristics of incurable diseases. Someone was talking about his bad dreams. Someone was telling a story about goblins. Someone was elucidating the teachings of astrologers. Someone was singing portents. Another was meditating on impermanence, condemning *saṃsāra*, lambasting the decadence of the Kali age, and censuring fate. Another was angry with the *dharma*, and scolding the deities of the royal family. Another was complaining about the fortune of the afflicted gentleman. In the palace all possessions were being offered. Devotional rites for the family deities were being performed. The cooking of nectar and barley had begun. The fire-sacrifice of six oblations was being performed. Tremulous shoots of *dūrvā* grass smeared with bits of ghee and curd were being offered. The *Great Peahen* was being recited, the house pacification rites were being performed, and the performance of the protective offerings to the *bhūtas* was completed. The utterance of the Saṃhitā propounded by the sages had been offered. The temple of Śiva was resounding with the *Eleven Verses to Rudra* being recited. The bathing of Virūpākṣa with thousands of pitchers of milk was being carried out by the very pure devotees of Śiva.[29]

There are clear differences between these two accounts. While Amoghavajra performs a mandala ritual (*tánfǎ* 壇法), the palace officiants in Kanyakubja were reciting (*paṭhyamāna*) the *Great Peahen*. There can also be no doubt that the literary record of these two moments was shaped by the limitations of the hagiographical genre and by the agenda of the authors. Zhàoqiān's account is unambiguously heroic, while Bāṇa's tale is much more ambivalent. In the *Harṣacarita*, the *Great Peahen* is but one of a panoply of rites performed across the spectrum of Indian religious traditions. The *Great Peahen*—along with all the other grain offerings and statue bathings and fire sacrifice and verses to Rudra—is so lamely ineffective that the servants outside the palace resort to darker thoughts, reflecting on the nature of incurable diseases or the inevitable corruption of our wicked Kali age. Despite these differences, there remains a remarkable continuity: in both seventh-century India and eighth-century China, the *Great Peahen Queen of Spells* was an eminently practical text, used at the highest levels in imperial courts to combat dire calamities.

The vicissitudes of the *Great Peahen* provide a rich set of data for thinking about the development of Buddhist tantra. The preservation of so many recensions in the Chinese canon is not simply a testament to the popularity and enduring value of the *Great Peahen*. It may also reveal the kinds of textual and ritual developments *generally applicable* in Buddhist history—developments usually obscured by a lack of data. Texts were not only circulating in easily remixable fragments, but even relatively stable texts could become a site of startlingly rapid ritual innovation. Instead of thinking of the *Great Peahen* as a strange aberration, an embarrassingly inconsistent or unphilosophical work, it is far more useful to think of it as a uniquely detailed example of the construction and evolution of a Buddhist scripture. We see the movement from a hodgepodge grimoire, a series of loosely joined lemmata, toward a more stable macroform whose singular identity is the focus of ritual veneration. Would this process be so different in the case of the *Lotus*, the *Flower Garland*, or the *Nirvāṇa Scripture*?

One might imagine a critical difference between the *Great Peahen* and a more "literary" or "philosophical" Mahāyāna scripture: perhaps it is the pragmatic nature of the *Great Peahen* that leads to such easy alteration, adaptation, and expansion. I am tempted to read the explosion of the *Great Peahen*'s pantheon and the mercurial shifts in its ritual manuals as a manifestation of the same kind of urge to comprehensiveness at work in Prabhākaravardhana's court. The denizens of Kanyakubja wielded every possible rite and every possible devotional practice in the service of their ailing king. An apotropaic text like the *Great Peahen* would be subject to the same universalizing impulses. The scripture's hodgepodge nature and its lack of literary coherence allowed it to rapidly spread throughout South and East Asia with an ever-expanding pantheon and ritual repertoire. It would later be used as a rain-summoning ritual even further East, in Heian and Kamakura Japan (Trenson 2003; de Visser 1919–1920, 385–387). The *Great Peahen* would also find its way into the *Pañcarakṣā*, a twelfth-century anthology of five protective spells popular in Tibet and Nepal.[30] *Vajrācāryas* to this day recite and transmit the *Great Peahen* as part of this ritual corpus, which is valued for its comprehensive powers of protection (Lewis 2000, 154ff.).

The *Great Peahen* did not confine itself to specifically Buddhist contexts. The scripture and many of its deities were absorbed into Daoist texts and rituals in the Míng 明 dynasty, appearing in the *Scripture Uttered by the Celestial Venerable Tàishàng Yuánshǐ on the Holy Mother Celestial Venerable Empress of Precious Moonlight and the Peahen Queen of Spells* (*Tàishàng Yuánshǐ tiānzūn shuō Bǎoyuèguāng huánghòu shèngmǔ tiānzūn Kǒngquè míngwáng jīng* 太上元始天尊說寶月光皇后聖母天尊孔雀明王經), the *Invocation Rite for the Venerable Scripture of the Holy Mother and the Peahen Queen of Spells* (*Shèngmǔ Kǒngquè míngwáng zūnjīng qǐbó yí* 聖母孔雀明王尊經啓白儀), and the *Invocation Text Uttered by Celestial Venerable Tàishàng Yuánshǐ on the Peahen Queen Scripture* (*Tàishàng Yuánshǐ tiānzūn shuō Kǒngquèjīng bówén* 太上元始天尊說孔雀經白文). Just as in the Buddhist *Great Peahen*, the texts feature an expansive pantheon of demons, dragons, and deities, but the specific names have changed, and the Buddhist elements have been fused into a Daoist context.[31]

The *Great Peahen*'s popularity extends even beyond the religious sphere. The text and its ritual power served as inspiration for a Japanese *manga* serialized from 1985–1989 called *Peacock King* (*Kujaku Ō*, 孔雀王), which later was adapted into an animated series, several video games, and even a live action kung-fu film.[32] In this new manifestation the Buddhist monk Kujaku, a reincarnation of *Mahāmāyūrī*, battles all manner of evil spirits using his esoteric mantras and *mudrās*. While we may be tempted to dismiss these popular incarnations of the *Great Peahen* as trivialities, the long history of this spell's transmission and its rapid changes should caution us from clinging too tightly to any monolithic vision of the tradition. Whether in art, literature, or liturgy, the only consistently unchanging feature of the *Great Peahen* has been its startling capacity for ready transmission and rapid transformation.

Table 6.1 Detailed Outline of the Earliest Recensions of the *Great Peahen*

	T. 986	T. 987	T. 988	T. 984	Skt. [Takubo]
Directional guardians			481c25–482b15		
Asking bodhisattvas for help			482b16–19		
Kings of various divinities			482b20–c7		
Intention to utter the spell			482c8–13		
Homage to spell, realms, and kings			482c14–483a3		
Homage to the Buddha, etc.		479a6–9	483a4–7	446b28–29	1.4–9
Exhortation to demons to listen		479a9–22	483a8–20	446b29–c15	1.10–2.8
Rākṣasīs		479a22–28	483a21–26	446c16–24	2.9–13
Story of Svāti		479a29–479b9		446c25–447a2	2.14–3.10
Buddha recommends MMVR to Ānanda		479b9–25	483a27–b16	447a2–15	3.11–4.9
Protective metrical verse: rātrau svasti divā svasti. . .		479b26–28	483b16–18	447a15	4.10–11
Spell iḍi viḍi kiḍi. . .		479b29–c19	483b18–c6	447a15–b7	4.12–5.8
Alliance magic (maitrī) verses for the Nāga Kings				447b7–c9	5.9–7.8
Story of the Golden Peacock King	477c6–9			447c9–12	7.9–12
Spell "hu hu hu. . ." #1	477c10–15	479c20–29		447c12–22	7.13–19
Spell "hu hu hu. . ." #2				447c23–448a9	7.20–8.12
Spell *siddhe susiddhe*				448a10–25	8.13–9.1
Spell *huci guci muci svāhā*				448a26–27	9.1–8

(continued)

Table 6.1 Continued

	T. 986	T. 987	T. 988	T. 984	Skt. [Takubo]
Heart *spell ili mitti tili mitti*. . .	477c16–478a4	480a1–17		448a27–c14	9.8–10.6
Spell *ilia mile kili*. . .				448c14–29	12.16–13.4
Spell *Citra mule Citra Citra male*. . .				449a1–19	13.4–16
Buddhas and their trees				449a20–b3	13.17–14.7
Great Yakṣas				449b4–23	15.6–17
Kings of the Directions				449b24–450a10	15.18–18.8
Great Yakṣa Generals				450a11–451c12	18.9–23.17
28 Yakṣa Generals				452a17–b22	24.13–26.13
Vaiśravaṇa's brothers				452b23–c27	26.14–29.5
Great Piśācīs				452c28–453c14	29.6–31.2
Great Rākṣasīs				453c15–454c10	31.3–39.4
Nāga Kings				454c11–455b23	39.5–42.23
Spells of the Buddhas				455b24–456a25	43.1–45.4
Maitreya spell	478a5–11	480a18–24		456a26–b7	45.5–9
Brahmā spell	478a12–17	480a25–b1		456b8–22	45.10–46.6
Indra spell	478a18–29	480b2–12		456b23–c5	46.7–14
Four Deva Kings				456c6–21	46.15–47.9
River Queens				456c22–457a12	47.10–48.14
Mountain Kings				457a13–b7	48.15–50.13
Constellations				457b8–26	50.14–52.2
Great Ṛṣis	478b1–26	480b13–c7		457b27–458a5	52.19–54.15

Great Poisons				458a6–19	55.14–56.4
Spell of Devarājas and demons: "akaṭe vikaṭe. . ."	478b27–c26	480c8–481a16	483c7–484a7	451c13–452a10	23.18–24.12
Plug for the Maṇiratna and *Mahāgandhabhikṣu scriptures	478c27–28				
Spell of Deva Kings			484a8–12		
Āṭāvaka Spell Scripture			484a13–c3		
Lineage and benefits of spell				458a20–c1	56.16–60.4
Ānanda cures Svāti				458c1–11	60.5–61.7
Ritual manuals			484c4–8	458c13–459a3	61.8–62.9
Spell "akaru arule. . ."		481a6–24			
Bandit Scripture		481a25–b11			
Lotus Scripture spells		481b12–c13			
Nirvāṇa Scripture spell		481c14–17			

Notes

1. My thanks to Janet Gyatso for comments on the first draft of this article, originally begun as a term paper for a graduate course in Buddhist Studies at Harvard University. I would also like to thank the graduate students at the University of California, Berkeley, who took my seminar on early Buddhist ritual literature in the autumn of 2014. Their critical and enthusiastic engagement with the *Great Peahen* corpus was inspiring. Special thanks to James Marks, whose gimlet eye spotted some potentially embarrassing errors in my comparative table. All that is good in this chapter comes from my teachers and students; all infelicities are mine alone.
2. The translation *Great Peahen Queen of Spells* for *Mahāmāyūrīvidyārājñī* is tentative. Lambert Schmithausen, noting that the text draws from an old tale about a peacock *king* named Suvarṇāvabhāsa, precisely translates *Mahāmāyūrīvidyārājñī* as the "Queen of Spells [called] the Great One of the Peacock" (Schmithausen 1997, 53). However, most iconography of Mahāmāyūrī in South and East Asia depict the figure as a female *bodhisattvā*, sometimes riding on a peacock. So should the reader take *Mahāmāyūrī* adjectivally (feminine in agreement with the noun *vidyārājñī*) or nominally (referring to the female embodiment of the spell itself)? Charles Orzech noted that the first explicit stance on this question was taken by Amoghavajra, whose eighth-century Chinese translations refers to Mahāmāyūrī as a Buddhist goddess (*fómǔ* 佛母; Orzech 2002, 82–83). As we shall see, not all versions of the text draw from the story of Suvarṇāvabhāsa. I use Schmithausen's interpretation when the context and grammar of the Chinese sources are clear, but when there is no clear answer I will, in deference to the iconography, refer to the spell as the *Great Peahen*.
3. The Chinese texts may be found in T. 982–988. Fragments of the Sanskrit text were found in the Bower Manuscript, on which see Hoernle (1893, 234ff). These fragments were first connected with the Chinese texts in Watanabe (1907). The earliest full Sanskrit edition may be found in Ol'denburg (1899). The most thorough Sanskrit edition to date is Takubo (1972). For detailed overviews of the many versions of the *Great Peahen*, see Waddell (1912); de Visser (1919–1920); Schmithausen (1997); DesJardins (2002, 20–28); and Sørensen (2006). DesJardins's dissertation remains the most comprehensive source on the antecedents and later reception of the *Great Peahen*.
4. This was put more charitably by J. F. Marc DesJardins in his dissertation on the *Great Peahen*: "Le MMVR est un ouvrage difficile à aborder à cause de son hermétisme, de son aspect de grimoire médiéval, et de son manque total de philosophie. Difficile à interpréter, il ne semble y avoir rien qui puisse valider idéologiquement sa popularité chez les prêtres de l'ésotérisme. En cela, le language du MMVR en est un de rituel, de magie, et de pouvoir. Le rituel fait le MMVR" (2002, 6).

5. *Dà jīnsè kǒngquèwáng zhòu jīng* 大金色孔雀王呪經. The Chinese title's use of *jīnsè* 金色 "Golden" probably translates Suvarṇāvabhāsa ("Golden Light"), the name of the Peacock King also found in the *Mūlasarvāstivādavinaya* (Dutt 1984, 3.1: 285–288). The text of T 986 varies in its titles considerably. The heart spell is entitled the "Heart of the Queen of Spells of the Great Peacock King" (*Dà kǒngquèwáng zhòuwáng xīn* 大孔雀王呪王心; T. 986, 19:477c16). Later the spell is called "Queen of Spells of the Great Peacock" (*Dà kǒngquè zhòuwáng* 大孔雀呪王; T. 986, 19:478a5, a12, a18, &c.), and later still the scripture itself is referred to as the "Scripture of the Spell of the Great Golden Peacock King" (*Dà kǒngquèwáng zhòu jīng* 大金色孔雀王呪經; T. 986, 19:478b19).
6. This spell (*vidyā*) contains mostly incomprehensible syllables transcribed into Chinese. When possible, I refer to the later Sanskrit version to interpret the Chinese transcriptions—often they are remarkably close. All the translations of the *Great Peahen* contain Chinese transcriptions of these Indian magical utterances, although occasionally the spells contain comprehensible injunctions that are translated into Chinese. For example, in the Sanskrit version the spell beginning with *akaṭe vikaṭe* . . . (Takubo 1972, 23–24) ends with the injunction *priyaṃkare rakṣa māṃ sarvasatvāṃś ca jīvatu varṣaśataṃ paśyatu śaradāśataṃ!* In T. 986 this portion of the spell is translated, not transcribed: *yōnghù mǒujiǎ, lìng déshòu bǎisuì, déjiàn bǎiqiū!* 擁護某甲，令得壽百歲，得見百秋！ (T. 986, 19:478c26).
7. In this translation I use . . . *[&c.]* to indicate a series of largely nonsensical Indic sounds phonetically transcribed into Chinese. I omit most of the translation for the sake of brevity.
8. The "Great Seers" of this spell are found in the later Sanskrit edition as *maharṣi*, the celebrated hearers of the Vedas. Sørensen claimed that this passage was one of the earliest references to *siddhis* in an East Asian text (2006, 95), but this claim rests on a dubious translation of the passage. For a detailed analysis of this passage see Overbey (2012, 132–135).
9. The characters *Móhēqiántuó bǐqiū* 摩訶乾陀比丘 probably refer to the scripture in one scroll, now lost, whose title in the early sixth-century *Chū sānzàng jìjí* 出三藏記集is recorded as *Móhēqiántuó wéiwèiluó jìnxìn bǐqiū děngdù jīng* 摩訶揵陀惟衛羅盡信比丘等度經. See T. 2145, 55:19c4–6. Sørensen (2006, 96) erroneously translates the characters 摩訶乾陀比丘 in the vocative as "Mahāmaudgalyāyana Bhikṣu," but nowhere in the canon is 摩訶乾陀 attested as a translation of Mahāmaudgalyāyana.
10. For example, Michel Strickmann called the *Great Peahen* "l'un des textes fondamentaux du prototantrisme" (1996, 296).
11. See Chou (1945, 241–245) for the argument that the various Buddhist spells and rituals translated in China during the first centuries CE constituted a kind of incipient tantrism.
12. See Strickmann (1996, 117–118); Sørensen (2006, 109–110).

13. For terminological reflections on the applicability of words like "tantra" to particular phenomena, see Lopez (1996, 83–104); Davidson (2002, 118ff). Both scholars rely on "polythetic classification" to define the word. This is a fancy way of saying that, given two different sets of defining characteristics for tantra A and B, one may choose to call x tantric if $x \in (A \cup B)$, rather than requiring $x \in (A \cap B)$. The term "polythetic classification" was introduced to anthropologists in the journal *Man* by Rodney Needham, who had noticed the similarity between Wittgenstein's family resemblances and the polythetic taxonomies of contemporary biologists (Needham 1975). Needham's article was written about one century after George Cantor invented naïve set theory.
14. McBride goes quite far in arguing against applying labels like "esoteric" or "tantric" to rites and scriptures labeled *mìjiào* 密教, since the term *mìjiào* often was used as a polemical device to announce the superiority of one's own tradition or lineage (McBride 2004, 354–356). On this reading, the scholar should always view any deployment of the term *mìjiào* with suspicion.
15. For reflections on the modular structure of esoteric Buddhism, see Orzech (1996).
16. Sørensen (2006, 99) discusses and translates the names of these fourteen demonesses. Unfortunately, his translations from the Chinese did not benefit from a comparison with the Sanskrit edition. To give one example, Sørensen's translation of "Naked Body" for Báijù 白具 is surely mistaken, as the name of the demoness in Sanskrit versions reads Śaṃkhinī. In English the Sanskrit would be translated as "She with the Conch." This should, in turn, lead us to emend the Chinese to Báibèi白貝, "White Shell." For the relevant Sanskrit passage, see Takubo (1972, 2).
17. See Lévi (1915, 118). Lévi also ventures a much bolder hypothesis in his article. By dating the list in the *Great Peahen*, and pointing out similarly named locales in the *Mahābhārata*, Lévi guessed that the *Mahābhārata* itself was finally redacted around the same time as the *Great Peahen* (122).
18. "Il est un document officiel, un registre d'état civil du monde spirituel bouddhique" (DesJardins 2002, 155).
19. A repeating formula throughout the text reads: "May they [the numina] protect the mendicant Svāti, myself, and all beings with this *Great Peahen Queen of Spells*! May they preserve, protect, surround, guard, pacify, bless, rescue from punishment, rescue from weapons, counteract poison, destroy poison, mark off the ritual arena, and mark off the earth! May they live a hundred years! May they see a hundred autumns!" See for example, Takubo (1972, 7, 10, 13, 15, etc.).
20. For archæological evidence on the complex relationship between Buddhist monasteries and *yakṣa* cults, see Decaroli (2004). For methodological reflections on the relationship between Buddhism and South Asian deities generally, see Ruegg (2008, especially pp. 19–29).
21. See Harper (1985, 2004). For further reflections on the demonology and spell literatures of Buddhism and Daoism in early medieval China, see Strickmann (2002, 58–122).

22. On the *Nǚqīng guìlǜ*, see Seidel (1987), Schipper (1994), and Lai (2002).
23. See T. 1393. Sørensen (2006, 95–97) argues that the *Maṇiratna Scripture* served as a liturgical complement to the *Great Peahen*, the former providing a list of demons and the latter describing the necessary rituals. Sørensen views T. 986 not as a full-fledged scripture, but rather as a short ritual guide. For an overview of the *Maṇiratna Scripture*, see Strickmann (2002, 109–113).
24. T. 987, 19:481a25–c17. See Sørensen (2006, 100–101) for more details on these excerpted spells. Sørensen argues that this sort of textual "mining" is evidence that "the formation of esoteric Buddhism as a distinct—although not separate—tradition in Chinese Buddhism was gradually taking shape" by the time of the text's redaction.
25. Many such grimoires are found throughout the Chinese Buddhist canon. One notable example, attributed to Xuánzàng 玄奘, is the *Scripture of Five Spells* (*Zhòu wǔshǒu jīng* 呪五首經; T. 1034), which contains five *mantras* completely stripped away from their original literary contexts. I am speaking here only of the materials that made it into the Chinese Buddhist canonical catalogues; the Dūnhuáng archives are full of non-canonical, practical ritual manuals. See Dalton's contribution to this volume (Chapter 4) for examples in the Tibetan materials from Dūnhuáng.
26. T. 988, 19:484a13ff. Sørensen (2006, 104) correctly notes that this version of the *Āṭakava Spell* is most useful for assigning a date of the early fifth century to the text. See Strickmann (2002, 143–151) for a description of an early scripture of magical seals devoted to Āṭavaka.
27. For a convenient diagram and list of these deities, see Giebel (2001, 12–14).
28. T. 2056, 50:293a21–24. This is from the biography of Amoghavajra written by his lay disciple Zhàoqiān 趙遷. Zhàoqiān's description of this incident was copied nearly verbatim in the hagiographical collection edited by Zànníng 贊寧 (919–1001), the *Sòng Biographies of Eminent Monks* (T. 2061, 50:712c14–17). For further details on the life and work of Amoghavajra, see Chou (1945, 284–307); Orlando (1981); and Orzech (1988, especially 135–167). For more details on the use of the purple robe in China, see Kieschnick (2003, 100–103).
29. See Kāṇe (1918, *ucchvāsa* 5, 21.25–22.7). This long passage translates a single sentence from Bāṇa's verbose Sanskrit prose. The sentencc reads: *mandaṃ mandaṃ dvārapālaiḥ praṇamyamānaś ca dīyamānasarvasvaṃ pūjyamānakuladevataṃ prārabdhâmṛtacarupacanakriyaṃ kriyamāṇaṣaḍāhutihomaṃ hūyamānapṛṣadājyalavaliptapracaladurvāpallavaṃ paṭhyamānamahāmāyūrīpravartyamānagṛhaśāntinirvartyamānabhūtarakṣābalividhānaṃ prayataviprastutasaṃhitājapaṃ japyamānarudrâikadaśīśabdāyamānaśivagṛham atiśuciśaivasamāpadyamānavirūpākṣakṣīrakalaśasahasrasnapanam ajirôpaviṣṭaiś cânāsāditasvāmidarśanadū yamānamānasair abhyantaraniṣpatitanikaṭavartiparijananivedyamānavārtair vārtībhūtasnānabhojanaśayanair ujjhitâtmasaṃskāramalinaveśair likhitair iva niścalair narapatibhir nīyamānanaktandivaṃduḥkhadīnavadanena ca praghaneṣu baddhamaṇḍalenopāṃśuvyāhṛtaiḥ kenacic cikitsakadoṣān udbhāvayatā kenacid*

asādhyavyādhilakṣaṇapadāni paṭhatā kenacid duḥkhasvapnān āvedayatā kenacit piśācavārtāṃ vivṛṇvatā kenacit kārtāntikādeśān prakāśayatā kenacid upaliṅgāni gāyatânyenânityatāṃ bhāvayatā saṃsāraṃ cāpavadatā kalikālavilasitāni ca nindatā daivaṃ côpālabhamānenâpareṇa dharmāya kupyatā rājakuladevatāś câdhikṣipatâpareṇa kliṣṭakulaputrakabhāgyāni garhayatā bāhyaparijanena kathyamānakaṣṭapārthivâvasthaṃ rājakulaṃ viveśa.

30. For more on *rakṣā* literature generally, see Skilling (1992).
31. For summaries of these works, see Schipper and Verellen (2005, 1233–1234).
32. The *manga*, written by Makoto Ogino 荻野真, was serialized in *Shūkan yangu jampu* 週刊ヤングジャンプ [*Weekly Young Jump*] magazine between 1985 and 1989.

References

Chou Yi-liang [Zhōu Yīliáng 周一良]. 1945. "Tantrism in China." *Harvard Journal of Asiatic Studies* 8 (3–4): 241–332.

Davidson, Ronald. 2002. *Indian Esoteric Buddhism: A Social History of the Tantric Movement*. New York: Columbia University Press.

Decaroli, Robert. 2004. *Haunting the Buddha: Indian Popular Religions and the Formation of Buddhism*. New York: Oxford University Press.

DesJardins, J. F. Marc. 2002. "*Mahāmāyūrī*: explorations sur la création dune scripture prototantrique." PhD dissertation, McGill University.

Dutt, Nalinaksha, ed. 1984. *Gilgit Manuscripts*. 2nd edition. 4 vols. Bibliotheca Indo-Buddhica 14–19, 22–24. Delhi: Sri Satguru Publications.

Giebel, Rolf W. 2001. *Two Esoteric Sūtras*. BDK English Tripiṭaka, vol. 29-II, 30-II. Berkeley, CA: Numata Center for Buddhist Translation and Research.

Harper, Donald. 1985. "A Chinese Demonography of the Third Century B.C." *Harvard Journal of Asiatic Studies* 45 (2): 459–498.

Harper, Donald. 2004. "Contracts with the Spirit World in Han Common Religion: The Xuning Prayer and Sacrifice Documents of A.D. 79." *Cahiers d'extrême-asie* 14: 227–267.

Hoernle, August Friedrich Rudolf, ed. 1893–1912. *The Bower Manuscript: Facsimile Leaves, Nagari Transcript, Romanised Transliteration and English Translation with Notes*. Archæological Survey of India New Imperial Series 22. Calcutta: Superintendent of Government Printing.

Kāṇe, Pāṇḍuraṅga Vāmana, ed. 1918. *Harshacharita of Bāṇabhaṭṭa (Uchchvāsas I–VIII)*. Bombay.

Kieschnick, John. 1997. *The Eminent Monk: Buddhist Ideals in Medieval Chinese Hagiography*. Kuroda Studies in East Asian Buddhism 10. Honolulu: University of Hawai'i Press.

Kieschnick, John. 2003. *The Impact of Buddhism on Chinese Material Culture*. Princeton, NJ: Princeton University Press.

Lai Chi-tim 黎志添. 2002. "The *Demon Statutes of Nüqing* and the Problem of the Bureaucratization of the Netherworld in Early Heavenly Master Daoism." *T'oung-Pao* 88 (4): 251–281.

Lévi, Sylvain. 1915. "La catalogue géographique des Yakṣa dans la Mahā-māyūrī." *Journal Asiatique* 5 (1): 19–138.

Lewis, Todd T. 2000. *Popular Buddhist Texts from Nepal: Narratives and Rituals of Newar Buddhism*. Albany: State University of New York Press.

Lopez, Donald S. 1996. *Elaborations on Emptiness: Uses of the Heart Sutra*. Princeton, NJ: Princeton University Press.

McBride, Richard Dewayne II. 2004. "Is There Really 'Esoteric' Buddhism?" *Journal of the International Association of Buddhist Studies* 27 (2): 329–356.

McBride, Richard Dewayne II. 2005. "*Dhāraṇī* and Spells in Medieval Sinitic Buddhism." *Journal of the International Association of Buddhist Studies* 28 (1): 85–114.

Ol'denburg, Sergej Fedorovič, ed. 1899. "Otryvki kašgarskix" i sansritskix" rukopisej iz" sobranija N. F. Petrovskago." *Zapiski Vostočnago Otdělenija Imperatorskago Russkago Arxeologičeskago Obščestva* 11: 207–264.

Needham, Rodney. 1975. "Polythetic Classification." *Man* n.s. 10 (3): 349–369.

Orlando, Raffaello. 1981. "A Study of Chinese Documents Concerning the Life of the Tantric Buddhist Patriarch Amoghavajra (A.D. 705–774)." PhD dissertation, Princeton University.

Orzech, Charles D. 1996. "Maṇḍalas on the Move: Reflections from Chinese Esoteric Buddhism circa 800 C.E." *Journal of the International Association of Buddhist Studies* 19 (2): 209–244.

Orzech, Charles D. 1998. *Politics and Transcendent Wisdom: The Scripture for Humane Kings in the Creation of Chinese Buddhism*. University Park: Pennsylvania State University Press.

Orzech, Charles D. 2002. "Metaphor, Translation, and the Construction of Kingship in *The Scripture for Humane Kings* and the *Mahāmāyūrī Vidyārājñī Sūtra*." *Cahiers d'Extrême-Asie* 13: 55–83.

Overbey, Ryan Richard. 2012. "On the Appearance of *Siddhis* in Chinese Buddhist Texts." In *Yoga Powers: Extraordinary Capacities Attained Through Meditation and Concentration*, edited by Knut Axel Jacobsen, 127–144. Leiden: Brill.

Ruegg, David Seyfort. 2008. *The Symbiosis of Buddhism with Brahmanism/Hinduism in South Asia and of Buddhism with 'Local Cults' in Tibet and the Himalayan Region*. Österreichische Akademie der Wissenschaften. Philosophisch-historische Klasse. Sitzungsberichte, 774 Band. Beiträge zur Kultur- und Geistesgeschichte Asiens 58. Wien: Verlag der Österreichischen Akademie der Wissenschaften.

Schipper, Kristofer. 1994. "Purity and Strangers: Shifting Boundaries in Medieval Taoism." *T'oung-Pao* 80 (1–3): 61–81.

Schipper, Kristofer, and Franciscus Verellen, eds. 2005. *The Taoist Canon*. Chicago: University of Chicago Press.

Schmithausen, Lambert. 1997. *Maitrī and Magic: Aspects of the Buddhist Attitude Toward the Dangerous in Nature.* Österreichische Akademie der Wissenschaften. Philosophisch-historische Klasse. Sitzungsberichte, 652 Band. Veröffentlichungen zu den Sprachen und Kulturen Südasiens 30. Wien: Verlag der Österreichischen Akademie der Wissenschaften.

Seidel, Anna. 1987. "Traces of Han Religion in Funeral Texts Found in Tombs." In *Dōkyō to shūkyō bunka*道教と宗教文化, edited by Akizuki Kan'ei秋月觀暎, 21–57. Tōkyō 東京: Hirakawa Shuppansha平河出版社.

Sharf, Robert. 2002. *Coming to Terms with Chinese Buddhism: A Reading of the* Treasure Store Treatise. Kuroda Institute Studies in East Asian Buddhism 14. Honolulu: University of Hawai'i Press.

Skilling, Peter. 1992. "The Rakṣā Literature of the Śrāvakayāna." *Journal of the Pali Text Society* 16: 109–182.

Sørensen, Henrik H. 2006. "The Spell of the Great, Golden Peacock Queen: The Origin, Practices, and Lore of an Early Esoteric Buddhist Tradition in China." *Pacific World* third series 8: 89–123.

Strickmann, Michel. 1996. *Mantras et mandarins: le bouddhisme tantrique en Chine.* Paris: Éditions Gallimard.

Strickmann, Michel. 2002. *Chinese Magical Medicine.* Ed. Bernard Faure. Stanford, CA: Stanford University Press.

Takubo Shūyo 田久保周誉, ed. 1972. *Ārya-Mahā-Māyūrī Vidyā-Rājñī.* Tōkyō 東京: Sankibō Busshorin 山喜房佛書林.

Takakusu Junjirō 高楠順 and Watanabe Kaikyoku 渡邊海旭, eds. 1924–1932. *Taishō shinshū daizōkyō* 大正新修大藏經. 85 vols. Tōkyō 東京: Taishō issaikyō kankōkai 大正一切經刊行會.

Trenson, Steven. 2001–2003. "Une analyse critique de l'histoire de *Shōugyōhō* et du *Kujakukyōhō*: rites ésotériques de la pluie dans le Japon de l'époque de Heian." *Cahiers d'Extrême-Asie* 13: 455–495.

de Visser, Marinus Willem. 1919–1920. "Die Pfauenkönigin (K'ung-tsioh ming-wang, Kujaku myō-ō) in China und Japan." *Ostasiatische Zeitschrift* 8: 370–387.

Waddell, Laurence Austine. 1912. *The "Dhāraṇī" Cult in Buddhism: Its Origin, Deified Literature and Images.* Berlin: Österheld.

Watanabe Kaikyoku 渡邊海旭. 1907. "A Chinese text corresponding to part of the Bower Manuscript." *Journal of the Royal Asiatic Society of Great Britain and Ireland* 1907: 261–266.

TEXTS FROM THE *TAISHŌ SHINSHŪ DAIZŌKYŌ* 大正新修大蔵経

T. 982. *Fómǔ dàkǒngquè míngwáng jīng* 佛母大孔雀明王經 [*Scripture on the Goddess Great Peahen Queen of Spells*]. Translated 8th c. by Amoghavajra.

T. 983a. *Fóshuō dà kǒngquè míngwáng huàxiàng táncháng yíguǐ* 佛說大孔雀明王畫像檀場儀軌 [*Ritual Manual Spoken by the Buddha on the Images and Maṇḍala for the Great Peahen Queen of Spells*]. Compiled 8th c. by Amoghavajra.

T. 983b. *Kǒngquè jīng zhēnyánděng fànběn* 孔雀經真言等梵本 [*Sanskrit Volume of Mantras &c. for the Peahen Scripture*]. Compiled 8th c. by Amoghavajra.

T. 984. *Kǒngquè wáng zhòu jīng* 孔雀王呪經. [*Peahen Queen Spell Scripture*]. Translated early 6th c. by Sēngqiépóluó 僧伽婆羅 [*Saṅghabhara].

T. 985. *Fóshuō dàkǒngquè zhòuwáng jīng* 佛說大孔雀呪王經. [*Scripture Spoken by the Buddha on the Great Peahen Queen of Spells*]. Translated 705 by Yìjìng 義淨.

T. 986. *Dà jīnsè kǒngquè wáng zhòu jīng* 大金色孔雀王呪經 [*Great Golden Peacock King Spell Scripture*]. Probably late 4th c. Attributed to Śrīmitra.

T. 987. *Fóshuō dà jīnsè kǒngquè wáng zhòu jīng* 佛說大金色孔雀王呪經 [*Scripture Spoken by the Buddha on the Great Golden Peahen Queen Spell*]. Probably early 5th c. Attributed to Śrīmitra.

T. 988. *Kǒngquè wáng zhòu jīng* 孔雀王呪經. [*Peahen Queen Spell Scripture*]. 5th c. Attributed to Kumārajīva.

T. 1034. *Zhòu wǔshǒu jīng* 咒五首經 [*Scripture of Five Spells*]. Translated 664 by Xuánzàng 玄奘.

T. 2056. *Dà Táng gù dàdé zèng sīkōng dàbiàn zhèng guǎngzhì Bùkōng sānzàng xíng-zhuàng* 大唐故大德贈司空大辨正廣智不空三藏行狀 [*Account of the Deeds of the Late Great Bhadanta Amoghavajra Trepiṭaka of the Great Táng, to Whom Was (Posthumously) Bestowed the Titles Sīkōng, He of Great Discrimination, He of Correct Vast Wisdom*]. Compiled 8th c. by Zhàoqiān 趙遷.

T. 2061. *Sòng gāosēng zhuàn* 宋高僧傳 [*Sòng Biographies of Eminent Monks*]. Compiled late 10th c. by Zànníng 贊寧.

T. 2145. *Chū sānzàng jìjí* 出三藏記集 [*Collected notes on the translation of the Tripiṭaka*]. Compiled circa 515 by Sēngyòu僧祐.

7

The Homa of the Northern Dipper

Richard K. Payne

Introduction

In private conversations, class lectures, and publications, Michel Strickmann repeatedly emphasized the importance of contemporary Japanese tantric traditions as sources of information about aspects of Chinese religious history that are no longer extant. In one of his posthumous works, *Mantras et mandarins*, for example, he discusses the tantric *homa* in China. In the course of this he states: "Pour le sinologue, les manifestations contemporaines les plus importantes du homa se trouvent à la frontière orientale de la diffusion du bouddhisme: au Japon" (1996, 339). At the same time, as Charles Orzech has pointed out, we cannot simply uncritically accept sectarian Shingon or Tendai historiography as a fully adequate representation of the history of Esoteric Buddhism in China (1989). Based on one of the names given to tantric Buddhism, *mantranaya*, the name of the movement is rendered into Chinese as "Zhenyan" (眞言, Jpn. *shingon*), meaning "true word." It is hoped that by examining one specific ritual, the Homa of the Northern Dipper of the Chūin ryū 北斗息災護摩供次第供中院, we can discern something of the characteristic processes by which Buddhist tantra interacted with Daoism in the formation of Zhenyan ritual in China, and which then became part of the Shingon ritual corpus in Japan.[1]

A Typology of the Appropriation of Ritual Elements?

In order to discuss the ways in which Daoism contributed to the development of Esoteric Buddhist ritual practices, it would be useful to have a terminology for categorizing the ways in which members of one tradition will appropriate ritual elements from another religious tradition. Erik Zürcher has proposed a typology of borrowing for literary elements, which appears to be adaptable for systematic discussions of the borrowing of ritual elements. On the basis of an examination of about 120 Daoist texts, Zürcher proposed four kinds of borrowing: (1) formal borrowing, (2) conceptual borrowing, (3) borrowed complexes, and (4) pervasive borrowing (1980).[2]

Formal borrowing includes such stylistic and terminological features as the textual frameworks of Buddhist sūtras, idiomatic expressions, and the appropriation of the exotic, mysterious, and magical potency of transcribed Sanskrit names and terms. An important element within this broader category, as indicated by Zürcher, would be the use of Sanskrit or pseudo-Sanskrit in the form of mantra and *dhāraṇī*. As understood by Zürcher, such borrowing involves the use of individual elements in isolation, without any particular reference to the significance they had in the tradition of origin. By "conceptual borrowing" Zürcher is referring to the appropriation of elements that do introduce a new meaning, but are still appropriated as an individual element. These instances point to "a general phenomenon fundamental to the whole mechanism of borrowing: the more an element is taken over in isolation, dissociated from its original context, the easier will be its complete digestion and its change of meaning and function" (Zürcher 1980, 112). Such isolated borrowings are relatively rare in Zürcher's sample. More common is the borrowing of a complex, in which the individual elements form a larger whole, maintaining its own intellectual context, and restraining the kind of "complete digestion" that occurs with formal and conceptual borrowing. In other words, this kind of borrowing involves "the absorption of a coherent cluster of ideas and/or practices, taken over from Buddhism as a complex in which at least part of the original constituent elements are maintained, even if the interpretation and function of those elements and of the complex as a whole may be quite different from the original ones" (87). Zürcher identifies three major complexes found in the Daoist literature: cosmology, morality, and karma and retribution. In the case of these major complexes, the "Buddhist elements . . . have deeply influenced the receiving system, and in some cases led to a complete reorientation" (119). The fourth category of borrowing, pervasive borrowing, appears almost speculative in Zürcher's discussion. He says that it "is so elusive that at this stage of investigation it is better not to speculate about it," though he does go on give some explanation of what he is thinking of as a pervasive borrowing when he says that it is "very probable that a number of fundamental notions and orientations in Taoism were reinforced or stimulated by analogous (or seemingly analogous) Buddhist ideas" (88). Here Zürcher seems to be attempting to formulate what I have called elsewhere the "overdetermined" way in which a religious culture into which Buddhism is moving selectively emphasizes aspects of Buddhist praxis that match its own presumptions and beliefs.[3] The dynamics here might only loosely be described as "borrowing," but rather as an interrogation of Buddhism by the religious culture into which it is moving, seeking answers to its own religious, philosophic, or existential questions.

Appropriation: At the Intersection of Trajectories

Zürcher's discussion focused on the borrowings from Buddhism by Daoism. Since, however, appropriations were made both from Buddhism to Daoism, and from Daoism to Buddhism, I believe that it is unproblematic that the same categories suggested by Zürcher in relation to Daoist borrowings from Buddhism could be applied equally well to Buddhist borrowings from Daoism. The question that this chapter will attempt to answer—at least in a preliminary fashion—is how these categories might be usefully adapted to discuss the appropriation of ritual practices per se. Ritual practices per se necessarily fall outside the first of Zürcher's categories, that is, formal appropriations, since they are not isolated elements that can simply be "plugged into" a larger religious framework. As we will see, however, elements of Indic religious practice have been both formally and conceptually appropriated into ritual. Following further introductory discussions of the place of the *homa* in tantric practice and the role of the Northern Dipper in Daoism, the Homa of the Northern Dipper's structure and contents will be examined in light of the four categories of borrowing proposed by Zürcher.

One metaphoric frame that might be applied to organize our considerations of the characteristics of appropriation of ritual practices and religious symbolism is to think of our present inquiry as existing at the intersection of two different trajectories. One trajectory involves the adoption of the *homa* ritual into Buddhist tantra and its spread across Buddhist Asia. The second trajectory is that of the Northern Dipper in Chinese religious culture, including popular religious culture, Daoism—both narrowly and broadly defined—tantric Buddhism in China, and the spread of Chinese religious culture to Japan. It is here at the intersection of the trajectory of the *homa* and the trajectory of the Northern Dipper that we find the Shingon Northern Dipper *homa*.

Instances of the Homa *in the Tantric Traditions of Asia*

The *homa* is a votive sacrifice in which offerings are made into a fire. The ritual, as it is known in tantric forms, is generally thought to derive from Vedic fire sacrifices. Recently, however, research on the relation between tantric and Zoroastrian fire rituals has suggested that there are direct influences on the tantric *homa* from those sources as well (Grether 2007). Although the details of the historical development of this ritual require further research, by the time that tantric Buddhism is codified, it is a well-established part of the tradition (Payne 2002). For example, the *Mahāvairocana sūtra*, one of the earliest tantric Buddhist texts, already distinguishes between internal (*naigoma* 内護摩, mentally visualized) and external (*gegoma* 外護摩, physically performed) forms of the *homa*,[4] a distinction that relates this text to broader shifts in Indian religions toward internalized forms of practice.[5]

The *homa* is found throughout tantric Buddhism, not only in China and Japan, but also Nepal, Tibet, Mongolia, and Bali. It is also found in almost all forms of South Asian tantra, including dualistic traditions such as Śaiva Siddhānta (Brunner-Lachaux 1963, vol. 1). This makes it one of the longest and most enduring threads running through any polythetic understanding of tantra.[6]

Contemporary Japanese esoteric Buddhism, both Shingon 眞言 (Tōmitsu 東密) and Tendai 天台 (Taimitsu 台密), retain rituals known from medieval China as part of a living corpus of practice. One of the Shingon rituals is the Homa of the Northern Dipper. Though known from the medieval Chinese tantric record, my understanding is that it is no longer an active part of institutionalized Chinese Buddhist practice, except in apparently revivalist and some hybrid forms among some expatriate Chinese communities.[7]

Mongolian Fire Rituals: At the Edge of the *Homa*'s Trajectory

In his re-examination of Mongolian fire rituals, Christopher Atwood has identified three different kinds, ranging from a domestic ritual evidencing almost no tantric character, to a clerical ritual that—while also not tantric—is much more fully integrated into the monastic Buddhist cosmos, and a clerical ritual that is tantric in character. Atwood notes that the domestic rituals make "occasional mention of the Sanskrit syllable *ram*" (1996, 124). In the Mongolian fire cult, the fire is feminine, and the occasional mention is to her being generated from the syllable RAM. This is the Sanskrit *bīja* mantra for the fire deity Agni. Given the fact that in this Mongolian instance the gender identification of fire contrasts with the Indic conception, this would seem to point to a clear instance of formal borrowing. The borrowed element has little effect on the ritual performance or the religious culture of which it is a part.

In the Mongolian domestic fire ritual, use of the syllable RAM is a purely formalistic appropriation. It seems, given Atwood's description, to simply have been introduced as an isolated item. It was included perhaps for the sake of the power of the exotic, as Zürcher mentions regarding the Daoist use of Sanskrit, or perhaps simply in emulation of tantric rituals. Despite its being the *bīja* mantra of the male fire deity Agni, the gender of the Mongolian fire deity remains unchanged by this introduction. To pursue the analysis of appropriations in the Mongolian fire cult further, a great deal more detailed information about the performance of the fire rituals would be needed.

The Northern Dipper: In and Out of Daoism

The Northern Dipper (*beidou* 北斗) plays a major role in the cosmology of China, seemingly throughout its entire history,[8] and although it is a multivalent symbol in Chinese culture generally, and even in Daoism per se, its location and relation to the Pole Star provide a common set of associations. It seems to have been one of the earliest constellations identified in the "Chinese sky" (Sun and Kistemaker 1997, 2). In the *Tianguan shu* 天官書, written by Sima Qian and considered to be the earliest systematic description of the stars and constellations, the Northern Dipper is described as the chariot of the emperor.[9] This chariot carries him around the Central Palace (*zhong gong* 中宮) at the North Pole (*beiji* 北極), traveling through each of the four palaces located in the four directions. Carrying the emperor through the entire circuit of the sky, the Northern Dipper as chariot is seen as providing the means by which the emperor controls the entire cosmos (Sun and Kistemaker 1997, 21–23, 133). The image here is a reflection of the imperial model, or goal, of "a central imperial court controlling the provinces" (22). As the establishment of centralized, imperial power during the Qin and Han led to the amplification of the Central Court, more constellations were constructed "which represented officials, institutions, facilities and deities in connection with the court" (133). In addition to other early sources, Livia Kohn calls attention to Han dynasty apocrypha. She indicates that these "describe the Dipper as part of the entourage and governing mechanism of the Celestial Sovereign (Tianhuang 天皇), who resides in the center of the sky and rules all from his palace of Purple Tenuity (Ziwei 紫微), often also simply called the Purple Palace (Zigong 紫宮). In human beings, this palace is located in the heart, the center of the human body" (2000, 156).

One example of the Daoist use of the Northern Dipper is the "Three Ways to Go Beyond the Heavenly Pass."[10] The concern with longevity and immortality found throughout Daoist thought characterizes this meditation text as well. Here one draws into oneself the residents of each of the seven stars of the Northern Dipper in sequence. Each time, they are requested to intervene to prolong the life of the practitioner. For example, the Great Star, first in the meditative sequence is asked to "Cut off my route to death at the Gate of Demons!" (Kohn 1993, 259), while the True Star, the third, is asked to "Cut off the source of death for me!" (261). This suggests that in addition to its sociopolitical role as the Emperor's Chariot, the importance of the Northern Dipper is that it was also understood as pointing the way to the unmoving Pole Star, which as unchanging is the key to immortality, or the gate through which one must pass to achieve immortality (Verellen 1994, s.v. "Beidou").

The names of the seven stars in the "Three Ways" differ from those found in the *homa* and Northern Dipper Sūtra discussed later in this chapter.[11] The structure of the constellation as understood in some of the Daoist traditions is more complex than just the visible constellation itself. In the Shangqing 上清 (Highest Clarity) tradition discussed by Isabelle Robinet, nine stars are said to form the Northern Dipper, the additional two being invisible. There was also thought to be an invisible mirror image, this dark complement to the Northern Dipper comprising "black stars" (Robinet 1989, 172, 179–180). Robinet identifies three kinds of practices within Shangqing that are directly related to the Northern Dipper: "invoking it for protective purposes; making its stars descend into one's body; ascending to and pacing on it" (175).[12] While the Northern Dipper may have been the most frequent constellation chosen for pacing, the practice of pacing through a constellation was applied to other constellations as well (Schafer 1977, 241–242).

Pointing to the center of the universe, it indicates the Great Unity (Taiyi 太乙, or 太一).[13] Its two invisible stars were in some instances associated with the Pole Star in a triadic unity, in turn homologized to the three original energies and the Three Ones (Robinet 1989, 179). Another organization of the stars of the Northern Dipper divided them into three pairs, known as the "Three Terraces" or the "Three Steps." This version of the constellation dates from the Han, being found, for example, in a text known as the "Scripture of the Six Tallies of the Great Steps" (Bokenkamp 1997, 210n). In a text preserved in Dunhuang, the "Scripture of Laozi's Transformations," Laozi says of himself, "Sur la tête je porte les constellations San-t'ai, je suis revêtu de ce qui n'a pas de forme" (Seidel [1957] 1992, 69). ("I wear the constellation Three Terraces on my head [as a crown], / I clothe myself in the formless" [Bokenkamp 1997, 210–211n]). While Laozi wears the Northern Dipper on his head in this text, in other instances, as noted by Robinet, the practitioner visualizes the constellation inside his body.

Such internal visualizations employ the frequently recurring conception of an integral relation between the celestial realm and the bodily realm, a relation in which each element in one has its reflex in the other. Again, the purposes for which this relation was employed are the familiar goals of longevity, vitality, and immortality. In his study of the Shangqing text "The Upper Scripture of Purple Texts Inscribed by Spirits," Bokenkamp has commented on the identification of the Northern Dipper, also referred to as the "Mainstay of Heaven," with the "Peach Child," referred to as the "Resplendent Mainstay" (1997, 327n). The practice described at this point in the Purple Texts is one in which the practitioner attempts to re-establish the placental connection by an invocation of the Peach Child who dwells in the Palace of Life, that is, "the passageway which joined the placenta to your viscera when you were first born." Regular practice of this invocation for eighteen years leads to the practitioner being able first to control the three Cinnabar Fields on the left and the three pneuma on the right, and then, finally, "to ascend to heaven in broad daylight" (327–328).

Veneration of the Northern Dipper and recitation of a "Northern Dipper Scripture" (*Beidou jing* 北斗徑) play key symbolic roles in the founding hagiography of Quanzhen 全真 Daoism in the twelfth century (Eskildsen 2004, 11, 92). Stephen Eskildsen notes that there are several texts that include the term *beidou* found in the Daozang 道藏, and suggests that the *Taishang xuanling beidou benming yansheng zhengjing*

(太上玄靈北斗本命延生真經; DT617/T341) is the text essential to the story of the early establishment of Quanzhen Daoism. The ritual that it describes "purports to expiate one's transgressions and prolong one's life span" (210n69). These goals—expiation of transgressions and prolonging of one's life span—recur frequently in relation to the Northern Dipper. The seven stars were seen to "systematically observe and record all the misdeeds of the living" (Strickmann 2002, 47). Being the ones to keep these records, they were also the ones who with proper veneration could be convinced to change the records. Strickmann describes a Mao Shan ritual visualization that "involved bringing down the stars of the Northern Dipper one by one, each on a different day and into a different organ of the body. Of each of the seven stars, the supplicant requests that all the faults and misdeeds of himself and his forebears to the seventh degree be expunged from the record" (47).

Christine Mollier refers to "augmenting the life account" and traces the idea of an account (suan 算) back to the Han dynasty, when in addition to a monetary payment of tax obligation, it "also carried a metaphorical significance, that to the 'celestial account,' the span of life allotted to each individual" (Mollier 2008, 101). The association of the Northern Dipper with the prolongation of life is matched with the imagery that the seven stars are "the awakeners of prenatal life. They attend to the opening of the embryo's seven orifices and insufflate it with its seven celestial souls (*hun* 魂)" (135–136).

Appropriations went on in both directions, of course, and even in the case of a figure as important in Chinese religious culture as the Northern Dipper, associations were drawn to it from Buddhist materials. One of the appropriations from Buddhism into Daoism occurs during the Yuan dynasty. This is the deity known as the Mother of the Dipper (Doumu 斗母) who, Kohn tells us, is still highly popular. "Shrines to her are found today in many major Daoist sanctuaries, from the Qingyang gong 青羊官 in Chengdu 成都 through Louguan 樓觀 (near Xi'an 西安) to Mount Tai 泰山 in Shandong" (Kohn 2000, 149). In a kind of escalation of essentialization, Doumu is characterized as representing "the germinal, creative power behind" the Northern Dipper, itself the "ruler of fates and central orderer of the universe" (149). Doumu is, however, a "dao-icized" version of Marīcī,[14] herself a later version of the Vedic goddess of the dawn, Uṣas.[15] Marīcī is widely popular in Tibetan Buddhism, with the Tibetan name 'Od zer can ma. In addition, she is also known under yet another name, Vajravārāhī—the Vajra Sow.[16]

It is also suggestive that the Northern Dipper also makes its appearance in Zen sources, such as the fifteenth-century set of Ten Oxherding Pictures from Shubun 周文. This set differs from others that have been made more familiar, in that the ninth is entitled "The Solitary Moon" (which corresponds to the seventh in the more familiar set, "The Bull Transcended"), and the tenth is entitled "Both Vanished" (which corresponds to the eighth, "Both Bull and Self Transcended"). The final two of the familiar set, "Reaching the Source" and "In the World," are not included in Shubun's set. In Shubun's ninth, however, the "Solitary Moon" is accompanied by the Northern Dipper. The accompanying verse says:

> Nowhere is the beast, and the oxherd is master of his time.
> He is a solitary cloud wafting lightly along the mountain peaks;
> Clapping his hands he sings joyfully in the moon-light,
> But remember a last wall is still left barring his homeward walk.[17]

The description sounds like that of a Daoist immortal, "cloud wafting lightly along the mountain peaks," while the closing line almost suggests a Buddhist warning that such extraordinary powers are not the same as awakening. The presence of the Northern Dipper in the sky strengthens the impression that the allusion here is to Daoist practices such as pacing the void.

We see, then, that over the many centuries of Chinese religious culture, the Northern Dipper has a variety of associations, forms, and names attributed to the stars it comprises, depending on the historical and religious contexts.[18] While many additional examples could be cited,[19] these give the reader an indication of the kinds of roles played by the Northern Dipper throughout the course of Daoist history and the history of Chinese religious culture generally. The cult of the Northern Dipper also spread into the rest of the greater Chinese cultural sphere, including Japan.[20]

The Northern Dipper in Yoshida Shintō

The cult of the Northern Dipper appears to have been introduced into Japan through Shingon, from which it extended into the medieval Shintō 神道 lineages. First Ōmiwa 太三輪 and then Yoshida 吉田 (also known as

Yuiitsu 唯一) Shintō formulated themselves as explicitly Shintō lineages. Despite this assertion of autonomy, both based their ritual practices on those of Shingon.[21] The Yoshida ritual corpus comprises three rituals.[22] One is an Eighteen Kami (*jūhachishintō* 十八神道) ritual, replicating in Shintō terms the Eighteen Stages ritual (*jūhachidō* 十八道), which is the starting point for the training of Shingon priests. Another is a Yuiitsu Shintō Goma, also replicating in Shintō terms the Shingon *homa*. And the third ritual, though not a *homa*, is a Northern Dipper ritual. Based first on the clear connection between the Eighteen Kami and Goma rituals of Yoshida Shintō and Shingon, and second on the known history of the Yoshida tradition, it seems reasonable to suggest that the Northern Dipper ritual was also adapted from Shingon precursors, rather than being based on Daoist rites brought to Japan earlier as part of the Onmyōdō 陰陽道 school (Way of Yin and Yang).

The creation of a Yoshida Shintō Northern Dipper ritual would perhaps fit into Zürcher's fourth category, which he called "pervasive borrowing." The religious culture of medieval Japan was deeply imbued with the ritual practices, beliefs, and symbolisms of tantric Buddhism, as well as those of Chinese Daoism. The construction of a ritual devoted to the Northern Dipper would in a sense be a "natural" consequence of the plurality of overlapping and mutually reinforcing influences.

At the Intersection: Creation of the Homa of the Northern Dipper

The Northern Dipper in Chinese Buddhist Tantra

Within the corpus of *homa* rituals found in the contemporary Shingon tradition of esoteric Buddhism in Japan is a "Homa of the Northern Dipper." Buddhist interest in the Northern Dipper is reflected in the Taishō canon, which contains several texts specifically including reference to the Northern Dipper in their titles (Orzech and Sanford 2000, 388; Demiéville et al. 1978, 114). These include the following:

- "Ritual Procedures for Invoking the Seven Stars of the Northern Dipper," translation attributed to Vajrabodhi (T. 1305: *Beidou qi zing niansong yigui / Hokuto shichishō nenju giki* 北斗七星念誦儀軌)
- "Secret Essentials for Performing Homa to the Seven Stars of the Northern Dipper," translation attributed to Amoghavajra

(T. 1306: *Beidou qi xing huma miyao yigui / Hokuto shichishō goma hiyō giki* 北斗七星護摩祕要儀軌),
- "Sūtra Expounded by the Buddha on Prolonging Life Through Worship of the Seven Stars of the Northern Dipper," (T. 1307: *Foshuo beidou qi xing yan ming jing / Hokuto shichishō enmyō kyō* 北斗七星延命經), and
- "Homa Ritual for the Seven Stars of the Northern Dipper," attributed to Yi Xing (T. 1310: *Beidou qi xing huma fa/Hokuto shichishō goma hō* 北斗七星護摩法).

Christine Mollier notes that in medieval China the seven stars of the Northern Dipper were identified with the seven hypostases of the Buddha Bhaiṣajyaguru, and that this association "was in itself sufficiently compelling in the eyes of the Chinese faithful to supply the *Sūtra of the Great Dipper* with its indisputable Buddhist certificate of authenticity" (2008, 140). In this, however, the "faithful" have been misguided by the symbolic association.

As suggested by our imagery of two intersecting trajectories, while the tantric Buddhist *homa* originates in India, the Northern Dipper per se is not an object of veneration in Indian Buddhist religious culture. An examination of the pantheon of Indian Buddhist tantra, for example, reveals no reference to the Northern Dipper.[23] Similarly, although a great deal remains to be studied in both cases, neither Tibet nor Dunhuang have provided any evidence of ritual practices devoted to the Northern Dipper.[24] Although a Tibetan translation of the Northern Dipper sūtra dating from 1137 exists, this seems to have been the product of a Mongol attempt to create a multi-ethnic religious culture in support of the Yuan dynasty. Elverskog tells us that this translation had "no lasting impact upon the Tibetans. Shorn of its religio-cultural, and most importantly, its political implications the *Big Dipper Sūtra* survived in the Tibetan milieu only as [a] cultural relic of the past" (2006, 101). While not probative, this negative data supports the claim that the Northern Dipper *homa* was a creation of tantric Buddhists in the Chinese milieu.

Popular conceptions—and until recently—scholarly as well, have often assumed that ritual is invariant, and that this invariance is constitutive of a ritual's efficacy. Such a view extends to both rituals as performances, and to the manuals that are the guides to ritual performance. Nicolas Sihlé says in his study of the ritual manuals of a tantric community in Mustang that "[g]enerally speaking, a ritual text is held to be invariable, and this is constitutive of its authority" (2010, 39). Yet given the evidence, what appears to be an unduly generalized claim regarding ritual invariance needs to be significantly nuanced. We also, however, need to discard the artificial segregation of ritual from other kinds of performative arts, as if by being "religious" it therefore embodies representations of something eternal and unchanging. For tantric rituals of this kind, the syntax remains highly consistent over time, and across religio-cultural boundaries. However, the contents—or lexicon—of the ritual, most prominently the deities evoked, are evidently much easier to change, thus allowing for much ritual creativity along what might be called the paradigmatic dimension of ritual performance.[25] This ritual creativity as a performing art was part of the ongoing adaptation of Buddhism in its historical development.

Chinese Astronomy, Indian Astronomy

Chinese astronomy was primarily concerned with "the circumpolar stars and meridians drawn from them to the 'lunar lodges'" (Orzech and Sanford 2000, 386). In contrast, Indian astronomy is generally concerned with "the ecliptic (the apparent motion of the sun against the background of fixed stars), the heliacal rising and setting of stars (which yields the twelve houses or the zodiacal band of stars confined to the apparent path of the sun in the sky), and the twenty-eight nakṣatras,"[26] that is, the twenty-eight days of the lunar cycle, the "lunar lodges" (*xiu* 宿) mentioned earlier. The Northern Dipper seems to play at best a peripheral role in the organization of the "Indian sky." Michael Witzel (1995) has noted that among the Indo-European peoples who all orientated themselves towards the east, the rising point of the sun, the Indo-Iranians alone exclude the northern direction from the scheme: while the east is "in front," the west "backwards," and the south "on the right,"—the north is "upwards": *uttara*, literally, "on the upper side," in Vedic, *upara* in Avestan, and *'brg* in Middle Persian.

Witzel then goes on to identify the "heavenly vessel" (*kośa*, bucket or casket) referred to in Vedic texts with the Northern Dipper. For example, "Varuna [*sic*] has poured out the cask, with its rim turned downwards, over heaven, earth and the interspace. Thereby the kind of the whole world sprinkles the soil, as the rain (sprinkles) the barley."[27] Despite the existence of numerous references, this heavenly vessel had remained unidentified. Witzel's argument is based on two key points. First, the heavenly vessel is described as pouring out its contents, or being turned over, each night, just as in the same way the Northern Dipper in its path around the Pole Star each night appears inverted. Second, the names of the seven *ṛṣis* who in an Upaniṣad are described as sitting on the rim of the vessel are the same as the names of the seven stars of the Northern Dipper. "The heavenly casket, the great ladle on which the seven ṛṣis sit according to the BAU [Bṛhadāraṇyaka Upaniṣad], turns round every night, emptying its (mythological) contents, the heavenly waters" (Witzel 1995).

In considering the apparent absence of the "heavenly vessel" in Indian Buddhist conceptions of the sky, the symbolic associations for the Northern Dipper, that is, the identification of the seven stars of the Northern Dipper with the Seven Sages of the Veda,[28] may be a key factor. Given Buddhism's status as a *nāstika* tradition, that is, one that does not acknowledge the authority of the Vedas, it seems unlikely that this grouping of the seven *ṛṣis* (*saptarṣaya*)[29] would have any appeal to Buddhist practitioners, even those such as the tantrikas who appear to have been quite willing to subsume Vedic deities, such as the twelve Vedic deities found in the fifth section of the Northern Dipper Homa described later in this chapter, into the pantheon as powerful upholders and protectors of the dharma.

The Northern Dipper Sūtra

The extent of the cult of the Northern Dipper throughout East and Central Asia is indicated by the spread of *The Northern Dipper Sūtra* (T. 1307). Herbert Franke, who renders the title as the *Great Bear Sūtra*, has examined the history of this sūtra, extant in Chinese, Tibetan, Mongolian, and Uighur versions (1990). His conclusion is that the text originates in China, based on Daoist models, and that it was this Chinese version that was translated into the other languages. Franke judges as simply fictitious the claims that an "Indian monk" was responsible for bringing it from India, found in the Uighur, and the even stronger claim attributing the work to Xuanzang, found in the Mongolian and Tibetan versions.[30]

The absence of any explicit references to the Northern Dipper in Indian or in Tibetan Buddhism, together with Franke's conclusion regarding the Northern Dipper sūtra, make a strong case for two conclusions: first, the narrow conclusion that the *homa* examined here has its origins in the use of Indic Buddhist *homa* ritual models to create a new *homa* ritual devoted to the Northern Dipper (Mollier 2008, 146); second, that tantric Buddhist interest in the Northern Dipper per se arose out of a competitive relation with Daoism. Based on her examination of both Daoist and Buddhist materials related to the cult of the Northern Dipper, Mollier concludes that

> the talismanic tradition of the seven stars of the Great Dipper originated in early medieval Daoism, which itself drew upon elements reaching back at least to the Eastern Han. By the eighth century, when the famed estoeric Buddhist masters settled in China, the worship of the Great Dipper that they integrated into their rites for longevity and protection, of both individual and state, therefore already had a long history. It had been maturing for several centuries in Daoist praxis, and had been profusely expounded, above all by the Shangqing movement. The religious rivalry that was then unfolding in court circles certainly prompted the Buddhist masters to appropriate this highly popular and firmly rooted Chinese cult in their liturgy and to promote it in interests of state ideology.[31]

The Contemporary Shingon Homa of the Northern Dipper

The "Hōtoku sokusai goma shiki shidai, Chūin" is a contemporary *homa* manual.[32] As a *sokusai* (息災, *śāntika*) *homa*, it is used for protection, and in contemporary Japan this kind of *homa* is the most commonly performed of the different kinds of *homas*. The other kinds of *homa* include *sōyaku* (増益, *pauṣṭika*), *gobuku* (降伏, *ābhicārika*), *keiai* (敬愛, *vaśīkaraṇa*), and *kōchō* (鉤召, *aṅkuśa*), each for different purposes, associated with different colors, to be performed at different times of the day, and utilizing different shapes of altar hearths.[33] These categories are not limited to *homas*, however, and are applied to a wide variety of different kinds of rituals. The notation "Chūin" in the title identifies this as a *homa* of the "Chūin ryū," the lineage of Kōyasan, which is presently the predominant lineage in Japan. This version of the Homa of the Northern Dipper is arranged into five sections, as is standard for contemporary gomas. These are

I. Agni: Ka ten 火天, Fire god;
II. Lord of the Assembly: Shaka Kinrin 釋迦金輪, Śākyamuni of the Golden Wheel; identified with Ichiji Kinrin 一字金輪, Ekākṣara-uṣṇīṣacakra;[34]

III. Seven Stars of the Northern Dipper;

IV. Various Deities: Hachi ji Monju 八字文殊, Eight syllable Mañjuśrī;[35] together with other celestial deities: the Seven Celestial Lights (*shichi yō* 七曜), the Twelve Birth Constellations (*jūni kū* 十二宮), and the Twenty-Eight Lunar Mansions (*nijūhachi shuku* 二十八宿);

V. Worldly Deities: Fudō Myōō 不動明王 and the Twelve Vedic Devas (Ishanaten 伊舎那天, Īśāna; Taishakuten 帝釈天, Śakra (Indra);[36] Katen 火天, Agni; Emmaten 焔魔天, Yama; Rasetsuten 羅刹天, Rākṣasa; Suiten 水天, Varuṇa; Fūten 風天, Vāyu; Tamonten 多聞天, Vaiśravaṇa; Bonten 梵天, Brahma; Jiten 地天, Pṛthivī; Nitten 日天, Āditya (Sūrya);[37] Gatten 月天, Candra), and then again the seven celestial lights, and the twenty-eight lunar mansions.

Opening with an offering to Agni, the Vedic Fire God, seems to be universal in the contemporary Shingon homas, and is indicative of the Vedic background of the tantric *homa*. The second section is identified as being for the Lord of the Assembly, who in this instance is the Golden Wheel Śākyamuni, ruler of one of the four disks (*cakra*) comprising the world system. The offerings to the Seven Stars of the Northern Dipper form the third and central set of offerings. The fourth section again is typically identified as being for "various deities," which in this case include one aspect of Mañjuśrī together with three sets of celestial deities: the Seven Celestial Lights, the Twenty-Eight Lunar Mansions, and the Twelve Constellations. These three groups refer to astrological calculations, having to do with the time of one's birth. The closing section, devoted to Fudō Myōō and twelve Vedic deities, is also very typically the last stage in contemporary Shingon *homas*. Structurally, this five-part arrangement is in no way distinct from other contemporary *homas*.

The names of the seven stars used in the *homa* are identical with those found in the Northern Dipper Sūtra. The ritual manual, however, identifies eight figures in its central rite. In addition to the seven individual stars, there first appears "Mysterious Vision" (*myōken*妙見), a name for the seven stars of the Northern Dipper taken together, which is also treated as a bodhisattva, "Myōken Bosatsu."[38] The names[39] of the eight figures of the central offering, together with their mantra in Japanese pronunciation and in Sanskrit as interpreted from the Siddham script,[40] are as follows:

1. Miaojian (Myōken) 妙見 Mysterious Vision (Sudarśana Bodhisattva)[41]
   ON SOCHIRI SYUTA SENJIKYA SOWAKA
   oṃ sudṛṣṭa śāntika svāhā

2. Tanlang (Tonrō) 貪狼 Greedy Wolf
   NAN CHIRA FURIKYA EI SENJIKYA SOWAKA
   nāṃ dhira pṛ ka ye śāntika svāhā[42]

3. Jumen (Kyomon) 巨門 Great Gate
   NAN TARA TARA TARA KA NI SENJIKYA SOWAKA
   nāṃ tra tra tra ha ṇi śāntika svāhā

4. Lucun (Rokuzen) 録存 Persistent Happiness
   NAN KA KA KA KARI YARI NI SENJIKYA SOWAKA
   nāṃ ka ka ka kari kari yari ṇi śāntika svāhā

5. Wenqu (Monkoku) 文曲 Civilian Song
   NAN HARA HARA BAYARA BAYARA NI SENJIKYA SOWAKA
   nāṃ pra pra bhayari ṇi śāntika svāhā

6. Lianzhen (Renjyō) 廉貞 Pure Virtue
   NAN KA KA KARI KAKARI KYARI NI SENJIKYA SOWAKA
   nāṃ ka ka kara hākara hāyari ṇi śāntika svāhā

7. Wuqu (Mukoku) 武曲 Military Song
   NAN TŌ TŌ RIRI KYA KYA SYARI KASYARI NI SENJIKYA SOWAKA
   nāṃ dhō dhō ri ri ka ka cari kacari ṇi śāntika svāhā

8. Pojun (Hagun) 破軍 Destroyer of the Army
   NAN BATEI TARA BATEI BARI BATEI BARI KARI SYARI NI SENJIKYA SOWAKA
   nāṃ bhate tra bhate bhari bhate bhari kari cari ṇi śāntika svāhā.

The visualization that forms the antecedent mental action to the mantric evocation of the eight figures reads as follows:

Imagine above the moon cakra of the heart, the syllable SU [in Siddham script] in the center, surrounded by seven RO syllables; these change, becoming "*SU BEI TARA KA HARA TORO NA BA*"; these change, becoming a jeweled priest's staff, a sun, a red jewel, a fire jewel, running water, a measuring rod, and a willow branch; next, these become

Mysterious Vision, comprising Greedy Wolf, Huge Gate, Happiness Retained, Civilian Corner, Pure Virtue, Military Corner, and Destroyer of the Army. As their physical form dims, their clear lights (*kōmyō* 光明) shine brightly.

The forms that each of the seven RO seed syllables take would seem to be important in understanding the sources for the Shingon Northern Dipper homa. As with other symbolic associations, such as that between the Daoist identification of the stars with different woods and grains and the kinds of offerings made into the *homa*, the issue remains uncertain (Mollier 2008, 158–59). It would seem reasonable to assume that the order of the visualized symbolic forms corresponds to the order of the seven stars:

Tanlang 貪狼, Greedy Wolf: a jeweled priest's staff, syllable BEI
Jumen 巨門, Great Gate: a sun, syllable TARA
Lucun 祿存, Persistent Happiness: a red jewel, syllable KA
Wenqu 文曲, Civilian Song: a fire jewel, syllable HARA
Lianzhen 廉貞, Pure Virtue: running water, syllable TORO
Wuqu 武曲, Military Song: a measuring rod, syllable NA
Pojun 破軍, Destroyer of Armies:[43] willow branch,[44] syllable BA.

This version of the Homa of the Northern Dipper demonstrates that ritual structure is less likely to change than are its contents, a principle regarding the movement of rituals across boundaries between religious cultures that I have elsewhere identified as the "conservation of structure" (Payne 2011a, 253). The appropriation of the seven stars of the Northern Dipper into this *homa* ritual was effected without transforming the ritual structure itself.

Conclusion

Zürcher's typology of literary appropriations by Daoists from Buddhist texts seems to hold promise for analyzing the appropriation of ritual elements as well. In the case of the Shingon Homa of the Northern Dipper we find something closer to the second of Zürcher's categories, a conceptual borrowing. Here the seven stars of the Northern Dipper are given a collective identity—Mysterious Vision Bodhisattva—which appears to be the Buddhist correlate to the Pole Star itself, as well as to the constellation of the Northern Dipper, that is, comprising the seven stars. At the same time, new associations to visualized objects and new mantras have been created to integrate the Northern Dipper into Buddhist ritual practice. Here we see a much more extensive adaptation of the existing ritual format in order to accommodate the new chief deity (*honzon* 本尊), that is, the inclusion of offerings to each of the seven stars together with the asterism as a whole. However, the adaptation has not been so great as to lead to any structural adaptation, that is, no changes to the organization or logic of the ritual actions. This particular ritual retains the five sets of offerings, and the order of deities evoked in each of them found in many other Shingon homa. Even the presence of the various sets of celestial deities (the Seven Celestial Lights, the Twenty-Eight Lunar Mansions, and the Twelve Constellations) in the fourth set of offerings is not unprecedented in other *homa*s, which do not have a celestial figure as the chief deity.

Zürcher's typology of borrowings provides a heuristically useful way of thinking about the ways in which appropriation of religious elements takes place. It does seem to require some further clarification, however. Although he talked about four different categories of borrowing, he also implies that borrowing is not such an easily categorized matter. He qualifies his claim that "[a]t least for the purpose of analysis we have to distinguish various types or levels of borrowing" by adding "even if it is obvious that there are many border cases and that, in principle, even the most formal loans to some extent do affect the content of the message" (1980, 86). More strongly, we can say that the categories do not identify distinctly different kinds of appropriation, and that the boundaries between the categories are not clearly demarcated. Rather, there appears to be a continuum of appropriations, such as the use of the *bija* mantra RAM in the Mongolian fire ritual at one end of the continuum, up to the creation of a Shinto version of the Shingon *homa* at the other.[45]

Johan Elverskog has noted that "the fixation on the 'Chineseness' of Big Dipper worship has obviated the fact that this work [the Mongolian translation of the Buddhist *Beidou jing*] was important among Mongols, and thus has led us to neglect what this worship among the Mongols tells us about Mongolian Buddhism and the process by which new ideas and practices cross both religious and cultural boundaries" (2006, 90). We can *mutatis mutandis* say the same for the Northern Dipper in Japan—an identification of this cult with Daoism has led to its being ignored as part of tantric Buddhist praxis across Buddhist Asia, including Japan. If we take as our concern, however, the appropriation of religious symbolism and the adaptation of ritual practice, it is an important instance.

Notes

1. Orzech has suggested the importance of studying the religious significance of fire as one of the potentially fruitful methodologies for developing a more adequate understanding of Zhenyan and its relations to the wider religious traditions of South and East Asia (1989, 113–114).
2. See also Kohn (1992, 126).
3. See, for example, Payne (2011b) and Payne (forthcoming).
4. See Giebel (2005, 152); Hodge (2003, 213–217).
5. The internalization of ritual practices is found in the Upaniṣads, and while it has come to be identified with mental visualization, as here, it comprises a broader category that includes esoteric physiology and sexual yogas.
6. See Davidson (2003, 119–123).
7. See, for example, the online publications of Yogi Chen: http://www.yogichen.org/ (accessed September 19, 2011).
8. Systematic astrological texts, which reference the movement of the Northern Dipper around the Pole Star, date from the mid-second century BCE. See Major (1980, 23). This is based on a very long tradition of interest in the relations between heaven and earth: "Archeological evidence from the fifth millennium B.C. Neolithic cultures of North China shows that burials and dwellings were already being oriented with particular attention to the diurnal and seasonal variations in the sun's position" (Pankenier 2004, 211).
9. See also Kohn (2000, 156). My thanks to Livia Kohn for providing me with a copy of this work. Regarding the role of portent astrology for the court, and for later tantric Buddhist influences on Chinese astrology, see Nakayama (1966).
10. "Tianguan santu," DZ 1366, fasc., 1040; tr. in Kohn (1993, 257–267). References to the Northern Dipper are also found throughout Lagerwey (1987).
11. In Kohn's translation they are: 1. Great Star, 2. Prime Star, 3. True Star, 4. Pivotal Star, 5. Net Star, 6. Mainstay Star, and 7. Passgate Star.
12. Cf. Schafer (1977, 239–240), for a discussion of the identity of the additional two stars.
13. See also Seidel ([1957] 1992).
14. See Strickmann (1996, 239, and illustration at p. 155).
15. An instance closely related to Doumu would be the Daoist appropriation of Avalokiteśvara (Guanyin 觀音) as Jiuku tianzun 救苦天尊, the Heavenly Venerable Savior from Suffering (Mollier 2008, 177).
16. Kohn (2000, 162). Kohn also suggests continuity with the Greco–Roman Aurora.

17. See Suzuki (1960); also http://www.sacred-texts.com/bud/mzb/oxherd.htm, accessed October 14, 2010.
18. Isabelle Robinet summarizes this variety as comprising four "major roles" that the Northern Dipper plays in Daoism, "all related to its dual aspect," that is, as a set of reflexes between the celestial dipper and the dipper within the human body. First, it provides guidance to the proper orientation for rituals and meditation. Second, it serves in exorcisms. Third, a petitionary function as the recipient of invocations for forgiveness of sins and the erasure of one's name from the "registers of death" (*siji* 死籍). And fourth, again in both meditation and ritual, it opens the path to the heavens for the practitioner. See Pregadio (2008, s.v. "beidou" [entry by Robinet]).
19. For example, Hymes (2002) includes several mentions of "pacing the dipper"; see also Mitamura (2002).
20. Elverskog (2006) gives a good general overview of the spread of the cult of the Dipper.
21. See Scheid (2000); Grapard (1992a, 1992b); and Payne (2011a).
22. The rare book collection in the Tenri Library contains a wealth of manuscripts on Yoshida Shintō. Although there may well be additional rituals, a review of the ritual section of this manuscript collection consistently found the three rituals discussed here. My thanks to Rev. Dr. Ikuo Higashibaba of the Tenri Foreign Mission Office for his assistance, without which I would not have been able to review the collection as I did in July 2001.
23. Orzech and Sanford do assert that "South Asian sources here parallel Daoist tradition in locating the Dipper in the head and associating it with the sun, moon, and the eyes" (385). This conclusion on their part would seem to require additional evidence, as the material cited does not make explicit reference to the Northern Dipper, but rather to the set of seven celestial bodies, comprising the sun, the moon, and the five visible planets.
24. Jacob Dalton, personal communication, November 12, 2009.
25. In semiotic usage, the syntagm (or syntax) refers to the order of texts, or in this case ritual performance, while the paradigmatic refers to the different symbolic elements that may be employed to create different rituals. "While syntagmatic relations are possibilities of combination, paradigmatic relations are functional contrasts—they involve *differentiation*" (Chandler 2002, 80; emphasis in original).
26. Orzech and Sanford (2000, 386). For a list of the names of the nakṣatras, and the presiding deity of each, as well as variant versions of each, see Achar (2000).
27. ṚV 5.85.3. Quoted from Witzel (1995).
28. Michael Witzel (1999) argues that an earlier name for the Northern Dipper, *ṛkṣāḥ* ("bears"), found in the *Śatapatha Brāhmaṇa* refers to an old term in the *Ṛg Veda*, which he in turn links to pre-Ṛg Vedic Indo-European lore, being a cognate for the Greek *arktos*, meaning "the bearess," together with her cubs.

29. Franke gives two different lists of the names of the seven sages (1990, 93n102).
30. Franke (1990, 93). Franke similarly rejects Needham's attribution of the sūtra to Yixing. Perhaps Needham was misled by T. 1310, which is attributed to Yixing.
31. Mollier (2008, 172).
32. The "Hōtoku sokusai goma shiki shidai," no. 56 of 65 *goma* manuals in Soeda (1998).
33. Payne (1991, 62). For altar hearth shapes, see Kamei (1967, 106–108).
34. Sawa (1975, 327, 25).
35. Sawa (1975, 565, 676).
36. Indra is identified with Śakra, the lord of Tuṣita heaven. In this case the mantra is very clearly directed to Indra.
37. Āditya is identified with Sūrya.
38. *Bukkyōgo daijiten*, (Nakamura), s.vv. "Myōken" and "Myōken bosatsu," 1303. See also *Bukkyō daijiten* (Mochizuki), s.v. "Myōken bosatsu," 5:4784.
39. The English rendering here follows that of Franke, which differs somewhat from that found in Orzech and Sanford.
40. The careful reader will note that there are some discrepancies between the Japanese and the Sanskrit. The *furigana* does not always closely match the Siddham syllable to which it is attached. Whether this is due to scribal error or shifts in the pronunciation can only be determined by a separate line of research. Regarding transcription of Siddham script, see *Mikkyō jiten* (Sawa 1975), s.v. "shittan," 308–310, and endpapers. More generally, see van Gulik (1980).
41. See Birnbaum (1980, 11).
42. The *dhāraṇī* for the seven stars here differ from those given in the Mongolian Big Dipper sūtra. See Elverskog (2006, 109–110).
43. English renderings of the names here follows Mollier (2008, 122).
44. Cf. Mollier (2008, 139–140), for other symbolic associations. The source of the symbols here does not match anything found in the *Big Dipper Sūtra*.
45. While Zürcher did not present the typology as explanatory, it may be worth noting that it is only descriptive, and of heuristic value. In other words, nothing in particular can be predicted on the basis of identifying an instance of appropriation as one kind of borrowing or another.

References

Achar, B. N. Narahari. 2000. "Searching for the nakSatras in the Rgveda." *Electronic Journal of Vedic Studies* 6 (2): n.p.

Atwood, Christopher P. 1996. "Buddhism and Popular Ritual in Mongolian Religion: A Reexamination of the Fire Cult." *History of Religions* 36 (2): 112–139.

Birnbaum, Raoul. 1980. "Introduction to the Study of T'ang Buddhist Astrology: Research Notes on Primary Sources and Basic Principles." *Society for the Study of Chinese Religion Bulletin* 8: 5–19.

Bokenkamp, Stephen R. 1997. *Early Daoist Scriptures*. Berkeley; London: University of California Press.

Brunner-Lachaux, Hélène, ed. and trans. 1963. *Somaśambhupaddhati*. 4 vols. Pondicherry: Institut Français d'Indologie and École Française d'Extrême-Orient.

Chandler, Daniel. 2002. *Semiotics: The Basics*. London; New York: Routledge.

Davidson, Ronald M. 2003. *Indian Esoteric Buddhism: A Social History of the Tantric Movement*. New York: Columbia University Press.

Demiéville, Paul, Hubert Durt, and Anna Seidel, eds. 1978. *Répertoire du canon bouddhique sino-japonais*, 2nd edition. Paris: Librarie d'Amérique et d'Orient, Adrien-Maisonneuve.

Elverskog, Johan. 2006. "The Mongolian Big Dipper Sūtra." *Journal of the International Association of Buddhist Studies* 29 (1): 87–123.

Eskildsen, Stephen. 2004. *The Teachings and Practices of the Early Quanzhen Taoist Masters*. Albany: State University of New York Press.

Franke, Herbert. 1990. "The Taoist Elements in the Buddhist *Great Bear Sūtra (Pei-tou ching)*." *Asia Major*, 3rd ser., 3 (1): 75–111.

Giebel, Rolf, trans. 2005. *The Vairocanābhisaṃbodhi Sutra*. BDK English Tripiṭaka 30-I. Berkeley: The Numata Center for Buddhist Translation and Research.

Grapard, Allan. 1992a. "The Shinto of Yoshida Kanetomo." *Monumenta Nipponica* 47 (1): 27–58.

Grapard, Allan, trans. 1992b. "*Yuiitsu Shintō Myōbō Yōshū*." *Monumenta Nipponica* 47 (2): 137–161.

Grether, Holly. 2007. "Tantric Homa Rites in the Indo-Iranian Ritual Paradigm." *Journal of Ritual Studies* 21 (1): 16–32.

van Gulik, R. H. 1980. *Siddham: An Essay on the History of Sanskrit Studies in China and Japan*. Śata-Piṭaka Series 247. New Delhi: Sharada Rani.

Hodge, Stephen, trans. 2003. *The Mahā-Vairocana-abhisaṃbodhi Tantra with Buddhaguhya's Commentary*. London and New York: Routledge.

Hymes, Robert. 2002. *Way and Byway: Taoism, Local Religion, and Models of Divinity in Sung and Modern China*. Berkeley; London: University of California Press.

Kamei Sōchū 亀井宗忠. 1967. *Goma no rekishiteki no kenkyū* 護摩の歴史的研究. Tokyo: Sankibō Busshorin 山喜房佛書林.

Kohn, Livia. 1992. *Early Chinese Mysticism: Philosophy and Soteriology in the Taoist Tradition*. Princeton, NJ: Princeton University Press.

Kohn, Livia. 1993. *The Taoist Experience: An Anthology*. Albany: State University of New York Press.

Kohn, Livia. 2000. "Doumu: The Mother of the Dipper." *Ming Qing yanjiu* 明清研究 8: 149–195.

Lagerwey, John. 1987. *Taoist Ritual in Chinese Society and History*. New York: Macmillan.

Major, John S. 1980. "Astrology in the *Huai-Nan-Tzu* and Some Related Texts." *Journal of Chinese Religions* 8 (1): 20–31.

Mitamura Keiko. 2002. "Daoist Hand Signs and Buddhist Mudras." In *Daoist Identity: History, Lineage, and Ritual*, edited by Livia Kohn and Harold D. Roth, 235–255. Honolulu: University of Hawai'i Press.

Mochizuki Shinkō 望月信亨. 1931–1963. *Bukkyō daijiten* 佛教大辞典. 10 vols. Tokyo: Bukkyō Daijiten Hakkōjo 佛教大辞典発行所.

Mollier, Christine. 2008. *Buddhism and Taoism Face to Face: Scripture, Ritual, and Iconographic Exchange in Medieval China*. Honolulu: University of Hawai'i Press.

Nakamura Hajime 中村元. 1975. *Bukkyōgo daijiten* 佛教語大辞典. Tokyo: Tōkyō Shoseki 東京書籍.

Nakayama Shigeru. 1966. "Characteristics of Chinese Astrology." *Isis* 57 (4): 442–454.

Orzech, Charles D. 1989. "Seeing Chen-Yen Buddhism: Traditional Scholarship and the Vajrayāna in China." *History of Religions* 29 (2): 88–93.

Orzech, Charles D., and James H. Sanford. 2000. "Worship of the Ladies of the Dipper." In *Tantra in Practice*, edited by David Gordon White, 383–395. Princeton, NJ: Princeton University Press.

Pankenier, David W. 2004. "A Brief History of Beiji 北極 (Northern Culmen), with an Excursus on the Origin of the Character *di* 帝." *Journal of the American Oriental Society* 124 (2): 211–227.

Payne, Richard K. 1991. *The Tantric Ritual of Japan: Feeding the Gods, the Shingon Fire Ritual*. Delhi: International Academy of Indian Culture and Aditya Prakashan.

Payne, Richard K. 2002. "Tongues of Flame: Homologies in the Tantric Homa." In *The Roots of Tantra*, edited by Katherine Anne Harper and Robert L. Brown, 193–210. Albany: State University of New York Press.

Payne, Richard K. 2011a. "Conversions of Tantric Buddhist Ritual: The Yoshida Shintō *Jūhachishintō* Ritual." In *Transformations and Transfer of Tantra in Asia and Beyond*, edited by István Keul, 365–398. New York: Walter de Gruyter.

Payne, Richard K. 2011b. "Soul as Process: Buddhist Reflections on Mark Graves' *Mind, Brain and the Elusive Soul*." *Pastoral Psychology* 60 (6): 883.

Payne, Richard K. Forthcoming. "'Japanese Buddhism' or 'Buddhism in Japan': The Category 'Japanese Buddhism.'" In *The Dao Companion to Japanese Buddhist Philosophy*, edited by Gereon Kopf. New York: Springer Verlag.

Pregadio, Fabrizio, ed. 2008. *Encyclopedia of Taoism*. 2 vols. New York: Routledge.

Robinet, Isabelle. 1989. "Visualization and Ecstatic Flight in Shangqing Taoism." In *Taoist Meditation and Longevity Techniques*, edited by Livia Kohn, 159–191. Michigan Monographs in Chinese Studies 61. Ann Arbor: Center for Chinese Studies, University of Michigan.

Sawa Ryūken 佐和隆研, ed. 1975. *Mikkyō jiten* 密教辞典. Kyoto: Hōzōkan 法蔵館.

Schafer, Edward H. 1977. *Pacing the Void: T'ang Approaches to the Stars*. Berkeley; London: University of California Press.

Scheid, Bernhard. 2000. "Reading the *Yuiitsu Shintō myōbō yōshū:* A Modern Exegesis of an Esoteric Shinto Text." In *Shinto in History: Ways ot the Kami*, edited by John Breen and Mark Teeuwen, 117–143. Honolulu: University of Hawai'i Press.

Seidel, Anna K. [1957] 1992. *La Divinisation de Lao Tseu dans le Taoisme des Han*. Reprint, Paris: École Française d'Extrême-Orient.

Sihlé, Nicolas. 2010. "Written Texts at the Juncture of the Local and the Global: Some Anthropological Considerations on a Local Corpus of Tantric Ritual Manuals (Lower Mustang, Nepal)." In *Tibetan Rituals*, edited by José Ignacio Cabezón, 35–52. Oxford: Oxford University Press.

Soeda Takatoshi 添田隆俊, ed. 1998. *Goma zenshū* 護摩全集. Osaka: Tōhō shuppan 東方出版.

Strickmann, Michel. 1996. *Mantras et mandarins: le bouddhisme tantrique en Chine*. Bibliothéque des sciences humaines. Paris: Éditions Gallimard.

Strickmann, Michel. 2002. *Chinese Magical Medicine*. Edited by Bernard Faure. Stanford, CA: Stanford University Press.

Sun Xiaochun and Jacob Kistemaker. 1997. *The Chinese Sky during the Han: Constellating Stars and Society*. Leiden; Cologne: Brill.

Suzuki, D. T. 1960. *A Manual of Zen Buddhism*. New York: Grove Press.

Verellen, Franciscus. 1994. "Die Mythologie des Taoismus." In *Wörterbuch der Mythologie*, edited by Egidius Schmalzriedt and Hans Wilhelm Haussig, 6:739–863. Stuttgart: Klett-Cotta.

Witzel, Michael. 1995. "Looking for the Heavenly Casket." *Electronic Journal of Vedic Studies* 1 (2): n.p.

Witzel, Michael. 1999. "The Pleiades and the Bears Viewed from Inside the Vedic Texts." *Electronic Journal of Vedic Studies* 5 (2): n.p.

Zürcher, Erik. 1980. "Buddhist Influence on Early Taoism: A Survey of Scriptural Evidence." *T'oung-pao* 66: 84–147.

8

The Tantric Teachings and Rituals of the True Buddha School

THE CHINESE TRANSFORMATION OF VAJRAYĀNA BUDDHISM

Tam Wai Lun

Introduction

For Vajrayāna Buddhism in China, we still have to rely on the foundational work by Chou Yi-liang (1913–2001), which examines the lives and works of the three "founders" of Chinese Tantrism and East Asian Tantrism (Chou 1945, 235–332).[1] As pointed out by Richard K. Payne, Chou's essay replicates the "founder school" model of religion, which reinforces the Shingon school's scholastic distinction between heteroprax and orthoprax Tantrism (Payne 2006, 27). Apart from Chou's remarkable work, Vajrayāna Buddhism in China has largely been neglected by Chinese scholars. One exception may be Lü Jianfu (Lü 1995). He, however, has devoted only twenty-eight pages on the modern period of his 718-page general history of Vajrayāna Buddhism in China. The purpose of this chapter is to examine the Tantric teaching and ritual of a new Vajrayāna Buddhist school called the True Buddha School with a following of more than five million all over the world but mostly in Taiwan, Malaysia, and Indonesia. It builds on the research of a previous paper (Tam 2007) in which we argue that in order not to participate in marginalizing the True Buddha School, a process initiated by the mainstream contemporary established schools of Chinese Buddhism, and not to take away the True Buddha School's right to claim themselves as part of an established religion, we should defer to the self-understanding of the True Buddha School. This means that in this chapter we will treat the school, on the basis of its own understanding, as a new Vajrayāna school of Chinese Buddhism, rather than a "new religion," and we will show how esoteric Buddhism has changed and adapted itself in a Chinese cultural context.

The True Buddha School has arisen out of the life and experience of Master Lu Sheng-Yen (盧勝彥, b. 1945). Born in Jiayi 嘉義 County, Taiwan, Master Lu is the author of more than 240 books, writing extensively on his own religious experience and cultivation. Lu received his tertiary education in a military college in Taiwan and was trained as a surveyor. He had a deep religious experience in 1969 that led him from his Presbyterian Christian upbringing to a period of seeking, studying, and learning Buddhism (Yao 1994; Tam 2001; Melton 2007). This period lasted for some twelve years during which time Master Lu began to openly accept disciples to teach them Buddhism. Near the end of this period, he also founded the True Buddha School (first known as the Lingxian 靈仙 School) and moved from his native Taiwan to the United States, a symbol of his intention to spread Buddhism internationally. The rise of the True Buddha School resembles the rise of a temple group in Taiwan called the Compassion Society, or the Cihui Tang 慈惠堂 (Jordan and Overmyer 1986, 129–212), which makes contact with the dead by inviting a medium to make a trip to hell, a practice known as *guanluo yin* 觀落陰. This temple group started in 1948 when an onlooker of the practice was suddenly possessed by the famous goddess Royal Mother of the West, Xi Wangmu 西王母. The onlooker soon became the medium for the goddess, and the community grew into a large system of temples. Much in the same fashion, Master Lu was an onlooker in 1969 when he accompanied his mother to a temple where there was a medium serving the community. Master Lu was suddenly "possessed" and was given, without his prior consent, the ability to see and communicate with the spiritual world. After this miraculous encounter, Master Lu continued to receive the nocturnal visits of an invisible master who transmitted to him Daoist and Tantric teachings. Under the direction of his invisible unknown spiritual teacher, Master Lu also sought out a highly accomplished Daoist master Qingzhen 清真 (d. 1971) on Mount Liantou in Taizhong. Qingzhen taught Master Lu various Daoist practices such as the writing of magical charms, spells, alchemy, geomancy, and the divination that later made him famous among the public. Meeting with invisible spiritual immortals is a very common mode of origin of a Daoist school.[2]

Master Lu later revealed that Qingzhen was also known as Liaoming (Lu 1985, Bk 57, 171), a Tantric monk who fled to Taiwan from Sichuan in mainland China around 1949, and he was both a friend and student of the reputable Lama Norlha Rinpoche (1865–1936) of the Nyingmapa school (*Randeng* 2009.9.1, 2009.4.15). This Buddho–Daoist master Liaoming (or Qingzhen) would prove to have a lasting influence on the development of the True Buddha School.

Starting from 1969 and for six years, Master Lu applied what he learned from Qingzhen to become a famous part-time diviner while serving in the military as a surveyor. Master Lu claimed to have received five hundred letters each month from his readers and more than a thousand requests for an appointment to see him (Lu 1976, Bk 21, 176), an indication that an "audience and client cult" (Stark and Bainbridge 1985) had formed around him. From 1975 onward, Master Lu spent less time on divination but more on telling the stories about his divination and his encounter with the world of spirits in book form and by writing columns in newspapers. His books were among the season's best sellers, making him even more famous. In 1970, Master Lu started to formally take refuge in Buddhism through the famous Chinese master Yinshun 印順(1906–2005) who had resided in Taiwan since 1953. He also studied with teachers from different forms of Buddhism, especially the different forms of Vajrayāna Buddhism. In 1979, when he had fulfilled his obligation of serving in the military, Master Lu started to become a full-time diviner and to receive disciples. In three years, he turned his "audience and client cult" into a "cult movement" (Stark and Bainbridge 1985) of a thousand members. Master Lu called his school the Lingxian School 靈仙宗 (School of Efficacious Immortals), a name with a strong Daoist connotation, and members engaged in the practice of waking their souls, enabling them to establish contact with the spiritual world (Lu 1976, Bk 22). Also in the same period (1979–1981), Master Lu started to receive different empowerments from Tantric masters. In 1984, Master Lu changed the name of his school to Lingxian True Buddha School (Lingxian Zhenfozong 靈仙真佛宗) because of a usurpation of the name of his school by others (Lu 1984, Bk 50, 1). Although he has used the name True Buddha School as early as 1986 (Lu 1986, Bk 62, 107), Master Lu officially shortened the name of his school to the True Buddha School for the sake of convenience in 1992 (Lu 1992, Bk 99, 80), indicating the full-fledged Buddhist orientation of his school.

The True Buddha School has, therefore, gradually transformed itself from a Daoist divination movement to a Vajrayāna school of Buddhism.

This choice of Vajrayāna Buddhism can be readily understood against the background of the history of Buddhism in Taiwan. In the early 1970s, which scholars call the period of the "pluralization of Buddhism" in Taiwan (Jones 1999, 179), two of the largest and most important Buddhist groups were founded. They were the Fo Kuang Shan 佛光山 (Mt. Buddha's Light) of Rev. Xingyun 星雲 (b. 1927) and the Buddhist Compassion Relief Tzu Chi Association of the nun Zhengyan 證嚴 (b. 1937). The lifting of martial law in 1987 and the passage of the Law on the Organization of Civic Groups in 1989 has further brought about a multitude of new Buddhist groups in Taiwan, notably the Dharma Drum Mountain Buddhist group of Rev. Shengyan 聖嚴 (1930–2009) and the Zhongtai Chan Monastery 中台禪寺 of Rev. Weijue 惟覺 (b. 1928). The members of the above-mentioned four Buddhist groups, the Fo Kuang Shan, the Tzu Chi, the Dharma Drum, and the Zhongtai Chan, constitute almost half the population of Taiwan. They all trace their origin back to schools of Chinese Mahāyāna Buddhism, notably the Chan School or the Pure Land School.

It would not be difficult to comprehend why the True Buddha School has chosen the Vajrayāna tradition to establish an alternative Buddhist organization in the context of the highly competitive Buddhist religious market in Taiwan. Nevertheless, the True Buddha School has never dropped its Daoist components or its magical dimension of divination practices. In most of the School's temples across the world, one finds both a Buddhist and a Daoist pantheon, making the sometimes exotic deities of the Vajrayāna tradition more readily acceptable to the general Chinese public. The mix of Daoist divination practices and the inner cultivation teachings of the Vajrayāna Buddhism (Tam 2001) have also contributed substantially to form the more familiar Chinese outlook of the school for the Chinese audience.

Master Lu, however, especially asserts his lineage through the Nyingmapa and Sakyapa instructors with whom he has studied and by whom he has been acknowledged. Equally important, and in the long run possibly more important, are his own personal contacts with supernatural entities. These invisible teachers include Śākyamuni Buddha, Padmasambhava, the founder of Nyingma Tibetan Buddhism, and Tsongkhapa (1357–1419), founder of the Gelugpa school (Lu 1993, Bk 103, 88). Lu's encounter with Tsongkhapa resulted in his long lecture on the famous Tantric text *The Great Exposition of Secret Mantra*, which was eventually published in twelve volumes (Lu 1994–1995).

Master Lu has also studied under various Vajrayāna masters living in this world. From 1995, Master Lu started to begin his sermons by listing his Tantric teachers (Lu 1995a, 162). Among them was a Chinese Buddho–Daoist monk mentioned earlier, Qingzhen or Liaoming, under whom Master Lu had studied Nyingmapa teachings during the period of 1969–1972. During his visits to Hong Kong in the 1990s, Master Lu also studied under another Chinese Tantric master called Li Tingguang 李廷光 (1931–2006), who is also known by a Tibetan religious name, Thubten Dargyay (Lu 1983, Bk 48, 193). Li Tingguang had studied under two Vajrayāna masters. The first one is referred to by his Tibetan religious name, Thubten Dali. He was the disciple of Thubten Nima (another Chinese Vajrayāna master with a Tibetan name), who had studied under the reputable Mongolian Living Buddha of Sweet Dew (Ganzhu VII) (1914–1978) of the Gelugpa tradition. Rev. Ganzhu VII fled to Taiwan in 1949. Li Tingguang had also studied under venerable Dudjom Rinpoche (1904–1987) of the Nyingmapa school, a Tibetan monk living in Nepal who established centers both in New York and Paris. Li Tingguang later became the head of the Jingyin Ge 淨音閣 (Tower of the Pure Sound) Temple located on Mount Furong in Tsuen Wan of the New Territories in Hong Kong.[3] Through Li Tingguan, Master Lu received teachings on both Gelugpa and Nyingmapa.

Apart from studying under Li Tingguang, Master Lu, from 1982 to 1985, while he was in Seattle, also received instructions and empowerments from Dezhung Rinpoche (1906–1987) of the Sakya School, whom Master Lu referred to in Chinese as Shakya Zhengkong (*Randeng* 2008.9.15, 2009.5.15a). Dezhung Rinpoche was the brother of the wife of H. H. Jigdal Dagchen Sakya (b. 1929), who was the head of the Sakya School. Early in 1980, during his trip to New York, Master Lu also received empowerment from another noted lama, H. H. the 16th (Gyalwa) Karmapa (1924–1981) of the Kagyupa (*Randeng* 2009.5.15b, 2010.6.1). Later in 1983, Master Lu received empowerment from the 12th Tai Situpa Rinpoche, Pema Donyo Nyinje Wangpo (b. 1954) of the Kagyu Karma School (Lu 1983, Bk 44, 165). In 1983, Master Lu studied with Pufang 普方, a Chinese master of the Shingon tradition who served as a priest of the Zhong Chi Temple in Taipei[4] from whom Lu received the Cundī empowerment (Lu 1983, Bk 46, 1). From each of the above-mentioned Tantric teachers, Master Lu claimed to have received ritual objects symbolic of his attainments. Thus, Master Lu had received advanced empowerments from teachers in all four Tibetan schools of Nyingma, Gelug, Kagyu, and Sakya. The lineage empowerment of Master Lu can, therefore, be summarized as follows:

The Red Sect (Nyingmapa): Ven. Liaoming
The Yellow Sect (Gelugpa): Ven. Thubten Dargyay
The White Sect (Kagyupa): H. H. The 16th Karmapa
The Flower Sect (Sakyapa): Dezhung Rinpoche (i.e., Lama Sakya Zhengkong)
The Shingon Sect: Ven. Pufang.

The result of Master Lu's wide exposure to Vajrayāna Buddhism is that we have, in the True Buddha, one of the most comprehensive systems of Tantric Buddhist practices integrating the various teachings of the four Tibetan school of Nyingmapa, Gelugpa, Kagyupa, Sakyapa, Chinese Vajrayāna, and Japanese Vajrayāna. After moving from his native Taiwan to Seattle in 1982, Master Lu concentrated more and more on teaching his followers Tantric teachings and rituals under the name of the True Buddha's Tantric Dharma, to which we will turn our attention in order to explore the Chinese adaptation of Vajrayāna Buddhism.

*The True Buddha's Tantric Dharma (*Zhenfo Mifa 真佛密法*)*

The most complete and detailed exposition of the Tantric practices and rituals of the True Buddha School, known as the True Buddha's Tantric Dharma, was given on November 24–30, 1992, at the Rainbow Villa in Seattle by the founder of the True Buddha School himself. It was later published in book form as the *Mijiao daguanghua* 密教大光華 (The Luminous Flower of Tantric Buddhism; Lu 1995d). The True Buddha Tantric Dharma was formulated in a tripartite model that consists of the preparatory practice, main practice, and concluding practice:

I. Preparatory practice
  Handclapping: "Wake-up Call" to alert the deity
  Reciting the Purification Mantras
  Invocation (by Mind, Speech, and Mudrā)
  The Great Homage (prostration by visualization)
  The Maṇḍala Offering

The Fourfold Refuge (Guru, Buddha, Dharma, saṅgha)
The Armor Protection (for the practitioner)
The Four Immeasurable Buddha-states of mind[5]
Reciting the *High King Avalokiteśvara Sūtra* and Rebirth Mantra

II. Main Practice
Visualizations of the Empowerment of the Three Lights
Mantra Recitation (and visualization)
The Entering into Samādhi
The Nine Round Buddha Breath Exercise
The Visualization of the Merging of Self and Deity
Breath-Counting Exercise
The Skeleton Visualization Method

III. Concluding Practice
Emerging from Samādhi
Empowerment Using the Bell and Vajra
Intoning the Buddhas
Dedication
Hundred-Syllable Mantra
Circle of Completion (A Final Dedication)
The Completion Mantra (Lu 1995d; 2005, Bk 81).

According to Master Lu's own exposition, the gist of the True Buddha Dharma consists of the merging of one's self with one's chosen deity. This practice is modeled on the *sādhana* practice (Personal Deity Yoga) of Tantric Buddhism. As Master Lu states,

> The entirety of Tantra can be found in the practice of Personal Deity Yoga *Benzun fa shi mijiao di quanbu* 本尊法是密法的全部). . . . In the final stage of external Tantra, the union of Personal Deity and practitioner occurs. In the final stage of internal Tantra, either the spiritual-consciousness transformed from light drops is transported to the Pure Land of the Personal Deity or it directly transmutes into the Personal Deity. Thus, it all has to do with Personal Deity Yoga, whether one is doing the external or internal practice (*buguan shi waimi huoshi benzun fa* 不管是外密還是本尊法). An accomplished spiritual cultivator (apart from being in continual union with one's Personal Deity) also has in his company the whole retinue of his

> Personal Deity. In addition, the Personal Deity's Dharma Protectors follow him. (Lu 1996, Bk 120, 116–117)

As we know, *sādhana* is the spiritual exercise by which the practitioner evokes a divinity, identifying with it and absorbing it into himself. It is a primary form of meditation in the Tantric Buddhism of Tibet. *Sādhana* involves the body in *mudrās* (sacred gestures), the voice in mantras (sacred utterances), and the mind in the vivid inner visualization of sacred designs and the figures of divinities. The mastery of visualizing the divinities in order of increasing complexity requires hours of practice each day for a period of years. A single cultivation session requiring three to four hours to complete in the Tibetan school of Tantric Buddhism is simplified, within the True Buddha School, to a process that takes about forty minutes, without losing its essence. In the words of the founder of the True Buddha School, True Buddha Dharma is a simplified version of the *sādhana* ritual of all deity practices as outlined in Tibetan Buddhism (Lu 2002, Bk 154, 188).

The True Buddha Dharma as a practice is prescribed by the founder of the True Buddha School to all his disciples as a daily practice routine at home and at weekly group practice in the temple. As the often-quoted motto of the school from Padmasambhava, "Honor the Guru, treasure the Dharma, and practice diligently," indicates, the True Buddha School puts a great deal of emphasis on daily practice. A lay disciple would practice the *sādhana* once every day, while a monk or nun is expected to do so four times a day (Lu 2003, Bk 164, 28). In the True Buddha School, the most important *sādhana* practice is called the Yoga of Padmakumāra. There are eighteen forms of Padmakumāra (literally, "the Lad of Lotus"), each of whom is associated with one color.

As Dalai Lamas were supposed to be the incarnation of Avalokiteśvara/Guanyin Bodhisattva, the founder of the True Buddha School claimed to be the incarnation of the White Padmakumāra. This deity is not commonly known but was found in caves 314 and 380 in the Mogao Grottoes in Dunhuang, dating back to the Sui Dynasty (581–618 CE; Lu 2007, Bk 194, 132).[6] In his book *Hudie de fengcai* 蝴蝶的風采 (*The Colorful Butterflies: A Collection*), Master Lu reveals that he is the Huaguang zizai fo 華光自在佛 or the Lotus Light Self-Mastery Buddha (Lu 1992, Bk 101, 142; 2001, Bk 145, 47). In 1996, Master Lu further revealed that the White Padmakumāra is Amitābha (Lu 1996, Bk 120, 179). Thus, both the Lotus Light Self-Mastery Buddha and the White Lad of Lotus are just different names of Amitābha. The importance of the Yoga of Padmakumāra in the True Buddha School is not only that Padmakumāra is an incarnation of Amitābha Buddha, but also that Padmakumāra is the root guru of the True Buddha School. In other words, the Yoga of Padmakumāra in the True Buddha School is Guru Yoga. As we know, the root guru in the Tantric Buddhism is the embodiment of all sources of refuge and devotion. The guru is the essence of all paths, so that Guru Yoga is the quickest, most effective method for attaining enlightenment; it is the one path in which all other paths are complete (Dilgo 1999, 18; Dalai Lama 1988). When one achieves yogic response with one's root guru, one will be a step nearer to a more advanced practice of achieving union with one's principal deity and later with one's protector deity. This is because when one achieves yogic response with one's root guru, the principal deity and protector will naturally come along and descend to bless one with joy (Lu 2002, Bk 154, 136). In order to engage in practicing a higher level of practice such as the *Mahāmudrā*, one must receive the necessary empowerments and oral personal instructions from one's root guru. The practitioner must first establish yogic response with the physical guru, and through him seek response from the lineage holders. Only by receiving this response in stages can one gain accomplishments. This is necessary for the practitioner of *Mahāmudrā*, who must rely on the blessings of the guru. When the practitioner gains a secret response, in which his mind is in tune with his guru's mind, he shall have great accomplishment (Lu 1984, Bk 51, 45). In the True Buddha School, there is a concept of the three roots of Vajrayāna:

1. The Guru is the main holder of all Dharma;
2. The Principal Deity is the self nature of the practitioner;
3. The Dharma Protector is the guardian of the human world (Lu 2003, Bk 163, 32).

Also, there is a special emphasis on the vital importance of staying with one guru, one Dharma, and one principal deity in the True Buddha School (Lu 2003, Bk 163, 80).

Varieties of True Buddha Dharma and Rituals

A total of 393 Tantric Dharmas were collected in one volume, published in 1997 by the Purple Lotus University of the school (Huaguang 1997). These

Dharmas are for the fulfillment of both mundane desires and soteriological aims. Tantric Dharmas for worldly purposes (*bhukti*) are known as *Shijian fa* 世間法, or literally "method for this world," and Tantric methods for spiritual purpose (*mukti*) are called *Chushijian fa* 出世間法, or "method for leaving this world" (Lu 2002, Bk 154, 172).

The Tantric Dharmas for worldly purpose could be divided into four main categories, according to intents:

1. Purification of sickness and negativity or to remove impending ill fortune (*xizai* 息災);
2. Enrichment and generosity so one may have abundance (*zengyi* 增益);
3. Magnetization to draw people together and harmonize human relationships (*jing'ai* 敬愛);
4. Subjugation of negative forces and demons (*xiangfu*降伏) (Lu 1984, Bk 54, 1).

The above four categories are sometimes called *Karma Yogas*. Like other practices in the True Buddha School involving talismans and incantations, the four Karma Yogas are "secular" and "magical" practices. Lu thinks that they can only be considered auxiliaries to one's cultivation to reach the "Right Path," that is, liberation from the cycle of birth and death (Lu 2001, Bk 145, 195). As Lu himself explains, "I have transcendental power. The power cannot change karma (*shubu dishu* 術不抵數)" (2000, Bk 142, 93).[7]

The True Buddha School does not reject the use of spiritual powers and the power of gods to perform divination, check the records of past lives, pray for rain, give healing, use chart astrology, and perform geomancy. Practices of this kind were known as "mixed esotericism" *zami* 雜密, a term first used by Japanese Buddhists (Sharf 2005, appendix). True Tantric teachings (*chunmi* 純密, literally "pure Tantra") involve the doctrines of Vajra disciplinary rules, the *bodhi* mind, liberation from *saṃsāra*, and attaining Buddhahood in this very body (Lu 2002, Bk 154, 114).

Traditionally in Japan, the "Pure Tantra" also refers to the Shingon and Tendai esotericism (White 2000, 21). Under the category of mixed esotericism, there are two popular practices in the True Buddha School:

1. The Wealth god's practice or the *Jambhala* practice;
2. The fire offering or pūjā (*homa*) practice.

The *Jambhala* practice, a practice for wealth, is especially popular among the Southeast Asian members of the True Buddha School. There are the practices of Yellow *Jambhala*, Red *Jambhala*, Green *Jambhala*, Black *Jambhala*, White *Jambhala*, and the Five *Jambhalas*. In addition, the Dragon Treasure Vase Practice, Earth God Practice, Mountain God Practice, and so forth, are all wealth deity practices (Lu 2002, Bk 154, 78; 1993, Bk 103, 222–233). An often-quoted story to explain the meaning of these practices is an ancient Chinese story of a father and son who tried to control a flood. The father, named Gun 鯀, who tried to control the flood by blocking it, is compared to the Sutric or exoteric tradition to save sentient beings, that is by stopping desires altogether. The approach of Esoteric Buddhism is compared to the method employed by Gun's son, Yu 禹, the legendary sage king in China, who controlled the flood by channeling the water. This story was recorded in many pre-Qin (that is, before 221 BCE) texts such as the *Book of Odes, Mozi, Mencius, Book of Documents*, and others. Moreover, the idea of Vimalakīrti that "without cutting off lust, anger and ignorance and yet not being part of them" (Thurman 1986, 27)[8] is also frequently quoted to explain the practice of True Buddha School's Tantric methods for worldly purpose. Such is the expedient approach of "first having attracting sentient beings through desire, and later leading them into the wisdom of the Buddha" (Thurman 1986, 71).[9] The cultivation of the *Jambhala* practice will also lead to the experience of Dharma taste, the bliss generated by visualizing a deity and merging with it, resulting in a natural transformation of desire. Eventually, it leads to a transformation of consciousness into wisdom, reaching a level of attainment.

The fire offering ritual *pūjā* (*homa*) was taught in 1993 (Lu 1993, Bk 103, 27). The ritual procedure of *pūjā*, which is characterized by consuming all offerings in a burning fire, could again be analyzed by means of a tripartite model:

I. The preparatory practices
  1. Purification and definition of boundary;
  2. Invocation and homage;
  3. Empowerment of rosary beads, *vajra* bell, and offerings;
  4. Armor protection ritual.

II. The main practices
  5. Visualization of root deity (and merging of self with deity);

6. Chanting mantra;
7. Lighting the fire;
8. Officially making offerings to the root deity.
   [the above are done with performance of *mudrā*]

III. The concluding practices
   9. Making wishes and transference of merit (Lu 1993, Bk 103, 27).

All practices and rituals in the True Buddha School, be it *Jambhala* practice or fire offering ritual, take different forms but follow the same tripartite model, with the merging of the self with the deity as the main practice. The deity could be a wealth god or any deity of one's choice. All practices aim at the same result: developing one's ability to visualize a deity and merge with it in meditation. As we will see, this would be the first level of attainment in the True Buddha School.

We should also mention the Yab-Yam or Consort Practice (*shuangshenfa* 雙身法), which Padmasambhava describes as "extracting the pearl from the mouth of the poisonous snake" (Lu 1991, Bk 92, 14). The view of the founder of the True Buddha School is that many of the techniques taught in this practice have long been lost. As the practice is shocking to most and is easily misunderstood by the uninitiated, it is best to avoid practicing it. Master Lu points out that Tsongkhapa himself only practiced with a visualized consort, a *jñāna-mudrā*. (Lu 2002, Bk 154, 82). Applying Daoist terminologies, Lu explains that each being is endowed with both masculine and feminine qualities, or yin and yang (*zishen yinyang* 自身陰陽), as well as the properties of water and fire. The true consort practice is the harmonizing of the yin and yang principles within and the blending of water and fire. This means that one can gain attainment within one's own body without having to resort to finding an actual female or male partner. This is comparable to the Daoist practice involving the male and female, which is not an occurrence involving a physical couple, but points to the masculine and feminine principles within oneself (*zishen nannü* 自身男女; Lu 1984, Bk 51, 83).

Why then are the images of Yab-Yum Buddha statues or Buddha of Pleasure statues (*huanxi foxiang* 歡喜佛相) used? Master Lu explains that this has to do with a more advanced level of practice in Tantric Buddhism known as the inner heat Yoga, which is a form of inner cultivation (*neifa*內法). When the drops and inner fire from the Yoga of Psychic Heat (*zhuohuo*拙火, Tib. *gtum mo*) pass through the seven nerve plexuses, or *cakras*, a wonderful bliss is produced. This bliss cannot be expressed in words, and this unparalleled state of bliss is sometimes compared to the comfort and ease experienced at the climax reached by a couple in sexual union. Therefore, Buddha of Pleasure statues simply symbolize the spiritual state of supreme bliss. Eventually, the state of bliss came to be symbolized by the union of man and woman.

Gradual Approach to Religious Practices

The True Buddha School adopts a gradual approach to religious practices. Master Lu always reminds his students of the necessity of practice in gradual steps, beginning with the practice of the Four Preliminaries, followed by Guru Yoga, Deity Yoga, the Vajra Practices, and finally the Highest Yoga Tantra, gaining realization through stages before one can cultivate the *Mahāmudrā* (Lu 1984, Bk 51, 13). It is a must, in the True Buddha School, to cultivate the Four Preliminaries: the Fourfold Refuge, the Great Homage, the Maṇḍala Offering, and the Vajrasattva Practice. Engaging in the Tantric Practice already presupposes the keeping of the Five Precepts and Ten Virtuous Deeds, and adhering to the Tantric disciplines. After cultivating the Four Preliminaries, one could proceed to cultivate the Guru Yoga. In the True Buddha School this is called the Yoga of Padmakumāra. Next is the Yoga for Principal Deity. The principal or personal deity is the deity for whom the individual has the greatest affinity in his or her cultivation. There are eight choices of such deity in the True Buddha School:

1. Buddha Amitābha
2. Bodhisattva Avalokiteśvara
3. Bodhisattva Kṣitigarbha
4. Mother of All Buddhas, Bodhisattva Cundī
5. Padmasambhava
6. Champara (Yellow Fortune God)
7. Medicine Buddha
8. Padmakumāra (the Lad of Lotus) (Lu, 2005, Bk 81).

The essence of the Principal Deity Yoga is that the practitioner invites the principal deity to "enter" into his or her body and "abide" in it. After this, the principal deity and the practitioner are mutually "absorbed" into each other. The next practice in the line would be the Dharma Protector Practice (guarding over one's cultivation). This is the practice of the Five Vajra Practices, or the Practices of the Eight Vidyārājas (*mingwang* 明王) (Lu 1984, Bk 51, 182).[10] These practices are all known as the external practice. The next level would be the internal practices, which are for advanced practitioners. The goal for external practice is the purification of the Three Secrets (one's body, speech, and mind). This is a preliminary for all practice and is repeatedly taught by Master Lu (Lu 2005–6, 1:40, 3:228). As Master Lu said when he lectured on the *Yuanjue Jing* 圓覺經, "it is from purity that all the other Buddhist teachings come" (Lu 1995c, 3:99; Lu 2005, Bk 181, 40).[11]

The advanced level of internal practice involves the cultivation practice of winds (*qi* 氣, Skt. *prāṇa*), channels, and drops. Central to the internal practice is the practice of wind, also known as the "Breath of a Precious Vase" (*baopingqi* 寶瓶氣), which has been repeatedly taught by Lu (Lu 1982, Bk 40, 170; 1994, Bk 111, 186). One has to inhale a breath of air (wind) and let it "enter" into the *dantian* 丹田 (lower abdomen) of the practitioner. This breath of air should constantly "abide" in the *dantian*. This breath of air is absorbed into all the meridians and channels, and reaches every pore. Lu quotes a saying of Padmasambhava, which states, "all the merits of Vajrayāna arise from the practice of Treasure Vase Breathing" (Lu 2002, Bk 154, 112). With the successful cultivation of winds, one could use this to ignite one's inner body heat. This spot of fire is seated right at the base of the central channel. Once this fire is ignited, it rises along the central channel and burns through every channel knot. When this fire burns the channel knots in our bodies, it is as good as burning away our karma. According to Master Lu, "whatever is to be gained or has yet to be gained (*xiudao di de yu weide* 修道的得與未得) hinges on the ignition and growth of this inner fire" (Lu 1984, Bk 51, 49).[12] This shows the centrality of the practice of inner body heat in the True Buddha Dharma. As it is commonly known, the inner heat yoga was understood to be the foundation of the Six Yogas of Nāropa (1016–1100) as taught by Tsongkhapa (Mullin 1996, p. 36; Lu 2002, Bk 154, 130). Here we could see how the True Buddha Dharma was constructed on the basis of Tsongkhapa and the Kagyu school of Nāropa. The highest level of the practice in the True Buddha School is the Highest Yoga Tantra and the Great Perfection (Lu 2002, Bk 154, 86).

Levels of Practices

There are different ways to express the different levels of practice in the True Buddha School. There are, for instance, four levels of empowerment in the True Buddha School:

1. The first level of empowerment is for the purity of body, speech, and mind.
2. The second level of empowerment is for the practice of winds, channels, and drops.
3. The third level of empowerment is for Highest Yoga Tantra.
4. The fourth level of empowerment is for the Great Perfection (Lu 2002, Bk 154, 26).

While the first level of empowerment is an initiation for all followers, the second level of empowerment is for fewer people. Their empowerments include the practice of inner fire, the practice of drops, and the method of non-leakage. The non-leakage method is only transmitted to selected students. According to the founder of the True Buddha School, the third level of empowerment—the Highest Yoga Tantra—has so far been given only to one individual, a certain *vajra* master whose identity is not revealed. The fourth level of empowerment—the Great Perfection—has not been given to anyone.

In other times, the stages of cultivation in the Kagyu School of Tibetan Buddhism are used:

1. The Yoga of One-Pointedness (*Zhuanyi* 專一)
2. The Yoga of Simplicity (*Lixi* 離戲)
3. The Yoga of One Taste (*Yiwei* 一味)
4. The Yoga of Non-Meditation (*Wuxiu* 無修) (Lu 2003, Bk 163, 64)

Similar to this scheme are the four levels of *Mahāmudrā*:

1. The first level is "warmth" (*wen* 溫). One ignites the fire within the body. This spot of fire is seated right at the base of the central channel. "Warmth" therefore refers to the inner heat Yoga.
2. The second level deals with "breaking" (*po* 破). When the inner fire rises to the area of the spiritual eye (between the two eyebrows), it produces light. When the spiritual eye radiates light, this is the spiritual eye practice of attaining realization through meditation (*zuochan tongming tianxin* 坐禪通明天心) (Lu 1983, Bk 45), which is described as "breaking."

3. The third level involves "preservation" (*chi* 持). Practitioners who are able to abide in the "unhindered mind" and reach the state of tranquility, unaffected by any outer influence, are said to reach the level of "preservation," where they always remain firm in their cultivation effort.
4. The fourth level is "attainment" (*zheng* 證). This refers to the state of nirvāṇa, in which an individual's light is merged with the light of the supreme consciousness (Lu 1984, Bk 51, 149).[13]

Another way to express the levels of practice used in the True Buddha School is the scheme of the Generation Stage and the Completion Stage of the Nyingmapa (Lingpa et al. 2006; Powers 1995, 245). In Generation Stage, one begins with the practice of purifying one's body, speech, and mind. After this, one should cultivate the winds, channels, and drops. And through the stages of cultivation, one approaches the Highest Yoga Tantra and finally enters into the Great Perfection of the Completion Stage.

A creative interpretation of the different levels of religious experience in Tantric Buddhism by the founder of the True Buddha School is that he matches them with the three levels of heaven in Buddhism: (1) the six heavens in the Realm of Desire (*yujie tian* 欲界天); (2) the eighteen heavens in the Realm of Form, which are further divided into four *dhyāna* regions (*sejie tian* 色界天); and (3) the four heavens in the Realm of Formlessness (*wusejie tian* 無色界天).

The Realm of Desire

Lu uses the term "blissful pleasure" (*xile* 喜樂) to represent the Realm of Desire. He said,

> When *Qi* [*prāṇa*] enters into the central channel and travels through it, a great blissful pleasure is generated as a result of the rubbing of *Qi* against the central channel. It is a kind of enraptured, soothing, yet divine ecstasy not unlike the euphoria engendered in sexual orgasms. However, bliss generated by the moving of *Qi* inside the central channel lasts longer and is more sublime. (Lu 1996, Bk 120, 71)

This bliss, Lu clarifies, is not the kind of "buoyant ease" (*qingan* 輕安) generally referred to as associated with meditation. It is instead the authentic "great bliss" (*damiao xile* 大妙喜樂) generated by the practice of wind. It is also known as the "Dharma Taste" (*fale* 法樂) enjoyed by devas in the

Realm of Desire. In other words, entering this level of practice virtually places one in Heaven. The blissful Realm of Desire is captivating because the sensations experienced there are solid, concrete, and, at the same time, sublime, according to Lu.

The Realm of Form: Clear Light

The Clear Light echoes the Clear Light Yoga in the Six Yogas of Nāropa. It builds upon the vase breathing technique and the inner heat yoga. Tsongkhapa described it as follows,

> One places the mind firmly . . . causing the energies from the side channels of *rasana* and *lalana* to enter, abide and dissolve within the central channel, arousing the four emptiness(es), and giving rise to the amazing clear light consciousness of the path. When this occurs one observes the mind of the great innate ecstasy and then holds to it. (Mullin 1996, 84)

The Clear Light Yoga essentially refers to engaging in the inner heat yoga in order to collect the vital energies into the central channel and cause them to abide and dissolve, melting the drops at the crown *cakra* and giving rise to the bliss. When the drops pass through the channels of the body, clear light is generated (Lu 1995c, 2:182–183). Generating the experience of this clear light through yogic endeavor is the main purpose of Highest Yoga Tantra. When this is achieved, according to Lu, one enters into the Realm of Form, where desires for food and sexual pleasure are transcended, but palaces (of form) still exist, thus giving rise to the name "Realm of Form." The sensations and awareness that one experiences throughout the eighteen heavens in the Realm of Form do overlap, although each has its own uniqueness. There is already the manifestation of clear light, as a result of one's practice, within the Realm of Form, and the heavens may be distinguished from one another by the scope, intensity, and color of the light. There are two kinds of light manifestation: self-engendered and other-engendered.

The Realm of Formlessness

The Realm of Formlessness is a realm without any material existence, body, or palace (of Deities). There is only the abiding of consciousness in a deep and subtle state of meditative stillness. Lu thinks that generally, perceptions experienced during *samādhi* consist of an incredible feeling of buoyant lightness or a sensation of bathing in an ocean of light. Or one may experience a loss of localization where there is no longer the duality of large versus small, outside versus inside. Contained within one is the whole, infinite universe, which is without any top or bottom, pervading everything. When all such sensations and perceptions cease to exist, when the euphoria and ecstasy vanish, when bathing in the clear light disappears, at such a moment one's Perfect and Bright Self Nature manifests itself (Lu 1996, Bk 120, 58). Lu uses the following metaphor:

> One's own pure *Dharmakāya* is the Child Light (*ziguang* 子光). The nature of the supreme cosmic consciousness is the Mother Light (*muguang* 母光). It is only when all discursive thoughts are eliminated and one abides in the realm of the light that the Child Light manifests itself. It is the very pure state of the Child Light that attracts the Mother Light of the supreme cosmic consciousness. As the Child Light spins and ascends through the central channel, both these lights merge into one, (*ziguang yu muguang heyi* 子光與母光合一) these two lights which in truth are of the same essence. Like old friends who meet again, these pure lights merge into each other. This is in essence the final return to the Ocean of Vairocana; (*huigui piluxinghai* 會歸毘盧性海) entering into Nirvana, achieving enlightenment. (Lu 1984, Bk 51, 113; Dilgo 1999, 59)[14]

The individual self is, therefore, infused with the cosmic spirit during his or her meditative absorption in *Mahāmudrā*. One then has become one with the Supreme Consciousness. The scheme of the True Buddha Dharma is such that one begins cultivating with devotion and giving. Devotion refers especially to the root guru through the practice of Guru Yoga, and moving on to the practice of inner cultivation and meditation. According to Lu, it helps to dissolve one's spirit and mind into the greater world of cosmic consciousness. This Samādhi of Observation has arisen from the accomplishment of realizing that all past, present, and future states are indivisible, that one is all and all is one, and that all phenomena of birth and extinction are illusory. Lu calls it the seeing of the very nature of all phenomena (*zhaojian yiqiefa de benxing* 照見一切法的本性) (Lu 1984, Bk 51, 132), which is the experience of enlightenment.

Concluding Remarks: The Chinese Feature of the True Buddha School's Tantric Dharma

I have argued elsewhere that the True Buddha School is a new school of Chinese Tantric Buddhism, rather than a new religion (Tam 2007). This is because the teachings as found in the True Buddha School are a continuation of a long tradition of Tantric Buddhism. Many Buddhist schools originating in Taiwan have eventually become international movements. Some of them would put emphasis solely on charity (Learman 2005, 185–209).[15] The True Buddha School, however, stresses the importance of daily religious cultivation. Lu teaches his lay disciples to engage in cultivation once a day, and monks and nuns to do so four times a day. As can be seen from the earlier discussion, the True Buddha School practice starts with the external practice that hinges on the purification of body, speech, and mind through the use of *mudrā*, mantra and maṇḍala. More concrete is the practice of Guru Yoga, that is, the Yoga of Padmakumāra, which is a form of *sādhana* (spiritual exercise). The internal practice for advanced practitioners has to do with the Inner Heat Yoga, the foundation for the Six Yogas of Nāropa as taught by the Tsongkhapa. The idea is to direct vital energies into the central channel, giving rise to the innate clear light (*jingguang* 淨光) in the heart *cakra* (Lu 2005–6, v2, 104).

All these teachings can be found in the Tantric Buddhist tradition. What makes the True Buddha School a Chinese Tantric School is that these teachings are now, for the first time, taught to the general public in lucid modern Chinese. Master Lu, through the publication of over 240 books, has worked to propagate his teachings to a very broad audience. Besides the medium of teaching and the fact that a great majority of the members of the school are Chinese or Chinese in diaspora, the Tantric doctrines of the school have become embedded in Chinese religiosity. In expounding Tantric doctrines, Daoist vocabularies and theologies are amply used. For the internal practice, for instance, Lu compares its elements with those in Daoism:

> *Jing* 精 is light drops (*mingdian* 明點).
>
> *Qi* 氣 is *prāṇa*.
>
> *Shen* 神 is the manifestation of light and wind in the channels (*guangming fengmai* 光明風脈).

And again, utilizing the vocabulary of the Daoist inner alchemy tradition, Lu explains,

> When the psychic heat reaches the crown chakra, the white *bodhicitta* (white drops) at the crown chakra melts and drips downwards via the path of the tongue that is pressing against the upper palate. This fluid is known in the Daoist teaching as the heavenly court water, and is called nectar in the Buddhist teaching. The fluid has the characteristic of cooling, and when mixed with the psychic heat produces a nurturing effect. This is known as the mixing of water and fire (*shuihuoji* 水火濟). The practice of psychic heat (*lingre* 靈熱) and the practice of inner fire and drops (*neihuo mingdian* 內火明點) are similar. (Lu 1984, Bk 51, 26)

Lu also matches many practices with the Daoist practices:

> The "Sword Tempering Method" (*zhujianfa* 鑄劍法) is a foundation practice of the Highest Tantra, the "Great Incubating Method" (*dawenyang* 大溫養) is equivalent to the Treasure Vase *Qi* and Psychic Heat practices, the "Pill Cauldron Practice" (*Dingdan fa* 丹田法) is the "light drop" practice, and the "Ultimate Correct Method" (*wuji zhengfa* 無極正法) results in the emergence of Clear Light and the Void (*Jingguang kongxing* 淨光空性). (Lu 1996, Bk 120, 44)

Master Lu once claimed, "I am an accomplished adept who epitomizes the teachings and practices of all Buddhist and Daoist schools" (2002, Bk 154, 44).

In analyzing the *sādhana* practice, Master Lu says,

> In my opinion, the "Self-Power Personal Deity" is what is referred to in Daoism as the "Original or Principal Spirit" [*yuan shen* 元神]. (*mijiao zilibenzun ji daojiao yuanshen* 密教自力本尊即道教元神) (Lu 1996, Bk 120, 153)
>
> In my [40th] book, *The Secret Daoist Method of Spiritual Communication*, I have written about the Daoist methods of cultivating the Original Spirit:

1. Observe one's own Original Spirit (spirit-viewing method; *guanshen* 觀神)
2. Respiration of the cosmic *qi* and light to reveal the spirit (spirit-nourishing method; *peishen* 培神)
3. True formula to reveal the image (spirit-manifestation method; *xianshen* 顯神)

4. Contracting and merging with the spirit (spirit-union method; *heshen* 合神)
5. The miracle of bi-location (spirit-traveling method; *chushen* 出神) (Lu 1982, Bk 40, 4 &43).

Lu believes the Self-Power Personal Deity is a luminous body that is engendered when *qi* enters into the central channel and transmutes into the five-fold rainbow light. Even on the level of external practice, one recognizes Daoist elements by simply walking into one of the temples of the True Buddha School. On the altar, one could easily find the Golden Mother of the Primordial Pond, the chief goddess of the immortals in the Daoist western paradise. Associated with the peach of immortality, she bestows longevity to beings. This is because the rise of the True Buddha School is closely related to a temple group in Taiwan called the Compassion Society (the Cihui Tang) that worships the Golden Mother of the Primordial Pond (Jordan and Overmyer 1986). Through a female medium who belonged to the Compassion Society temple, Qiandai 青代 (d. 2006), Master Lu was suddenly given, without his prior consent, the ability to see and communicate with the spiritual world (Lu 2006, Bk 186, 42; Tam 2001). Some of the temples even have a separate altar for Daoist gods and goddesses, such as the city god, the Jade Emperor, and the dragon god. An altar for the Taisui 太歲, or the Year Planetary Ruler, who is a Daoist star deity, and for the earth god is a must in all the temples of the True Buddha School. A Chinese device for divination is also sure to be found. This consists of a canister with 108 long strips of bamboo together with divination blocks, which are two moon-shaped pieces of wood with one side convex and the other flat, used to check with the right choice of bamboo strips.

More important is the ritual cycle of the School. Using the True Buddha School temple in Hong Kong as an example, we found the following rituals common to most True Buddha School temples:

Ritual for burning the first incense in a year (*shang touzhuxiang* 上頭炷香)
Ritual to celebrate the Chinese New Year (*xinchun tuanbai fahui* 新春團拜法會)
Ritual to bless the tablets for the living (*changsheng luwei* 長生祿位)
Ritual to install the Year Planetary Ruler (*anfeng taisui* 安奉太歲)
Ritual for deliverance of the souls during the Qingming Festival (*Qingming chaodu fahui* 清明超度法會)

> Ritual for deliverance of the souls during the Yu-Lan Pen-Hui (Feeding the Hungry Ghost Festival) (*Yulan chaodu fahui* 盂蘭超度法會).[16]

In most cases, "ritual" means a standard *sādhana* ritual in a tripartite model that lasts for one to two hours. These rituals reveal the nature of Tantric ritual in a Chinese setting. This was most obvious in our participatory observation of the ritual to celebrate Chinese New Year in the Hong Kong temple, when the chief deity is the Golden Mother. It was a *homa* ritual in which the mantra used was a combination of Sanskrit and Chinese: "*oṃ jinmu siddhi hūṃ*." Here only the word *jinmu* 金母 (Golden Mother) is Chinese, the others being Sanskrit.

Fang Litian方立天 (1933–2014), a renowned scholar in the field of Chinese Buddhist philosophy teaching in the Renmin University of China in Beijing, had identified three basic features of Chinese Buddhism.

1. The tendency to harmonize different trends of thoughts;
2. The tendency to integrate different schools of thinking;
3. The tendency to simplify complicated doctrines and practices (1988, 378–411).

The fact that a single cultivation session requiring three to four hours to complete in the Tibetan schools of Tantric Buddhism is simplified, within the True Buddha School, to a process that takes about forty minutes, without losing its essence, is an important feature of the sinification of Tantric Buddhism. Another feature of sinification is revealed by the fact that the True Buddha School itself is one of the most comprehensive systems of Tantric Buddhism, integrating the practices of different Tantric systems. Lu claimed to have integrated Tibetan, Chinese, and Japanese Esoteric Buddhist traditions. The popularity of the Tantric *dharma*s and rituals for worldly purpose (*bhukti*) or the *Shijian fa* 世間法 in the True Buddha School, especially the wealth god's practice or the *Jambhala* practice, is another feature of Chinese Buddhism, namely a positive evaluation of the phenomenal world and a vision of Buddhism that affirms life in this world (Gregory 1991, 7, 13). I have also argued elsewhere that there is an integration of a magical discourse with a cultivational discourse in the True Buddha School (Tam 2001). These are some of the recurring themes in Chinese intellectual history, and they also serve as evidence that the Tantric Buddhism of the True Buddha School has accommodated itself to Chinese cultural values.

A recent development in the teachings of the True Buddha School is an attempt to integrate the Chan School of thought with the Tantric teachings in the form of commentary on the Chan text *Wudeng Huiyuan* 五燈會元 (Lu 2005, Bk 182; 2006, Bk 184, 188; 2007 Bk 192, 195; 2008, Bk 199; 2009, Bk 207, 211).[17] Emphasis is put on the potentiality for Buddhahood that existed embryonically within all sentient beings as the womb of the Tathāgata (*tathāgatagarbha*). This new development uses Chan concepts, such as the idea of a teaching that does not rely on the written word but instead points directly to the human mind. The analysis of this process of integration of Chan Buddhism with Tantric Buddhism in the True Buddha School, however, has to be addressed in a future publication.

Notes

1. The three founders of Chinese Tantrism are Śubhākarasiṃha (Shan Wuwei 善無畏) (d. 735), Vajrabodhi, and Amoghavajra as recorded by Zanning 贊寧 (919–1001) in his *Song Gaoseng zhuan* 宋高僧傳 [*Eminent Monks during the Song Dynasty*] in *Taishō Shinshū Daizōkyō* 50:709ff.
2. Zhang Daoling 張道陵 (34–156) met spiritual Laozi at Mt. Heming and later founded the Way of the Celestial Masters (Tianshi Dao 天師道) school of Daoism. The female Daoist Wei Huacun 魏華存 (251–334) met the spiritual immortal Qingxu 清虚, who transmitted to her various Daoist texts, on the basis of which she formed the Maoshan 茅山 School of Daoism. Gexuan 葛玄 (164–244) met three spiritual immortals sent by Laozi at Mt. Tiantai, who transmitted to him the Lingbao texts, based on which he founded the Lingbao 靈寶 school of Daoism.
3. It is listed under the World Directory of Buddhist Organization Hong Kong given in http://www.mba.net.my/BuddDatabase/Contact/World/w-address-hongkong.htm. The address of the Jingyin temple was also given in Lu 1983, Bk 48, 193.
4. The address of the temple is Zhongheshi zhongshanlu erduan 中和市中山路 568 xiang 巷 66 hao 號. For a brief introduction to the temple, see http://library.taiwanschoolnet.org/cyberfair2002/C0216220096/page/zong-chi-si/zong-chi-si.htm.
5. (1) Boundless kindness or bestowing of joy or happiness; (2) boundless pity to save from suffering; (3) boundless joy on seeing others rescued from suffering; (4) limitless indifference, i.e. rising above these emotions, or giving up all things. See Soothill and Hodous ([1937] 1982, 178).
6. The Mogao Grottoes, also known as the Caves of the Thousand Buddhas and Dunhuang Caves, form a system of 492 temples 25 km (15.5 miles) from the center of Dunhuang, an oasis strategically located at a religious and culture crossroads on the Silk Road, in Gansu province, China. The cave contains some of the finest examples of Buddhist art spanning a period of 1,000 years. Construction of the Buddhist cave shrines began in 366 CE as places to store scriptures and art.

7. Despite the fact that Deliverance Ritual (*Bardo*) in the True Buddha School is known to be very effective, Master Lu admitted in a lecture delivered on January 5, 1999, in Seattle that he was not able to save the soul of one relative of his former wife, Rev. Master Lianxiang 蓮香. Lu said he chanted the scripture but he knew that he was not able to deliver the soul of the relative of his wife (Lu 2006b, 4:174–175).
8. In Chinese, *buduanyinnuchi yibuyuju* 不斷婬怒癡,亦不與俱. See *Weimojie suoshuo jing* 維摩詰所說經 [*Scripture Spoken by Vimalakīrti*], T. 475, 14:p540b24.
9. In Chinese, *xianyiyugouqian houlingrufodao* 先以欲鉤牽,後令入佛道. See *Weimojie suoshuo jing*, T. 475, 14: 550b7.
10. Practices of the Vidyārājas that had been taught by master Lu includes the Practice of Yamāntaka 大威德金剛 (Seattle 1995), Hevajra 喜金剛 (Seattle 2008), Ucchuṣma 穢跡金剛 (New York 1997), Kālacakra 時輪金剛 (Hong Kong 2000), Acala 不動明王 (Seattle 1997), Rāgarāja 愛染明王 (Hong Kong 1998), and Hayagrīva 馬頭明王 (Seattle 2000).
11. The full title for *Yuanjue jing* is *Dafangguang yuanyue xiuduoluo liaoyijing* 大方廣圓覺修多羅了義經 found at T. 842, 17:913a21–922a24.
12. The inner heat Yoga was taught by Master Lu in an annual ceremony in Seattle, which took place in September 1994.
13. The four levels of Mahāmudrā were revealed by the retinues of Mañjuśrī called the Eight Youths of Mañjuśrī, whom Master Lu met on a pilgrimage to Mt. Wutai in his meditation.
14. Cf. the metaphor of uniting the "Mother luminosity" and "Child luminosity" in order to liberated into the *dharmakāya* in his discussion of *Atiyoga* by Dilgo Khyentse Rinpoche (1999, 59).
15. The most representative group is the Ciji Gongde Hui 慈濟功德會, founded by the Buddhist nun Zhengyan 證嚴 (b. 1937). See the study of this group by C. Julia Huang (Learman 2005, 185–209).
16. For a timetable of the True Buddha School Temple in Hong Kong from the period of 2003 to 2007, see http://www.hklts.org.hk/Main/index.php?option=com_content&view=category&id=39&Itemid=69.
17. The Chan text *Wudeng Huiyuan* consists of five works: *Jingde Chuandenglu* 景德傳燈錄, *Tiansheng Guangdenglu* 天聖廣燈錄, *Liandeng huiyao* 聯燈會要, *Jianzhong jingguo xudenglu* 建中靖國續燈錄, and *Jiatai pudenglu* 嘉泰普燈錄. The anthology is found in 卍 *Xuzangjing* v. 138 (Puji 1905–1912).

References

Chou, Yi-Liang. 1945. "Tantrism in China." *Harvard Journal of Asiatic Studies* 8 (3–4): 235–332.

Dalai Lama. 1988. *The Union of Bliss and Emptiness: A commentary on Guru Yoga Practice*, trans. by Geshe Thupten Jinpa. Ithaca, NY: Snow Lion Publications.

Dilgo, Khyentse Rinpoche. 1999. *Guru Yoga: According to the Preliminary Practice of Longchen Nyingtik*. Translated by Matthieu Ricard. Ithaca, NY: Snow Lion Publications.

Fang Litian. 1988. *Zhongguo fojiao yu chuantong wenhua* 中國佛教與傳統文化 [*Chinese Buddhism and Traditional Culture*]. Shanghai: Shanghai renmin chubanshe.

Gregory, Peter N. 1991. *Tsung-mi and the Sinification of Buddhism*. Princeton, NJ: Princeton University Press.

Huaguang Purple Lotus University Education Committee, ed. 1997. *Zhenfo miaobao* 真佛妙寶. Taipei: Liankuei Publishing House.

Jordan, David K., and Daniel L. Overmyer, eds. 1986. *The Flying Phoenix: Aspects of Chinese Sectarianism in Taiwan*. Princeton, NJ: Princeton University Press.

Jones, Charles Brewer. 1999. *Buddhism in Taiwan: Religion and the State 1660–1990*. Honolulu: University of Hawai'i Press.

Learman, Linda, ed. 2005. *Buddhist Missionaries in the Era of Globalization*. Honolulu: University of Hawai'i Press.

Lingpa, Jigme, Patrul Rinpoche, and Getse Mahāpandita. 2006. *Deity, Mantra and Wisdom: Development Stage Meditation in Tibetan Buddhist Tantra*. Translated by Dharmachakra Translation Committee. Ithaca: Snow Lion Publications.

Lü Jianfu. 1995. *Zhongguo mijiao shi* 中國密教史. Beijing: Zhongguo shehui kexue chubanshe.

Lu Sheng-yen. 1976. Book #21. *Linghun di chaojue* 靈魂的超越 [*The Transcendental Awareness of our Soul*]. Hong Kong: Qingshan chubanshe.

Lu Sheng-yen. 1976. Book #22. *Qilingxue* 啟靈學 [*Awakening of the Soul*]. Hong Kong: Qingshan chubanshe.

Lu Sheng-yen. 1982. Book #40. *Tongling mifashu* 通靈妙法書 [*A Book of the Secret Teachings on Communicating with Sprits*]. Hong Kong: Qingshan chubanshe.

Lu Sheng-yen. 1983. Book #44. *Fumo pingyao chuan* 伏魔平妖傳 [*Exorcising Demons and Subduing Evil Spirits*]. Singapore: Siang Ching Trading PET.

Lu Sheng-yen. 1983. Book #45. *Zuochan tongmingfa* 坐禪通明法 [*The Art of Meditation*]. Hong Kong: Qingshan chubanshe.

Lu Sheng-yen. 1983. Book #46. *Xiyatu de xingzhe* 西雅圖的行者 [*Practitioner in Seattle*]. Hong Kong: Qingshan chubanshe.

Lu Sheng-yen. 1983. Book #48. *Shangshi de zhengwu* 上師的證悟 [*The Guru's Enlightenment*]. Hong Kong: Qingshan chubanshe.

Lu Sheng-yen. 1984. Book #50. *Jingang numuji* 金剛怒目集 [*The Glaring Eyes of the Guardian Warriors*]. Hong Kong: Qingshan chubanshe.

Lu Sheng-yen. 1984. Book #51. *Wushangmi yu dashouyin* 無上密與大手印 [*Highest Yoga Tantra and Mahāmudrā*]. Hong Kong: Qingshan chubanshe.

Lu Sheng-yen. 1984. Book #54. *Mizong jiemofa* 密宗羯摩法 [*Tantric Karma Practices*]. Hong Kong: Qingshan chubanshe.

Lu Sheng-yen. 1985. Book #57. *Daofazhuanqi lu* 道法傳奇錄 [*Tales of Marvels in Daoist Methods*]. Hong Kong: Qingshan chubanshe.

Lu Sheng-yen. 1986. Book #62. *Daodi buke siyi* 道的不可思議 [*The Incredible Dao*]. Hong Kong: Qingshan chubanshe.

Lu Sheng-yen. 1991. Book #92. *Chanding di yunjian* 禪定的雲箋 [*Remarks on Meditation*]. Hong Kong: Majianji tushu gongsi.

Lu Sheng-yen. 1992. Book #99. *Xicheng yeyu* 西城夜雨 [*Rain at Night in Seattle*]. Hong Kong: Majianji tushu gongsi.

Lu Sheng-yen. 1992. Book #101. *Hudie de fengcai* 蝴蝶的風采 [*The Colorful Butterflies: A Collection*]. Hong Kong: Majianji tushu gongsi.

Lu Sheng-yen. 1993. Book #103. *Mijiao daxiangying* 密教大相應 [*The Great Spiritual Response of Tantrayāna*]. Hong Kong: Xinfatang.

Lu Sheng-yen. 1994. Book #111. *Zouguo tianya* 走過天涯 [*Roving over the World*]. Hong Kong: Mingchuang chubanshe.

Lu Sheng-yen. 1994–1995. *Mijiao zhihui jian* 密教智慧劍 [*The Sword of Wisdom in Tantra*]. Hong Kong: Majianji tushu gongsi.

Lu Sheng-yen. 1995a. *Mijiao di fashu* 密教的法術 [*The Magic of Tantrism*]. Hong Kong: Majianji tushu gongsi.

Lu Sheng-yen. 1995b. *A Complete and Detailed Exposition on the True Buddha Tantric Dharma*. Translated by Janny Chow. San Bruno: Purple Lotus Society.

Lu Sheng-yen. 1995c. *Qingjingde yuanjing* 清淨的圓鏡 [*The Pure Round Mirror (II) & (III): Yuanjue Jing as Taught by the Living Buddha Liansheng*]. Taipei: Dari chupanshe.

Lu Sheng-yen. 1995d. *Mijiao daguanghua* 密教大光華 [*The Luminous Flower of Tantric Buddhism*]. Hong Kong: Majianji tushu gongsi.

Lu Sheng-yen. 1996. Book #120. *Fowang xinjingjie* 佛王新境界 [*New Revelations from the Buddha King*]. Hong Kong: Majianji tushu gongsi.

Lu Sheng-yen. [1997] 2005. Book #81. *Zhenfo yigui Jing* 真佛儀軌經 [*A Scripture on the Ritual Procedure of the True Buddha School*]. Taiwan, Taoyuan: Daden Culture.

Lu Sheng-yen. 2000. Book #142. *Yeshen renjingshi* 夜深人靜時 [*In the Stillness of Night*]. Taiwan, Taoyuan: Daden Culture.

Lu Sheng-yen. 2001. Book #145. *Dangxia de qingliang xin* 當下的清涼心 [*Living this Moment in Purity*]. Taiwan, Taoyuan: Daden Culture.

Lu Sheng-yen. 2002. Book #154. *Zhihui de guanghuan* 智慧的光環 [*The Aura of Wisdom*]. Taiwan, Taoyuan: Daden Culture.

Lu Sheng-yen. 2003. Book #163. *Duguo shengsi de dahai* 渡過生死的大海 [*Crossing the Ocean of Life and Death*]. Taiwan, Taoyuan: Daden Culture.

Lu Sheng-yen. 2003. Book #164. *Yiri yishouyu* 一日一小語 [*Daily Wisdom*]. Taiwan, Taoyuan: Daden Culture.

Lu Sheng-yen. 2005–2006. *Huofo zhige* 活佛之歌 [*Songs of the Living Buddha*]. 4 vols. Taiwan, Taoyuan: Daden Culture.

Lu Sheng-yen. 2005. Book #181. *Zhijin yitiao minglu* 指引一條明路 [*Point Towards a Sunny Path*]. Taiwan, Taoyuan: Daden Culture.

Lu Sheng-yen. 2005. Book #182. *Bukeshuo zhi shuo* 不可說之說 [*The Unspoken Dharma*]. Taiwan, Taoyuan: Daden Culture.

Lu Sheng-yen. 2006. Book #184. *Geini dianshang xindeng* 給你點上心燈 [*Illuminating Your Hear—A Reading of the Chan Text Wudeng Huiyuan* 五燈會元]. Taiwan, Taoyuan: Daden Culture.

Lu Sheng-yen. 2006. Book #186. *Jimo de jiaoyin* 寂寞的腳印 [*Lonesome Footprints*]. Taiwan, Taoyuan: Daden Culture.

Lu Sheng-yen. 2006. Book #188. *Songni yizhan mingdeng* 送你一盞明燈 [*A Bright Lamp for You—A Second Re-reading of the Chan Text* Wudeng Huiyuan]. Taiwan, Taoyuan: Daden Culture.

Lu Sheng-yen. 2007. Book #192. *Tianxia diyi jingcai* 天下第一精采 [*Lamp of Utmost Brilliance—A Third Re-reading of the Chan Text* Wudeng Huiyuan]. Taiwan, Taoyuan: Daden Culture.

Lu Sheng-yen. 2007. Book #194. *Menghuan de suixiang* 夢幻的隨想 [*Illusory Journal*]. Taiwan, Taoyuan: Daden Culture.

Lu Sheng-yen. 2007. Book #195. *Shiguren di yahui* 拾古人的牙慧 [*Ancient Wisdom—A Fourth Re-reading of the Chan Text* Wudeng Huiyuan]. Taiwan, Taoyuan: Daden Culture.

Lu Sheng-yen. 2008. Book #199. *Fenglai bolangqi* 風來波浪起 [*The Billowing Waves—A Fifth Re-reading of the Chan Text* Wudeng Huiyuan]. Taiwan, Taoyuan: Daden Culture.

Lu Sheng-yen. 2008. Book #203. *Guying di duihua* 孤影的對話 [*Conversing with the Lonesome Shadow—A Sixth Re-reading of the Chan Text* Wudeng Huiyuan]. Taiwan, Taoyuan: Daden Culture.

Lu Sheng-yen. 2009. Book #207. *Nianhuashou di mimi* 蓮花手的秘密 [*Unlocking the Flower Koan—A Fifth Re-reading of the Chan Text* Wudeng Huiyuan]. Taiwan, Taoyuan: Daden Culture.

Lu Sheng-yen. 2009. Book #211. *Yizhijian shexiang cangtian* 一支箭射向蒼天 [*An Arrow Shooting to the Sky—A Eighth Re-reading of the Chan Text* Wudeng Huiyuan]. Taiwan, Taoyuan: Daden Culture.

Melton, Gordon. 2007. "The Emergence of the True Buddha School in Taiwan and the West." Paper presented at the annual meeting (June 7, 2007) of the Center for Studies on New Religions (CESNUR), University of Bordeaux, Bordeaux, France.

Mullin, Glenn H. 1996. *Tsongkhapa's Six Yogas of Naropa*. Ithaca, NY: Snow Lion Publications.

Payne, Richard K., ed. 2006. *Tantric Buddhism in East Asia*. Boston: Wisdom Publications.

Powers, John. 1995. *Introduction to Tibetan Buddhism*. Ithaca, NY: Snow Lion Publication.

Puji. 1905–1912. *Wudeng huiyuan* 五燈會元 [The Five History on Transmission of the Lamp in the Chan School of Buddhism] Collected in *Dai Nippin zokuzōkyō*. Kyoto: Zōkyō shoin. Reprint, Taipei: Xin wenfeng chuban gongsi, 138: 1–832.

Randeng 燃燈 [*Enlightenment Magazine*]. Taizhong: Taiwan Leizang si.

Sharf, Robert H. 2005. *Coming to Terms with Chinese Buddhism: A Reading of the Treasure Store Treatise*. Honolulu: University of Hawai'i Press.

Soothill, William Edward, and Lewis Hodous. [1937] 1982. *A Dictionary of Chinese Buddhist Terms with Sanskirt and English Equivalents and a Sanskrit-Pali Index*. London: K. Paul, Trench, Trubner. Reprint, Taipei: Xin wenfeng chuban gongsi. Taiwan, Taoyuan: Daden Culture.

Stark, Rodney, and W. S. Bainbridge. 1985. *The Future of Religion: Secularization, Revival and Cult Formation*. Berkeley: University of California Press.

Takakusu Junjirō and Watanabe Kaigyoku, eds. 1924–1932. *Taishō shinshū daizōkyō*. 85 vols. Tokyo: Taishō Issaikyō Kankōkai.

Tam Wai Lun. 2001. "Integration of the Magical and Cultivational Discourses: A Study of the New Religious Movement Called the True Buddha School." *Monumenta Serica* 49: 141–169.

Tam Wai Lun. 2007. "Re-examining the True Buddha School: A 'New Religion' or a New 'Buddhist Movement'?" *Australian Religion Studies Review: The Journal of the Australian Association for the Study of Religion* 20 (3): 286–302.

Thurman, Robert A. F. 1986. *The Holy Teaching of Vimalakirti*. University Park; London: Pennsylvania State University Press.

White, David Gordon, ed. 2000. *Tantra in Practice*. Princeton, NJ: Princeton University Press.

Yao Yu-shuang. 1994. *A Study of Two Chinese Buddhist Movements in London: The London Buddha's Light Temple and the Real Greatest Chapel*. MA thesis, University of London.

Index

Page numbers followed by *t* or *f* indicate tables or figures, respectively. Page numbers followed by n indicate notes.